Metaframeworks

DOUGLAS C. BREUNLIN
RICHARD C. SCHWARTZ
BETTY MAC KUNE-KARRER

Metaframeworks

Transcending
the Models of
Family Therapy

Jossey-Bass Publishers · San Francisco

FIRST PAPERBACK EDITION PUBLISHED IN 1997.

For sales outside the United States, please contact your local Simon & Schuster International Office.

Jossey-Bass Web address: http://www.josseybass.com

TCF Manufactured in the United States of America on Lyons Falls Turin Book. This paper is acid-free and 100 percent totally chlorine-free.

Library of Congress Cataloging-in-Publication Data

Breunlin, Douglas C.
    Metaframeworks : transcending the models of family therapy /
Douglas C. Breunlin, Richard C. Schwartz, Betty Mac Kune-Karrer.—
1st ed.
        p.   cm.—(The Jossey-Bass social and behavioral science
series)
    Includes bibliographical references and index.
    ISBN 1-55542-426-0 (cloth)
    ISBN 0-7879-1070-8 (paper)
    1. Family psychotherapy.   I. Schwartz, Richard C.   II. Mac Kune-
Karrer, Betty, date.   III. Title.   IV. Series.
RC488.5.B683   1992
616.89'156—dc20   91-32317

FIRST EDITION
HB Printing   10 9 8 7 6 5 4
PB Printing   10 9 8 7 6 5 4 3 2 1

Contents

Preface to the Paperback Edition ix

Preface xi

The Authors xix

Part One: Foundations of the Metaframeworks Perspective

1. A Conversation About Metaframeworks 3

2. The Metaframeworks Perspective 19

Part Two: Six Core Metaframeworks

3. Of Mind and Self: The Internal
   Family Systems Metaframework 57

4. Patterns of Interaction: The Sequences
   Metaframework 90

5. Leadership, Balance, and Harmony:
   The Organization Metaframework 125

- Family therapy has absorbed the impact of postmodernism, which has produced an important clinical derivative: narrative therapy.
- Psychotherapy is now regulated by the system of managed care, which mandates time-limited therapies and increases the popularity of the brief therapies, particularly solution-focused therapy.
- Psychiatry's emphasis on biomedicine has ushered in the mass distribution of such "miracle drugs" as Prozac.
- Census projections indicate that American clinicians in years to come will see an increasing number of minority and immigrant families.
- Multiculturalism, feminism, and individualism have had impacts that are producing tension around such issues as equality of opportunity and privilege.
- The viability of marriage as an institution continues to concern clinicians and families, as does the importance of safety from all forms of abuse.
- Many people are turning away from secular solutions to their problems and moving toward a reawakening of their spirituality.

All these developments have challenged the metaframeworks perspective to assimilate them and remain cohesive while continuing to evolve.

This new edition of *Metaframeworks* affords us the opportunity to share the ways in which we have elaborated the metaframeworks perspective. Specifically, Chapter Eleven, which replaces the final chapter of the hardcover edition, discusses how we have refined the metaframeworks perspective and attempted to incorporate new trends in the field of family therapy. In all other respects, the hardcover edition and this one are identical.

June 1997   Douglas C. Breunlin
                                      La Grange, Illinois

                                      Richard C. Schwartz
                                      Oak Park, Illinois

                                      Betty Mac Kune-Karrer
                                      Highland Park, Illinois

Preface to the
Paperback Edition

Eight years have passed since we originally embarked on the hard-cover edition of *Metaframeworks*. As family therapy trainers, we had decided that students needed a way to transcend the myriad of family therapy models that inevitably confused rather than clarified this complex field. With *Metaframeworks* we were able to provide that alternative, and we were delighted to find that our students liked and felt comfortable with this transcendent approach, which has come to be known as the *metaframeworks perspective*.

   Metaframeworks has proved to be more than a book that gets read once and then gathers dust on a shelf. It offers a living, evolving perspective, one that has grown as we and others have applied it to our teaching and practice. Since the publication of the hard-cover edition, in 1992, *Metaframeworks* has been central to both our clinical work and our teaching. The metaframeworks perspective has also been adopted in other training settings: some of our students have themselves become teachers of the metaframeworks perspective, and other professors have adopted *Metaframeworks* as a core text.

   One result of all this intense scrutiny of the metaframeworks perspective has been elaboration and refinement of some of the concepts and ideas that we presented in the original work. Moreover, the field of family therapy itself has evolved, and the face of American society continues to change:

- Family therapy has absorbed the impact of postmodernism, which has produced an important clinical derivative: narrative therapy.
- Psychotherapy is now regulated by the system of managed care, which mandates time-limited therapies and increases the popularity of the brief therapies, particularly solution-focused therapy.
- Psychiatry's emphasis on biomedicine has ushered in the mass distribution of such "miracle drugs" as Prozac.
- Census projections indicate that American clinicians in years to come will see an increasing number of minority and immigrant families.
- Multiculturalism, feminism, and individualism have had impacts that are producing tension around such issues as equality of opportunity and privilege.
- The viability of marriage as an institution continues to concern clinicians and families, as does the importance of safety from all forms of abuse.
- Many people are turning away from secular solutions to their problems and moving toward a reawakening of their spirituality.

All these developments have challenged the metaframeworks perspective to assimilate them and remain cohesive while continuing to evolve.

This new edition of *Metaframeworks* affords us the opportunity to share the ways in which we have elaborated the metaframeworks perspective. Specifically, Chapter Eleven, which replaces the final chapter of the hardcover edition, discusses how we have refined the metaframeworks perspective and attempted to incorporate new trends in the field of family therapy. In all other respects, the hardcover edition and this one are identical.

June 1997

Douglas C. Breunlin
La Grange, Illinois

Richard C. Schwartz
Oak Park, Illinois

Betty Mac Kune-Karrer
Highland Park, Illinois

Contents

Preface to the Paperback Edition   ix

Preface   xi

The Authors   xix

Part One: Foundations of the Metaframeworks Perspective

1. A Conversation About Metaframeworks   3

2. The Metaframeworks Perspective   19

Part Two: Six Core Metaframeworks

3. Of Mind and Self: The Internal
    Family Systems Metaframework   57

4. Patterns of Interaction: The Sequences
    Metaframework   90

5. Leadership, Balance, and Harmony:
    The Organization Metaframework   125

6. Beyond the One-Dimensional Life Cycle:
   The Development Metaframework   158

7. Unifying Diverse Parameters:
   The Multicultural Metaframework   193

8. Reweaving Feminism and Systems:
   The Gender Metaframework   237

Part Three: From Theory to Practice

9. A Blueprint for Therapy   281

10. A Case in Point   317

11. Refining the Metaframeworks Perspective   354

    References   373

    Index   384

Preface

For the past decade and a half, we have devoted our professional lives to the field of family therapy. Family therapy has gone through several developmental stages during this period, and the same is true for each of us. We wrote this book because we believe that the field of family therapy is ready to step beyond the boundaries that constrain it. Rather than creating yet another school of therapy, we have created an orientation—to people and to therapy— that attempts to expand the field's horizons and contribute new concepts and methods.

To do this, we took two steps. The first step was to distill the central ideas (such as sequences, boundaries, and structure) from the many systems-based models of family therapy, add some concepts that had not been widely used before in family therapy (such as leadership, balance, harmony, and perspectivism), and connect them all to one another in a new way. The second step was to apply these ideas to domains that family therapists have not explored (or have just begun to explore) from a systems perspective—domains such as intrapsychic process, human development, gender, and culture. The result is the present volume.

This is a book intended for clinicians and theorists of every kind. In addition to offering new ways to understand families, it moves systems ideas beyond the boundaries of the family, in two directions: downward, to the individual's internal process; and outward, to gender and culture. Why is this important? When we entered the field, there were only a few approaches to family therapy, each led by a charismatic pioneer. Theory and practice for each approach were, by today's standards, relatively simple and clear, easily differentiated from those of the other approaches. The followers of each approach were very enthusiastic, but they were also often rigid and self-righteous. All of this was taking place in a formative period, during which lines were being drawn and discoveries were being made. Everyone involved had the sense of being part of a new movement that would revolutionize mental health. We enthusiastically joined those revolutionaries, promoting a hybrid of structural and strategic family therapy that we thought could handle most of life's problems.

This decade has brought a number of rude awakenings to us and to the field. It is increasingly clear that any one approach to family therapy is limited and incomplete. Each has made valuable contributions, but none has lived up to its initial great expectations. Moreover, each of these early approaches has been "deconstructed"—that is, its basic assumptions have been challenged by feminist family therapists, who have uncovered underlying patriarchal biases, and by "constructionists," who have questioned theorists' claims to be representing the reality of families. Finally, revolutionary zeal has abated, as has polarization among traditional models, and these developments have allowed the absorption of many family therapy ideas or techniques into the mental health mainstream.

All these recent changes have left family therapy with an identity crisis. The original approaches still exist, but they do not generate the same excitement or attract as many adherents. New approaches have emerged; but, since "true-believerhood" is passé, it is hard for them to coalesce into discrete schools with which people in the field can identify. As the original charismatic leaders age and die, few new ones have emerged to replace them.

We, along with the rest of the field, suffered through these disconcerting periods, routinely questioning our own and others' most cherished beliefs. We responded to our anomie in two ways. First, we began to peek outside the comfort and simplicity of our structural and strategic bastion to see what we could bring to or take from other levels of systems. Each of us focused on different levels.

Betty Mac Kune-Karrer explored gender and culture, Douglas Breunlin explored development, and Richard Schwartz explored intrapsychic process. Second, we began to look for common elements within the existing models of family therapy that could resolve those models' contradictions and polarizations. We also took another look at cybernetics and at the work of other systems theorists such as Ludwig von Bertalanffy to see how the family therapy pioneers had used and abused their ideas. We began to recognize some underlying principles—what we call *presuppositions*—that seemed to transcend the apparent differences among warring models of family therapy.

This book is a snapshot of our evolution. It contains the fruits of our soul-searching, the temporary resolution of our individual identity crises. It has allowed us to transcend the limitations of particular models of family therapy without having to give up the valuable core of family therapy and systems thinking. It has allowed us to extend systems thinking into new domains—intrapsychic process, cultural and gender relations, and development. In turn, these explorations have resulted in new discoveries that we have fed back into our understanding of families.

Audience

As we have said, the audience for this book is clinicians and theorists. The book is full of clinical ideas, methods, and examples. Nevertheless, it is not a standardized "cookbook" for therapy; it is more like an orientation to thinking about human systems at many levels. Rather than spelling out each step for therapists, it guides the process of therapy. In this respect, it is not a book for therapists who are looking for simple, easy answers and practices; the field already offers enough such books. Our own students find that, once they understand the ideas developed here, our approach offers both flexibility and comprehensiveness that repay the effort of mastering these concepts.

Foundation of This Book

With respect to the specific elements of the metaframeworks perspective, we begin with six topics: internal process, sequences, organization, development, culture, and gender. These are core ideas in any consideration of human systems. To a greater or lesser degree, they are woven into the conceptual frameworks of most models of psychotherapy.

Each different model of family therapy has interpreted each of these core ideas differently. For example, structural family therapy had a particular slant on family organization involving concepts of hierarchy. The strategic therapy of Haley and Madanes also used the concept of hierarchy, but in a different way. Bowen used many organizational ideas, as did the Milan model.

We decided there was nothing to prevent our distilling core ideas from the various models and examining them in their own right. Once we had extracted each core idea from the models and freed it of the various theorists' idiosyncratic uses of it, we began to notice the underlying patterns connecting the approaches. For example, we saw that each of the models seemed to use the concept of sequences, but that each one was concerned with sequences of different length. Whereas structural family therapy focused on short, in-session sequences, Bowen focused on long, transgenerational sequences. Our view of sequences constitutes one of six *metaframeworks:* it transcends each model of family therapy, and it provides a comprehensive view of patterning in families. When the sequences metaframework is interwoven with the other five, the perspective on families expands. These six metaframeworks and our descriptions of the ways we use them in therapy are the foundation of this book. The metaframeworks bring together, in a new way, much of the knowledge base of family therapy. They have also led to new ideas and techniques (for example, the internal family systems model, or IFS, originally developed by Richard Schwartz; the concept of developmental oscillation; and the multiperspective approach to culture).

This book contains a considerable amount of theory, but we have tried to translate theory into methods that practicing clinicians can understand and use. Toward this end, we have illustrated each metaframework with many case examples, and we include a set of guidelines that we call a *blueprint for therapy*. One advantage of this approach is that clinicians of all kinds can use the book, perhaps expanding their horizons somewhat without having to abandon their training.

Overview of the Contents

The book is divided into three parts. In Part One (Chapters One and Two), we set the stage for the discussion of metaframeworks. To introduce all these ideas and the ways in which they differ from more traditional approaches to family therapy, in Chapter One we invite the reader to eavesdrop on a dialogue between two former colleagues. In Chapter Two, we introduce the basic presuppositions that run through and connect all six metaframeworks. We provide background information on each presupposition, so that the reader has some idea of how each was derived.

Part Two (Chapters Three through Eight) devotes one chapter apiece to the six metaframeworks. Each chapter provides a rationale for a particular metaframework, for its underlying constructs, and for the metaframework itself. Each metaframework is illustrated with clinical examples. Our metaframework for *internal family systems* is the topic of Chapter Three. Using presuppositions of systems theory and a view that the mind consists of a multiplicity of subpersonalities (what we call parts) and a Self, this metaframework provides an empowering way to access and work with internal process in the context of the family. The *sequences* metaframework described in Chapter Four, using the construct of periodicity, classifies and interrelates all the relevant sequences essential to family therapy and provides a decision tree for using them in any given case. The metaframework on *organization* is presented in Chapter Five. In this metaframework, we modify the organizational concepts of hierarchy and boundaries and replace them with leadership, balance, and harmony, since we believe that the latter concepts successfully address concerns of power and control. Our organization metaframework also reexamines the function of the symptom by explaining how a problem can oppress a system while still being maintained by the constraints that the system imposes. In Chapter Six, our metaframework on *development* expands the traditional concept of the family life cycle by building on the premise that, in multilevel organic systems, development takes place at the biological, individual, relational, family, and societal levels. This metaframework also examines recursive relationships among the levels of development. The *multicultural* metaframework presented in Chapter Seven seeks to unify the many ideas about culture—based on notions of ethnicity, race, class, economics, religion, region, and gender, and on the processes of cultural fit, acculturation, and transition—that have informed family therapy in the past decade. The *gender* metaframework presented in Chapter Eight builds on the

multivocal feminist discourse in the field of family therapy, seeking
to reconcile feminism and systems theory in a gender-balanced
approach.

Part Three (Chapters Nine, Ten, and Eleven) applies the six
metaframeworks to clinical practice. In Chapter Nine, we present a
blueprint that allows therapists to apply the metaframeworks to their
own practice. The blueprint involves four interrelated clinical processes, each one described in detail, with the relationships among
them illustrated with clinical material. Chapter Ten provides a detailed description of the application of the metaframeworks approach
to a specific case, and we follow the therapist session by session. In
Chapter Eleven, we conclude with personal statements and a statement from a colleague regarding our use of this perspective.

Acknowledgments

All three of us contributed to the thinking that went into each
chapter, but we each took primary responsibility for different chapters. Breunlin was the primary author of Chapters Four, Six, Nine,
and Ten. Schwartz was the primary author of Chapters One, Three,
and Five. Mac Kune-Karrer wrote Chapters Seven and Eight, and
Breunlin and Schwartz coauthored Chapter Two. Each of us wrote
a section of Chapter Eleven. In addition, a colleague, Rocco Cimmarusti, contributed a section to this last chapter.

We feel very fortunate to have worked together and learned
from each other as teachers and therapists through this turbulent
decade. Having to constantly revise a postgraduate curriculum and
stay abreast of developments in the field has kept us perpetually
generating and reviewing ideas. We have been blessed with stimu-
lating, challenging students who stirred the stew and an environment at the Institute for Juvenile Research (IJR) under the
directorship of Lee Combrinck-Graham that supported this process.
Within IJR we would especially like to thank the adjunct and core
faculty of the Family Systems Program for their many ideas and
challenges over the years.

Thanks also go to the many people who critiqued various
chapters of this book, including Lois Braverman, Nancy Burgoyne,
Celia Falicov, Debbie Gorman-Smith, Bart Mann, Kelly Naylor,
Cheryl Rampage, Virginia Simmons, Kathy Statos, Linda Webb-

Watson, and Cathy Weigel-Foy. Linda Stone-Fish and an anonymous reviewer read the entire manuscript and their feedback led to improvements. We also thank those who helped prepare the manuscript, particularly Nikki Settles and Royce Warren.

Special thanks go to Gracia Alkema and her successor at Jossey-Bass, Becky McGovern, for their sage editorial guidance and unwavering support. Finally, our colleague Rocco Cimmarusti has our undying gratitude, not only for contributing to many of the ideas in this book but also for mediating the sometimes heated disputes that arose as we negotiated what was to go in it. As mentioned earlier, Rocco also wrote a section of the last chapter.

We also want to thank our many students for sharing their clinical work with us. Several of the case examples and anecdotes in this book are based on their work.

Finally, we want to express our appreciation to the many families who have helped us to develop a collaborative approach to family therapy.

January 1992

Douglas C. Breunlin
La Grange, Illinois

Richard C. Schwartz
Oak Park, Illinois

Betty Mac Kune-Karrer
Highland Park, Illinois

To Cyndy, my wife, and Rachel and Gareth,
my children, for enriching my ideas about
the family. —Douglas C. Breunlin

To my families (both internal and external)
for their support and patience.
—Richard C. Schwartz

To the memory of my son, Phillip Fabregat
Mac Kune (1956–1986), and in celebration
of his life. To my mother Alicia Mac Manus,
whose strength supported my freedom to
explore, challenge, and believe in myself.
—Betty Mac Kune-Karrer

The Authors

Douglas C. Breunlin is vice president and chief operating officer of the Family Institute at Northwestern University. He is also associate professor in the School of Education and Social Policy at Northwestern University. He received his B.A. degree (1969) in arts and letters and his B.S. degree (1970) in aeronautical engineering from the University of Notre Dame and his M.S.S.A. degree (1975) in social work from Case Western Reserve University.

Author of more than forty articles and book chapters, Breunlin's main interest is family therapy training. He is coauthor of *The Family Therapy Assessment Exercise* (1980), a research instrument for evaluating the outcome of family therapy training, and coeditor of *The Handbook of Family Therapy Training and Supervision* (1988, with H. A. Liddle and R. C. Schwartz). Breunlin is the associate editor of the *Journal of Family Therapy* and serves on the editorial board of the *Journal of Marital and Family Therapy*.

Breunlin was on the faculty of the Family Institute, Cardiff, Wales, from 1975 to 1978. He was director of the Family Systems Program at the Institute for Juvenile Research, Chicago, from 1982 to 1989 and director of professional education there from 1989 to 1990.

Richard C. Schwartz is a member of the senior faculty of the Family Institute at Northwestern University. Schwartz was coordinator of training for the Family Systems Program at the Institute for Juvenile Research in Chicago from 1979 to 1996. He received his B.A. degree

(1971) from Knox College in psychology and graduated in 1980 from Purdue University's doctoral program in marital and family therapy. He is a fellow of the American Association of Marriage and Family Therapy.

Author of over thirty articles and book chapters, Schwartz has developed a systemic model of intrapsychic process called the internal family systems model, described in *Internal Family Systems Therapy* (1995). He has written extensively on eating disorders, family therapy training, and family therapy in general. He is also coauthor of *Family Therapy: Concepts and Methods* (1997, 4th ed., with M. Nichols), coeditor of *The Handbook of Family Therapy: Training and Supervision* (1988, with H. A. Liddle and D. C. Breunlin), and coauthor of *Mosaic Mind: Empowering the Tormented Selves of Child Sexual Abuse Survivors*.

Betty Mac Kune-Karrer is director of the Family Systems Program of the Institute for Juvenile Research (IJR), and clinical associate in psychiatry at the University of Illinois, Chicago. She is a clinical member and approved supervisor and a member of the board of directors of the American Association of Marriage and Family Therapy. Mac Kune-Karrer is editor of the *Journal of Feminism and Family Therapy* and a member of the advisory board of the *Journal of Marriage and Family Therapy*. She has M.A. degrees from the University of Mexico (1955) and from Roosevelt University (1971), both in psychology.

In addition to cultural and gender issues in family therapy, Mac Kune-Karrer is interested in promoting family therapy internationally. To this end, she has taught family therapy in Mexico, South America, and Europe. Mac Kune-Karrer has published in the area of structural family therapy, acculturation, cultural variation of the life cycle, and early intervention. She is coeditor of *Minorities and Family Therapy* (1989, with G. W. Saba and K. V. Hardy).

Mac Kune-Karrer was previously director of the Multicultural Early Intervention Program at IJR, a program for infants, toddlers, and kindergarten-age children and their families.

PART 1

Foundations
of the Metaframeworks
Perspective

ONE

A Conversation
About Metaframeworks

This book contains a large number of relatively abstract clinical concepts, some of which are borrowed from the family therapy field and some of which are new. After struggling with various ways of introducing this complexity and not overwhelming the reader, we settled on a dialogue format for the first chapter.

The following is a discussion between two clinicians, Al (A) and Barbara (B). They worked together in an agency some years ago, and they shared similar ideas about therapy in those days. This is their first encounter since that time. After catching up on their personal changes, they turn to clinical issues.

A: It's been a long time since we talked about therapy. I'm curious to know what you've been up to, but first let me ask you about a case I'm stuck on. Nancy is a fifteen-year-old girl who has been anorexic for six months. Her parents are split on how to get her to eat, and her mother is very intrusive on her life. I've been trying to get the parents to work together and stop undermining each other, but they don't seem to be able to do this for more than a few days. As a result, Nancy eats pretty well for a while and then, after gaining a pound or two, goes back to starving herself. I suspect that Nancy is distracting them from their issues, but they contend that she's their only problem. I meet with Nancy individually, and she will talk to me about her social life or about how her parents don't understand her, but she is denying that she is too thin or has an

3

eating problem. I'm feeling stuck, and I'm thinking about directing the parents to pretend they don't care about her eating and to start going out with each other mysteriously. What do you think?

B: Before I answer, let me ask you what you think is constraining each of these people to behave and think in the ways they do.

A: Well, I think the mother is enmeshed with Nancy and doesn't want her to grow up and leave home. The father is afraid that if Nancy did grow up, he'd have to deal with his wife, who would be after him for more attention. The parents probably have underlying resentments that keep them from working together effectively to get Nancy to eat. I think Nancy is also afraid to grow up and is rebelling against her mother's controlling.

B: So you believe they each have parts of them that fear Nancy's growing up. What do you think might be activating these scared parts? For example, what's their ethnicity, and how isolated are they from a network of family or friends?

A: From their name, I think they're Greek. I don't know about friends, but the father's family is around. So you think I should look at this multigenerationally, or you think it's related to their ethnicity? What makes you want to look in that direction?

B: It's nothing in particular about your case. It's just that I believe that when people are acting in extreme ways, it's because they are constrained, by aspects of their context, from behaving or thinking in valuable, health-promoting ways. A family that is isolated, or whose ethnic values don't fit with the surroundings, is likely to be severely constrained, so I often explore those issues with the family. I might also discuss with them the degree to which they are victimized by patriarchal values, which lead to imbalances in responsibility, influence, and access to resources. All of this would be in the context of exploring what was keeping them from relating in competent ways. Since people are also constrained by mental processes, I would ask about that as well.

A: But what about getting them to change the family structure or the sequences around the problem? It sounds like your therapy has moved away from giving directives or reframes, to a kind of exploration process with families.

B: It's true that I no longer focus so exclusively on the family interactions that I see in the session as the primary targets of change. I still might ask questions about those patterns, but I am less certain that my interpretation of them is the correct or best one. Instead of diagnosing a family and then thinking up a directive or reframe to give them on the basis of my diagnosis, I try to create an atmosphere in sessions in which the fearful or angry parts of people are calmed and their resources can emerge. When this happens, therapy becomes a kind of collaborative discussion of constraints and negotiation of ways to release those constraints. The constraints might be related to the common structural problems that I used to focus on, but I find that those structural problems are often related to the developmental, cultural, or gender issues that we all face.

A: This constraint-releasing process still sounds too vague and optimistic to me. Do you really believe that just by talking about these things you call constraints, people will change? If I have an open conversation with Nancy's family about ethnic heritage or division of responsibilities, how does this get her parents to change the way they relate to her?

B: I agree that unstructured conversations are not necessarily going to produce change, and that's not what I do. I'll tell you more about what I do a little later, but first it might help if I tell you how and why I changed my thinking about therapy. You're right that this is an optimistic view. It's based on a belief that people are, at their core, competent and compassionate. For example, even if there are parts of the mother that fear Nancy's growing up and want to control Nancy's life, I know that at the mother's core is a self that wants her daughter to thrive and can deal with her own fearful parts. So, in addition to discussing with family members the constraints they face from various levels of the systems surrounding them, I talk with them about internal constraints—that is, the parts of them that have become extreme and are interfering with their lives. And I can show them specific ways to get those parts of them to stop interfering. This idea alone—that the extreme things people feel, think, or do are caused by little parts of them, and there is much more to them than just those extreme parts—is very empowering for people and keeps me seeing them in a positive way.

A: But I've found that focusing on intrapsychic issues distracts me from focusing on family relationships. My clients and I get too involved in looking inside each family member and miss crucial interactions.

B: This is a danger, but if you take this constraint-releasing approach seriously, then the internal work is closely linked to the work with the family or other levels of the system. For example, in asking Nancy's mother what keeps her fearful part extreme, issues like her isolation or conflicts with her husband are likely to emerge. Or you can go the other way and start with these environmental issues and then ask how they affect each family member's parts. In other words, discussions of constraints will shift back and forth among various levels of the system, and the family will have a say in which level seems the most constraining or should be focused on first. It may be decided that the best way to calm the mother's fearful part is for her husband to react differently to her when that part has taken over. Or it may be that she needs to be less overworked, so she can develop more of a life of her own, in which case the father will be asked to do more. In this way, environmental changes are used to effect specific internal changes. Similarly, they may decide that the best way to change a family relationship is for all the people in it to work on the parts of themselves that are interfering, in which case internal change is used in the service of relationship change. In thinking this way, I can break the artificial barrier between the intrapsychic and the family or social levels of the system and incorporate all these levels into my and the family's conceptualizing and acting.

A: It sounds interesting, but I'd need to hear more about this parts stuff before I could really evaluate this approach. Is the parts perspective the main thing that is new about your approach?

B: The parts stuff is probably the biggest departure for me from the family therapy mainstream, but it is just one of several interrelated frameworks that I use to think about cases. The others—sequences, development, organization, gender, and culture—are probably more familiar to you because these are core domains that have appeared throughout the family therapy literature. I have changed or expanded each of these, however, and have tied them together by using the same set of presuppositions throughout each. In this sense, they are not just different frameworks. They are metaframeworks in that they create a way to transcend individual models of therapy. They become six different lenses through which to view a family or problem. Each lens examines the problem from a different angle or has a different focal point, but the lenses are all ground from the same piece of glass, and so they are highly compatible. In fact, several of them can be used simultaneously.

A: You mean that you can put on the lens of sequences as you look at the family, and then the lens of gender or structure or parts, and all these views would be tied together somehow? That's an attractive idea because I always felt that if I wanted to think about sequences, I would use strategic models of therapy, and then if I wanted to think about organizations, I'd have to shift to the structural model, with all its different assumptions. And to think about intrapsychic process, I'd have to shift again, to object relations or self-psychology, and so on.

B: Exactly. That's one big advantage of this metaframework perspective. It takes some of the most useful ideas from seemingly disparate models and links them with common underlying assumptions, so that you can move fluidly from one to another. For example, you can work one session with Nancy on the extreme parts of her that are constraining her from eating the way she wants to, and in the next session you can explore with her and her family how our culture's gender values affect those parts of Nancy. All the while, you can ask questions about sequences among Nancy's parts or among these three family members. Or you can help them look at structural or developmental issues that might be creating these sequences. If one of these metaframeworks seems more relevant to or useful with a particular case, I will stay with it, but the others are still in the back of my mind.

A: It seems that these common assumptions—what you call presuppositions—among the frameworks are keys to making this perspective work. What are they, and where did they come from?

B: The first and, in a sense, most basic presupposition is about the nature of reality, and it asserts that my perspective limits what I can see and understand of reality. Before I became so aware of the impact of my perspective on what I saw, if Nancy and her mother spoke for each other in a session, I would see an enmeshed relationship, and I thought that was a relatively objective description of something real that needed to be changed. On the basis of that belief, I would tell them to stop speaking for each other. Now that I am more aware of the limitations and biases of any particular perspective, I am slower to assume that I see the reality of the family, and I'm more interested in their perspectives. This leads to a more collaborative form of therapy.

A: That sounds like constructivism—the idea that there is no objective reality, only various constructions that people carry around in their heads. Constructivist therapists like to have conversations with families that lead to new, more useful constructions of their problems. Is your position different from constructivism?

B: There are many versions of constructivism, ranging from the position that reality exists, but we can only know approximations of it that are more or less distorted or incomplete, to the radical position that there *is* no reality to approximate. I subscribe to the former position—what von Bertalanffy called perspectivism. With perspectivism, one's perspective—that is, one's presuppositions—determines what one can see. That's why I'm so concerned with understanding and being clear about my own presuppositions and finding ones that are health-promoting.

A: So what are some of these other health-promoting presuppositions?

B: Another is related to Arthur Koestler's concept of holons—that systems are multileveled, and that each level can be viewed as a system in itself while also being part of a larger system. To understand and treat a problem, then, the therapist may start at one level but have to shift to either smaller or larger levels along the way, in order to deal with enough constraints to allow lasting change. For example, Nancy's anorexia can be seen and treated as the result of polarized internal parts of her, one wanting her to binge and the other terrified of getting fat. It can also be seen as an escalating sequence between Nancy and her mother over control, where the battleground is food. The more Mom insists that she eat, the more she refuses. The anorexia can also be seen as a way to distract her parents from issues between or inside them that threaten the family, or as the product of our culture's extreme views of women and the way Nancy and her family have ingested them. If I were to ask about the sequences within any one level of the system, I would hear, if I were listening for them, about related sequences between that level and other levels around it. For example, suppose that while I asked questions of Nancy and her mother about their sequences around Nancy's eating, they said that they are okay with each other until the mother's mother comments on Nancy's thin appearance. I would then shift temporarily to explore the sequences between the mother and her mother, both in the present and in the past. Throughout these discussions, I would also shift to sequences at the internal level, by asking about how parts of each of them reacted to the external sequences between them or with the grandmother. Thus, tracking sequences becomes a way to find the constraints at each level of the system and to move between levels. There are many other ways to view Nancy's problem—many other perspectives. Each of these, while incomplete in itself, may be potent enough to initiate change and, in some cases, to maintain change. In many cases, however, I find that I have to examine and work with the constraints imposed by many different levels of the system. That's one reason to have all these frameworks—to have ways of understanding and treating these different levels.

A: With all these frameworks for all these different levels, it seems as if therapy would be so complex that I could get lost with all the choices. There is something comforting about limiting my purview. I may not cover everything, but at least I know where I'm going most of the time.

B: When I used to limit myself to focusing on only one or two levels, therapy was simpler but also less successful and less rewarding. As Einstein once said, "Everything should be made as simple as possible, but not simpler." In many cases, my limited perspective limited my effectiveness. This metaframeworks perspective involves thinking about more levels, but because each level is examined with the same presuppositions, the complexity is not overwhelming. In addition, when I felt responsible for getting people to change, my model had to be simpler because I'd be overwhelmed by a large number of choices at each point in therapy. This new approach allows me to collaborate more with families in determining the direction of therapy, so I don't always have to decide what we should be doing or which level we should focus on. I trust their judgment more than I did before, so I help them look at their predicament from various levels, and they help me choose the direction to go.

A: You really *have* changed! I remember when you were more of a brief therapist than I am. So you no longer think that people can change quickly?

B: No, I just think that it isn't always possible. In other words, I still have cases that seem to improve and remain improved after only a handful of sessions. Usually these problems are embedded in only one or two levels of the systems, and the systems are not terribly polarized. For example, after Nancy and her mother begin to get along better, Nancy may consistently eat healthfully and give up her body-image delusion. In cases where the problem is embedded in many levels, and the systems at each level are highly polarized, the process of therapy takes longer—sometimes several years. Thus, I am no longer constrained by considering myself either a brief or a long-term therapist. In fact, pressure to be brief can actually prolong the process.

A: Okay, so you presume that systems are multileveled. Do you still consider boundaries an important concept, too? That is, are there boundaries between systems and subsystems that need to be improved?

B: Yes, that side of my thinking hasn't changed much, in the sense that I believe healthy systems have healthy internal and external boundaries. With perspectivism, however, I no longer make those boundary assessments or boundary-making interventions as a detached observer of the family. Instead, I help families or individuals evaluate and change their own boundaries.

A: I think that the most basic of the presuppositions would relate to your view of human nature, and I haven't heard much about that yet.

B: You're right. The mind is the most basic level of any multilevel human system, and I've already mentioned one presupposition about it—that it is multiple, having many different subpersonalities or parts that interact as a system. I believe that each of these parts has a valuable intention and role for the person, but that they can become extreme and constraining of the person when they are polarized with each other. I also believe that, in addition to these parts, everyone has a self that has all the qualities of good leadership. The goal becomes helping people differentiate this self, so that it can become like a therapist to the person's system of parts.

A: Differentiation of self—now you're sounding like Murray Bowen.

B: Well, actually, the goal is not that different from Bowen's concept of a differentiated self. By understanding the network of relationships among parts, however, I can achieve that differentiation in clients far more quickly than Bowen suggested. My belief in the existence of this compassionate, competent, and confident self in everyone leads to another presupposition that I've referred to frequently in our discussion—constraints. I believe that all human systems contain this resourcefulness, so when they are not functioning well, it is because they are constrained from exercising this resource. Therapy becomes a search for these constraints at different levels of the system, and an attempt to release them. This contrasts with the way I used to search for defects in individuals or in families and then fix them with corrective reframes or directives.

A: Well, I think I search for strengths in my clients, too. I guess I haven't clarified as much as you have the reasons why I do that.

Your focus on internal leadership tells me that there's still some structural family therapy in you, and that you've imported the structural idea of hierarchy to the level of people's minds.

B: That's true, except that I prefer the term *leadership* to hierarchy because hierarchy connotes a power arrangement and emphasizes the control side of leadership. Leadership, then, is another presupposition, because I believe all levels of human systems require effective leadership to be healthy. But good leadership means all kinds of things, including nurturance, encouragement, self-sacrifice, wisdom, and compassion. When leaders exercise these qualities, there is little need for control or discipline. Fortunately, when differentiated, a person's self already has these abilities. Good leaders are also careful to balance resources, responsibilities, and influence among the members of the system. Balance, in this sense, is another presupposition. Healthy systems are balanced in these areas—not in the sense that all members get the same level of resources, responsibilities, and influence at all times, but that they do receive the amount that they need for their own internal balance, and amounts similar to what others in the same position in the system receive. To make this less abstract, in Nancy's family it may be that the father has more influence over family decisions, spends more money on himself, and has fewer responsibilities around the home than the mother does. This imbalance will lead to chronic polarization between father and mother. This is a good example of how this balance presupposition links several metaframeworks. That is, this imbalance between the mother and the father will create or reflect parallel imbalances in each one's internal systems— the father will listen mainly to his assertive, entitled parts and push away his caretaking parts, while the mother becomes highly identified with her caretaker and blocks out her asserter. In addition, this imbalance will reflect and maintain similar imbalances throughout the surrounding system—for example, between Nancy and her brother, and between men and women generally in our culture.

A: So is this how you tie the feminist movement in family therapy to systems thinking, through this concept of balance?

B: Yes, that's one way. The version of systems theory that had the largest impact on family therapy was derived from cybernetics, which was developed from studying nonhuman systems, and so the concept of balance was virtually absent from the systems literature in family therapy. Balance is not particularly relevant to the functioning of machines. As you know, Gregory Bateson disdained the metaphor of power in describing systems, implying that all elements influence one another mutually and recursively. This led several family therapy theorists to devise models in which all family members were seen as equally responsible for the family's problems. These models have been criticized by feminist family therapists, who were outraged at, among other things, the implication that victims of abuse were as much to blame for the abuse as the abusers. As a result, many feminist theorists have suggested that we reject systems thinking as the conceptual basis for the field. But if we include the concept of balance as a central presupposition in systems thinking, then we resolve this conflict, because issues of influence and responsibility are placed in the foreground, rather than dismissed.

A: Now that you mention it, the idea from the ecology movement that living systems need to be balanced seems almost second nature. It's interesting that family therapy never really picked up on it. Along those lines, then, I suppose you believe that when systems have good leadership and are balanced, the members of the system live in harmony.

B: Exactly. Harmony is the last of these presuppositions. Harmony implies that the members of the system relate with an overall sense of trust, connectedness, and mutuality of goal, so that communication is clear and differences are faced and resolved fairly. The opposite of harmony is polarization, in which members of the system shift from their valuable, harmonious state and take extreme and opposite positions relative to one another. When two members of a system are polarized, they become rigidly locked into roles that are often a far cry from their natural desires, because they fear that if they back down from these extreme positions, the counterpart will gain the upper hand. Each one often believes that his or her extreme behavior is the only way to protect the system from the extremes of

the other and will escalate these extremes in response to any perceived escalation on the other side. As a result, the behavior of each
polarized member is destructive to the health of the system, even
though each member's intention is protective. Thus, highly polarized systems are delicate, with any change likely to trigger escalations. Consequently, they are fearful of and resistant to change. I see
these principles at work at all levels of human systems, from the
international level down to the intrapsychic.

A: So, for example, Nancy is afraid that if she eats, her mother
will control all aspects of her life. Is that the kind of polarization
you're talking about? It sounds similar to positive feedback loops—
more-of-the-same sequences—but with the addition of intentional-
ity. That is, rather than just describing these escalations, you're
interested in why each member is escalating. You're interested in the
polarizing beliefs under which each one operates.

B: That's probably a fair comparison. But the concept of polarization also applies to structural concepts. Polarization helps me
understand how alliances form and grow in families. The polarization between Nancy and her mother that you mention may exist,
but it's likely to be only one of many polarizations in the family,
as well as within each family member. Each polarization constrains
the resources of the system that contains it and creates similar polarizations in the systems around it. This is why you see parallel
processes or isomorphic sequences in systems that interface each
other.

A: Okay, I think I follow most of that, and I can see some value
to both the metaframeworks and these presuppositions you've been
describing, but this is all very conceptual and abstract. You said
earlier that you'd tell me more about what you would do with my
case.

B: Well, as you can imagine, the specifics of what I would do are
more difficult to predict than when I operated from one simple
model. I can tell you that I would approach the family with these
metaframeworks in mind, and I would encourage them to discuss
the constraints that kept them from relating to themselves internally, and to each other, in ways that could eliminate Nancy's eat-

ing disorder. Suppose Nancy says that she's afraid to grow up and leave home. I would ask the family about polarization at various levels that may be contributing to Nancy's fears. For example, I might ask Nancy if there were other parts of her that strongly wanted her to leave home or take more control of her life. Many kids like Nancy oscillate between dependent, younger parts and aloof, rebellious, independent parts. Such a developmental oscillation between acting younger than one's age and then acting older confuses parents enormously. I would ask the parents about their reactions to Nancy's eating or oscillating. They might reveal cultural constraints—beliefs about the age at which young women should begin to act and think for themselves—that conflict with the dominant American middle-class values. Or they might discuss long-term sequences through their families of origin, regarding the way women separated from their families. Each of these discussions of constraints—developmental oscillation, sequences, culture, gender—contains entry points to different metaframeworks. I would discuss with Nancy and her parents which metaframework seemed most salient and then focus on it for a period of time. While focused on that metaframework, I would ask about how it affected the family's leadership, balance, and harmony. Suppose we focused on the gender metaframework. I would ask how family members' views of the relationship between men and women affected the balance of influence, responsibility, and resources in the family. I'd also ask how that balance affected their leadership in terms of polarization between the parents and the ability of each parent to show a full range of leadership skills. I would also ask about the parts of each of them that carried constraining gender beliefs and whether they all wanted to help those parts change. If they did, I might work with each family member's internal system while the others watched, or we might generally discuss how they could help one another change those parts. For example, Nancy may have parts that tell her that she is only valuable to the extent that she is attractive to boys, which makes her weight so central to her self-esteem. In the family discussion, her mother may acknowledge similar parts, and they may discuss the parts of the father that reinforce appearance-oriented values. This discussion could trigger a shift to the culture metaframework and a discussion of American middle-class values and their impact on the family. Or it could shift to the sequences meta-framework and a recalling of events in the family's history that may have contributed to certain beliefs.

A: I think that the father's high-pressure and demanding job is, to use your language, a big constraint. How would you get to an environmental constraint like that?

B: It could come up through discussions of any of the metaframe-works, especially as the issue of balance is addressed in that meta-framework. For example, in discussing the family's organization or gender relations, it would become clear that the mother is overbur-dened and lonely because of the father's job. In discussing the fa-ther's internal system, the imbalance between his striving parts and his intimacy parts would be apparent. From discussions of our cul-ture's impact on the family, the need for the father to work so hard would be evaluated. Out of any or all of these discussions, the fam-ily would recognize the imbalances caused by the father's job and could then discuss how to improve things.

A: This does seem like a highly flexible way to work, but it almost seems too flexible in that I'd have trouble deciding which meta-framework to use at any given point.

B: Initially, it felt that way for me at times. Since all these levels of systems are interrelated and affect each other, however, I find that no matter which level I focus on, I am affecting the imbalances and polarizations that constrain the family. In other words, there isn't any essential core that one has to get the family to address, and so important work done with any of the metaframeworks will affect the others. As long as constraints are being released, I don't worry if I'm working at the crucial level with the family. I also give the family some responsibility for selecting the metaframework with me, so I don't always have to make all the decisions regarding focus. If family members feel that they have some control over the content, and if they experience me as respecting their judgment and valuing their opinions, then they will be less fearful of the therapy process.

A: That raises a good question. How do you handle resistance in this kind of therapy?

B: Well, I think of resistance as coming from protective parts of people. Those parts may be fighting the therapist for any number of reasons, and those reasons are often valid. People may not trust that I know what I'm doing enough to let me muck around with their internal or external family. They may not trust that I really like or care about them, or that I will stay committed to them as long as necessary. They may not trust that they can handle the information or feelings that may emerge if they open up their family or themselves. They may fear that change will bring unpredictable problems and would rather live with the familiar ones than risk potential loss or harm. Some family members may fear that they will lose some privileged status if things change. Rather than see this resistance antagonistically, as something to override or maneuver around, I see it as the result of protective parts' fears, which need to be respected and addressed. I want to know what they are afraid of, and I take those fears seriously. Those fears may also lead to various metaframework discussions. I may find, for example, parts of the father that believe his daughter's young behavior proves that she is too frail to handle life on her own, and that she will be hurt if they let her drift too far from the family. Other parts of the father know that he must let her learn through painful mistakes, but his fearful parts always override them. The mother, accustomed to a traditional family where mother and daughter remain close, may fear that her daughter will become a "modern" woman who "never comes around," so she speaks of her own isolation and the parts of her that are afraid of losing her daughter's company. Nancy speaks of the parts of her that make her feel responsible for preventing her mother's loneliness, and of other parts that contribute to her oscillation and fear of growing up. After discussing these fears, family members may collaboratively decide that it is best not to rush into removing the constraints, and that the kinds of changes that would foster the daughter's independence should be put off until the fearful parts of each of them are ready, or until they are ready to fully override those parts. In this scenario, I might eventually take a restraining position similar to that of the strategic therapist, yet there is no deception involved in my position. I genuinely believe that it is best not to rush ahead with changes until the family's fears have been respected and dealt with.

A: I see how what we used to call paradoxical restraining techniques fit into your approach. How about other techniques?

B: I still ask people to talk to each other. So, in that sense, I still create enactments. But it doesn't feel like I'm using a technique when I do that, so much as that being a natural part of my role as the leader of these discussions. I still ask people to do things between sessions, but I don't have to dream up these tasks, because they usually emerge from the collaborative discussions. Similarly, I rarely have to reframe a problem for the family or come up with a clever metaphor about it, because people naturally see things differently as they do this work—as their selves emerge. I still do some boundary setting—getting people to speak for themselves, or not to interfere in relationships between two others—but even in doing that, I am less frequently directive. More often, I'm asking questions about what kinds of boundaries the family wants. I find that I don't have to deliberately provoke intense interactions in therapy, because as constraints are released, things often heat up on their own. I am most directive when I am working with one family member's parts, because there are specific techniques needed to get that work going. Even there, however, I shift as soon as possible to a suggestive stance, asking the person's self about what should change, and how. I guess the main difference that underlies a lot of this change in my therapy is that I trust people, more than I used to, to change themselves and their families in healthful ways if they are released from constraints. So my job is a lot simpler—to help them find these constraints and find how to release them, rather than come up with solutions to or new ways of viewing their problems. That trust is what allows me to be so collaborative.

A: Well, you won't be surprised to hear that parts of me are intrigued by what you're saying, while other parts are very skeptical and are comfortable with the way I do therapy now.

B: I wouldn't have it any other way.

TWO

The Metaframeworks
Perspective

The discussion of the case in the previous chapter illustrates the complexity of the human condition and how it brings forth human suffering. Confronted with this complexity, clinicians can easily become overwhelmed. They are understandably attracted to therapies that circumscribe that complexity by focusing on just one aspect of it. Many traditional therapies do this by locating the cause of problems within the individual; for example, depression may be viewed as being caused by a biochemical imbalance, by ego deficits, or by anger turned inward. Family therapy ostensibly increased complexity by replacing this focus on the individual with a focus on the family, thereby making a problem a function of an interpersonal context. Most family therapy models, however, dealt with complexity by adopting simplified definitions of the family while totally ignoring the internal process of family members; for example, the brief therapy model of the Mental Research Institute (MRI) (Watzlawick, Weakland, and Fisch, 1974) focuses on interactions that constitute attempted solutions to the problem. In this mode, depression may be seen as the by-product of an attempted solution, whereby the family's attempt to solve the problem of sadness unwittingly creates a vicious cycle that transforms sadness into depression through the way in which the sadness is handled. For instance, the family may try repeatedly to cheer up or minimize the sad feelings, only making them worse.

The narrowing of clinical purview in both individual and family models does keep therapists from becoming overwhelmed, but such narrowing also has limitations. Individual therapies have ways of conceptualizing internal process, but they have difficulty looking at the family. Family therapies have ways of looking at the family, but not at the individual. Neither fully considers the larger context in which the individual and the family are embedded.

When therapists working with either of these models are successful, it may not be because they are working with the essence of human problems but rather because they have applied curative factors common to all psychotherapies. What happens when therapy is not successful? In that case, therapists working within a particular model are being handicapped by blind spots that prevent thinking and acting in ways that could be more helpful. For example, a cognitive therapist may not see how behavior affects the problem. Conversely, a behavioral therapist dismisses cognition. In pure form, neither type of therapy can account for the interaction between cognition and behavior. A family therapist may not be able to see how something internal to the individual may be affecting the problem. As the following example illustrates, however, problems are often embedded within the individual, the family, and the larger context:

> Rod, an eighteen-year-old African-American male, was hospitalized after he threatened to commit suicide. At the time of his admission, Rod was depressed, and he exhibited bizarre behaviors. One of these was to insist on always wearing a towel around his face, which covered all but his eyes. Throughout the hospitalization, he refused to remove the towel. His psychiatrist diagnosed him first as delusional and, later, as obsessive-compulsive.
>
> After his discharge, Rod was medicated and placed in individual and family therapy. The family therapist was open to viewing Rod's problems as related to Rod's internal process, to the family, and to the larger context in which Rod and his family lived. The therapist, wondering how Rod's problems (in-

cluding his need for the towel) could be meaningful within his context, asked the family whether it was more approrpriate to think of the towel as a mask. As Rod and his family members pursued this question, they revealed a complex picture of the situation.

Rod had grown up in an intact family, but his parents separated a year before his hospitalization. The father stated in therapy that Rod was a fearful young man, lacking in "street smarts." He accused the mother of being too protective and never allowing Rod to "stand on the corner." When gangs moved into the neighborhood, his mother had intensified her protection, and Rod, as an adolescent, found his routine strictly controlled. Rod did not rebel. (In therapy, he admitted that part of him was fearful of street dangers, and that he liked being able to use his mother's strictness as an excuse not to get involved with the tougher kids.)

Without his parents' knowledge, however, Rod was recruited into a gang. As part of his initiation, he assaulted two members of a rival gang. Several months later, the rival gang retaliated by mugging Rod and breaking his jaw. Rod was hospitalized, and his jaw was heavily bandaged for some time. He missed a month of school, during which time he fretted over what he should do when he got better. His father pushed for him to go back to school. His mother pushed for him to remain at home until he felt ready to return. Meanwhile, Rod feared for his life. He wanted to get out of the gang, but he knew that his gang would not let him walk away. He also feared what would happen if his parents learned that he was in the gang. Not only would they be upset with him, they would also blame each other and intensify their conflict. As Rod became more and more isolated, he became extremely fearful, obsessed with his own safety, and depressed. He began to experience delusions.

At this point, he threatened suicide and was placed in a psychiatric unit.

His father once stated in family therapy that Rod had become totally "wrapped up in himself." When he was released from the hospital, Rod continued to be wrapped up—in a towel, and in himself. He fought with his mother, who felt he had been discharged prematurely from the hospital. Of course, his father sided with Rod. But if Rod got better, then one of his parents would be right and the other would be wrong. He would also have to go back to school and face the gangs. By being defined as an emotional cripple, Rod could avoid both dilemmas.

Building Blocks for a Metaframeworks Perspective

To understand the unique context that constitutes Rod's human condition, we need to include his internal process, his family, and the gangs in his community. These factors were interacting in a way that produced an effect greater than the sum of the factors themselves. If Rod, his family, and the gang had interacted differently, Rod might not have become depressed and delusional. For example, if Rod could have told his parents about the gang, he might not have been so fearful. If the gangs had not been in the neighborhood, the mother might not have been so protective. If the parents had not been at war over the proper way to bring Rod up, they could have been more supportive of each other and made it possible for Rod to come to them. If Rod had developed more autonomy, he might have known how to stay out of the gang. These factors, all interacting in a complex way, constrained Rod. In this context, the towel was meaningful: it was both a disguise and a metaphor for being "wrapped up in himself."

No single model of therapy can adequately conceptualize and treat the complex context in which Rod's problems are embedded. One solution would be to abandon all existing models and create a new, more comprehensive one. We believe that this solution would be shortsighted, however, because it would force us to abandon much of what we have found valuable in the existing models. It would also make us just one more "competitor" in the already crowded world of psychotherapy models. We could attempt to integrate existing models, but this project would require us not only to retain the limitations, incompatibilities, and contradictions of the models but also to add sophisticated guidelines for moving among them. Moreover, using the product of such an endeavor would prove overwhelming to the average clinician.

We adopt a different approach in this book. Rather than rely on existing models, we conceptualize the human condition broadly and propose a therapeutic approach that enables families to collaborate with a therapist in ameliorating the psychological suffering that arises from the human condition. We do this by means of three building blocks. First, we use systems theory to describe human systems as complex, multilevel entities. Second, we set forth presuppositions concerning the human condition, and we hold them constant throughout our work. Third, to understand the specifics of the human condition as it is related to therapy, we use six core domains: internal process, sequences, organization, development, culture, and gender. Each one contains ideas pertinent to the human condition, at the level of theory and/or knowledge about it. In the domain of development, for example, we would expect to find ideas about biological, individual, relational, and family development.

Any theory or idea can be placed in one of these domains, as long as it is consistent with our presuppositions. Not surprisingly, some theories and ideas favored by existing models fit readily into the domains; others fit only with some modification. We have also added many of our own theories and ideas to the domains. Because our approach begins with the domains and, as appropriate, examines existing models through the lens of the domains (rather than the other way around), the domains can be said to transcend the models.

Placing theories within particular domains essentially classifies them and allows us to search for underlying patterns among the ideas represented by the theories. These underlying patterns are in fact metapatterns, or what we call *metaframeworks*. Hence, each metaframework is a metapattern for the domain that it represents. The metaframeworks allow us to break free of the limitations of existing models, without abandoning the useful theories that can be drawn from them.

Systems theory and our presuppositions provide the scaffolding or underlying structure for our approach, and the metaframeworks provide the specifics for thinking about the human condition. To complete this approach, we need yet another building block: a flexible blueprint for therapy, a blueprint that replaces the clinical logic of any one model. The approach constructed from these four building blocks allows us to see and address the complexity of the human condition, without becoming overwhelmed by it. We call this approach the *metaframeworks perspective*.

Systems Theory

Systems theory is a generic term for several concepts, which, taken together, enable therapists to address problems by working with the contexts in which they occur. These concepts began to influence the field of psychotherapy in the 1950s and were instrumental in challenging the prevailing notion of mental illness as a disease caused by defects in the individual. The core concepts of systems theory include *pattern, information, relationship, level, context, feedback, recursiveness,* and *circularity.* The intellectual roots of systems theory can be traced to many disciplines: to biology and the general systems theory of Ludwig von Bertalanffy (1968); to medicine and the biopsychosocial model of George Engel (1977); to mathematics, through the theory of logical types (Whitehead and Russell, 1910); and to cybernetics (Wiener, 1967) and physics, through the theories of relativity and quantum mechanics (Capra, 1982). Many models of family therapy, as well as some individual theory models, are grounded in systems theory. The basic concepts are often overshadowed, however, by the ways in which the models have translated concepts into specific, limited understandings of a human system. More careful attention to the basics of systems theory enables us to establish a firm foundation for grappling with the complexity of human systems.

We adopt Hall and Fagan's simple definition of a system: a set of objects, together with the interaction between the objects and their attributes (Hall and Fagan, 1956). A human system, then, is not just a collection of individuals, or an individual with a set of attributes; it is a complex entity wherein interactions are just as important as the interacting parts. In any human system, the whole is greater than the sum of the parts. We have found the following characteristics of systems particularly relevant to understanding human systems.

Organization

Any collection of objects can be a system, as long as the objects bear some relation to one another and are separated from their environment by a boundary. The relationships that the parts have with one another over time is maintained within certain parameters by the system's organization. For example, the human skin constantly loses and replaces cells, but the exterior of the person remains constant. A system's organization is a set of rules defining how the various parts are structured together, as well as the function that each part of the system serves for the whole.

Levels

Complex human systems are, as Engel (1977) has noted, multilevel entities with biological, psychological, and social levels. To have a broad perspective on the human condition, it is useful to assess and have access to all levels and to the interactions among levels. As therapists, we are particularly interested in human systems at the following levels: the biological and mental processes within the individual; the individual, dyadic, or triadic relational systems within the family; the nuclear family; the extended family; the family's immediate social context, including helping systems, such as therapy and community influences; the family's historical and current cultural context; the national social system in which the family exists; and the international system.

In this multilevel system, smaller units or levels are nested within and are part of larger units. This view of systems allows us to think about parts and wholes flexibly, without becoming reductionistic—that is, without having to see one level as the cause of the problem—because each level is both a whole in itself and a part of the next level up. Koestler (1967) coined the term *holon* (from the Greek prefix *hólos,* meaning *whole,* and the Greek suffix *on,* meaning *part*) as a way "to supply the missing link between atomism and holism, and to supplant the dualistic way of thinking in terms of 'parts' and 'wholes,' which is so deeply ingrained in our mental habits, by a multi-level, stratified approach. A hierarchically-organized whole cannot be 'reduced' to its elementary parts; but it can be 'dissected' into its constituent branches of holons" (p. 197). Applying this term to a family, we consider adults and children to be holons, with adults affiliating in a *parental* holon and children in a *sibling* holon. These holons in turn are part of the *family* holon. Families are part of a *community* holon, and communities are part of a *society* holon. Koestler sees holons as semiautonomous units, capable of functioning as wholes at their own level but also of being influenced by the rules governing the larger levels to which each holon is subordinate. Using the concept of the holon, we can view any level of a system as a system in itself, and we can apply systemic principles to it (the sibling holon, for example, can be viewed as a whole system or as part of the family system). Consider the following case example:

> A mother, her fourteen-year-old son, and her ten-year-old daughter came for therapy after the death of the children's father. The son was depressed and had angry outbursts toward the mother, which sometimes became physical. The children were biracial; the mother was European-American, and the father had been African-American. It quickly became apparent that the mother was also depressed. She had been ostracized from her family because of her marriage, and she had relied exclusively on her husband and his family for support. When her husband died, she felt overwhelmed, abandoned, and angry. She also felt trapped: as a white woman with biracial children, cut off from her European roots and without her husband, she lost access to the African-American community. The son was confused as well. He wanted to protect his mother but was

angry when she withdrew from him, and he felt shame about his skin color.

The therapist focused on four levels. First, sessions were held with the whole family, to help them mourn the loss of the children's father. Second, sessions were held with the mother alone and the son alone, to help each of them with the impact of this loss on their identity. Third, sessions were held with the siblings, because the son improved much more quickly than the mother did, and the therapist worked with the siblings to help them convince the mother that they were getting over the loss of their father. Fourth, sessions were held to help reconnect the mother with her family of origin.

Boundaries

To distinguish one holon from another, it is necessary to demarcate a system by a boundary that specifies what is part of the system and what is not. Anything inside the boundary has the properties of a subsystem and obeys the rules of the system; anything outside becomes part of the system's environment. The environment of any system serves as a context for the system, placing constraints on the system by limiting what the system can import and how it can function.

Human systems, like all living systems, are open; therefore, their boundaries must be permeable, to allow resources to enter from the environment. These resources are sources of energy, matter, and information. Every system, however, also has an acceptable range of boundary permeability, below or above which the system's transport of resources will be adversely affected. For example, the boundary around the sibling subsystem must allow for some parental intrusion. If the intrusion becomes too great, however, sibling conflict will be exacerbated rather than resolved.

Interaction

Initially, systems-based therapies ignored objects and attributes and focused exclusively on interaction. Any process of a human system that shows regularity can represent an interaction. Sequences of behavior (action sequences) were initially of greatest interest to family therapists. Over the past decade, however, family therapy has also become interested in patterns of beliefs (meaning). We are now beginning to see the importance of the interaction of action with meaning. For example, a wife complains that her husband never shows affection. Reacting to this complaint and to the demand to show affection, he often disappoints her, and she responds by constantly being angry. Fearful of her anger, he withdraws. Occasionally, when he does try to be affectionate, she rejects him, believing that he is doing it only to get back in her good graces. He withdraws again, and she complains again that he never shows affection.

The husband may indeed have a problem showing affection. It is also crucial, however, to understand how the wife's difficulty in trusting his sincerity makes it impossible for her ever to experience his affection as genuine. Both the action and beliefs are part of the interaction.

Interaction relevant to a problem can occur at all levels of a system. Family therapists are most familiar with interaction among family members, but internal process also involves mental interactions. These define the person's world-view and guide how he or she chooses to act. If we look at larger systems, we can examine cultural and political patterns that affect the ways in which families and individuals behave and think.

Objects

When the pioneers of family therapy turned to systems theory, they were trying to build a paradigm for therapy that could overcome what they considered to be the limitations of the prevailing psychodynamic therapies. In so doing, they went out of their way to take the focus off the individual, emphasizing only the interactional properties of human systems. A system is not just a pattern, however, because it includes its objects and their attributes. The objects of a human system are specified by the way in which boundaries are drawn—that is, by the level of the system under analysis. People are the most obvious objects of human systems; and, ultimately, human systems cannot be understood without reference to the people who make them. Fortunately, we see nothing in systems theory to prevent our including the individual as part of the system. According to the level of analysis, there will be different objects. For example, the objects may be the various subsystems of a family, such as parents and siblings. If the boundary is drawn around the community, then the objects may be several institutions (school, gangs, the legal system). If the boundary is drawn around an individual, then the objects may be the parts that constitute the psyche, or they may be some relevant system of organs.

Attributes

For the most part, family therapy has ignored attributes. Early applications of systems theory to families did not account, in any significant way, for the fact that families are composed of males and females and that gender affords different, unequal biological and social roles, expectations, and privileges. Temperament is another significant attribute. A young mother ambivalent about her mothering ability will have more difficulty interacting with an infant who has a "slow to warm up" temperament than she will interacting with one who has an "easy" temperament (Chess, Thomas, and Birch, 1972; Guerin and Gordon, 1986).

Mechanism Versus Organism

Human systems can be conceived of as either mechanistic or organismic (Ritterman, 1977). Much of modern science, including much of psychotherapy, is based on mechanistic assumptions. From the standpoint of such assumptions, human systems are seen as operating like machines. For example, Freud applied a hydraulic metaphor, derived from Newton's law of the conservation of energy, to conceptualize the human psyche. Behaviorism, by contrast, eschewed the mind but reduced the individual to the status of a machine responding to the contingencies of its environment.

Von Bertalanffy believed that the life, behavioral, and social sciences should be based on organismic rather than mechanistic presuppositions, because living systems have characteristics that distinguish them from machines. First, they violate the second law of thermodynamics, which states that the entropy of an inanimate system will always move in the direction of maximum disorder. Living systems, however, evidence negentropy: over time, they become more ordered and complex, rather than random and disordered. Second, human systems obey the law of equifinality, which states that the same end state can be arrived at from many initial conditions. A couple, for example, ends up with the same style of arguing, regardless of the initial conditions of the argument. Third, unlike mechanistic systems, which are fully specified by the initial conditions of operation, organic systems develop and change over time. Interaction with the environment does ensure the input of the resources essential to growth, but organic systems also possess an internal blueprint for development. Fourth, organic systems exhibit spontaneous, novel, and creative activity that cannot be totally predicted. Fifth, human systems employ symbolism through the use of language, as expressed in communication, art, music, religion, literature, ritual, and so on. Using symbolism, humans create systems of meaning, which become central to the regulation of the systems in which they participate (von Bertalanffy, 1968).

Recursion

The interactions, objects, and attributes of each system level are related to the various levels of a human system in a recursive fashion, so that each factor influences the others. For example, a fifteen-year-old has temper tantrums when he does homework. He admits that a part of him is very lazy, and another part is easily frustrated. He often receives assistance from his mother, and so he never has to deal with challenges on his own. He attends a prep school where competition is intense. His mother states that the other parents help their children, and that if she did not, her son would be at a disadvantage among his peers. In this example, the tantrums are embedded within a set of recursive factors, and these include the learning style of the son, the relationship of the son and his mother, and the competitive striving of other parents of students in the son's school.

We prefer the term *recursiveness* to another systems term, *circularity*, because the latter has too often been construed to mean

that behaviors repeat themselves as identical sequences, in an
a,b,c,d,a . . . fashion. This is a mechanistic idea. It presupposes that
the family, like a machine, has unchanging parts and organization,
much as in the overused example of a household thermostat. Circularity came to be equated with regularity, wherein a sequence is
like the motion of a pendulum, highly predictable and regular.
Chaos theory (Gleick, 1988) has shown that even simple mechanical
systems are not regular. Like families, they never repeat behaviors
in exactly the same sequence. The notion of recursiveness, by contrast, rests on the idea that, over time, behaviors or beliefs consistently and reciprocally influence one another, even though the
order, frequency, and intensity with which they appear may vary.

Stability and Change

To preserve itself, a system must possess both stability and the capacity for change. Stability and change are two sides of the same
coin: there can be no change without an underlying stability (otherwise, the system dies), and there can be no stability without
change (Keeney, 1983). A system's equilibrium is preserved by this
balance of stability and change, which can be described as "order
through fluctuation" (Jackson, 1957), and is referred to in the family therapy literature as *homeostasis*. For example, a tightrope
walker maintains stability on the rope by constantly changing the
position of the balance pole. For several decades, family therapy
emphasized the stability side of the homeostatic equation, on the
basis of the belief that symptoms served a homeostatic function,
which caused disturbed families to resist change. It was believed
that the family would change only if powerful interventions disrupted its homeostasis, but this view underestimated the change side
of the equation. More recently, family therapy has recognized that
systems are always changing, and that when therapy focuses on
change of change—that is, on the system's pattern of fluctuation—
change can be achieved without the need for crisis-inducing interventions (Keeney, 1983). We share this more recent view.

Presuppositions

Every theory of therapy is essentially a world-view that involves
beliefs about the nature of the human condition, the circumstances

in which it causes human suffering, and the ingredients that can be drawn from it to facilitate health. World-views are always supported by presuppositions, which answer fundamental questions: about human systems, the nature of the mind and reality, how change occurs, the nature of power, and the functioning of systems. Many therapy models are presented so pragmatically that their presuppositions are never clearly stated. Nevertheless, presuppositions are implicit in every model; that is, one cannot *not* have presuppositions. The presuppositions of the various models of family therapy often differ from or contradict one another and that is one of the main arguments against model integration (Fraser, 1982). Therefore, if we are to move among the metaframeworks without introducing theoretical inconsistencies into our work, we must define our presuppositions and hold them constant.

Reality

Like the average layperson, many therapists give little thought to the nature of reality. They take for granted that the world in which they live is real and knowable. Inadvertently and uncritically, they accept a presupposition known as *objectivism*. This position, which philosophers refer to as "naïve realism" (Held and Pols, 1985), asserts a reality that can be grasped through direct experience. Two family therapists who adopted this view would believe that they could both watch a family interact and both see the same thing.

Objectivism permeated most of the early family therapy literature. By the late 1970s, however, many family therapists began to question the legitimacy of this view and embraced the presupposition of *constructivism*. The nature of reality, as perceived under the umbrella of constructivism, varied considerably, however. Some writers, to whom we refer as *radical constructivists*, have asserted that there is no reality except what exists in the mind (Efran, Lukens, and Lukens, 1988). Radical constructivists claim that problems exist only in the way in which they are "languaged"—that is, only in the frames or stories we believe and tell ourselves and one another about those problems. Another position, also called *constructivism* by many, is that reality does exist, but we cannot come close to knowing it objectively because of our sensory and conceptual limitations, or because of the closed nature of our sensory system, and so one map of reality is as good as another. We might call this position *pessimistic realism.*

Our own position begins with the proposition that we cannot know reality objectively. By contrast with the assumptions of radical constructivism, however, this is not because reality is only an internal construct; rather, a reality does exist "out there," but we cannot know it objectively because our perceptual apparatus and our system of internal parts provide incomplete access to it and distort any data we receive from it. But unlike the pessimistic realists, we believe that it is possible to achieve closer or more complete and less distorted approximations of reality, so that some maps actually are better than others. This position is similar to what von Bertalanffy (1968) called *perspectivism*—that one's view of reality depends on one's perspective, which sets the initial conditions for any observation. "The same table is to the physicist an aggregate of electrons, protons, and neurons; to the chemist, a composition of certain organic compounds; to the biologist, a complex of wood cells; to the art historian, a baroque object; to the economist, a utility of certain monetary value" (von Bertalanffy, cited in Davidson, 1983, p. 211). Likewise, several therapists asked to interview the same family may see very different families. The initial condition—in this case, the therapist's theory—will define the distinctions that each therapist draws and, therefore, how the therapist interacts with the family. One therapist may have a theory that the family's problems have to do with poor parenting. That therapist may ask questions that elicit parental deficits. Another therapist may believe that problems involve unresolved mourning, and that therapist may ask questions that reveal past losses. Still another therapist may see the problem as one of discipline, and that therapist may seek to show that the parents are not in charge of their children.

Perspectivism calls our attention to the importance of our theories in determining how we draw distinctions about human systems and, therefore, what we elicit in a therapy session. For example, in an initial interview with a single parent and her two children, a six-year-old encopretic girl and her two-year-old sister, the therapist asks about the presenting problem. The six-year-old picks up the recording microphone and, interrupting, says, "I been using it on myself" (an expression for wetting or soiling oneself). The therapist draws his distinctions from organizational theory, such as that reflected in Haley's strategic therapy (Haley, 1976), which suggests that the encopresis is caused by a faulty family hierarchy. Therefore, the therapist assumes that the girl's behavior is a function of lack of parental control, and he asks the mother whether that sort of thing happens at home, and the mother answers yes. Shortly thereafter, the girl interrupts again and asks if she and her sister can play with the toys. Once again viewing this behavior as a challenge to the mother's authority, the therapist asks the mother to tell the girl that she has to listen, not interrupt. The mother complies, using a stern voice, and the girl sits down and begins to suck her thumb. The therapist asks whether the thumb sucking is also a problem, and again the mother answers yes. The therapist views the thumb sucking as part of the same constellation of behaviors as the encopresis, and he concludes that his hypothesis—about hierarchy, and its relationship to the problem—is correct. In this way, the therapist's distinctions partly created the outcome, which he then took as proof of his theory.

If the therapist had used a developmental framework instead, viewing the girl's use of the microphone as an attempt to be helpful by confessing her problem, and seeing the request to play as an attempt to show that she could be helpful with her sister, then he would have viewed the situation quite differently. Consequently, he would have asked different questions; for example, he might have asked whether the girl was always so helpful. Had he done so, she might have continued to act in age-appropriate ways and might not have reached a point where she was sucking her thumb.

The Mind

Many ideas about mental process can be drawn from theories of cognition and neuroanatomy. Family therapy initially adopted a "black box" view of the mind, to avoid the complexity and speculation that accompanied these theories (Watzlawick, Beavin, and Jackson, 1967). We believe, however, that any attempt to understand the human condition must not ignore internal process. Any such approach must be straightforward enough so that therapists can work simultaneously with internal process and other levels of human systems.

Most views of the mind are monolithic—that is, they posit a monolithic model of the mind. We believe that this monolithic model is less useful than one based on the concept of multiplicity, by which we mean that people are interacting systems of an indeterminate number of autonomous and interconnected minds. Other models have called these smaller "minds" subpersonalities, but we call them *parts* because that is the word that people commonly use to describe them ("A part of me wants to go, but another part doesn't"). These parts have internal dialogues. Therefore, because they interact in sequences similar to the ways in which "external" family members interact, we can apply systems principles to internal systems as well.

Each part wants something positive, something different from what the other parts want, and will use a variety of strategies to gain influence. Parts may be forced into extreme and destructive roles, however, when the internal system becomes polarized or lacks leadership, for any number of reasons. The parts can quickly revert to their natural, nonextreme, positive state when effective internal leadership is restored and the system is depolarized.

In addition to parts, we each have a *Self,* which is a different-level entity than the parts. The Self can and should lead the internal system. It is the best leader because, unlike any one part, it has a "meta" perspective, as well as other qualities (such as compassion and moderation) that are needed for effective leadership. We find that the Self exists, with all these qualities of leadership, even in severely disturbed clients. The goal of internal work, then, is to help people differentiate the Self from the parts and, within the internal system, elevate it to a point where it can lead. In a Self-led system, the parts cooperate with one another and are there to assist the Self, lending feelings and talents as it deals with the external world.

From these assumptions, we derive an optimistic view of people. Despite the fact that people may behave in disturbing ways, have many problems, are unable to control themselves, and lack regard for themselves, they still possess the equipment they need to solve problems, control and like themselves, and behave and feel in nonextreme ways.

Constraints

If people are capable of being resourceful, then how can we explain their often not behaving in that way? For us, the answer lies in the theory of constraints, which derives from Bateson's notion of negative explanation (Bateson, 1972; White, 1986). The theory of constraints simply states that people do what they do or think what they think because they are prevented (that is, constrained) from doing or thinking something else. As in a game of checkers, in which a player is forced to a move a piece, which then gets jumped, people often find themselves in contexts where it appears to them that only limited behaviors are possible.

The concept of constraints is easy to derive from systems theory. The fact that systems are patterned means that the events and the beliefs of the system are recursively related—that is, over time, they bear some relations to one another, with each influencing the others in a reciprocal way. This recursiveness also increases the probability that events will occur and beliefs will develop. As probability for *one* event or belief increases, probability for *other* events or beliefs decreases. Consequently, options also decrease. In this way, the people in the system become constrained because their options are limited.

The notion of negative explanation can be distinguished from theories that are based on positive explanation. The latter state that people are propelled to do things by some kind of force or motivation. For example, a student is being live-supervised while interviewing a family in which the mother and a teenage daughter are fighting because the mother grants the daughter almost no autonomy, to the point where the mother will not let the daughter have her own room, even though a room is available. During a break, when the student therapist says that the mother needs the daughter to be close to her, she is evoking positive explanation. The student's supervisor responds by asking the student to consider what keeps the mother from allowing the daughter to have more autonomy: What *constrains* the mother from granting autonomy? When the student returns to the interview and asks this question, she learns that the mother was sexually abused by an uncle who lives in their home. The uncle's presence and the mother's previous experience with him create a fear that poses both a real and a psychological constraint. Positive explanation would require the therapist to understand why the mother needs the daughter to be dependent. Negative explanation suggests that the mother would allow the daughter to be more autonomous if her fears about her daughter's safety were resolved—that is, if the constraints were lifted.

Constraints can exist at any level of a human system. Within the internal system, extreme or polarized parts may constrain the range of beliefs a person can hold. Patterns of family interaction may also constrain the options available to the people in the system. For example, consider the classic sequence of a cross-generational coalition. In this sequence, one parent is too harsh and the other is too soft, with each behaving in more of the same fashion in response to the other's behavior. The harsh parent, believing that the "spoiled" child must be controlled, and in the absence of controlling behavior from the other parent, is constrained from nurturing. The nurturing parent, believing that the child is overcontrolled by the harsh parent, cannot be controlling.

The situations in which people live may also pose constraints. For example, a mother sought therapy for her daughter, who was described as agoraphobic. The mother reported that the family lived in a high-rise housing project and that her daughter would not leave their apartment. She had missed months of school and appeared quite depressed. Further exploration revealed that a son was a gang member and that rival gangs were after him. The mother and the daughter were terrified that the daughter would be harmed if she left the apartment. When police raided the apartment, searching for weapons, they removed the daughter. Her agoraphobia disappeared when she moved in with an aunt.

If constraints exist at only one level and are not serious, the problem is simple and easily solved. If many levels are involved, and if the interactions among them are complex, the problem is complex and not so easily solved, because constraints are interlocked. Just as a spider web derives great strength from its complex weave of many silk threads, so does a web of constraints powerfully limit what people can do. If constraints are of long standing, the problem becomes even more entrenched because the people involved despair of their capacity to solve it. This is particularly true of long-standing marital strife, when each party has become convinced that the other cannot or will not change. Both have given up, and their withdrawal creates a barrier that constitutes yet another constraint.

Human systems may seem very difficult and resistant to change when they are multiply constrained, and individuals who are multiply constrained by polarized or extreme parts may seem quite pathological. For example, Sid, an adolescent male living in a group home, was referred for therapy because he repeatedly ran away and refused to go to school. He had been placed in the home when he became violent toward his mother. The intake information described Sid as very disturbed. Sid was initially reticent but became animated when the therapist learned of his affection for his girl-friend's infant son. The girlfriend used drugs and did not provide adequate care for the baby, and so Sid often slipped out of the group home and missed school in order to help. When the therapist commented on Sid's caretaker part, he added that, before his placement, he had cared for his younger siblings because his mother was constantly drunk. His confrontations with her over alcohol had gradually escalated to violence. Unfortunately, the welfare authorities tried to solve the problem by removing Sid, which activated his caretaker parts and made them extreme. Putting Sid in a group home stripped him of what was meaningful to him and further impoverished the family. Continued exploration of Sid's caretaking revealed that, in trying to help so many people, he could see no future for himself. When he was helped to locate his assertive parts, Sid's attitude changed. He realized that he could not sacrifice his own life for his girlfriend and her infant. He settled into life at the group home, returned to school, and was considered by the staff to be a "miracle cure."

Regardless of the number and kinds of constraints, we believe that families feel oppressed by them and aspire to rid themselves of the difficulties that bring them to therapy. Families may be understandably cautious about taking risks, believing that their system will be destroyed by change, or they may believe that nothing can be done to lift the constraints. Either position can look like resistance and may lead the therapist to believe the family opposes therapy. Our view of therapy is straightforward: develop a relationship with family members, and collaborate with them to remove the constraints that limit their functioning. When such a collaborative relationship exists, family and therapist struggle together against the constraints, rather than against one another. The following case example illustrates the oppressive power of a web of constraints:

> A young couple was referred for therapy when the husband announced that he wanted a divorce. The husband and the wife were seen together for several sessions. The husband revealed that he had had affairs, and it became apparent that the marriage would end. The wife went into crisis and asked to be seen individually. The therapy helped her accept the end of her marriage and reconstruct her life in the postdivorce period.
>
> A major theme of this work was her inability to trust people. She feared that if she made herself vulnerable in any way, someone would take advantage of her. This issue surfaced at work (where she held a managerial position), with her friends, and particularly with a man she was dating.
>
> The therapist could easily have traced this crisis of trust to the betrayal that the woman had experienced in her marriage, and this was a major constraint; it would take time for her to trust again. But the situation was more complex. The woman originally had come from a small town in rural Kansas. Part of her wanted to remain what she called a "small-town girl." Another part of her wanted to be a "big-city woman." Growing up in a small community, she had seen people as basically trustworthy and saw no reason to be either suspicious of or aggressive toward others.
>
> Shortly after marrying, she moved to a major metropolitan area. She was successful but found urban living stressful. The city was dangerous, and the pace of life was frenetic. By comparison to people she had known in Kansas, people in the city seemed aggressive and self-centered. She was unable to "read"

them and became uneasy about their motivations. When her dreams about security in marriage were shattered, extreme and very protective suspicious parts came to her defense, telling her that the city and its people were not safe. When she felt wronged, these suspicious and aggressive parts became extreme, and she became rigid and demanding. People reacted to this extreme behavior in ways that convinced her that she had a right to be suspicious.

Over the course of therapy, the therapist helped her not only to resolve her feelings about the divorce and move on but also to learn that she was being constrained whenever suspicious and aggressive parts of her became extreme and polarized. As she learned to lead with her Self and to calm these parts, she found it much easier to trust. The therapy also examined the distinction between her small-town and big-city parts. As the woman understood her ambivalence, she realized that life in the big city would always constrain her sense of well-being. In the end, she remarried and returned to her home town.

Hierarchy, Power, and Control Versus Leadership, Balance, and Harmony

Human systems are fraught with issues of power and control, and so therapy must adopt a presupposition about these issues. Beginning with the famous differences between Bateson and Haley over power, and continuing with the feminist critique of gender imbalance, the issue of power has troubled and threatened to polarize the field of family therapy. Issues of power and control in therapy are related to generational hierarchy, to gender, and to the ways in which symptoms can be used to manipulate. Some models have tried to ignore power by asserting that is a linear concept and therefore not systemic; others are heavily grounded in power metaphors and view relationships as essentially governed by power games. Both positions create unnecessary problems: to ignore the fact that people try to control or have power over one another seems as naïve as the belief that power is all that motivates their behavior.

We resolve this dilemma by replacing the concept of unilateral control with concepts of balance and harmony. In human systems, some parts have more influence than others. For example, men have more access to the material resources of society and, therefore, more influence than women; men can leave a marriage and survive economically, while many women cannot; parents can and should have more influence than children.

Like all other ecologies, human systems are healthiest when they are balanced. This state exists when each holon of a multileveled system (1) has the degree of influence, the access to resources, and the responsibility appropriate to its needs and to its level in the system and (2) is equal to other holons at the same level. As human systems evolve, temporary departures from balance are inevitable, but healthy systems quickly regain their balance. In an unhealthy system, any departure from balance may trigger an escalating polarization among its members, so that the system moves either toward disharmonious balance (symmetrical escalation) or toward stable imbalance (rigid complementarity). For example, a sibling holon is balanced when the siblings believe that they all have appropriate access to the parents. In the absence of balance, the siblings may compete for parental attention (disharmonious balance), or one may acquiese to getting less while others enjoy parental preference (stable imbalance). In balanced systems, harmony exists among holons—that is, they cooperate, are willing to sacrifice some individual interests for the sake of the greater good, care about one another, feel valued by the larger system, and have clear boundaries that allow a balance between belonging and separateness. This does not mean that harmony is a constant state; human systems are always in flux. But the system retains, as a basic belief and value, the idea that it is possible and desirable to restore harmony.

Human systems cannot achieve or maintain balance and harmony without effective leadership. Some holon of the system is invested with responsibility for carrying out the following functions of leadership:

- Mediating conflicts between other holons
- Making sure that other holons get their needs met and feel valued
- Allocating resources, responsibilities, or influence fairly
- Providing firm and fair limits and controls
- Encouraging the growth of other holons while considering the needs of the whole system
- Representing the system in interactions with other systems
- Coordinating plans for the system's future.

In families, this task usually falls to parental figures; in classrooms, to teachers; in schools, to principals; in organizations, to bosses. Within the individual, the Self provides leadership to the parts.

Rigid and extreme leadership creates imbalances, which create polarizations, which constrain leadership, and so on. Effective leadership corrects imbalances, a correction that depolarizes and harmonizes the system, which in turn supports effective leadership. At any level of a human system, effective leadership includes the ability to be firm and set limits but also to be nurturing, encouraging, fair, and flexible. For example, the "tough love" movement, in our view, is misguided leadership. To advocate the threat of expulsion to parents of an out-of-control adolescent, without first evaluating the history of nurturance in the parent-child relationship, is dangerous. Many such adolescents are angry and uncooperative partly because they have not been adequately nurtured by their parents and think they are unwanted. "Tough love" runs the risk of confirming this belief and intensifying the vicious cycle of acting out.

Human Nature

Implicit or explicit in any model of therapy are presuppositions about human nature. Many models operate with the presupposition that human suffering is the product of human defects; consequently, therapists are taught to search for and label pathology. Such presuppositions lead to the view that people must be "fixed" before they can solve their problems, or that therapy must somehow accommodate their deficits. Our presuppositions about the mind, constraints, balance, harmony, and leadership offer explanations of human suffering that do not require a deficit-based view of human nature .

This does not mean that all people are capable of functioning to the same capacity, or that people are incapable of doing reprehensible things. Rather, it means that we take people for what they are and believe that, if constraints are lifted, they will use their talents, strengths, and resources to solve their problems. Nor does it mean that the removal of constraints will automatically produce psychologically sophisticated people. For example, a severely depressed man in his late fifties was admitted to a Veterans Administration hospital. After a month, he had not responded to medication and would not talk, and electrochemical therapy was being considered. A family therapist inquired about the man's family and learned that after World War II, when he received a psychiatric discharge, the man had moved in with his brother and his sister-in-law. He had never worked, and he spent his days doing odd jobs around the house and talking with his sister-in-law. In the year before the man was hospitalized, his brother died. His sister-in-law sold the house, and she and the man moved in with her adult son and his family. In this arrangement, the man shared a room with a teenage grandnephew. He felt displaced. He had no useful function and found himself cut off from his sister-in-law. He deteriorated rapidly, until he was hospitalized. The therapist hypothesized that the man and his sister-in-law had a long-standing affection for each other, which they never acted on. When the man's brother died, the new possibilities terrified the two, and they panicked. They sold the house and moved to a safer situation, not realizing that it would impose many constraints that would jeopardize the man's mental health. Over the course of several sessions with the family, decisions were made for the man and his sister-in-law to rent a small house near the woman's son. The man's depression lifted, and he was discharged without medication.

People sometimes do bad things, sometimes for bad reasons. Sexual abuse, domestic violence, marital betrayal, and many other unsavory acts do push us to confront the dark side of family life. But whenever we examine these acts within the multileveled systems in which they occur, we can see how the people who perpetuate them are constrained, in either their internal or their external systems. Our systemic view and our health-oriented focus allow us to retain our optimism—our belief that people can change—even in the face of gruesome stories.

We can summarize our presuppositions as follows: We hold to a part/whole view of human systems as multilevel entities, wherein each level recursively influences and is influenced by the other levels, and where problems arise from constraints that exist at one or more levels. We see change occurring through a collaborative effort, between the therapist and the family, to remove the constraints. We subscribe to a view of the mind's multiplicity, informed by a perspectivism that is neither radical constructivism nor naive realism. We accept power as a variable in human systems, but we do not approach it through the concepts of hierarchy and control; rather, we approach it through concepts of leadership, balance, and harmony.

Metaframeworks

Von Bertalanffy believed that structural similarity, or *isomorphism*, exists among systems levels; that is, "there are correspondences in the principles that govern the behavior of entities that are, intrinsically, widely different" (von Bertalanffy, 1968, p. 33). Isomorphism allows us to use the same concepts to describe different levels of systems. Therefore, we can expect to find pattern, organization, and development at each level of a system. Systems theory provides only the scaffolding for describing complex human systems, however. To understand any particular level, specific knowledge about that level's functioning must also be added. For example, organization is a systems property of both a cell and a family, but understanding the organization of a cell and that of a family will require different knowledge.

Metaframeworks are our vehicle for the specific ideas that therapists need in working with human systems. Each metaframework classifies a domain of ideas and organizes it into metapatterns. The domains derive from the considerations of systems theory. *Sequences* and *organization* are fundamental properties of systems, just as *development* is fundamental to living systems. To understand a human system, we must also have knowledge about its objects—the people who make up the system—and we gain this knowledge through the domain of *internal process*. We have found it impossible to understand human systems without serious consideration of *gender*, the core attribute that distinguishes males from females. Finally, at the broadest level, human systems are defined by *culture*. Other domains could have been included in our perspective, but we have limited our scheme to these six because they map our clinical experience so well.

Internal Process

Our view of the mind is both a presupposition and a metaframework. In creating this metaframework, we had little help from existing models of family therapy or from traditional intrapsychic models. As we mentioned a few pages back, family therapy models that derive from systems theory initially ignored internal process by using the "black box" metaphor, according to which only the inputs and the outputs of a system are important. Anything inside the "black box," including internal process, was ignored. Over the past decade, however, systemic family therapy models have revealed an interest in internal process, largely through the inclusion of meaning (belief systems) as an important part of human systems. But these models still offer no specific way of understanding the origin and nature of meaning as it emanates from internal process, and even when they do focus on internal process (either individual or family), their presuppositions about internal process either are nonsystemic or view individuals from a deficit orientation.

Schwartz (1987), the architect of the internal family systems (IFS) model, applied the basic principles of systems theory to his own clinical experience, to elaborate a model of internal process that views the mind systemically. In keeping with our presuppositions about the mind, we reject the notion of a monolithic self. We view mind as a multiplicity of subpersonalities (what we call *parts*) led by a Self. With this metaframework, any internal process, even one fraught with contradictions, can be understood and addressed. Moreover, the relationship between internal and external process can be mapped and understood, without the need to shift back and forth among conflicting models.

Sequences

Constructing metaframeworks for sequences required a different approach because all systemic family therapies used this domain, and there is already a wealth of knowledge about sequences in existing family therapy models. The problem is how to assemble these disparate fragments of knowledge into a metaframework. Building on the work of Breunlin and Schwartz (1986), we first distilled knowledge about sequences from the models, and we examined it in its own right. We then detected underlying patterns connecting various sequences. We created four classes of sequences of different periodicity, with shorter sequences also embedded in longer ones. In this way, periodicity became an overarching variable that tied all the sequences together. Using this variable, we can develop hypotheses about the complex patterning of a family and assess which sequences are relevant and how they are related.

Organization

Organizational principles are an inherent characteristic of all living systems. They are also the hallmark of structural family therapy and of Haley's version of strategic therapy. To some extent, they are included in all models of family therapy.

Hierarchy is the salient organizational concept of the structural and strategic models. In our metaframework, however, we replace it with the concepts of leadership, balance, and harmony, as already described. Our organizational metaframework, as we have said, also reexamines the function of symptoms, which can both oppress a system and be maintained by its constraints.

Development

In the 1970s, family therapy began to recognize the importance of development, and most models of family therapy came to incorporate views about development, under the rubric of the family life cycle. The development metaframework considerably expands the traditional concept of the family life cycle by building on the premise that development in human systems takes place at each level: biological, individual, relational, family, and societal. This metaframework also examines recursive relationships among levels in terms of development, making it possible to see how developmental problems at one level can constrain development at others and contribute to the emergence and maintenance of problems. The development metaframework builds on the work of Breunlin (1988, 1989), which posits that symptoms can be a function of developmental oscillations, whereby an identified patient acts older or younger than his or her age.

Culture

Family therapy acknowledges that families are bounded by and live in an environment, but theories of problem formation and change have focused almost exclusively on the family itself, without regard to the context in which the family is embedded. This trend has been tempered, however, by a body of literature that views culture as a primary context for understanding a family's environment. Building on the work of Karrer (1989), we construct a multicultural metaframework that adopts a broad definition of culture. More than a description of specific sociocultural characteristics, our definition reflects sensitivity to the multiple contexts in which people are embedded and learn a variety of ways to be human. These contexts are classified by economics, education, ethnicity, religion, gender, generation, race, minority or majority status, and regional background. The contexts themselves change and evolve as a result of cultural transition, immigration, and acculturation. Within each level of a human system, as well as across levels, similarities and differences in contexts and rates of change produce opportunities or constraints, according to the degree to which contexts fit together. The multicultural metaframework allows therapists to identify and lift cultural constraints, as well as to use therapeutic opportunities presented by placement(s) in various contexts.

Gender

No movement has affected family therapy in the past decade as dramatically (and, at times, as divisively) as feminism has. As already mentioned, some feminist family therapy theorists have argued that systems theory is inappropriate to family therapy. Our gender metaframework builds on the multivocal feminist discourse in family therapy but also seeks to reconcile feminism and systems theory in a gender-balanced approach to family therapy.

Combining Metaframeworks

The metaframeworks are a recursive set of ideas that interact with and complement one another. To understand a human system, we often draw on more than one metaframework, and our hypotheses are often hybrids, constructed from the ideas contained in several metaframeworks. For example, we may hypothesize that a child with a problem at school is caught in an oscillation (*development*), which cannot be resolved because the leadership in the family (*organization*) is compromised by parents with polarized parts (*internal process*) and male-female imbalances (*gender*). If we disregard any of these metaframeworks, our hypothesis is weakened and we limit the possible points of entry for therapy. For the following case example, we combined elements of the internal process, sequences, and culture metaframeworks:

> A psychiatrist referred Joe for what was called a serious problem with lying. Joe had been a professor at a small Christian college. Through the course of an affair, Joe had lied both to his wife, Joan, and to his lover, Karen. Since infidelity always involves lying, why was the lying so serious in this instance? The basic question for the therapist was not "Is Joe a pathological liar?" or even "Why does Joe lie?" but rather "What keeps Joe from telling the truth?"
>
> Joe reported that he and Karen, feeling dishonest about the secrecy of their affair, had decided to make it public. When they told the truth, the Chris-

tian community immediately ostracized them. Joe lost his job, and friends and neighbors shunned them. The culture of fundamentalist Christianity had placed Joe in a double bind: while professing honesty as the best policy, the culture had punished Joe for being honest. Cut off from his support network, and under intense pressure from his parents to give up the affair and go back to his wife, Joe was riddled with doubt. He wanted to give his marriage another try, but he hoped not to lose Karen, and so he lied to both women. Karen learned of Joe's lies and was devastated, particularly because she had relied on Joe for the only support she could get. She decided to break off the relationship with him.

When the therapist explored the lying with Joe, he learned that part of Joe had always rebelled against the strict religious teachings of his parents, but another part felt very guilty whenever he went against their wishes. Not wanting to let them down, and constantly feeling pressure from them to conform, Joe fell into a pattern of telling small lies, to conceal his "non-Christian" behavior. For years he lived a public life of conformity, particularly in his marriage. He described his wife as being just like his mother, always pushing him to be something that he felt he was not. Joe felt that his marriage had become a lie, and that what he and Karen had done was his first honest act.

When Joe experienced the isolation and pressure from his parents, his wife, and the community, however, he buckled. The part of himself that told him to be a good Christian pushed him back toward his marriage. The part that told him to be honest with himself pushed him toward Karen. For a while, lying enabled Joe to do what he had done for much of his previous life: attempt to satisfy both parts. Therefore, Joe's lying can be understood as a function of culture, of the marital relationship, and of Joe's internal process. When the therapist helped Joe see the context of

his lying, Joe decided that his marriage really was
dead, and that he truly did want a relationship with
Karen. But could he ever redeem himself?

Karen eventually agreed to see Joe again, provided that they went into therapy. Karen asserted that
she still loved Joe but was terrified that he was a liar,
or that he might succumb to religious pressure to preserve his marriage and leave her. She was intensely
suspicious of Joe. While willing to talk about a relationship, she was afraid to commit herself to it. The
therapist wondered whether Karen had always had extreme suspicious parts, and he learned that the opposite was true. Karen said that she had always been a
trusting person, perhaps even naïve. When people
close to Karen rejected her because she had an affair
and her marriage ended tragically, she began to experience suspiciousness, which was quite unfamiliar to
her. She also said that she had never been very assertive
and did not know how to deal with Joe so that she
would not be hurt again. The good intention of the
suspicious part, therefore, was to ensure that Karen
would not get hurt again.

Joe pursued his divorce. As in most divorces,
however, there were inevitable delays and complica-
tions, each of which aroused Karen's suspicious part.
When this part became extreme, she would pressure
Joe to act and to tell her what was causing the delays.
Joe reacted by being evasive or withholding information, which only fueled Karen's suspicious part, leading to yet more pressure on Joe. This polarization
always culminated in bitter arguments that made the
couple question the viability of their relationship.
Several sequences of this sort brought the relationship
to a crisis, and it looked as if it would end. When the
therapist helped the couple see how their extreme
parts, the repeating sequence, and the constant oppression from the fundamentalist Christian community was defeating their relationship, they began to

move forward. The therapist also helped Joe separate from his parents and stop tolerating the emotional abuse of their religious pressure. After several months of ups and downs, Joe's divorce became final. Joe and Karen entered a period of stability, which allowed their relationship to flourish.

A Blueprint for Therapy

The metaframeworks enable us to transcend the narrowness of the theories that form the basis of existing family therapy models. In the same way, we need a clinical approach that transcends the limitations of those models' interventions and techniques. We need a basic blueprint for therapy, on which we can map a clinical practice that is consistent with our presuppositions.

The blueprint proposed here is very simple. It recognizes four interrelated processes of therapy: *hypothesizing, planning, conversing,* and *reading feedback.* The metaframeworks and our presuppositions form the basis for hypothesizing, and our collaborative approach forms the basis for planning. The process of therapy itself is a conversation in which the therapist draws distinctions by asking questions, making statements, and giving directives while constantly attempting to make sense of and use the family's feedback.

The blueprint must also be flexible enough to let us select whatever locus of change we feel is appropriate. (Psychotherapy models, by contrast, have often specified a limited focus of change.) The therapy literature has tended to make distinctions between action and meaning, as well as among the domains of experience, description, and explanation. We take a *both/and* rather than an *either/or* position on such foci.

Action and Meaning

Since its inception, family therapy, like all the rest of psychotherapy has struggled with the relationship between action and meaning (Pearce and Cronen, 1980). Synonyms for the term *action* are *behaviors, sequences,* and *interactions.* Synonyms for *meaning* are *beliefs, cognitions, premises, perceptions,* and *ideas.* The debate often centers on whether action or meaning is the appropriate locus of change in therapy. A causal relationship is sometimes attributed to the two: if meanings change, behaviors will change, and vice versa. Psychoanalysis has relied exclusively on meaning changes; pure behaviorism, on behavior. As already noted, family therapy initially favored action but has been increasingly interested in meaning. We believe that good therapy relies on both action and meaning.

When people relate to one another, they engage in a recursive process, whereby they attribute certain meanings to their interactions. The interactions in turn create certain meanings. Over time, meanings and actions fit together in an organized pattern (Bogden, 1984a; 1984b). People may not see the same meanings, but meanings do become coordinated, so that meaning for one family member elicits complementary meanings for other family members (Pearce and Cronen, 1980). For example, a man may have been brought up in a family where teasing served to establish the good feelings that defined positive relationships, while a woman may have come from a family in which the parents used teasing as a form of ridicule. If the man initiates an episode of teasing, to show friendliness, the woman will take his behavior to mean that she is being ridiculed. She may also believe that the best thing to do is not to show that she feels ridiculed. The man, for his part, may believe that her lack of overt response is an invitation to more teasing, and so he continues to tease her, and on they go. They may develop a relationship that becomes strained whenever they engage in an episode of teasing (ridicule). Change in this relationship may occur if the teasing stops, or if the meaning attributed to teasing changes.

Because no one model of family therapy provides all the tools necessary to address action, meaning, and the relationship between them, we must transcend the models, drawing on the best that each one has to offer. We still must have skills of observation, to see patterns of interaction, but we must also be able to perceive the internal process of family members, to see how they attribute meaning to specific actions. Sometimes we want family members to begin acting differently, whether we suggest the use of enactment or a ritual or the changing of a sequence. At other times, we try to work with meaning: altering, through circular questioning, the way one person's meaning system contextualizes an action, or working with conflicting beliefs in one or more parts of a system. Giving ourselves permission to focus on both action and meaning helps us practice what family therapy preaches: namely, flexibility.

Experience, Description, and Explanation

Psychotherapy is an encounter between a client system and a therapist, which takes place within the domains of experience, description, and explanation (Dell, 1986). *Experience* is the affective impact of an event in an individual's environment. *Description* is the way in which the individual recounts experience. *Explanation* is the meaning attributed to experience, on the basis of a particular description of it. Experience, description, and explanation are recursively related to one another. We may experience an event, describe it, and give it an explanation, but subsequent and similar events will be sought or avoided partly on the basis of the affect associated with it and the explanation or description given of it. How an experience is described can influence its explanation, and vice versa. How we describe one event colors how we experience subsequent and similar events.

Clients bring experiences, descriptions, and explanations to therapy, which itself becomes an experience that solves problems by means of these three domains. Some therapies emphasize one domain over another. Some even eschew the use of certain domains. We believe that all three domains provide useful points of entry for therapy. We can validate the experience of one family member, and we can help other family members accept that all experience is real for the one who undergoes it. We can help people examine and change the descriptions that they give of experiences, and we can challenge explanations that produce counterproductive beliefs.

Techniques and Interventions

With our blueprint for therapy, we can use any technique or intervention, as long as it is consistent with our presuppositions and with the collaborative nature of our therapy. To do this, however, we often have to modify interventions. For example, we are still fond of what the structural family therapists call *enactment* (Minu-

chin and Fishman, 1981). We ask family members to interact with
one another, but we recognize that enactment is not just a behavioral dance. It also activates parts of people that attribute meaning
to the events and evoke feeling responses to it. Enactment allows us
to focus on both action and meaning, as well as to address several
levels of the system. The use of a blueprint allows us to be flexible
without falling into a woolly eclecticism, because the plan is always
tied to the metaframeworks.

Our metaframeworks perspective grew out of our frustration
with the limitations of the existing family therapy models and out
of our belief that the best way to overcome those limitations was to
transcend the models themselves. We sought to preserve valuable
aspects of the models, however, and fill the gaps without having to
create yet another model with its own limitations. Using the metaframeworks, we can grapple with a large amount of complexity but
not get confused and overwhelmed. The complexity, and our way
of approaching it, help us remain curious about and appreciative
of the human condition, as well as respectful of the struggle that
humans undergo to live healthy lives. Because we respect them, we
can collaborate with families in their efforts to remove the constraints that have come to oppress them.

PART 2

Six Core Metaframeworks

THREE

Of Mind and Self:
The Internal Family Systems
Metaframework

There are many reasons why systems-oriented family therapists and theorists traditionally have eschewed theories of personality and, like the behaviorists before them, have tried to construct models of human functioning that have no intrapsychic base. The reason most frequently cited is that the addition of an intrapsychic layer of complexity to the already complex phenomena of family interaction would overwhelm therapists.

It is true that while the pioneers of family therapy were struggling to develop maps of the totally unfamiliar territory of family process, they needed to focus on these "external" interactions exclusively and could not afford to be distracted or confounded by efforts to incorporate each family member's internal dynamics into their formulations. Furthermore, many of these pioneers had become interested in families largely because of what they perceived as the failure of existing models of intrapsychic process to produce an effective approach to therapy. They sought the creation of a new, more optimistic, and more practical approach. Consequently, they had little patience with the pace and pessimism of analytically derived models, which they identified as linear and based in the medical model. It seems that, to differentiate themselves from the individual therapy establishment, from which many of them had come, these pioneers in family therapy became rigidly external in focus and felt justified in doing so, because they had discovered the power of external context and believed that changing a person's family would sufficiently change his or her internal life.

Such "psychephobia" can be seen as a necessary and natural stage in the development of family therapy, but the question arises of whether the field can move beyond that stage, to incorporate a more complete view of human systems that includes internal as well as external process. There is nothing inherent in systems theory (or in cybernetics) to preclude its application to internal process, but it does seem to take time for some systems thinkers to accept that possibility. Many of the reluctant are dyed-in-the-wool Batesonians, who were steered away from viewing the psyche as a system by Bateson's attempt to expand the notion of mind:

> The basic rule of systems theory is that, if you want to understand some phenomenon or appearance, you must consider that phenomenon within the context of all *completed* circuits which are relevant to it. The emphasis is on the concept of the completed communicational circuit and implicit in the theory is the expectation that all units containing completed circuits will show mental characteristics. The mind, in other words, is immanent in the circuitry. We are accustomed to thinking of the mind as somehow contained within the skin of an organism, but the circuitry is *not* contained within the skin.
>
> Consider the case of a man felling a tree with an ax. Each stroke of the ax must be corrected for the state of the cut-face of the tree after each chip flies. In other words, the system which shows mental characteristics is the whole circuit from the tree to the man's sense organs, through his brain to his muscles and the ax, and back to the tree. This is not the unit that psychologists are accustomed to considering but it is the unit which systems theory will force them to consider.
>
> Very little thought will show that this change in relevance from thinking of man versus tree will

change our ideas of the nature of the self, the nature
of power, responsibility, and so on [1970, p. 244].

This is an odd view of mind, which does not square with
Bateson's view of other systems; for example, he does not prohibit
the study of a family as a system of parents and children. To be
consistent, he should have advocated giving up the notion of a
family as parents and children and instead asserted that we ought
to think of a family only as family members plus all the "completed
circuits that are relevant to" the family, which may include schools,
work environments, helpers, extended family, and so on. By contrast with his position on mind, Bateson has been instrumental in
stressing the importance of both understanding the family as a unit
and viewing it within all its relevant "circuits."

A clue to the reason for Bateson's odd treatment of mind is
found in the last paragraph of the passage just cited. Bateson was
passionately interested in finding a new way for humankind to view
its relationship to nature. It was his hope, obviously, that this mind-
as-circuits notion would make us feel more connected to one
another and to nature (much as the Buddhist or Taoist traditions
advocate) and therefore more sensitive to the consequences of our
actions. His next paragraph is even more telling of these motives:
"[This view of mind] might even lead the human race to a sort of
wisdom that would preclude the wanton destruction of our biological environment and preclude some of the very peculiar attitudes
we exhibit towards patients, foreigners, minorities, our spouses, and
our children—and even each other" (p. 244).

It is interesting to note that while Bateson's intention to get
humanity to think more ecologically was similar to Buddhist or
Taoist intentions, his modus operandi was different from that of
those traditions. Those philosophies encourage people to work on
themselves through such techniques as meditation and, through
that inner work, to find that they have come to feel more ecologically connected. Bateson's approach is more similar to that of fundamentalist religions. Just as they may ban the very thought of lust
or other sins, in the hope that people who are not thinking about
something will behave differently, Bateson seems to have believed
that if we could banish our ordinary conceptions of such things as

mind or power, we would behave more ecologically. The problem with this approach is that it orders people not to experience things that they cannot help experiencing, and this puts them at odds with the parts of themselves that do experience those things.

We have the same goal as Bateson did, but not the same approach to its achievement. We contend that the internal level of system deserves and must receive the same treatment that other levels (such as the family) have received, so that we can understand how mind operates as a system within the boundaries of an organism, as well as how that system interacts with external systems. Instead of banning traditional uses of the concepts of mind or power, we try to help people see and use them in a different way, a way that eliminates many negative consequences. It is our hope and has been our experience that if we can construct a systemic map of internal process that enables people to balance and harmonize themselves, they will become more ecologically sensitive and will feel more connected to other people and to nature. The model described in this chapter seems to help people quickly access the place in themselves where their connection to other people and to nature is experienced.

Family Therapy and Internal Process

In family therapy, the time seems right to revisit internal systems. Through the work of the family therapy pioneers and the generation that followed them, and with the help of systems thinking, we have devised useful maps for the territory of family process, and we are perhaps in less danger of being overwhelmed by its complexity. The field also now seems so differentiated and established that it no longer needs to continue staking and guarding its claim to difference from models that have centered on intrapsychic formulations.

As a sign of this change, there have been several attempts to integrate family systems approaches with existing psychodynamic models. Object relations theory has been the primary target of integrationists because its shift away from Freudian drives as the basis for behavior and toward relationships with inner and outer "objects" seems compatible with the relationship focus of family therapy (Wachtel and Wachtel, 1986; Scharff and Scharff, 1987; Nichols,

1987; Slipp, 1988; Luepnitz, 1988). Nevertheless, despite family therapy's burgeoning interest in the individual, this integrationist movement is problematic because, we believe, object relations still contains many of the assumptions (about individual defectiveness and pathology) that originally turned the family therapy pioneers away from psychoanalysis.

Expanding Systems Thinking Inward

Instead of trying to integrate family systems principles and techniques with a preexisting model, why not see what happens if systems thinking is extended into the individual's inner domain? The same Bateson who argued against a mind-within-organism concept foreshadowed this question (and seemingly contradicted his own position) in this passage:

> [T]he ways of thinking evolved by psychiatrists in order to understand the family as a system will come to be applied in understanding the individual as a system. This will be a fundamental change within the home territory of psychology, i.e., in the study of the individual, and a corresponding change in the philosophy and practice of individual psychotherapy . . . many parts of conventional individual psychology have long been ready for framing within systems theory, notably the Freudian concept of psychological conflict where the contrasting poles of thought or motivation are conventionally assumed to be interactive, each promoting the other [Bateson, 1970, p. 243].

Perhaps a different "part" of Bateson wrote that passage.

In 1983, Schwartz began to take a fresh, systemic look at internal process. The resulting internal family systems (IFS) model (Schwartz, 1987) will be described in this chapter and provides many of the ingredients necessary to a more effective and comprehensive systems therapy. For example, it fills a gap in family therapy's conceptualizations and language, which have been rife with such "dormative principles" (Bateson, 1972) as enmeshment and homeostasis. These concepts have value as descriptors of process but, because of the lack of alternatives, they have been given explanatory power: "Why are mother and daughter so close?" "Because they are enmeshed." "Why do they resist change?" "Because of the homeostasis in the system." Because we could not talk about characteristics of individuals in the family, we were forced to bastardize our family concepts and use them in circular explanations barren of empathy for and understanding of the human condition.

Minuchin (Simon, 1984, p. 14) agrees that we need another language: "When family therapy wrapped itself in the words of systems thinking, we lost in the translation. We lost in our understanding of the emotional world of human beings, with their complexities and painful contradictions. . . . The theories of family therapy were increasingly expressed in a dry, dehumanized, predictable babble, all too similar in many ways to the language of psychoanalysis." When family therapists do discuss individuals, they try, admirably, to avoid traditional diagnostic categorizing. But since they lack a language that conveys their optimistic and systemic philosophy on the individual level, such discussions can easily become pessimistic: "Johnny is a needy, dependent child who is trying to protect his parents' marriage. His mother is enmeshed with him and afraid to let him grow up. His father is overly rational and afraid to deal with his wife's feelings." Depictions like this are presented in case conferences across the country and portray family members unidimensionally, with the focus on the aspects of their personalities that are thought to be causing the problem.

As we will demonstrate, the IFS model provides a rich, empowering, and optimistic language that captures the multidimensional and resourceful nature of people and allows therapists to see the continuity of patterns of interaction within and among family members. The model reflects an understanding of people that is derived from and is totally compatible with systemic assumptions (see Chapter Two) and so allows therapists to see connections, as well as opportunities to intervene, between the internal and external worlds.

But how, with the addition of this internal level of conceptualization, does a therapist decide which level of system to focus on? "External only" family therapists have always had to choose whether to focus on the whole family, on various subsystems of the nuclear or extended family, or on the family's relationship with other systems. These choices made things complex enough, without the addition of each family member's inner life to the menu. We find that using the IFS model reduces rather than compounds the complexity of the task facing a family therapist, because it is easier to choose a focus when one clearly understands the aspects of each family member that are involved in the family's problematic inter-actions. Let us return to the example of Johnny. It may be clear, from talking with the family about the problem, that the needy, childlike part of Johnny takes over whenever his mother tells him what to do, and that her controlling part, which tells Johnny what to do, is activated by an apathetic part of her husband, which takes over in response to Johnny's needy part, and so on. With a map like this one, the therapist and the family can discuss together the best level on which to focus, to get these parts of each person to back off and let everyone function competently.

The resulting treatment is likely to include intervention at a combination of levels. The therapist discusses with family members what changes can be made in their relationships, so that these parts will interfere less. The therapist may also help family members work on their own parts, individually or while the others watch. The point is that this model offers the understanding and the lan-guage to allow the direction of therapy to emerge collaboratively, through asking about the best way to keep various parts from im-posing constraints. There is usually no need to know about the entire system of each family member's parts; only those parts par-ticularly involved in the problem need to be considered, so that complexity is not overwhelming.

In addition to its value in providing direction and a general language for therapy, the IFS model has enabled us to stumble onto the discovery that, when we apply systemic principles and tech-niques to people's internal processes, people are able to change their internal systems more rapidly than has been thought possible. In light of this discovery, the therapist can trust family members more to be able to change themselves, and this heightened trust forms the basis of a collaborative, strengths-oriented therapy. Thus, instead of having to come up with and "sell" a good reframing of a problem, the therapist need only help family members make some internal shifts, and they will see one another differently and come up with solutions on their own.

The Internal Family of Parts

The IFS model is based on a view of the mind that, while still quite controversial, is increasingly becoming accepted in the world of psychotherapy. This is the view that the mind, rather than being a unitary entity, is a collection of subminds or subpersonalities, each of which operates with relative autonomy and whose characteristics, intentions, and feelings are different from those of the others. After spending many years trying to understand "external" families and ignoring internal process, we stumbled onto this phenomenon of multiplicity when, out of frustration with the limits of the "external-only" models, we began to interview bulimic clients about their inner selves (Schwartz, 1987). We became excited by the prospect that a client's inner system might operate and change in much the same way that family systems do. Although we were unaware of it at the time, the multiplicity phenomenon had been perceived and studied by a number of nontraditional models of psychotherapy for many years. These included psychosynthesis (Assagioli, 1973); two Jungian derivatives, voice dialogue (Stone and Winkelman, 1985) and archetypal psychology (Hillman, 1975); ego state therapy, derived from hypnotherapy (Watkins and Watkins, 1982); and, within family therapy, the internal cast of characters (Watanabe, 1986). Encountering each of these models, we experienced an odd mixture of confidence (since each of these models confirmed aspects of the IFS model) and trepidation (since we feared that we had perhaps merely rediscovered the wheel). It was increasingly clear, however, that the application of systemic principles and techniques to the "society" of subpersonalities had produced a novel model and was leading to discoveries and possibilities that had not been described elsewhere.

What do we mean by the subpersonality or multiplicity phenomenon? Throughout the day, people pass regularly (and often imperceptibly) from subpersonality to subpersonality. Given the speed and fluidity of this process, as well as the fact that we are conditioned to view these changes simply as mood shifts within our unitary personality, we do not usually attend to the ways in which our inner community conducts its business. In observing client families, it is very easy to become absorbed in content and ignore process. In the same way, we may notice thoughts running through our heads but fail to recognize that they emerge from a range of recurrent conversations that we carry on with ourselves. Of course, the exact quality of these conversations can be extraordinarily elusive. We are capable of having any number going on at the same time. What is more, we can converse with ourselves in many "languages," some of which consist of images or body sensations rather than words.

Living as a human being is a very complex enterprise. We have to do and think many things at once. We need specialized minds, which operate with a certain amount of autonomy and internal communication, to accomplish all this simultaneous activity. The evidence for multiplicity is abundant. How else are we to understand the "spontaneous inspiration" involved in creativity, in which the answer to problems come to us "out of the blue," in the middle of the night? Religious conversions, the "out of character" behavior triggered by drug or alcohol intoxication, the experience of suddenly falling in or out of love, the various phenomena of multiple personality disorder are all examples of people's capacity to undergo dramatic and sudden personality changes. We see such changes not simply as shifting sets of emotions or thought patterns; instead, they often seem to represent shifts to a completely different world-view, complete with its own consistency of values, interests, beliefs, and feelings.

The more we explored the nuances of our clients' subjective experiences of themselves, the more the analogy to a family or a community seemed to make sense in understanding this inner world. The subpersonalities (called *parts* here, because that is what most people call them) that inhabit this world are both interconnected and autonomous. These parts, like members of an "external" family, vie for control, interact sequentially, organize into alliances, and sometimes go to war with one another.

Often the most important (but not the only) factor shaping the organization of our inner community is our experience in our family of origin. We tend to identify with, rely on, and listen to the parts of us that our family valued, or that helped us play a particular role while growing up. At the same time, we tend to distance ourselves from or stifle parts that our families disapproved of. Some of our parts relate to us in the same way that one or the other parent did, while other parts battle those parental replicas. Each of these parts is a discrete, autonomous mental system, with an idiosyncratic range of emotion, style of communication, and set of abilities, intentions, and functions. Each is organized around a particular premise or set of premises about the world and how to survive or thrive within it.

To give a common example, most people can identify an assertive part that tells them to stand up for themselves and go after what they want. This part is organized around the premise that it is best to confront problems and people directly. Most people are also aware of a cautious part that tells them to be careful, so as to not get hurt emotionally or physically. This cautious part's organizing premise is that the world holds dangers that must be considered.

Some people grow up in "angerphobic" families, where their assertive parts are disdained or feared. Jane was one of these people, and the harmonious balance between her normal assertive and cautious parts was disturbed because she was taught to fear her assertive part, and so she tried not to listen to it. Instead, she always followed the advice of her cautious part, which told her that she should never think of herself first. Jane's assertive part, after years of frustration at its lack of access to her, years during which she was continually exploited by people, became increasingly angry. Thus, on the rare occasions when the cautious part's hold on Jane weakened and the assertive part was able to take control, Jane turned into a raving maniac. These outbursts redoubled her conviction that her assertive part should be feared and isolated, and that she should follow the cautious part's lead.

This example highlights two primary assumptions of the IFS model. First, all parts, in their nonextreme, natural state, want something positive for the person and desire to play a valuable role in the internal system. Since each part's positive intentions are different from the positive intentions of other parts, conflict among parts is inevitable. How conflict is handled often determines whether the inner selves polarize (and, in the process, become extreme and destructive) or remain valuable resources. Even when parts become extreme, however, they want to return to their non-extreme, valuable state, and often can do so quickly when internal polarization is reduced. If Jane could have seen her angry, assertive part with less fear and had been able to give it more access to her, she would have seen a dramatic shift in how it presented itself.

The second assumption is that the same positive feedback escalations that characterize polarization in "external" families also characterize polarization in internal families. For example, the more Johnny is excluded by his family, the more he, attempting to protect himself from feeling hurt, acts apathetic and distant toward the family, and the more his family, interpreting his apathy as his not wanting to be in the family, excludes him, and so on. Similarly, the more Jane excludes her assertive part, the more extreme it becomes, which furthers her commitment to exclude it, and so on. Family therapy has shown that such escalation can be reversed quickly in many cases, and when it is, things quickly return to their nonextreme state. The same is true of inner "family" systems.

The Self

In the example of Jane, we saw two parts in conflict. But who is "Jane"? Who excludes the one part and elevates the other? Our picture of the inner world is still incomplete. We will now discuss a crucial participant in the internal family: the Self.

In applying the techniques of family therapy to internal systems, we repeatedly observed that when a person was dealing with one part, other parts would frequently interrupt the process or otherwise interfere. Using a simple boundary-setting technique taken from structural family therapy, we asked the person to keep those interfering parts away from the action. We often found that, immediately after the person was able to differentiate from the interfering parts, his or her perspective on the original part would shift. Instead of seeing the original part in some extreme way, the person would suddenly have compassion for or curiosity about it. It seemed that people, when they could differentiate from their parts, all had a similar experience, described as feeling "calm," "lighthearteded," "confident," and "in the present." It also seemed that people in this state were able to change their relationships with each part, as well as the relationships among parts, with relative ease. We found that the experience of being in this state is comparable to what people experience while meditating: an experience of being centered and outside the flux of moment-to-moment identification with particular parts of themselves. Yet we found that the Self is more than a passive state of consciousness. The Self can be highly active in a person's internal politics, assuming leadership in reorganizing the internal family and in dealing with the external world.

We began to focus on differentiating the Self in clients, so that it could assume a position of leadership as quickly as possible. We found that the Self, in that position, could comfort and soothe parts that felt and looked like frightened or sad children, calm raging defenders, and redirect overzealous strivers. The Self could become a therapist to the internal family by getting the polarized inner antagonists to deal with one another and by helping the whole inner community depolarize and restructure itself. We found that, in general, the various parts of clients welcomed this kind of leadership, once they were convinced that the Self could be trusted. Moreover, clients could do this work on themselves, between sessions, once they knew what to do, and so they were less dependent on us, and they felt empowered.

The goal, then, of the IFS model is to help people reorganize their internal systems, so that the Self is generally in the lead and the parts are there to advise, lend feelings or talents, or otherwise assist. Schwartz uses the metaphor of an orchestra, in which the parts are analogous to the musicians and the Self to the conductor:

> A good conductor has a sense of the value of each instrument and the ability of every musician, and is so familiar with music theory that he or she can sense the best point in a symphony to draw out one section and mute another. Indeed, it is often as important for a musician to be able to silence his or her instrument at the right time as it is to play the melody skillfully. Each musician, while waiting to spotlight his or her own

talent or have the piece played in a way that emphasizes his or her section, has enough respect [for] the conductor's judgment that he or she remains in the role of following the conductor yet playing as well as possible. This kind of a system is (literally) harmonious. . . .

Thus, I am suggesting that we all have within us a capable conductor. One implication of this assumption is that the goal of therapy shifts from the gradual development of the Self to the elevation and differentiation of the Self, much as a family therapist helps . . . parent[s] to elevate [themselves] to a position of unbiased and non-extreme leadership in a family. Thus, the length and difficulty of treatment will often depend on where the Self begins in the hiearchy of the internal system rather than how many stages it is behind in its development [1987, p. 31].

Summary of IFS Assumptions

At this point, we will try to help the reader grasp the IFS model's view of people, as well as how it differs from views offered by other models, by providing a summary of the model's major assumptions.

Multiplicity

It is the nature of the human mind to be subdivided into an indeterminant number of subpersonalities, or parts, that interact internally in sequences and styles that are similar to the ways in which "external" people interact (most clients identify and work with between five and fifteen parts through the course of therapy). Each part wants something positive and different for the person and will use a variety of strategies to gain influence within this internal system, to get its desires attended to. This multiplicity or differentiation is inherent in the nature of the mind. It is not caused by introjection of external phenomena (although the images and behavior of parts are affected by the external world) or by the fragmenting, through trauma, of a once unitary personality.

The Self

In addition to this collection of parts, a person has a Self, a different-level entity from the parts, which is often at the center of the "you" that the parts are talking to, and which likes or dislikes, listens to or shuts out, various parts. The Self can and should lead the person's internal system: unlike any part, it has a systemic perspective, as well as other abilities that permit its leadership. The Self comes fully equipped to lead and does not have to develop through stages or be introjected or strengthened. Instead, the Self needs to be differentiated from the network of its relationships with the various parts that prevent its effective leadership.

Self Leadership

All systems—families, organizations, nations—function best when leadership is clearly designated, respected, fair, and capable. The internal family system is no different. When the Self is in a position to lead, it will do so, in the sense of taking care of and disciplining the parts in an equitable, firm and compassionate way, making major decisions regarding the direction of the person's life, and dealing with the external world. With Self leadership, the parts do not disappear. Instead, they are there to advise, remind, work on solutions to problems, lend talents or emotions, or otherwise help. Each one has a different, valuable role and set of abilities. The parts will generally cooperate, rather than compete or conflict with one another. When conflicts do arise, the Self will mediate. When this is the case, the person will be less aware of the existence of the parts because the system is operating harmoniously.

Internal Interaction Patterns

Since the parts are relatively autonomous, they form relationships with one another that can have major impacts on the whole system. Often, for example, these internal relationships must be addressed before the Self can be fully differentiated. Moreover, if a person attempts to change one part or its relationship to the Self without also considering the network of internal relationships in which it is embedded, other parts are liable to interfere or try to reverse the change. Some models interpret this kind of ecological reaction as resistance. The client's motivation to change is questioned, and the client is encouraged to slowly "work through" this resistance. In the larger picture of the internal family, however, one can perceive the internal relationships that are most amenable to changes, predict which other parts are likely to be activated by those changes, and deal, directly with those parts when they are activated.

Polarization and Positive Feedback Loops

Like external systems, internal family systems operate according to systemic principles. For example, because of historical or current events or interaction patterns, the Self may not be trusted to lead, or one or more parts may become extreme. When this is the case, the internal system polarizes, and parts become extreme in opposite directions, to counter one another. The more extreme a part is, the more will the extreme assumptions that other parts or the Self have about it be confirmed; thus is polarization perpetuated.

Depolarization

Extreme parts do not enjoy their extreme roles. They want to return to their nonextreme, valuable, appreciated roles, but they are afraid. They fear elimination or punishment. They are so identified with their current roles, they believe that there is nothing else they can do, or that they will be punished by other parts if they back down. They also fear revolution—if they back down, parts or other people whom they oppose will take over and harm the person or make him or her extreme in the opposite way. If the Self can demonstrate the power to prevent such consequences, the part often gladly adopts a valuable role and maintains it as long as the Self maintains effective leadership. For change to last, one cannot change one part in isolation. One must consider and change the part's relationship to the Self and to other parts.

Internal and External Parallels

Changes in the external systems in which one is embedded bring about parallel changes in one's internal system, and vice versa. This recursiveness between the internal and external levels of a system has important implications. One should not work with a client's internal systems without also thoroughly considering and/or dealing with the person's external context. One can, however, work only with a client's external family—to improve its leadership, and without directly addressing the client's internal family—and still create major internal shifts in internal leadership. Thus, in choosing the level on which to focus therapy, one assesses both the external and the internal level of the system, focusing on whichever level of change will have the greater impact or be more expedient, and shifts levels fluidly, as necessary.

The assumption of internal and external parallels directs us outward, toward the client's current and past environment, with an eye toward the impact of the external world on his or her internal society. The techniques that have evolved from the IFS model are powerful, but they are less effective when the client is embedded in an external context that countinually activates his or her inner polarizations.

IFS as a Metaframework

The IFS model informs our therapy at many levels. At the conceptual level, it provides our basic understanding of people and a basic language for talking about them. We rarely speak or think about people monolithically. Phrases that used to characterize our assessments, such as "He is depressed," "She acts younger than her age," or "He wants to control the family," are replaced by "He seems to have a passive or sad part that takes over frequently," "She shows a young part in this situation," and "There may be a part of him that wants to control his family."

As the reader may notice, the second set of depictions convey the sense that there is much more to our clients than the parts that they show. These formulations are also generally quite tentative or hypothetical, because the IFS model has taught us to respect our client's reports of the nature of their parts, rather than prejudge their parts' intentions or actions and impose our prejudices on our clients in the form of interpretation or reframing. In this way, the IFS model takes the therapist out of the position of having to construct and "sell" a new reality to the family. Instead, the therapist inquires about the parts of each family member that are involved in a problem: "What do you think that part wants for you?" "How hard is it for you to control or calm that part?" "How might the problem be affected if you could remain in your Self, rather than letting that part take over?" "Do you want to change your relationship with that interfering part?" As is evident in this line of questioning, the IFS model also provides a language for therapy that allows family members to see themselves, one another, and the presenting problem quite differently. In the course of the therapist's using this language, these changes occur naturally, so that the therapist need impose no more than the most basic assumptions of the model: that people have parts and a Self. Often, those assumptions need not even be stated overtly in order to start the process, because this is a language that most people use intuitively and fall into easily.

This language also encourages self-disclosure and assumption of responsibility for unsavory thoughts or behavior. For example, in admitting that a small part of himself sometimes takes over and makes him act in rebellious or irresponsible ways, an adolescent loses less face than if he is asked to admit that *he* does those things. He is further disarmed if, in the same session, he has watched his mother acknowledge that she has a part that makes her attack him too much, or if he has heard his father disclose that one of his parts makes him so disappointed that he gives up on the boy, and if he sees that both parents want to keep their parts from doing these things to him.

The reader may also have noticed that this model and language create a collaborative atmosphere, not only between the therapist and the family but also among family members. The frame for therapy shifts—for example, from "How can the parents control their rebellious, irresponsible son?" to "How can the Selves of all the family members work together, so that all of them can keep their extreme parts from interfering in the family's life?" In such an atmosphere, free of coercion or recriminations and full of empowerment and hope, a family's resources surface.

Another benefit of using the IFS model as a metaframework is that it helps us view and handle "resistance." We are more sensitive to the ecological impact we have on people. So-called resistance can be seen, through the IFS model, as the activation of protective parts of family members. Therefore, instead of searching for techniques to overpower or bypass "resistant" clients, the therapist can simply ask clients to focus on and listen to their protective parts and try to find out what those parts fear. The therapist may try to reassure those parts directly or may respect the parts' fear and slow the pace. We find that when protective parts are given respect and consideration, they become less protective, and we encounter less "resistance."

Sensitivity to the concerns of protective parts reflects a larger awareness, derived from our experience with this model: that internal families, like external families, are delicate ecologies. As we have learned more about common relationship patterns within internal family systems, we have learned better timing of our interventions. For example, if certain parts, or relationships among parts, are addressed too early, other parts react protectively and may try to sabotage the change. If a therapist tries to elicit a vulnerable, childlike part of a client before having dealt with other parts that try to keep that one away from the client's Self or from other people, "resistance" will be encountered, and the client may be punished internally for allowing the intrusion. A family therapist who tries prematurely to get at a family secret or vulnerability encounters the same process.

In some ways, the IFS model is a meta-metaframework, because it informs our conception of the most fundamental unit of family systems: the individual. With a tentative map of internal relationships (and land mines), we can anticipate and deal with the consequences of internal and external change, and we can time the process of therapy accordingly. Our understanding of all the other metaframeworks is influenced by the IFS model. Such an ecological outlook on the internal and external levels of the system can make family therapy not only easier and quicker but also less disturbing to clients.

Applying the IFS Model to Therapy

Using the IFS model, one assumes that a person who has a problem is embedded in internal as well as external sequences of interaction (see Chapter Four), which activate each other. Let us return to Jane, the woman who feared her assertive part and let her fearful part lead. Her fearful approach to life encouraged her husband, John, to overprotect her and do things for her. His behavior confirmed her fearful part's assumptions that she was not competent and needed to depend on him, as well as the belief that if she asserted herself, she might lose him. Parts of John resented Jane's dependence on him; other parts worried that if Jane felt more competent, she would not put up with his moodiness and would leave him. Therefore, he continued to do things for her, while sending the message that she was a tremendous burden, which provided more ammunition to Jane's fearful part, whose argument was that Jane was lucky to have John. In this way, Jane's fearfulness was tightly embedded in internal and external sequences that confirmed and activated each other. Assertiveness on Jane's part was countered not only by her own fearful part but also by John's. For Jane to be able to change, both her internal and external systems needed to reorganize themselves, to some degree. As mentioned earlier, we have found that changes at either the internal or the external level effect parallel changes at the other level.

Internal and External Levels of Focus

It is possible to focus only on the external interactions between Jane and John and find simultaneous changes occurring in each of their internal systems, changes that parallel and promote the external changes. If, in therapy, Jane is encouraged to do more for herself and stand up to John, and if John is reassured by seeing that she becomes closer to him as this happens, then Jane is likely to become closer to her assertive part, and both Jane and John will probably be better able to calm their fearful parts.

It is also possible to focus only on the internal interactions of Jane and John and find simultaneous changes occurring in the external interactions between them. If, in therapy, Jane and John both learn that they can calm down and take care of their fearful parts, then their Selves will have more access to leadership, and they will communicate very differently.

From this perspective, the initial job of the therapist becomes to assess, in collaboration with clients, which level of system (internal or external) is most amenable to change and, in most cases, to shift the focus of therapy back and forth from internal to external, as indicated by feedback from changes. (The external level can also be subdivided, of course, among family of origin, family of procreation, and larger systems or cultural factors that affect the family.) For example, if a client is financially or emotionally dependent on and/or living with a family whose interaction sequences are highly activating of the client's parts, then working exclusively with the client's internal system is likely to result only in slow or temporary improvement, at best. The external sequences can often trigger extreme internal sequences among parts that the client is struggling to change. If the client were to improve rapidly and start to become more independent, the untreated external family might actively undermine the changes, given the family members' mixed feelings about the client's independence. Therefore, unless a client has plenty of room to change, without having to encounter a great deal of external activation (in general, or in reaction to the change), it is wise to focus initially on the external context, with an eye toward creating more room to change. When a client does have plenty of room to change, it is possible and often expedient to work directly with the internal system, but always being mindful of and ready to shift focus to unexpected external reactions.

Such flexibility of focus reflects another difference between the IFS model and the "external only" structural, strategic, and systemic family therapy models. Unlike those models, the IFS model does not assume that there is always some aspect of a client's current external context that is maintaining his or her problems, or that when a client's external context does seem to be involved, external interactions are more powerful and influential than internal ones. We find that some problems seem to be maintained primarily by a client's polarized internal system. The polarizations may have originated in the past, in the client's life within a polarized external system, but they have become self-maintaining, and they can be changed without a great amount of attention to the external context, as long as it allows room to change.

If Jane had been living alone and supporting herself, we might have begun by working with her individually, focusing on her internal life and using particular techniques, until her internal family's improvement had been hampered by some reaction in her external family. At that point, we might have continued to see her individually but shifted our focus to strategies for dealing with the external constraints, or we might have brought the family members involved into therapy and focused on their sequences or organization, until more room had been cleared for Jane to change. During some of this external family work, the focus might have shifted to parts of her family members that were activated by and interfered with Jane's changes and to how those parts could be handled. Our therapy rarely remains exclusively external for long.

Promoting Self Leadership in a Dyad

In reality, Jane did not have much room to change, because of the intensity of her relationship with John, and so therapy focused initially on the couple's external interaction sequences, on their boundaries with respect to other family members, and on the parts of each of them that interfered with their lives. They began to discuss what kept Jane from asserting herself in their relationship, and Jane brought up John's overprotectiveness. John reacted defensively. He claimed that he wished he did not have to do those things, but he had to because Jane was so fearful. Jane quickly retreated into agreement with John, and she apologized for being such a burden.

At that point, the therapist asked each of them to focus, internally, on what they were saying to themselves. Jane was criticizing herself for being so fearful and for trying to blame John for her problems. She was feeling very guilty and weak. Her assertiveness was nowhere to be found. John was saying, "Why am I stuck with such a helpless person?" and "How dare she say that, considering all I do for her?"

As the therapist asked questions about the parts of each of them that were saying these things or giving them these feelings, Jane identified a self-critical part that she called "the witch," as well as a guilty, frail little girl whom the witch attacked and an anxious woman who made her fearful. John found an angry, self-righteous defender who was ready to pounce on Jane. The therapist asked a series of questions about how Jane and John thought their conversations would be different if these parts did not take over and interfere. Without interpretation from the therapist, they described how John's defender triggered Jane's witch, who in turn triggered Jane's little girl and anxious woman, who in turn made John's defender feel even more burdened and self-righteous. They agreed that things would be better if these sequences could be eliminated, but both felt at the mercy of their parts. They had no clue about how to keep those parts from taking over and perpetuating these patterns.

We find that many people, once they identify parts that have been leading in certain situations, and once they firmly request that the Self be trusted, have far more capacity for Self leadership than they believed. The therapist asked both Jane and John to take a second and tell these parts to let their Selves talk to each other, without the parts' interfering or taking over, and then to resume their discussion of obstacles to Jane's assertiveness. The ensuing discussion began in a different spirit. Before long, however, John's defender leaped forward and triggered Jane's witch. Again the therapist asked them to stop the external sequence and get back to having their Selves in the lead.

Through this process of quickly catching and calming parts as they appeared in external interaction, Jane and John found that things did indeed go better when their parts trusted their Selves to lead. By the end of the session, John had agreed to try to keep his defender from attacking Jane and to rein in his overresponsible part, which made him do so much for her. Jane had agreed to try to protect her little girl from her critical witch and, in so doing, to keep the fearful part that wanted to protect the girl from dominating her so much. While they did agree to make these attempts to change, they both confessed that they still did not know exactly how to change.

So far, the therapy had focused on the complementarity of internal and external sequences (that is, on how John's overprotectiveness and anger affected Jane's internal sequences, which caused Jane's fearfulness and dependence, which in turn furthered the extremes of John's angry and overresponsible parts and his consequent external behavior, and so on). The therapist used the parts language to shift the frame for therapy—from how to get Jane to be less fearful to how they could each work on themselves. John and Jane arrived at this new frame on their own, without the therapist's imposing it. The therapist simply asked a series of questions that were based on the assumptions of the IFS model. With this new frame, each spouse would have more room to change, because each would be less bombarded by the other's extreme parts, and the therapy could shift temporarily to an internal focus, so that each spouse could actively change his or her own inner system. Such a shift does not necessarily imply the need for the therapist to meet individually with each family member; it may be highly productive to have one family member watch another work on his or her own parts. For example, while John watched Jane find a new, more supportive role for her witch and nurture her little girl, he became agitated. Asked to focus on that feeling, John found a childlike part of himself, which worried that if Jane became more independent, she would leave him. In the next session, he was able to show his worried little boy that even if Jane did leave, John would take care of him, in a way that he had not before. Similarly, as Jane watched John struggle to convince his defender that it did not have to protect him from every sign of criticism, she felt empathy for his vulnerability and allied with his Self in this struggle, instead of living in fear of the defender.

When it is acceptable to the family members involved, and when being observed does not seem to interfere with people's work, we work with one family member in front of the others. If the person doing the work has reservations, however, we will ask the others to leave the room. We work with that person alone, and we may ask that person later to give a summary of the parts work to the others. We almost always find it useful for family members to share their struggles with one another. In some cases, however, and for any number of reasons, someone requests, and we give, total confidentiality and privacy. In many such instances, people become less concerned about confidentiality as they work on themselves, and they increasingly want to share their internal changes with family members. In other cases, one or more family members work with the therapist individually on their internal systems, without any disclosure to other family members.

IFS with an Individual

Family therapists traditionally have been reluctant not only to consider intrapsychic issues but also to work with the individual, for fear that the rest of the family would see and treat that person as "the problem" and not feel any responsibility to change. The IFS model eliminates that dilemma because, in the initial meeting with the family, it becomes clear that everyone has parts that interfere. Those who want or agree to work on their parts are seen as the most courageous or the most interested in changing the problem, rather than being seen *as* the problem.

The therapist may encourage every family member to do some internal work, either individually or in front of the others. Many people seem able to reorganize aspects of their internal families quickly enough so that therapy does not have to become a long-term endeavor, even when everyone takes a turn at doing the work. Many problems can also be improved lastingly even though only one or two family members (or no family members) work directly on their internal families, because external changes effect parallel internal changes in all members.

In this space, we cannot present all the considerations and guidelines for doing this work with an individual. [For a more detailed description of this work, see Schwartz (forthcoming)]. Because a person's mind is a delicate ecology, which may become more polarized if the therapist is not careful, we recommend that the following technique be applied, at least in the beginning, only to less internally extreme or polarized clients, until the therapist has more experience in dealing with the inner world of parts.

Once a client has identified a few parts, we begin by asking him which part he would like to work with first. After he selects one, we ask him to focus on that part exclusively, however he experiences it—it may be a thought pattern or an inner voice or a feeling state. As he isolates the part, the therapist asks him if he can see what it looks like. Once he gets an image of it, he is asked to put the part in a room by itself. He is then outside the room, looking at the part through a window. The therapist asks the client how he feels toward the part in the room and whether he feels anything extreme toward it (anger, envy, extreme sadness, fear, hopelessness).

If so, he is asked to find a part that is outside the room with him and is influencing him to feel extremely toward the original part. He then moves this second part into another room, so that it does not interfere with the Self's ability to see clearly and work with the original part.

Jane's critical part looked to her like an old, misshapen witch. As she looked at it through the window, she was afraid of the witch, and the witch leered at her menacingly. Asked to find the part that made her fear the witch, Jane found the fearful, anxious woman and the little girl. She put those parts in another room, reassuring them that she would return soon. With the little girl out of harm's way, Jane returned to the witch's room and immediately felt anger toward the witch. She was able to locate and move this angry part, which looked like a dragon, into still another room. Upon returning again to face the witch, she suddenly felt compassion for it and could see that it did not like having to attack her all the time.

Jane's experience—of sudden shifts of feeling toward a part, to the point of compassion or curiosity, as other parts were differentiated from her Self—seems to be universal and is the most empowering discovery of the IFS model. We generally find that the Self, once differentiated in this way, is able to change its relationship with the parts and help them change with respect to one another. With her newfound compassion for the witch, Jane entered the room as her Self and asked the witch why she attacked the little girl so much and what she really wanted for Jane. The witch initially responded defensively, saying that the girl was weak and she hated weakness. As Jane remained her Self, the witch admitted that she did not want Jane to get close to the little girl: when she had done so in the past, the little girl took over and made Jane rush into relationships and get hurt. Jane asked the witch whether she would like to find a different role, if Jane could show her that she, Jane, could take care of the little girl, make her less needy, and control her impulse to look desperately for others to take care of her. The witch was very interested in taking on a supportive, problem-solving role but was skeptical about Jane's ability to control the little girl.

This dialogue between Jane and her witch illustrates the

principle of depolarization: parts cannot change in isolation and often become less extreme only when assured that the parts they are polarized with will also become less extreme. To borrow a metaphor from Watzlawick, Weakland, and Fisch (1974), if two sailors are leaning out on opposite sides of a boat and trying to keep it balanced, one of them is not going to move in unilaterally, because of the realistic fear that the boat will capsize. The sailors can move in only together and will not do so unless a trusted leader can ensure such coordination. Before the sailors move in—while they are both still leaning out in opposite directions (polarized)—they are stuck in their extreme positions. They cannot move freely around the boat and must counter each other's every move. Once they both move in, they are both free to do what they want to do on the boat, regardless of the other's behavior. This is the difference between the rigidity of any polarized system (family, corporation), in which all parts occupy extreme, opposed positions, and the flexibility and freedom of a harmonious system, in which all parts have a much wider range of roles.

Jane's witch agreed to suspend her attacks temporarily, to see whether Jane could deal with the little girl. Jane then moved to the room in which she had put the little girl and the fearful woman. The girl was hiding behind the woman, who looked very nervous. Jane said that she felt compassion for the girl but anger toward the woman, because the woman dominated Jane's life so much. Once again, this was the dragon making Jane feel angry. After she moved the dragon back to its room, she felt sorry for the woman for having to worry so much about protecting the little girl. Jane entered the room and negotiated with the woman to let her, Jane, try to nurture the little girl. During these negotiations, Jane respected and addressed all the woman's fears, both the extreme and the realistic ones, before the two of them decided that Jane could spend time alone with the little girl.

One of the deals made during these negotiations was that Jane would protect the girl directly from John's angry defender, and that she would not have sex with him for a while, until the little girl felt less vulnerable. To ensure that these deals would be kept, Jane had to get the fearful part to reconcile its differences with the dragon, so that the dragon could help Jane stand up for herself with

John. Jane took the fearful woman to the dragon's room and had the two of them sit facing each other, while she acted as their therapist and encouraged them to come to some resolution. The woman agreed not to interfere with Jane's access to the dragon. The dragon agreed that when it was upset, it would tell Jane what it was upset about and let her speak for it, rather than taking over and exploding at John or at anyone else who was its target.

These negotiations illustrate the importance of being sensitive to the client's ecology before making major interventions. If the therapist had pushed Jane to disregard the woman and approach the girl directly, the system would have reacted severely. (We have learned this principle the hard way.) With this model, encouraging Jane and her parts to consider all the negative consequences of change is not a paradoxical, "outpositioning," maneuver; rather, it is good ecological practice. The negotiations also illustrate the use of structural family therapy techniques with the internal family. Jane (as her Self) was becoming the therapist to this internal family and was surprised at how easily the parts could resolve what had seemed to be huge differences, once they were forced to face one another without the interference of other parts and with her calm, confident leadership.

The little girl, when Jane approached her, was wary at first. But as Jane patiently stayed with her, both in and between sessions, gradually the girl came to trust her and cried deeply in Jane's arms. The girl spoke of messages she had received from Jane's parents, which made her feel unlovable and evil. Jane asked the girl if she was stuck somewhere in time. The girl showed a scene where, when she was five years old, her parents were fighting and she was terrified. Jane went to her in the middle of that scene, comforted her there, and asked the girl if she wanted to leave that time and live with her in the present. The girl was eager to leave and came to live in Jane's bedroom, where Jane visited her frequently and occasionally returned with her to the past, to help the girl understand that her parents' fights were not her fault. In addition, Jane and the girl decided that Jane would talk to her parents about those early (and occasionally current) messages, to get more information about why they were given.

This work demonstrates one way in which the IFS model

handles the deeply embedded beliefs that parts hold. Unlike many other systems-based models of family therapy, this one respects the impact that a client's history can have on his or her current beliefs and behavior. If a part acquired a strong belief when the client was young, we encourage the process of rescuing that part from the past and then helping it understand from the standpoint of the present. Fortunately, many parts are able to specify precisely where they are stuck, and so the exploration does not become a long-term wild-goose chase. If a part can let go of a belief without knowing its origin, it is not always necessary to explore the belief's history. In other words, therapy goes in whatever direction will best help the parts change and clear the constraints to Self leadership.

Jane, in preparing to speak to her parents about these issues, imagined her mother in one room and her father in another. Next, the therapist had Jane talk with her parts about what they each wanted Jane, as her Self, to say for them to each parent. She also talked with them about not interfering and staying out of the rooms while she talked to each parent. Upon reaching agreement with her parts, Jane entered each imaged room and found that, after an initial defensiveness, both her mother and her father were able to discuss their relationships with her in a surprisingly open way. Afterwards, Jane's parts were impressed with how well she had done without their help or interference, and they were more inclined to trust her to lead when she met with her actual parents.

Jane had an actual conversation with her mother during the week after that session. It did not go quite as well as it had in Jane's imagery, but Jane's mother was able to hear how the hurtful messages had affected Jane, without defending herself in the way that she always had in the past. Instead, she apologized and told Jane about how critical she was of herself. This conversation seemed to help Jane's little girl a great deal, and Jane decided that she did not need to talk directly with her father.

Here again, we see how work at the internal and external levels is complementary and how therapy can move back and forth between these two levels. The more Jane can lead with her Self externally (in her interactions with her mother, her father, John), the more her parts trust her to lead internally, and vice versa. We generally find that when a person maintains Self leadership in the face of the extreme parts of another person, the other person's Self gradually surfaces, and their interaction becomes more productive. Therefore, it was not surprising that as Jane remained her Self in the lead, her mother's defensiveness melted, and they were able to interact in a new way that was better for each of them. In some ways, this technique is similar to Bowen's (1978) family voyages.

As Jane's little girl let go of beliefs about being unlovable or evil, and as Jane continued to nurture that part, the little girl changed from being such a source of sadness and vulnerability to being a source of elation and sensitivity. The fearful woman also found a different role, because she no longer had to worry about protecting the little girl, since the Self, with the help of the dragon, was doing that. The witch also changed, since she no longer had to keep Jane from the little girl.

In step with all these internal changes, Jane became increasingly assertive with John. She spoke frequently with her parts (by this time, Jane had found many more parts than the four we have reported so far) about whether they all wanted to stay married to him. Some of her parts did not know whether they could forgive him for having dominated her and making her feel so ashamed of her fears. Other parts saw and trusted the changes he was making as he worked on his parts, and they realized that the couple's history was the product of their polarization among their parts and their lack of Self leadership, for which neither spouse could be held unilaterally accountable.

Since John witnessed most of these changes and debates within Jane, and since she also witnessed his parts work, they frequently talked, in and out of sessions, about these changes and the implications for their relationship. John realized that parts of Jane felt brutalized by some of his parts, and that he needed to be patient sexually, until Jane felt better able to take care of those brutalized parts and could trust John's patience. He retreated from making demands on her. Instead, he focused on his own polarizations. Once Jane and her parts began to trust that John could control the parts of himself that they feared, forgiveness came easily, and the parts that had affection for him emerged.

If John had not been privy to Jane's changes and had not been working on himself simultaneously, their relationship probably would not have survived. John would have become increasingly confused and threatened by her assertiveness; with Jane persisting in therapy and not retreating into fearfulness, John's angry defender would have become unbearable. We say this because using the IFS with an individual can be so fascinating and powerful that a therapist may be tempted to ignore or underestimate the impact of the person's external context, or to ignore the impact on that context of the changes in that one person. In Jane's case, the goal of liberating her from her fearful life had to supersede the goal of keeping the marriage intact. If John had refused to participate, the marriage probably would have ended. It is often possible, however, to achieve both a primary and a secondary goal if the therapist engages all the Selves involved in the change process and does not neglect some out of fascination with others.

IFS with Families

For the sake of simplicity, we have described work with a couple, rather than with a family, to illustrate the IFS model. We hope that the reader can extrapolate from what we have said, to imagine how the model would apply to working with families. To facilitate this extrapolation, we will summarize some of the steps involved.

First, the therapist tracks the problem but translates what the family says into the "parts language." When the father says that Johnny is rebellious, the father is asked about how his parts react to the rebellious part of Johnny, whether he thinks it is good that his parts react in that way, and whether he wants to change his relationship with those parts of himself. Every other family member, including Johnny, is asked similar questions about their own parts and about how their parts are affected by those of others.

Next, the family members may discuss with one another how they can all best deal with their own interfering parts, so that they can all be their Selves with one another. They also discuss how they can help one another in this process. During these discussions, interactions between a family member's internal sequences among parts and other, external sequences among family members often become apparent. People come to understand how they can avoid triggering internal sequences within one another.

Johnny describes how his rebellious part protects him from the pain of his sad part, which is activated by his inner critic, which in turn is activated by the critical parts of either parent. His father describes how his critical part attacks Johnny more brutally after the mother's nurturer has minimized Johnny's transgression and tried to protect Johnny from the father's critic. The mother says that her nurturer becomes extremely protective of Johnny: there is another part of her that identifies with the hurt that Johnny feels at the hands of the father's critic, because that critic is sometimes aimed at her, too. Both parents agree to try to keep their own extreme parts from taking over and see more clearly the ecological effects of letting their parts take the lead.

Such discussions frequently elicit information about structural problems within a family (for example, an alliance between many parts of the mother and of Johnny against the father's critic) and about problems with systems outside the family, problems that keep family members' parts extreme and must be changed. (For example, the father describes how his stressful job makes it more difficult to control his critic at home.) Again, however, these issues are easier to discuss and act on when they are framed in the parts language: only *parts* of the mother and the son are allied against *part* of the father.

From this point on, therapy combines two phases. In one, various family members work on their own internal systems, either in the presence of the others or individually. In the other, family members discuss their differences or plans with one another and try to lead with their Selves during such discussions. These two phases reinforce and overlap with each other, and therapy shifts between them, according to which family members are struggling the most with their parts and what factors are creating obstacles. The progress of therapy is now more apparent, since the therapist does not have to rely solely on external signs of change but can also check on the internal systems of key family members, to see how far the family has come and still needs to go. Therapists who use the IFS model often report that, in the past, they always wondered whether a family had really improved; with the IFS model, however, they have greater confidence in results because they can assess changes at several levels.

Therapist-Client Relationship

An important implication of the IFS model is that, to be effective, the therapist must also be able to lead with his or her Self. Some systems-based schools of family therapy have described techniques for engaging or "joining with" families. Other schools have basically ignored issues that have to do with the person of the therapist and with the therapist-family relationship. In using the IFS model, however, the way the therapist interacts with the family is vitally important. The therapist, to varying degrees, must be able to elicit the Selves of all family members. For this to happen, the therapist must be able to lead with his or her own Self and control any parts that the therapy process may activate. We find that most therapists do not need to learn techniques for "joining" with people; instead they need to work on themselves, to the point where they can keep their parts from interfering with therapy. We do not mean to evoke a scenario analogous to the situation in psychoanalysis, whereby a novice family therapist would have to receive years of IFS-based therapy before he or she could be effective. Many therapists, once they know the basic techniques and assumptions of the IFS model, are able to work on themselves—by themselves, or with some help from a therapist—to the point where they achieve the necessary Self leadership relatively quickly. Moreover, doing therapy becomes therapeutic in itself, because one must work continually to keep one's parts under control in order to maintain one's clinical effectiveness.

Perhaps more than people working with other systems-based family therapy approaches, we emphasize the importance of the person of the therapist and of his or her relationship with clients. We do not require a trainee to receive personal therapy, but when we notice parts of the trainee interfering with his or her work, we may inquire about those parts and recommend that he or she work on changing his or her relationship with them.

Because the IFS model informs our basic conception of people, it provides the foundation on which our larger model rests. The IFS model has implications for all aspects of therapy, from techniques for working with individuals, couples, and families to the therapist-client relationship. In general, these implications lead us toward a therapy that can be described as collaborative, normalizing, and empowering.

FOUR

Patterns of Interaction:
The Sequences Metaframework

Family therapy has always recognized and stressed the importance of the interactional component of systems. Thus, structural family therapy defines a family as "a natural group which over time evolves patterns of interacting" (Minuchin and Fishman, 1981, p. 11). Haley (1976) has defined a problem as a "type of behavior that is part of a sequence of acts between several people" (p. 2). This concept of patterning has been identified by others who have used terms such as "feedback loops" (Hoffman, 1981; Watzlawick, Beavin, and Jackson, 1967), "homeostatic cycle" (Hoffman, 1976), "recursiveness" (Keeney and Sprenkle, 1982), "problem-maintaining behavior" (Fisch, Weakland, and Segal, 1982; Watzlawick, Weakland, and Fisch, 1974), "sequences" (Haley, 1981, 1980; Madanes, 1981), "system of interaction" (Madanes, 1981), and "morphostatic and morphogenic processes" (Maruyama, 1963). The concept that families are patterned is so pervasive that it can be seen as one of family therapy's common denominators.

While patterning is an important systems concept, it cannot be operationalized without a decision about which patterns are relevant to particular human systems. As Hoffman (1976, p. 50) has noted, "How is one to know which patterns to look for, let alone

Note: Portions of this chapter are adapted and reprinted, with permission, from Douglas C. Breunlin and Richard C. Schwartz, "Sequences: Toward a Common Denominator of Family Therapy," *Family Process*, 1986, *25*, 67–88.

identify, when one is in the presence of a strange family, peering into the gloom of its manifold transactions?" Family therapists must make distinctions about these "manifold transactions," punctuating a family's highly complex pattern into manageable sequences that are somehow related to the presenting problem. As Haley (1980) suggests, "The chief merit of systems theory is that it allows the therapist to recognize repeating sequences and so make predictions. . . . There remains the problem of how to simplify the sequences so they become recognizable and useful" (p. 24).

Families transact their business in real time by emitting a stream of behaviors, as shown in Figure 4.1. An untrained therapist attempting to employ the systems concept of interaction will note that some of these behaviors appear to repeat themselves over time and to be related to one another. He or she will then derive a sequence from these behaviors. For example, the therapist may note that the parents fight, the child misbehaves, a grandparent interferes, things settle down, life returns to normal, and then the child misbehaves again.

We should note, however, that other events also occur between those that are selected to be part of the sequence, and the other events may themselves constitute another sequence. Several therapists seeing the same family could each come up with a different set of behaviors in the sequence. How do we know which sequences are relevant to the process of change? Some theorists would argue that it does not really matter: because all the sequences are recursively connected, change of some sort will occur as long as the therapy manages to interrupt one of them. But such thinking has perpetuated a casual and sometimes careless attitude toward the use of

Figure 4.1. Events over Time.

— a — b — c ——— d — e ——— f ——— n — n+1 — n+2 ——— n+ —

      Time — — — — — — — — —

sequences. Moreover, we have found that sometimes significant change does not occur unless the therapist is careful to work with a number of related sequences, some of which are not readily distinguished at the outset of therapy. Therefore, we believe that the selection of relevant sequences should be based on more than the idiosyncratic ways in which therapists choose to punctuate events.

The models of family therapy, by evoking theories that specify which sequences are important, help to bring order to this randomness. For instance, structural family therapists explore brief, in-session sequences believed to be isomorphic with respect to the family's structure (Minuchin, 1974; Minuchin and Fishman, 1981). Brief therapists limit their focus to behaviors that constitute attempted solutions to problems (Fisch, Weakland, and Segal, 1982; Watzlawick, Weakland, and Fisch, 1974). Strategic therapists look for a sequence of interaction that is analogous to an incongruous hierarchy (Haley, 1976, 1980; Madanes, 1981). Such preselection provides guidelines that help to separate the central from the peripheral (Haley, 1976), and it makes therapy manageable and pragmatic. But it also represents a form of "ecology chopping" that has contributed to fragmentation in the field, creating a "Tower of Babel" (Hoffman, 1981) and weakening the potential for the concept of patterning to serve as a common denominator of effective family therapy. We have also found that preselection of sequences on the basis of a model often limits the therapist's field of vision and creates blind spots, which may severely limit therapeutic potential. Often, not just one but several sequences impose constraints that make it difficult for the system to solve the problem.

The interactional family therapies have also been criticized for their pragmatism. Critics argue, for example, that the selection of a simple sequence, which is altered to "fix" the problem, amounts to a mechanistic, engineering-based approach to families. Keeney (1983) has said that pragmatism, while it is an essential aspect of therapy, must be contextualized by an aesthetic appreciation of the complexity of human systems; hence, if we select a specific sequence for therapy, we should do so with an understanding of how that sequence is related to the incredibly complex real-time pattern of the system.

For the concept of patterning to serve as a true common

denominator of family therapy (Breunlin and Schwartz, 1986), we need a *metaframework* that transcends the whims of the therapist's perceptions and the parochial preferences of the models, one that enables us to grasp the aesthetic complexity of patterning while providing pragmatic guidelines for how specific sequences, which make up partial arcs of that pattern, can be extracted from it and used for therapeutic purposes. With the construct of *periodicity*, events in the same time frame can be related to one another in particular sequences, and several sequences from different periods can also be related to one another. For example, we are familiar with the "nag and withdraw" sequence: the more the husband withdraws, the more the wife nags, and vice versa. There are different versions of this sequence, however. In one, the wife nags her husband to help with the children, and he responds by sticking his face in the newspaper. In another, she tries to get him to leave work early and take the kids to the dentist, and he withdraws by staying late at the office. The first version captures the couple's style of communication; the second specifies one dimension of how they manage their family routine. In still another version, several times a year the wife may become so exhausted that she falls ill, thus forcing the husband to withdraw less, only to see him withdraw again as her health returns. And what about the patterns of contact and withdrawal that each spouse witnessed in his or her family of origin? These sequences are isomorphic with respect to each other, because they involve a pattern of nagging and withdrawing. But they also cover very different periods of time. The various sequences can be combined if we recognize that sequences of shorter duration are partial arcs of—and therefore nest in—sequences of longer duration.

The number of relevant classes of sequences that we select depends on the range of periodicity that we select. We have limited our metaframework to four classes, having found that these four map our clinical experience well and correspond closely to the types of sequences used by the popular family therapies.

The first class, which we label *S1*, includes relatively brief sequences of face-to-face interaction. The second class, *S2*, represents aspects of the family's routine and periods that range from one day to a week. The third class, *S3*, represents the ebb and flow of

some condition or problem in the family and periods ranging from several weeks to a year. The fourth class, *S4*, represents transgenerational sequences, wherein events occur from one generation to the next. The internal parts system of each family member also contains sequences of internal dialogue, and these internal sequences interact with the four classes of external sequences. Consider the following case example:

> A professor sought therapy for a writing block. Each day, he would attempt to write but instead engaged for several hours in a typical sequence (S1) of procrastination: sharpening pencils, making phone calls, and finding other small tasks. He complained that he could never hit a writing stride. These sequences of procrastination occurred both at home and in his office.
>
> Examination of the professor's daily routine (S2) also revealed a problematic sequence. Having failed to write, he would experience a range of emotions, from guilt and anger to self-pity, and was therefore moody at home. He would bitterly chastise his wife for her failings and then remain awake well into the night, eating and watching television. The next day, he would sleep late but still feel physically drained. Criticizing himself for such irresponsible behavior, he would once again sit down and attempt to write.
>
> Two sequences of yet longer duration (S3) were also related to the writing problem. Several times a year, the professor took trips abroad. As departure time approached, he would become increasingly preoccupied with the trip and anxious about unmet publication deadlines. Upon his return, many work-related demands would have accumulated, and so once again he could not find time to write. As his frustration mounted, at about eight-month intervals, he experienced episodes of excruciating cluster headaches, which persisted for several weeks, totally incapacitated

him, and left him unable to work at all. When the headaches passed, he was physically drained for several more weeks.

Discussions about the professor's family of origin (S4) eventually revealed that his father had possessed considerable potential but never realized it. His mother was more success-oriented and had groomed her son to succeed where her husband had failed. The professor replicated his father's struggle with success, but he also felt that to succeed or fail clearly would ultimately force him into loyalty toward one parent over the other.

The writer's block can be seen as embedded in any one or all of these sequences. The sequences combined to pose massive constraints on the professor, so that, even if he could interrupt one of the sequences, others could still prevent him from following a productive writing schedule. Moreover, each of these four represents just one sequence from each class; many other sequences, related to the marriage, to parent-child interactions, and to professional relationships, also existed. These sequences influenced and were influenced by the sequences directly related to the writing block. Taken together all the sequences constituted the total pattern.

The relevant question (posed throughout this chapter) is, How can a therapist select from such a pattern of sequence or sequences that, if changed, would allow the constraints to be lifted?

Characteristics of Sequences

Although the sequences metaframework allows us to draw on any sequence of interest to any model, we do so with a particular understanding of the nature of sequences. This understanding is guided by our presupposition of perspectivism and by our acknowledgment that sequences include patterns of action as well as meaning. The relevance of sequences to problems in human systems, and the way in which several sequences may be related to one another, can be clarified through reference to several important characteristics of sequences: recursiveness, probability, constraint, embeddedness, generation, calibration, and resilience.

Sequences and Perspectivism

We believe that family life is not entirely random, and that its order does not depend on an observer. Families are indeed patterned, but the distinctions that the therapist makes are what highlight one sequence over others. This view is confirmed every time we show our students an excerpt of a videotape and then marvel at the many different sequences they construct from the same data. We believe that the sequences metaframework, because it includes classes of sequences and hypothesized relationships among them, is more useful as a map of family patterns than are the parsimonious maps of models that use only one class of sequences.

Meaning and Sequences

Family therapy originally defined sequences simply as patterns of action, but we believe that sequences involve both action and meaning, with each recursively contextualizing the other. The action component is more apparent in shorter sequences (S1 and S2). Actions often occur so rapidly that interactants appear to be on "automatic pilot," and it is difficult to see how they can consciously attribute meaning to their behavior before initiating it. Sequences, however, may activate parts that spontaneously express beliefs about what should be done in a given situation. For example, a husband has an easily polarized blamer, while his wife has an easily polarized defendant, which immediately calls in her lawyer part. In an argument, the wife's defendant activates her lawyer, which in turn activates a more polarized blamer, which polarizes the wife's defendant, and so forth. This S1 interaction will be one of nonproductive blame and justification.

In longer sequences, it is easier to see how meaning and action interact recursively. For example, the ebb and flow of a key variable in an S3 interaction is often significantly affected by meaning. Say that a woman in couples therapy experiences intense anger toward her husband, who she believes is not committed to their relationship. She derives this meaning from the fact that he periodically loses his job, creating financial instability and great stress for the family. The job loss itself is a significant event within an annual S3 pattern. With each recurrence of the S3, the woman's anger over her husband's lack of commitment intensifies until she is living with an ever-present anger that burns like hot coals. As she convinces herself of his lack of commitment, she also sees lack of commitment in his day-to-day behavior. If he fails to fold the laundry, that indicates a lack of commitment. His not folding the laundry is analogous to his throwing a small stick onto the hot coals: the tremendous heat of the coals immediately ignites the stick, just as she herself "ignites" in intense anger. Finally, the anger takes on a life of its own and is managed by what the wife comes to recognize as her anger part. She knows that it is irrational to get so angry if her husband does not fold the laundry, particularly when there are often good reasons why, but her anger is out of control and fueled by her beliefs about his lack of commitment. Until she understands how she attributes meaning about commitment to various acts, and how this meaning fuels her anger, she cannot alter S1 and S2 sequences with her husband.

From Circularity to Recursiveness

A sequence can be represented by a circle, a shape that illustrates how the acts within a sequence return to the same starting point. This notion of circularity is rather simplistic, however. It suggests that the acts repeat themselves with regularity in an unchanging manner, like the movements of a clock's hands. Events may actually repeat themselves, but rarely in exactly the same manner; small irregularities are associated with the sequence, and their existence in apparently patterned events has been the focus of the new science of chaos. Gleick (1988) notes that, before chaos theory, the essence of the physical sciences was the attempt to find those regularities in nature that could be described in simple linear equations, to produce exact solutions to problems. Newton's laws of motion are a classic example, and the swinging of a pendulum can also be described in simple equations. By contrast, chaos theory has demonstrated that there are small irregularities even in an apparently regular system—that is, there is chaos. The pendulum does not traverse its path in an unchanging pattern. An even more startling finding of chaos theory is that chaos itself, previously thought to occur at random and without a pattern, shows pattern. Because chaos theory forces us to recognize that we do not live in a world of exactly repeating sequences, the circle is an inadequate image of a sequence. The irregularities that scientists once simply discarded as "noise" have a strange regularity and may themselves constitute important sequences. We are forced to abandon the search for one simple unchanging sequence and must rethink how we define pattern in human systems.

Rather than say that therapists search for the magic sequence, with its defined set of related behaviors, we prefer to say that some events bear recursive relationships to one another, each event influencing and being influenced by other events in the sequence. The events need not appear in exactly the same order every time, nor need one event always occur when a related event has occurred. For example, a daughter's running away may be recursively related to the mother's going out with a man whom the daughter hates, but there may also be times when the mother goes out with him and the daughter does not run away. When events bear a strong recursive relationship to one another, it becomes convenient to say that they constitute a sequence, but we must remember that the therapist is the one making this distinction.

Probability

Recursiveness, since it increases the probability that some events will remain related, decreases the probability that others can occur, and so a sequence becomes predictable. For example, if a mother objects to her teenage daughter's behavior, and if the daughter immediately becomes upset and unreasonable, it is probable that the mother will respond by intensifying her objection, and that the sequence will then escalate. Probability implies only that an event is likely to occur, not that it is destined to occur. Therefore, in any given sequence of recursive events, there is always a small probability that some new event will occur. For example, there is always a small probability that the mother may object in a way that does not upset the daughter, or that the daughter will decide not to get upset when the mother objects.

Constraint

When events become recursively related, and when a high probability exists that a sequence will occur, the sequence can be said to impose a constraint on the system, since its occurrence precludes the occurrence of other events. Constraints can exist at all levels of sequence, from S1 through S4. We frequently hear people say, "He always does such and such" or "She never lets me do such and such." These statements capture the experience of constraint. Therapists, of course, are quick to detect the language of such absolutes as *never* and *always* because they convey an individual's belief that a sequence is 100 percent probable; therefore, the person is fully constrained by it.

Embeddedness

Sequences of shorter duration constitute partial arcs of sequences of longer duration; therefore, they are viewed as being embedded in the longer sequences. For example, a conflictual exchange between a mother and a daughter (S1) always occurs late in the evening, when the mother arrives home after working long hours and the daughter has spent her evening being in charge of younger siblings (S2). We can hypothesize the embeddedness of all four classes of sequences, as shown in Figure 4.2, which we refer to as the "fallen snowman." An embedded sequence may generate or calibrate another sequence.

Generation

A sequence may have a set of initial conditions that trigger it. These initial conditions are often longer or shorter sequences; hence, one sequence may generate other shorter or longer sequences. For example, short sequences of conflict (S1) may erupt between spouses over certain issues if the wife is suffering from premenstrual syndrome

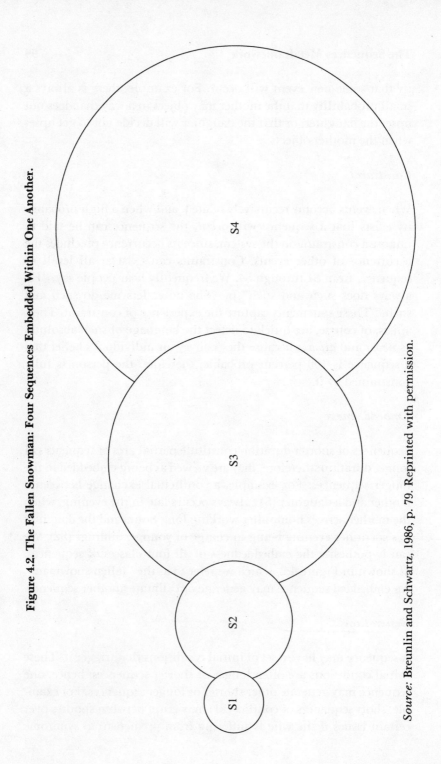

Figure 4.2. The Fallen Snowman: Four Sequences Embedded Within One Another.

Source: Breunlin and Schwartz, 1986, p. 79. Reprinted with permission.

(PMS) while the same issues would not precipitate conflict during the latter part of her menstrual cycle: an argument (S1) may precipitate a pattern of withdrawal (S2) that persists for weeks (S3). To take another example, a child may bring home one report card after another with failing grades. With each report card (S3), the parents experience disappointment and frustration, and with each successive report card their disappointment and frustration mount, to the point where they clamp down on the child and change the routine around homework for an entire marking period. When the grades improve, the parents feel less frustrated and give up the new homework routine. The child then begins to slack off, and the grades fall again.

Calibration

A hotly debated question in family therapy is whether sequences serve regulatory functions. Hoffman (1976, p. 505) has labeled such sequences "homeostatic cycles": "If one speaks of a homeostatic cycle, one should be able to define the factors which are being monitored by this cycle. It is too general to say 'tension between the parents' and let it go at that. Presumably, there are essential variables which the parents—or whatever executive dyad is operating— must maintain within certain limits if they are to function together successfully. What might such variables be?" These hypothesized regulatory functions of a sequence can be depicted visually, if we draw an analogy from the mathematics of periodic motion (Cooklin, 1982; Thomas, 1979), as shown in Figure 4.3. At each point in time (t) along the horizontal axis, there also exists a corresponding point on the vertical axis, which measures a variable (C), such as intimacy, tension, conflict, and so on. Over time, the variable will ebb and flow but will stay within certain limits. This sort of regulatory theory has been criticized as a type of systemic animism whereby a system is said to be imbued with mindlike qualities that enable it to take protective action on its own behalf (Dell, 1982). It can be argued that the system does not regulate itself in this way, but it does seem to us that key variables in families do ebb and flow in a predictable (and therefore patterned) manner. People often say such things as "You could cut the tension with a knife" and "It's

Figure 4.3. The Relationship Between the Regulated Variable and Time.

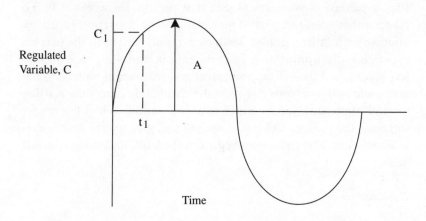

Source: Breunlin and Schwartz, 1986, p. 72. Reprinted with permission.

a real pressure-cooker situation." If the system itself does not regulate these variables, then perhaps the people do. As time passes, the intensity of a particular variable increases, to the point where the experience becomes intolerable for one or more interactants. That person, or those persons, will act to reduce the intensity, and someone will act in a complementary manner, so that both experience the variable as decreasing. These behaviors, taken together, constitute another sequence and can be said to calibrate the ebb-and-flow sequence. Two such sequences are depicted in Figure 4.4. Each of these sequences involves some variable (C). We can combine the sequences by adopting another analogy from mathematics: the Fourier theorem, which states, "Any periodic motion (sequence) can be obtained by the superposition of a number of simple harmonic motions which may differ in amplitude and period" (Weidner and Sells, 1965, p. 89). For example, a chord played on a piano is heard as one sound but is actually the simultaneous sounding of several notes. With the Fourier theorem, the chord can be understood and analyzed as the summation of the sound waves generated by the vibrations of the strings that are set in motion when the chord is played (Feynman, Leighton, and Sands, 1963). By

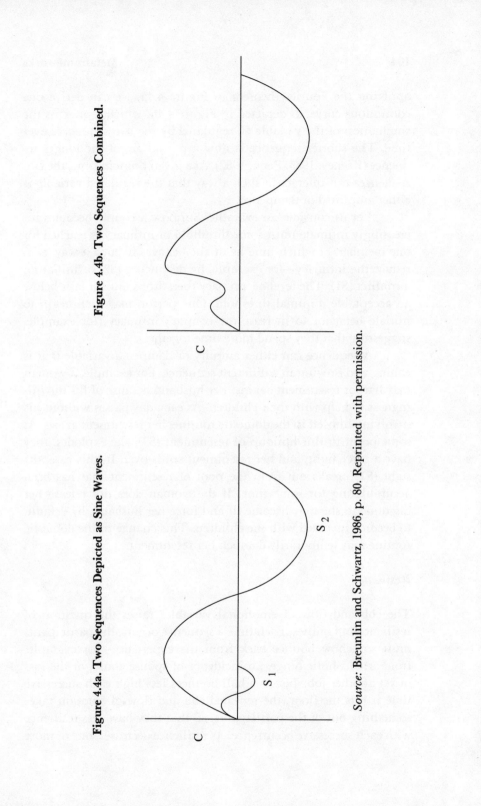

Figure 4.4a. Two Sequences Depicted as Sine Waves.

Figure 4.4b. Two Sequences Combined.

Source: Breunlin and Schwartz, 1986, p. 80. Reprinted with permission.

applying the Fourier theorem to Figure 4.4a, we can derive one continuous curve, as depicted in Figure 4.4b, which represents the summation of the variable C, regulated by the two sequences over time. The shorter sequence is now a partial arc of the longer sequence (Keeney, 1983; Penn, 1982). At a given point in time, the two sequences can interact in such a way that the regulated variable is either amplified or dampened.

Let us consider an example. Suppose a couple becomes increasingly intimate until some threshold of intimacy is reached for one member, at which time he or she behaves in such a way as to reduce the intimacy—for example, by distancing (S2) or initiating a conflict (S1). The level of intimacy then drops until it falls below an acceptable minimal threshold. One person may then begin to initiate behavior to increase the couple's intimacy (for example, suggesting that they spend more time together).

A sequence can either amplify or dampen a variable that is ebbing and flowing in a different sequence. For example, a woman may harbor resentment against her husband because of his unwillingness to help with their children. As each day passes without his involving himself in the domestic routine, her resentment grows. At some point in this buildup of resentment (S3), she explodes, they have a huge fight, and her resentment spills over. In this case, the fight (S1) breaks out from the pool of resentment that has been accumulating for some time. If the woman does not release her resentment, she may become ill and force her husband, by default, to become involved with the children. This change in the domestic routine may temporarily dampen her resentment.

Resilience

The ebb and flow of emotional variables raises the question of resilience in families. Each time a sequence occurs, the participants must somehow bounce back from the experience—for example, from an alcoholic binge, an incidence of spouse abuse, or the loss of yet another job. Just as a ball bounces less high each successive time it hits the floor, the repeated ebb and flow of emotion takes something out of the participants, so that they have less resilience with each successive occurrence. As resilience decreases, one or more parties may begin to contemplate giving up. We frequently hear people say, "I can't take much more of this" or "I don't think I can go on any longer." Therefore, knowing the history of such sequences helps us know more about just how constraining the sequence has become over time.

The Four Classes of Sequences

An infinite number of sequences can be constructed for each of the four classes. The following discussion of the classes is intended only as an overview and a sampler. With experience, therapists learn to use small bits of feedback in guiding themselves to the relevant sequences from each class.

Class 1 (S1): Face-to-Face Interaction

When two or more family members engage in face-to-face interaction, their acts constitute a sequence. These sequences define the characteristic process or style of relating. Many such sequences are not context-specific, and so they may occur at home, in the grocery store, or in a therapist's office. As such, they are readily observable and available for intervention in the context of a therapy session. An S1 interaction that lasts a few seconds may be repeated over and over during one interaction; or the interaction may involve only one sequence, which lasts from several minutes to several hours. S1 interactions include the entire range of nonverbal behavior. For instance, a couple may talk to each other but never make eye contact, or a mother may smile while she chastises a child. An S1 interaction may also involve such transactions as a mother's sitting with a six-year-old until the child falls asleep. The style of S1 interaction is also important. For instance, a mother and her daughter may argue the way two sisters do, or a father may address an adolescent son in a way that treats the son like a child. The acts that are missing from an S1 interaction are often as important as the ones that are there: if a couple argues and neither party listens to the other, then the absence of listening is an important dimension of the sequence. When research attempts to attribute outcomes to changes in a family's interaction, by coding and scoring videotapes of family therapy sessions, it essentially focuses on S1 interactions. Structural family therapists use S1 interactions as the basic sequence around which enactments are constructed.

Nonproductive S1 interactions place enormous constraints on the people involved, because they limit the direct means by which relationships can be negotiated and problems solved. They also generate negative beliefs and feelings about the relationship as the people involved make attributions: "He wouldn't say that if he cared about me" or "She never listens." Once such meanings become rigidly held, it becomes more difficult for the interactants to believe that anything productive can be done about the relationship or the problems.

The communication-oriented schools of family therapy elevate the S1 interaction to a position of primary importance, in the belief that if communication skills are improved, relationships can be improved and problems can be solved. Therefore, we have many techniques that are designed to make communication clear and congruent. We have found, however, that people sometimes cannot easily alter their relevant S1 interactions until attention is paid to other sequences. We have also found that changing an S1 interaction is sometimes not enough to solve the problem, since other classes of sequence are involved.

Class 2 (S2): Routines

Face-to-face interaction is embedded within longer sequences, which make up the routine of the family. Such sequences usually cover a period of twenty-four hours. S2 interactions are very important because they constitute the patterns by which the family carries out the functions necessary to its existence. Varela (1989, p. 23) has commented on this issue: "In my exposure to family therapy, I have come across an almost exclusive reliance on linguistic practices as the basis of theorizing. . . . It also seems to me that more detailed studies of micropractices of time, space and nonverbal connecting in the family home—following the example of the ethnologist and anthropologist—would increase an understanding of the relevant dynamics and sharpen therapeutic insights."

Failure of the family routine creates enormous constraints.

For example, in many cases of child abuse, a single mother lives chronically on the border of exhaustion and depression. The mother's physical and mental health are recursively related to how successfully she manages the family routine. Her exhaustion impairs her routine, and her routine exacerbates her exhaustion, in an endless cycle. Such a mother may have trouble getting her children to bed until late at night. The next morning, she may be unable to get up before the children do, in which case they may be running around the house unsupervised, increasing the risk of harm to themselves or of the mother's displeasure. The problem here is not so much that the mother cannot communicate with her children (S1) as that she does not have a routine that allows her to be effective.

As another example, two parents may work different shifts and never see each other during the week, and their children may take advantage of any confusion engendered by different and/or conflicting parenting styles. Or one parent may sleep during the day, forcing the other parent to keep several small children quiet. Consider still another example, of a mother who has four children and provides day care for other children. By the time her own children arrive home from school, her energy is depleted, and she finds it difficult to deal with their normal demands. The constraint imposed by the day care makes it difficult for this mother to improve her relationship with her own children.

In a complex society such as ours, few families follow such traditional routines as having one parent work while the other serves as homemaker. Instead, we have a vast array of alternative family arrangements. Most involve two parents who juggle work schedules around domestic routines that include the demands of school and children's peers. Some involve single parents or stepparents, and children who relate in many different ways to adults. Therapists must be skilled at recognizing a kaleidoscope of S2 interactions, many of which have the inherent potential to constrain the family's capacity to carry out its functions.

One dimension of the modern family that has greatly influenced the family routine is the degree of autonomy that family members have. When both parents work and children are involved in many activities outside the home, there is far less contact among

family members than there was a generation ago. The autonomy of
family members creates sets of individual agendas, which are not
easily coordinated. Moreover, children learn when their parents are
not available, and they protect their parents by getting busy with
friends and activities. When the family does come together in an
effort to share so called quality time, the hoped-for good feeling
often does not materialize, given conflicting needs and lack of
practice.

The acts of an S2 interaction may calibrate a given S1 interaction. For example, a mother may have difficulty setting limits on
a young daughter throughout the day (S1). When the father comes
home, he may criticize the mother for being ineffective. His criticism calibrates the S1 interaction between mother and daughter by
undermining the mother's confidence and making her resentful that
she, not he, must be home all day with a demanding child. The
amount of time that the father spends with their daughter also
calibrates the S1 interaction. If he spends little time with her, his
wife will be more frustrated and less willing to listen to his suggestions. If he were to spend all day with the daughter, his response
might change, because he would experience the strain of dealing
with a small child for a long period, and this experience might
make him more supportive of his wife's predicament.

The routine of a family is very complex. In many instances,
the way an S2 interaction calibrates an S1 interaction may be quite
subtle. For example, a mother may complain bitterly to her son that
he does not obey her (S1), but then she stays away from home until
late in the evening (S2), leaving the son with no adult supervisor.
A father may seem very intrusive and overinvolved when he speaks
to his daughter (S1), but he works two jobs and is rarely being
available to talk to her (S2). In both instances, the children read
more from the absence than they do from the direct communication.

S2 interactions may also generate S1 interactions. For instance, if a parent expresses constant displeasure with one child,
that child may engage in a conflictual S1 interaction with a sibling.
A father's absence from home in the evening may generate overinvolvement of a mother with a son. S1 interactions can also calibrate
S2 interactions. For example, a mother's interaction with an infant
may be so distressing, she believes that a sitter could not handle the

baby, and so she does not use sitters and never gets a break, which only increases the time that she must spend with the baby, and this intensifies her distress. S2 interactions may have periods that exceed one day. A child may have a weekend-long visit with a divorced parent. An event that occurs during the visit may generate an S1 interaction in the blended family, and the child may return from the visit upset and fight with the mother.

    S2 interactions cannot be discerned solely on the basis of direct observation. Questions that elicit information about a typical day, or that track the daily occurrence of a symptom, provide clues to S2 interactions. For example, a child may be encopretic at the same time each day. Frequently, when the therapist addresses S1 interactions directly in a session, by asking family members to change their face-to-face interaction, they reveal spontaneously how that interaction is calibrated by S2 interactions. For instance, if she is asked to get her child to sit quietly, a mother may try, fail, and then reveal that the child runs to the grandmother's apartment whenever the mother tries to impose discipline.

Class 3 (S3): Ebb and Flow

Family life unfolds across time, and patterns emerge that have much longer periods. It is more difficult to articulate how these longer sequences (what we call S3 patterns) affect family life, but we do know that they contextualize the S1 and S2 interactions embedded in them. There are two interlocking ways in which S3 patterns become important. First, they may contain a crucial intermittent event, which also includes the buildup and aftermath of the event. Second, they may reflect the ebb and flow of a significant emotional or interpersonal variable.

    Some intermittent events are imposed; others are voluntary. For example, a husband may have periodic business trips, which create patterns of absence from the family and may contribute to differences in parenting styles between father and mother. The menstrual cycle is a biologically imposed event for women, and PMS may trigger powerful changes in some women's bodies and in their relationships. Women have reported much more difficulty in managing their S2 interactions under the influence of PMS, and the intensity of conflict with a spouse (S1) may also be greater. Report cards are also imposed. Other kinds of events are voluntary in that the interactants have some control over whether they occur. Intermittent episodes of violence or drinking are examples.

Symptoms or problems rarely manifest themselves in a constant manner. They are more often intermittent, or they ebb and flow in their intensity. A behavior-disordered child usually shows "runs" of problem behavior, marked by intensification of the bad behavior, which in turn is followed by a hiatus, when behavior is better. Affective disorders ebb and flow over time, sometimes with periods of remission that are followed by sudden exacerbations of mood. A well-known example of an S3 pattern of intermittent events is Haley's (1980) leaving-home cycle, in which a young adult who is involved in a parental conflict attempts to leave home. Perhaps he succeeds for several months, until the parents threaten to separate. He then returns home—because of symptoms or job or school failure—until the marriage stabilizes. He then improves again and attempts to leave home once more.

S3 patterns connect the family to its ecology, and so they often include participants other than immediate family members (in-laws, schools, and hospital personnel, or agents of social control, such as probation officers). For instance, a foster family may take foster children to an agency once a month, to visit their natural mother. This event, its buildup, and its aftermath constitute an S3 pattern that profoundly affects the family.

Intermittent events live in the memory of the interactants. Both the memory and the expectation of the event create an experience that contributes to the affective tone of living. For example, a spouse remembers an alcoholic binge and wonders daily when another may occur again. Memories and expectations generate tension, which constantly impinges on relationships. Intermittent events also take on meanings, which then become part of the sequence. For example, if an adolescent intermittently violates an important family rule, then parents may conclude from these events that the adolescent is defective in some way (bad, lazy, mentally ill, and so on). This belief colors the way the parents interact with the adolescent on a daily basis, whether or not the adolescent has broken the rule on any given day.

"Normal" families may seem quite boring because the sequences of face-to-face interaction (S1) and family routine (S2) effectively resolve tensions and meet the needs of family members. Tension or stress either is not built up to threatening proportions (as perceived by one or more members) that require more drastic calibration or, where the system is distressed (at a new life stage, for example), self-corrects through adjusting of the S1 and S2 interactions. When S1 and S2 interactions do not resolve tensions or meet needs, the system is periodically threatened, to the point where symptomatic calibration may be required. The symptoms temporarily reduce the perceived threat but are usually ineffective in resolving it. Therefore, they wax and wane over weeks, months, or even years, as calibrations are needed.

Although every family demonstrates S3 patterns, not every problem is necessarily connected to such a sequence. Part of the challenge of therapy is to determine whether a relevant S3 pattern exists. Sometimes this determination can be made from information available at intake (multiple hospitalizations, for example). Questions regarding the onset of the symptom, its chronicity, and any periods of its remission are also useful. Sometimes families are unable to articulate a relevant S3 pattern. In such cases, its existence may become apparent only at some point during therapy, when symptoms or relationships appear to change independently of therapy. The sudden or drastic improvement or worsening of a situation at the outset of therapy may be more related to the timing of therapy, with respect to the ebb and flow of an S3 pattern, than to the brilliance or ineffectiveness of the therapist.

Class 4 (S4): Transgenerational Sequences

All families transmit patterns from one generation to the next (Boszormenyi-Nagy and Spark, 1973; Bowen, 1978). Because these transgenerational patterns have such long periods, they are not easily recognized and are often not classified as sequences. Bowen (1978), for example, has demonstrated that the way in which a couple relate is closely connected to the level of the spouses' differentiation from their respective families of origin. In our view, family patterns repeated from one generation to the next, which may stem from encoded differentiation levels, constitute a transgenerational sequence in which shorter sequences are embedded.

These transgenerational sequences are also encoded as values, rules, and beliefs and may derive from the evolution of the family's culture, or they may be idiosyncratic to a particular family. Commenting on how history can be recreated in the present, Sluzki (1983) has noted, "Part of it [history] may be prehistory, that is, elements of the members' own original family histories that persist through time as they keep symbolizing and actualized standing agreements, representing them, i.e., keeping them present. Thus, the shared history is one of the reservoirs of interactional rules and a coding manual of how to construct a reality that is activated whenever a corresponding fragment of that history is activated" (p. 473).

Transgenerational sequences may calibrate and/or generate shorter S1, S2, or S3 interactions. Consider, for example, an S4 pattern repeated in some single-parent African-American families. An adolescent becomes pregnant and bears a child. The grandmother initially functions as the primary parent, bringing the child up while its mother has the status of older sibling. As the child grows older and its mother reaches adulthood, the mother and the grandmother struggle for parenting rights. The living arrangements for the child (S2) may vary over time as the child moves back and forth between the mother's home and the grandmother's (S3). The child, caught in this struggle, begins to rebel and, upon reaching adolescence also has a baby. The mother, now a grandmother, takes over the rearing of the new baby, and the sequence is repeated. In this sequence, a woman can have the status of a mother only by becoming a grandmother (Boyd-Franklin, 1989).

It is not uncommon for events in one generation to mirror the events in a previous generation. For example, a father who has no history of psychiatric illness may become depressed when he reaches the same age at which his own father first developed similar symptoms. In this example, the S4 event will generate many sequences of shorter duration: the S1 interactions that regulate how the family treats the father, those (S2) that involve changes of routine, and those (S3) that regulate the ebb and flow of the father's depression.

A pattern in one generation may also be rejected in the next generation. For example, a couple sought therapy because the husband was not expressive to his wife. The wife reported that her own father was a wimp, and that she had been determined to marry a strong and dependable man who would provide for her and never let her down. Her husband was a good provider but, like many other men who are preoccupied with their work, he was indeed not very expressive. The woman had generated a transgenerational sequence in which she got half of what she wanted.

In traditional societies, such sequences may pass from one generation to the next with little change. In rapidly evolving societies such as our own, however, sequences that were adaptive in one generation may create stress if they are replicated in a subsequent generation. One could even hypothesize a set of S5 events, which would reflect the shifting values of a whole culture or society. They would span several generations and might involve changes in moral values, rates of divorce, levels of economic well-being, or the status of women. Such patterns have been noted in long-term observations of investments, weather, international conflict, and so on.

Sequences: A Pattern That Connects

We view interaction as an interlocking web of sequences that constitute the real-time living of a system. Interaction includes the past, the present, and expectations about the future; the here-and-now sequences of face-to-face interaction (S1); the daily routine of a family (S2); longer sequences, which include the ebb and flow of variables, symptoms, or relationships (S3); and transgenerational sequences (S4). Adaptive sequences support leadership, balance, and harmony, which in turn nurture the growth of all a family's members. Nonadaptive sequences impose constraints that threaten the health of the system and its members.

Therapists encountering systems are confronted with enormous interactional complexity. We find it hard to believe that the alteration of one simple sequence will always remove constraints in a manner necessary and sufficient to the changes that a family requires. Our clinical experience and follow-up of our cases have convinced us that more than this is often needed. For example, three brothers constantly fought, and the mother repeatedly intervened to defend the youngest. This action only fueled the conflict, for the older brothers then got even. The therapist initially interrupted this S1 interaction by having the mother charge the youngest brother a quarter for her protective services. The change did not last, however, because this S1 interaction was embedded in an S3 pattern, in which the mother periodically became depressed and was cared for by the youngest son, and the other sons became jealous. We have found that what once seemed to us to be dramatic changes, based on interventions designed to alter a single sequence, proved upon follow-up not to have lasted; or sometimes the family found itself in new difficulties, without the tools to solve its new problems. We now proceed more cautiously, using the sequences metaframework to navigate the maze of complexity.

Applications to Therapy

The sequences metaframework provides an opportunity to understand the total pattern of a human system. It also operates as a vehicle for therapists' making distinctions that reveal sequences, which are partial arcs of that pattern and can be used as the focus of therapy. Sometimes only one sequence has to be extracted. At other times, more than one is needed, or sometimes one or more sequences from each of the four classes may be needed. Moreover, if focusing on a specific sequence fails to remove enough constraints, the sequence can be examined through the sequences metaframework, and therapy can be modified, or alternative sequences can be focused on. We believe that this metaframework allows examination of sequences to function as a common denominator of effective family therapy.

Assessment

Some problems involve only S1 and/or S2 interactions, while others also involve S3 and S4 patterns. In some cases, an S3 pattern may be involved, but a change in an S1 or S2 interaction may be enough to interrupt it because the degree of embeddedness is not severe. Where it is severe, and when the S3 pattern continues to impose constraints, therapy must focus on it directly. Therefore, the degree of embeddedness—that is, the number of classes of sequence involved in a problem—correlates positively with the problem's intractability. In general, when several classes of sequence are significantly involved, therapy must be directed to each of them, and there must be a plan for the order and manner in which the sequences are addressed.

Elaborate assessment procedures can be constructed to obtain information pertinent to all four classes of sequence, but such procedures are time-consuming. They set a pace for therapy that is passive. Moreover, they are often unnecessary, since the problem may involve only one class of sequence. We have found it preferable to teach therapists to attune their listening to information relevant to all four classes of sequence. When the family tells its story, such information inevitably emerges. It is important that therapists not restrict their field of vision, as happens most often when they focus narrowly on one class of sequence (for example in adopting a particular model of therapy). Structural family therapy, for instance, emphasizes S1 interactions, which can be seen as isomorphic of structure. Such sequences are easily identified through observation of the pattern of interaction in the session. Once an S1 interaction has been detected, the structural therapist usually initiates an enactment, to change that sequence. Family members usually resist such enactments, often by offering additional information about themselves. Structural therapists are taught to maintain a focus on the relevant S1 interaction and ignore the new information (Minuchin and Fishman, 1981). This exclusive focus may be a mistake, however, because the new information may reveal other relevant sequences.

For example, a father complained in a session that his adolescent son refused to cooperate around the house. The relevant S1 interaction was one in which the father made halfhearted attempts to get his son to talk, and the son acted uninterested, giving only "yes" or "no" answers. This sequence could be seen as isomorphic of a structure in which the son refused to acknowledge the father as one of the executives in the family, and an enactment was initiated to intensify the sequence, until the father acted like a father and the son acted like a son. During the enactment, however, another son interrupted and revealed that the father did make demands and did set effective limits, but that eventually the sons could count on his inconsistency (S3). At this point, the therapist defocused from the S1 interaction and asked the father why he fell into patterns of inconsistency. The father replied that he believed he should not have to set limits: having left home himself at the age of his son (S4), he had learned self-sufficiency, and he secretly expected the same level of maturity from his son. This crucial belief on the father's part enabled the therapist to reposition the father, so that he could assess more realistically what his sons needed from him. We must keep in mind, however, that family members sometimes volunteer even important information to distract the therapist. The sequences metaframework helps therapists recognize when such information really is important.

Several conclusions can be drawn from this discussion of problems and sequences. First, despite their having a very similar symptom profile, two problems from different cases may be embedded within different classes of sequences, and so diagnoses that are based only on such profiles can be misleading. Second, an intervention that produces a quick and easy improvement in one family may have little impact on a similar problem in a second family: in the second family, there may be other relevant sequences involved, which are not addressed. Third, sometimes competent, well-intentioned people find it virtually impossible to solve a simple problem because it is embedded in many sequences; at other times, families that appear to be highly disturbed solve serious problems, once they are freed from the constraints imposed by just one or two sequences. Therefore, we must be careful not to get into situations where canaries are being killed by cannons and elephants are being hunted with slingshots. In other words, if we fail to appreciate the degree of a problem's embeddedness in various classes of sequence, our treatment approach may be poorly matched to the problem.

An important question is how to prioritize the importance of several sequences. We have developed several rules of thumb, but they should not be applied rigidly.

First, because longer sequences are always embedded in shorter sequences (at least theoretically), there exists the possibility that changing S1 or S2 interactions may also interrupt S3 or S4 interactions. Therefore, when the S3 and S4 patterns do not appear to be crippling the system, it is worthwhile to work initially on the S1 and

S2 interactions. Even when S3 patterns exist, particularly when they involve the ebb and flow of a variable such as resentment, correcting communication itself sometimes helps. In this case, the resentment can be dealt with directly, so that it does not build up over time.

Second, if a therapist works hard on an S1 interaction and no change occurs, the therapist should question whether the hoped-for change is being constrained by an S3 or S4 pattern. In such a case, the S3 or S4 pattern may involve beliefs that, if unaltered, will continue to impose constraints. In this situation, it is often productive to shift to the level of beliefs, using the IFS metaframework in conjunction with the culture and gender metaframeworks. For example, if resentment does not abate in the face of improved communication, a part that feels justified in its resentment may be unable to trust or accept that the communication changes are real.

Third, sometimes therapy must tack back and forth among efforts on several sequences, with small shifts in each sequence producing further small shifts in the others.

The interactional data revealed by the sequences metaframework also provides information about the other metaframeworks. For example, Minuchin and Fishman (1981) note that "the family is a natural group which over time has evolved patterns of interacting. These patterns make up the family structure" (p. 11). Hence, sequences can also access the organization metaframework, as well as provide clues about how the family is developing and how gender and culture are manifested in the family.

Treatment

When the sequences metaframework is used, the objective is to remove constraints by altering sequences. In this way, the family gains flexibility and access to new behaviors and beliefs, which were previously unavailable because of the high probability that a problematic sequence would occur.

Family therapy's heavy emphasis on interaction has produced a plethora of techniques and interventions designed to change sequences. Most such interventions originated under the umbrella of one of the popular models of family therapy. If we analyze the models' predilections for sequences, we see that differ-

ences among models of family therapy can be accounted for by the
different classes of sequence that the models emphasize. Some models have developed effective techniques for blocking or reorganizing
S1 or S2 interactions, while others have aimed more at S3 or S4
patterns and the beliefs and world-views that maintain them. These
techniques can be thought of as unique to the models; with the
sequences metaframework, however, we are always transcending
particular models, and so we can use techniques drawn from any
of them. While some theorists argue that mixing models creates
confusion, we have found that, as long as therapists hold their
presuppositions constant and maintain collaborative relationships
with families, techniques originally associated with divergent models can be used. Because this view liberates therapists from the constraints of model purity, therapists are free to select among any
number of techniques but also to maintain a conceptual grounding,
so that the process of selection and implementation is organized,
rather than random. We have employed techniques from the structural, strategic, Milan, and Bowen models of family therapy, often
in the same case.

Likewise, because we take a ''both/and'' rather than an
''either/or'' position about action and meaning and see them as
recursively involved in sequences, we feel comfortable changing
sequences by means of both action and meaning techniques. Obviously, the shorter S1 interactions lend themselves more readily to
action techniques (such as enactments), while the longer sequences
more often involve both an action change and a meaning change.
For example, confronted with an S2 interaction, in which the parents do not provide adequate supervision of their children because
of long working hours, the therapist may first have to create a
meaning change associated with the importance of supervision. Ultimately, however, the parents must find a way to be more available
at home. When an S3 pattern that involves an intermittent event
must be interrupted, therapy may center on a plan for keeping that
event from happening. The plan often involves a decision that requires a change in priorities. For example, a traveling husband may
literally have to decide between his job and the viability of his
marriage. With S3 patterns that involve a variable that ebbs and
flows, we identify the part of the person that is activated by the

variable: a spouse may identify a part that is fearful of intimacy and may track that part's response to the ebb and flow of intimacy in the marital relationship.

The sequences metaframework forces therapy to account for the complexity of human systems and to recognize that quick and easy changes are sometimes not possible. Therapists must respect the natural timing of families and pace therapy to it. For example, a couple entering therapy with ambivalence about the future of the marriage may show an S3 pattern around commitment, one that has ebbed and flowed for several years and has gradually reduced the resilience of the relationship. Assessment will include the events, beliefs, and variables involved in that sequence, as well as the degree of commitment and viability of the relationship. In such a case, therapy must often "ride out" at least one cycle of the S3 pattern before the therapist is in a position to know how to help. We have found that the sequences metaframework does increase the length of therapy, but it also increases our satisfaction with the outcome, as in the following case example:

> Joe, age forty-two, sought help for a sleep disturbance. He had no history of sleep disturbances but reported a sudden onset of the problem after he and his fifteen-year-old son had gone camping with a group of fathers and sons. The sons had stayed awake late into the night, and none of the fathers got much sleep. Upon arriving home, Joe found that he still could not sleep, and he reported being very anxious. Curiously, the camp was the same one that Joe and his own father had gone to when Joe himself was fifteen. Joe reported that being at the camp had freaked him out: he had suddenly realized that he could not really account for the past twenty-five years of his life; they had just happened, and he felt like an adolescent trapped in a middle-aged body.
>
> Joe's wife, Bernice, was supportive and accompanied him to the interview. In addition to his son, he had a college-age daughter. Joe worked as a plant

manager at a factory and said that work in the summer
was always slow.

Joe reported that he went to bed every night
and tried to sleep. After he tossed and turned for several hours, he and his wife would both get up, and
they would talk in an effort to get to the bottom of the
problem. During the day, Joe ruminated about the
source of the problem and worried whether he would
sleep that night. He could feel himself getting more
and more tense as the night approached.

With just these few details, we can use the sequences metaframework to hypothesize several relevant sequences. We know that
sleep is a spontaneous behavior that cannot be willed. By attempting to will himself to sleep, Joe unwittingly created a "be spontaneous" paradox (Watzlawick, Beavin, and Jackson, 1967). When that
failed, he and his wife would get up and talk about it, engaging in
a failed "attempted solution," whereby talking only created more
anxiety (Watzlawick, Weakland, and Fisch, 1974). Both the "be
spontaneous" paradox and the "attempted solution" were counterproductive S1 interactions.

Throughout the day, Joe thought and worried about the existential nature of the problem, so that he was approaching each
night with considerable tension and dread. He had abandoned
many of the behaviors normally associated with his routine, such
as exercise and leisure activity. The problem, then, had disrupted
Joe's normal routines (S2), replacing them with a buildup of tension that further impaired his sleep reflex.

The seasonal nature of Joe's work disrupted his normal pattern of energy expenditure. He could have expected to be less tired
during the summer and, but for this seasonal variation (S3), might
not have fallen into a sleep disturbance.

Finally, a transgenerational pattern (S4) seemed to be present. Returning to the scene of a childhood experience had created
an existential crisis for Joe that was both midlife and transgenerational in nature. Joe's father's success in business had given Joe a
privileged childhood and the belief that someday he would be the
vice-president of one of his father's companies. This dream was

shattered when the father began to drink while Joe was an adolescent. By the time Joe reached young adulthood, the companies had been lost, and Joe spent much of his time dragging his father out of bars. Joe started college but dropped out to protect his mother. He went to work in a factory, worked his way up until he became plant manager, and was currently working in a relatively easy job that did not challenge his potential. The owners of the factory were meanspirited individuals whom Joe resented, both for their style and for the fact that, but for fate, Joe would have been an owner, too, not a manager.

The two camping trips were significant in several ways. The first was one of the last happy times that Joe had with his father. The second reconnected the first part of Joe's life, when his father had been successful, with his current life, where Joe was beginning to question his own success. At midlife, he was forced to recognize "missing chapters" between the two camping trips.

Therapy for Joe could have taken many directions. Some models would simply have interrupted the S1 interactions and called therapy successful if Joe's sleep patterns had returned to normal. Other models would have focused on Joe's midlife crisis or examined the transgenerational issues. With the sequences metaframework, the therapist could hypothesize that the sleep disturbance was embedded within several sequences. Interruption of the S1 and S2 interactions might or might not prove sufficient to eliminate the sleep disturbance. Even if they did, the question would remain of whether therapy should address the midlife and transgenerational issues. With the sequences model and the developmental metaframework, all relevant sequences could be addressed.

The first step was to establish priorities. Clearly, Joe needed to get some sleep, but it was also important not to lose the urgency for therapy provided by the presenting problem. Joe agreed that he was anxious to sleep but also wanted therapy that would address what was happening to him. Therefore, therapy initially focused on interrupting the sleep-inhibiting S1 and S2 interactions while leaving some time in the sessions to begin exploring the transgenerational issues.

To interrupt the "be spontaneous" paradox proved straightforward. The therapist discussed the nature of sleep and suggested that when Joe went to bed and failed to sleep, he should get up and do something boring until he felt drowsy, and then he should return to bed. Interrupting the "attempted solution" of searching for explanations with Bernice was more difficult, because Joe was obsessed with finding the answer. The therapist explained that Joe was obviously searching for explanations, but the harder he looked, the more elusive they became. If Joe stopped trying so hard, important clues were more likely to pop into his head. An arrangement was made whereby Joe and Bernice would have time-limited discussions at breakfast and then forget about the problem for the rest of the day.

This plan also reduced Joe's daytime ruminations, which were contributing to a tension-building routine (S2) whereby he went to bed in a very tense state. Joe was taught progressive muscle relaxation, which he practiced in abbreviated form throughout the day whenever he felt himself wanting to ruminate or getting tense. He also performed a full-relaxation exercise before going to bed. Joe was encouraged to resume some of the behaviors of his normal routine as well. These plans produced partial success. Within a week, Joe began to get some sleep, but he fell into a pattern of good days and bad days. The therapist explained that as Joe came to grips with his existential crisis, the good days would outnumber and eventually replace the bad days.

Joe agreed, and he seemed in no hurry for the sleep disturbance to remit entirely. It called attention to many issues that had remained dormant for twenty years. So powerful were these issues that Joe had lived his adult life in a fog, barely aware of the passing of two decades. The sleep disturbance forced Joe to reconcile his past with his future.

Regarding the past, Joe had never acknowledged his anger toward his father for having squandered his inheritance and constrained him to drop out of college and forsake his potential. Twenty years later, Joe found himself trapped in a job he hated. He craved a change that would allow him to live up to his potential. But would such a change merely replicate his father's actions by throwing away his family's security? The transgenerational issues imposed massive constraints on Joe, threatening his psychological security and limiting his options for the future. The therapist suggested that Joe could account for the missing years by releasing himself from the past and deciding about his future. Joe's embittered beliefs about his father were constraining him from letting go.

A session with Joe's adult siblings was suggested, to provide Joe with a different perspective from which to reexamine his past. Two siblings who were close to Joe's age and two who were much younger attended this session. The elder siblings, including Joe, expressed intense feelings about their father. Joe had always believed that his father's alcoholism and failure had caused him, as the eldest, to suffer the most. In fact, however, the next-eldest son appeared to be the most disabled by anger. The younger siblings, who had never known a successful father, were more accepting of the father they did know and helped Joe see the father as a frail human being whose luck had gone bad. All the other siblings offered views of their mother that Joe had never considered in his own beliefs about the past. In the end, all but the next-eldest brother encouraged Joe to go and see the father and to forgive and forget.

After the session, Joe and the youngest brother made a pilgrimage to their father. Joe asked his father to explain what had happened and received an apology from his father for the pain he had caused. Joe returned to the next session feeling less bitter about the past. Both the session with Joe's siblings and the pilgrimage are examples of how action can help to change meaning.

Less plagued by the lost opportunities of the past, Joe could turn his attention to the future. He was asked to list the pros and cons of staying in his current job versus making a fresh start. A session was held with the whole family, which served to focus Joe on his non–job-related achievements. Several sessions later, Joe announced that he had decided to stay in his job. He said that the security and financial benefits of the job outweighed the hassles. He seemed relieved. The therapist understood this as a decision to interrupt the transgenerational patterns, which could have replicated his father's abandonment of his responsibilities. To stabilize the changes, Joe was encouraged to find greater satisfaction outside his job and he and Bernice began to find new activities.

Therapy lasted for fifteen sessions. Joe's sleep disturbance abated significantly after five sessions. By the end of therapy, his sleep pattern had returned to normal. In a one-year follow-up, conducted after the slow time in the summer, Joe had no further sleep disturbance. He reported being satisfied with his life and did not have periods of anxiety and indecision.

We have come a long way from the time when we believed we could solve a problem by changing one simple behavioral sequence in which the problem was embedded. We now believe that problems may be embedded in several sequences, and that sequences involve both action and meaning. We also see that the sequences metaframework provides only one perspective on the family, which must often be complemented by perspectives from the other metaframeworks.

The sequences metaframework is like a kaleidoscope for the shifting perspective of the therapist, which creates a rich array of sequences from the colorful fragments that make up family life. We were intimidated by the complexity of the sequences metaframework at first, but as we gained experience with it, we began to appreciate the interactional richness it could provide. We remain curious about families, knowing that a small twist of the metaframework can bring a brilliant pattern into view, one that further illuminates the constraints that lock the family into its dilemma.

FIVE

Leadership, Balance, and Harmony: The Organization Metaframework

Systems theory has encouraged researchers in psychotherapy, as it has those in many other fields, to move from studying the component parts of an entity, in isolation, to trying to understand the entity as a whole. In studying the whole, researchers found that there seemed to be something more to systems than the sum of their parts. For example, a person is a collection of cells, and people endure as constant organisms, despite repeatedly losing and replacing all their cells. The essence of an organism, then, is not its components but rather its organization—that is, how it fits together as a whole. A system's organization defines how its various parts are structured, as well as the function that each part of the system serves for the whole.

Von Bertalanffy believed that living organisms possess an organizing force that establishes and preserves relationships among their component parts and gives them integrity. Maturana and Varela (1980) called this force *autopoiesis,* or self-creation, and saw it as an internal blueprint that allows an organism to maintain itself. This internal blueprint has been referred to as a *code,* as in the term *genetic code,* or as a set of rules that govern the relationships among components. Any system—a society, a corporation, a motor, a living cell, or a family—can be studied, to find the patterns that reflect the rules guiding the way in which the parts are interrelated (that is, the *structure*).

Social scientists have long been interested in the concept of organization, and the well-known sociological theory of structural-functionalism has influenced anthropology, sociology, and psychology. The organizational view has also played an important role in the evolution of family systems theory. In shifting the focus from individuals to families, researchers in family therapy were interested at first in pathological communication among family members. Only later did they recognize that problems of communication occur when the organization of a system is confused.

Organization and structure became the dominant focus of some of family therapy's most influential models. The best-known of these are structural family therapy, developed by Minuchin and his colleagues (Minuchin, 1974; Minuchin and Fishman, 1981) and the brand of strategic therapy developed by Haley (1976, 1980) and Madanes (1981, 1983, 1990). Other prominent models also used organizational concepts: triangles (Bowen, 1978), for example, and coalitions (Selvini-Palazzoli, Cecchin, Prata, and Boscolo, 1978).

Multilevel Perspective

Since family therapists have been primarily interested in understanding families, they have applied ideas about systems organization primarily to family systems. As a result, when most family therapists examine a problem, they see the family level of the system as the most important one. They give lip service to the inclusion of other levels, but they shift focus to other levels only with reluctance and difficulty. This happens partly because the organizational principles that have been applied to families have not been applied to other system levels, and so shifting to other levels has often entailed changes to other conceptual models.

We believe that family therapy's emphasis on the family as the most important system, and the consequent reluctance to shift levels, has been an unnecessary constraint on therapists. We subscribe to a multilevel view of human problems, informed by Koestler's concept of the holon: any system can be conceived of as being both part of a larger system and a system in itself, with its own parts (see Chapter Two). From this perspective, the family is an important system, but we are also interested in its parts (for example, the marital and sibling subsystems) and the parts of its subsystems (the individuals within them and their internal parts, as described in Chapter Three), as well as in the systems in which the family is embedded (the community, systems of other helping agents, the systems formed by national conditions) and in the belief systems in which those larger systems are embedded (for example, cultural values; see Chapters Seven and Eight).

If one accepts the premise that all these levels of a system are interrelated—that they affect and are affected by one another—then it follows that people can be constrained by imbalances at any level. It also follows that each level can be understood according to the same organizational principles, so that one can shift fluidly up and down this "holarchy," rather than focusing exclusively on constraints within the family, which may be more easily understood and lifted from some other level.

Family therapy in general, and structural family therapy in particular, have operated on the premise that the key to changing individuals is to change their families—that is, to change the network of relationships in which they are embedded. Therefore, instead of working directly with a child's inner conflicts, the therapist assumes that the intrapsychic conflicts will be resolved when the family conflicts that surround the child are resolved. We agree with this premise, but we would say that *one* key to changing individuals is to change their families. We still believe that the family level is very influential and cannot be ignored, but we do not believe that it is the only level (or, in some cases, even the most important level) to explore.

Family therapy's rigidity over this top-down stance—that to change a system, one should work on a problem that exists at one level by working on the level above it—can be seen as a reaction to the rigid bottom-up stance of psychoanalysis, against which family therapy rebelled. We believe that both stances are correct; it is each one's exclusiveness that is limiting. We find it possible to change whole families by working only with a marital or a sibling subsystem—or, on a level lower yet, only with the internal lives of individual members. It is also possible to change families by working with the larger systems that impose constraints on them from above (such as the welfare system, patriarchal belief systems, or the economic system that imposes deprivation on a community). It is interesting that, because family therapy has been so focused on the family level, the field has only recently begun to pay more than lip service to the importance of considering these larger constraints, despite all the top-down rhetoric.

Freed from the constraints of exclusively top-down or bottom-up assumptions about change, therapists can scan the whole range of systems involved in a problem and assess, with a family, which level would be the most efficient and ecological starting point. (The focus may shift frequently among levels, however, no matter where one starts.) It should be remembered that when there is imbalance at one level of a system, the other levels are also likely to be imbalanced, because each level is interrelated with every other level. Therefore, a therapist can always do valuable work, no matter what level of the system is selected. The work may proceed more rapidly or smoothly, however, if certain levels are attended to before others.

How do we decide about level of focus? Consider Tim, a nineteen-year-old high school dropout who lives with his parents and his sixteen-year-old brother. He works part-time as a janitor and is depressed enough to have attempted suicide recently. When he is not at work, Tim mopes around the house or fights with his brother, who is a straight-A student. Their father works in sales for a big corporation and frequently travels. When he is home, he hounds Tim about being lazy, which distresses Tim's mother, who thinks that her husband's temper is the root of Tim's problem. Many family therapists would try to get the family to focus initially on the divisive relationship between Tim's parents and the way they fight their battles over Tim. Many individual therapists would focus on Tim's internal struggles and lack of differentiation from his family. It is also possible, however, to focus on Tim's relationship with his brother or with his peers, or on the impact of the father's pressure-packed and absence-making job on the whole family, or on the family's relationship with the physician who is prescribing drugs for Tim, or on the family's beliefs about children leaving home, or about the gender roles that derive from the family's Irish heritage, or on the fact that the mother's fear of provoking Tim stems from her own father's suicide, and so on. Each of these levels is likely to contain constraints related to Tim's problem, and releasing constraints from any of them could have an immediate impact.

It is also likely, however, that there will be ways to minimize resistance to and maximize the staying power of such an impact if one is aware of several considerations.

First, some levels of a system are easier to access than others. For example, family members may be less interested in talking about the marital issues or problems that are due to the father's job than they are in talking about Tim's internal state.

Second, change at some levels will be difficult to achieve or maintain if other levels do not change simultaneously. For example, Tim's internal system will be difficult to change as long as his parts are continually activated by extreme interactions with his family. The parents' marital issues will be difficult to resolve as long as the father holds such a stressful job. The father will be unlikely to change jobs as long as he is dominated by his achievement-oriented parts, and so on.

Third, change at some levels may be countered or overridden by lack of change at other levels. For example, Tim's efforts to become more independent may threaten his mother, since she has seen him as her only ally in dealing with her husband. The father's attempts to travel less will be countered by his boss. The parents' attempts to redefine their relationship will be countered by parts of themselves that hold traditional beliefs about men and women, and so on.

It is certainly possible to ignore these considerations, work at only one level, and have such a powerful impact that a change perseveres. For example, we could see Tim in individual therapy and help him hold the changes steady in his internal system, through all the activation from other levels, until those other levels adjusted to his changes. Similarly, we could work only with the protective triangular sequences among Tim, his mother, and his father and struggle to help them hold the improvements steady in the face of activation from systems above and below. Many therapists try one or the other of these two strategies. The point, however, is that if one can shift fluidly and, often, rhythmically from level to level, one encounters less resistance, because each level can be helped to adjust to and can even facilitate changes at other levels.

Sometimes such shifting of levels is not so necessary, because the person's problem does not seem to be so tightly embedded in multisystem imbalances. For example, if all the facts in Tim's case were the same except that he worked full-time and was living independently, then his internal system would have more room to change, without activation or constraint by his family members and their environment. In that situation, it would be less crucial to work at all levels, although we would still advocate giving all the other levels some attention, at least.

The Structural View of Organization

Structural family therapy (SFT), which provided the field with its first clear map of organization at the family level, was the model around which the field was organized for at least a decade. Minuchin eschewed speculation about the inner lives of family members and emphasized the power of the family as the "matrix of identity"—as what determined the individual's sense of self. In this way, SFT fixed therapists' focus primarily on the level of current family process and constrained flexible shifting among levels by declaring internal process off limits. Nevertheless, SFT did introduce many basic concepts and techniques that we use to understand and help change other levels of systems. For this reason, we will summarize and critique aspects of the structural conceptualization of family organization.

Although Minuchin does not give much credit to others for his views on structure, the concepts on which his organizational perspective is based were in the air, particularly in the work of such social scientists as von Bertalanffy (1968) and Talcott Parsons. For example, to appreciate SFT's debt to Parsons, consider the following passage (Parsons and Bales, 1955, p. 37):

> That the [nuclear family] is itself a subsystem of a larger system is of course a sociological commonplace. But to break it in turn down into subsystems is a less familiar way of looking at it. Yet we will treat the family in this way and say that, in certain crucially important respects, the very young child does not participate in, is not fully a "member," of his whole family, but only of a subsystem of it, the mother-child

subsystem. The marriage pair constitute another subsystem, as may, for certain purposes, also the child
with all his siblings, all the males in the family, all the
females, etc. In fact, any combination of two or more
members as differentiated from one or more other
members may be treated as a social system which is a
subsystem of the family as a whole.

Minuchin (1974) has defined family structure as "the invisible set of functional demands that organizes the ways in which
family members interact" (p. 51). The family is differentiated into
subsystems, each of which can contain any number of family
members and is defined by its function or its membership. Thus, for
example, there is the spousal subsystem and the sibling subsystem.
In addition, the spousal subsystem may or may not be the executive
subsystem, according to who in the family makes decisions or takes
care of others.

Minuchin concretized the rules that determine who partici-
pates in a subsystem when and how by using the organismic metaphor of a semipermeable boundary around the subsystem. If the
boundary around a subsystem is too diffuse, then it is too easy for
other family members to intrude into that subsystem and disrupt its
functioning. If the boundary is too rigid, then the subsystem will
become isolated and dysfunctional. From these premises follows a
basic tenet of SFT: if the boundaries around a subsystem are improved—made either less diffuse or less rigid—the functioning of
the subsystem will improve. For example, if a father is prevented
from interfering in the conflicts between his wife and his daughter
(if the boundary around the mother/daughter subsystem is made
less diffuse), and if the therapist prevents the mother and the daughter from avoiding their differences in their usual ways (if the boundary between mother and daughter is made less rigid), then mother
and daughter will be better able to resolve their differences and
become closer. This simple concept of the boundary is central and
powerful. SFT basically consists of improving the boundaries
among the various subsystems within a family, or between a family
and its environment. This boundary-improving process involves
two operations: improving the *proximity* of members of a subsys-

tem, and improving the generational *hierarchy* between subsystems (Wood and Talmon, 1983; Wood, 1985).

Drawing on the work of Erving Goffman (1971), Wood (1985) distinguishes six dimensions that define the proximity of members within a subsystem: the amount of time the members spend together, how physically close they allow each other to be (touching or standing closely), how differentiated they are emotionally, how much general information they share with one another, how much personal information they confide to one another, and how they handle decisions within the subsystem. The therapist can track these dimensions, within or between family subsystems, to assess the proximity component of boundaries. Wood also identifies several dimensions of generational hierarchy, the other component of boundaries: the degree to which parents nurture their children, are able to control their children, are in peerlike relationships with their children rather than with each other, or are in coalition with their children against each other.

A structural family therapist scans the interactions of family members, with an eye for extremes on any of these dimensions of proximity or generational hierarchy. For example, the mother speaks for and always sits next to eight-year-old Lisa (proximity extreme of enmeshment), and she sits passively while Lisa races around the therapist's office (generational hierarchy extreme of peerlike relationship). The father screams at Lisa when she acts up (generational hierarchy extreme of overcontrol) and reports that he rarely spends time with her (proximity extreme of disengagement). Having spotted these boundary problems, the therapist tries to improve the boundaries by getting the parents to work together in controlling Lisa (generational hierarchy) while also directing the father to spend time playing with Lisa while the mother spends more time with Nathan, their son (proximity).

The SFT principle of complementarity implies that members of a subsystem often adopt opposite positions or behaviors, in a complementary fashion. Therefore, the more enmeshed the mother is with Lisa, the more disengaged the father becomes (proximity). The more peerlike the mother is with Lisa, the more authoritarian the father will be (generational hierarchy). This principle also implies that if changes are to last, both sides of the complementarity must be addressed. For the mother to become firmer, the father must become softer; for the mother to distance, the father must approach.

In a family where boundaries around subsystems are clear, a child will be a part of all the subsystems that he or she needs in developing competence. Those subsystems will also function well enough to provide a balance between the sense of belonging and the sense of separateness. When this is not the case, a child will miss opportunities to develop competence and will suffer from either too much nurturance and protection or not enough. Thus, SFT is not just a theory of therapy; it is a theory of normative family and individual development.

SFT views problems as arising from or being maintained by boundary disturbances within families. From this perspective, improvements in boundaries (at the level of both proximity and generational hierarchy) can be expected to eliminate problems. Therefore, all the SFT techniques are designed to enable the therapist to use his or her relationship with family members to improve these boundaries.

The literature from which we have derived this summary of structural family therapy was published before 1985; most of it comes from the 1970s or the early 1980s. The family therapy field has evolved since that time, and we suspect that many of those who practice structural family therapy have evolved along with the field. There is a lack of written evidence of this evolution, however, Minuchin himself has shifted his focus, from families to larger systems (Elizur and Minuchin, 1989), and his departure has left SFT without a prolific spokesperson. In this chapter, we criticize several aspects of structural family therapy, but we do so with the recognition that we are challenging old ideas. We hope to update rather than replace the SFT model.

The Strategic View of Organization

Jay Haley spent ten years working with Minuchin in Philadelphia, and so his writings reflect many of the same organizational concepts that SFT does: boundaries, hierarchy, cross-generational coalition, and so on. Haley did use many of these concepts, but he emphasized them differently and produced a different model of therapy. As already discussed, a boundary is understood to have two components, proximity and generational hierarchy. Haley, choosing to focus on the latter in his theorizing, turned family therapy into a study of hierarchy.

Initially, Haley (1976) concentrated on triangular power relations in families, particularly on the cross-generational coalitions that occur when one parent allies with a child against the other parent. He believed that all problems were embedded in such triangles, which sometimes involved grandparents as well as other helpers, and would be resolved once the generations were properly realigned. For this reason, Haley focused on the sequences of family interaction that surround the problem (what, in Chapter Four, we call S1 or S2 interactions) as a way to expose the dysfunctional hierarchy. Returning to the example of Lisa's family, we can say that Haley might have family members describe the details of their behavior before, during, and after Lisa's outbursts at home (S1), as well as the details of the family's daily schedule (S2), and would search for points at which to intervene in these sequences and thereby shift the hierarchy. Haley, more than Minuchin, would also be listening for evidence that Lisa's behavior was serving some kind of distractive or protective function for the family; that is, Lisa's tantrums would be seen as the product of hierarchical issues between her parents, but she might also be using her tantrums to distract her parents from their conflicts with each other and thereby protect them from each other. (Madanes, 1981, increased strategic family therapy's emphasis on this function of symptoms, by building her theory around what she calls "incongruous hierarchies," in which children are in the position of trying to take care of their parents in indirect ways.)

Later, Haley (1981) expanded the temporal scope of his search for hierarchy problems and for the function of symptoms, by considering family sequences of longer duration (S3). In particular, he described symptoms of severely disturbed young adults as being embedded in a sequence precipitated by the threat that the young adult's impending departure poses to the parents. The distressed parents begin to fight with each other. The patient acts crazy. The parents unite to deal with the patient and hospitalize him or her. The patient improves while in the hospital and considers becoming independent. The parents are again threatened and fight. The patient acts crazy again, and so on. In outlining this leaving-home sequence, Haley broke with the ahistoric tradition of SFT, with its emphasis on current family process, and opened the door to consideration of the historic evolution of family organization and the different levels of sequence involved. We have elaborated on this work by designing a multilevel model of sequences, as described in Chapter Four.

The Organization Metaframework

Our views owe a great deal to the thinking that came before. Yet, because we emphasize or interpret many of these basic organizational concepts differently, our views have different implications for therapy. We retain the powerful concepts of boundary and holon; as a result, we remain interested in assessing which parts of a system, at any level, are allied, enmeshed, or disengaged. We have many differences with these traditional organizational maps, however. We will summarize our differences first, and then we will describe them in more detail.

To summarize our differences, we add the concepts of *balance* and *harmony* in understanding how holons interact; we take a different view of hierarchy and replace it with the concept of *leadership;* we take a multilevel perspective, which expands the therapist's purview in two directions and leads to a new view of individuals (see Chapter Three) and of a family's environment (see Chapters Seven and Eight); we connect organization with the sequences metaframework described in Chapter Four and thereby also expand the therapist's temporal purview, allowing for greater understanding of a system's evolution and greater ability to predict future patterns; we take a less pathology-oriented position regarding the function of the symptom; and we use the concept of perspectivism (see Chapter Two), aware that the distinctions we make about families are not maps of their real structure but are maps limited and distorted by our perspective.

Balance and Harmony

In Chapter Two, we discussed balance and harmony as antidotes to the troubling aspects of the concepts of power and control. Here, we will return to balance and harmony, to understand the interactions among holons within a system and between systems.

We use the concept of balance in relation to three dimensions within systems: the degree of influence that a holon of a system has in the system's decision-making process; the degree of access that a holon has to the system's resources; and the level of responsibility that a holon has within the system. When each holon is allowed the degree of influence, the access to resources, and the responsibility appropriate to its needs and to its level in the system, and equal to that of other holons at the same level, the system is considered to be balanced.

We use the concept of harmony with respect to relationships among holons. In balanced systems, holons usually relate harmoniously—that is, they cooperate, are willing to sacrifice some of their individual interests for the greater good, care about one another and feel valued by the larger system, and have clear boundaries that allow a balance between belonging and separateness.

If we reflect on the earlier discussion of boundaries, we see how improving a holon's boundaries can improve balance and harmony within the system. For example, a diffuse holon boundary will create relationships that are too close, too influential, or too responsible. Given the limits imposed by the zero-sum nature of any system's resources or decision-making process, this will mean that other relationships are too distant, disenfranchised, or irresponsible.

To take the discussion another step forward, imbalances or unclear boundaries in systems create polarization and disharmony. By *polarization,* we mean a shift in two holons relative to each other, whereby each moves from a nonextreme, flexible, harmonious position or role to a rigid, extreme position or role that is opposite to that of the other. As a couple argues, for example, one spouse may find herself taking an increasingly extreme and rigid position in response to the rigidity and extremity of the other spouse, even to the point where each spouse is saying things that he or she does not really believe. In this example, the couple's positions regarding some issue are polarized, and each spouse is defending his or her own position and attacking the other's. Drawing on Bateson's (1972) distinction between symmetry and complementarity, we consider this couple's conflict to be an example of symmetrical polarization because each spouse, in challenging the other, is doing the same thing: defending himself or herself and blaming the other. The two are polarizing in a symmetrical manner. Complementary polarizations occur when holons do or think complementary or opposite things, to the point where their differences are ossified and exaggerated. Consider a wife who takes an authoritarian approach to the children, while her husband is consistently permissive. In this example, there is a complementary polarization in their roles (hard versus soft), while their conflict over whether children respond best to hardness or softness is a symmetrical polarization because of the similarity of their styles of conflict.

Polarization has several negative effects on a system, First, each holon is constrained by the rigidity of its positions or roles and by the need to counterbalance the other's (recall the example of two sailors balancing a boat, in Chapter Three). Second, polarized holons not only cooperate poorly but also can become so competitive that they actively try to sabotage each other or even the whole system. Third, the tension generated by polarized holons can create the need for some kind of distraction or detouring, frequently involving a third holon or some other focus external to the system. In this way, polarizations at one level of a system often create polarizations at other levels as holons from those other levels are pulled in.

We end this discussion of polarization with the reminder that polarization is generally reflective of or responding to (1) imbalances in the system that allocates influence, resources, or responsibility or (2) boundary problems. It follows, then, that one way to depolarize systems is to correct such imbalances, as implied in the slogan, "If you want peace, work for justice." (The gender metaframework, discussed in Chapter Eight, is concerned largely with correcting one particular and pervasive imbalance.)

Leadership

Systems cannot achieve or maintain balance or harmony without effective leadership. Some holon within a system must be in a position to mediate conflicts among other holons, to make sure that the other holons are getting their needs met and feel valued, to allocate resources fairly, to allocate responsibilities and influence fairly, to provide firm and fair discipline, to encourage the growth of other holons while considering the needs of the whole system, to represent the system in interactions with other systems, and to coordinate planning for the system's future. Fortunately, biological systems seem to come equipped with the resources necessary to this kind of leadership. Unfortunately, the same resources are often constrained by polarizations within or outside the system, so that the system's leadership also becomes rigid and extreme. Rigid and extreme leadership creates imbalances, which create polarizations, which constrain leadership, and so on. Effective leadership corrects imbalances and thus depolarizes and harmonizes the system, and this harmony supports effective leadership.

In families, we generally assume that parents are capable of effective leadership, but we also find that they are often constrained by polarizations. The constraining polarizations may exist at any or all levels of interfacing systems, including the internal systems of either or both parents, the nuclear family holon and/or the parental holon within it, the extended family, the family/school holon, the family/work or family/community holons, and the national and international environments, which affect all lower levels of the system.

Family therapists have been confronted repeatedly with families where the children are out of control and where parents' discipline is excessively weak or harsh, and so it is easy to see why the control aspects of leadership have been emphasized in the field. Many therapists have assumed that once parents are back in control, the other aspects of good parenting will flow naturally, and, in many cases, the shoring up of parental discipline has been enough, at least temporarily, to resolve the presenting problem, at which point therapy has stopped. We believe in the importance of the disciplinary aspects of family leadership (a phrase we prefer to *family hierarchy*, which has power-structure connotations), but they are only one aspect of effective leadership.

Effective family leaders, like effective leaders of any other system, have the qualities that maintain balance and harmony within the system. These include the ability to be firm and to set age-appropriate limits for children but also to be nurturant, encouraging, fair, and flexible. Effective family leaders help children attain a balance of autonomy from and connectedness to the family, a balance that fits with the family's cultural context and needs. They neither fear excessively nor eagerly await the day when the children will leave. They are able to shift their leadership style as the children grow. They are able to put the needs of the children above any issues that they themselves have with other family leaders, so that family leadership is cooperative, consistent, and accessible. They are able to take care of themselves, so that the children do not feel responsible for their well-being. In short, when family leadership is effective, children receive the message that they are cared about and for, not just controlled.

Most family therapists would agree with these family leadership goals. Our contention, however, is that, because of the field's overconcern with control, many of the other, nondisciplinary, aspects of family leadership have been undervalued. It has also been assumed that they will follow improvements in the power structure automatically, without benefit of any direct attention. As a result, the primary technique of many therapists has been to prod parents or other family leaders into seizing control over children, or to strategize with parents about how to get control indirectly.

It is often true that a family calms down and its symptoms abate after parents regain disciplinary control over their children. It is also often true, however, that the struggle to regain control may not succeed, because disciplinary deficits are only one aspect of ineffective leadership in the family, and that this struggle may involve pain, deception, or rage that could be avoided if the family could change other, nondisciplinary, aspects of its leadership.

Isomorphism and the Temporal Dimension of Therapy

Traditionally, a family therapist whose work was informed by an interest in the structure of a family has been interested primarily in the current functioning of the family and has believed that, by watching certain family transactions, he or she could obtain the information needed for understanding the family's structure. Such a therapist would also believe that short interaction sequences among family members are reflective of the larger structure of the family, since all the family's behavior is governed by the rules governing the entire system, which also determine its structure: "Family structure is manifested in a variety of transactions that obey the same system rules and which are therefore dynamically equivalent" (Minuchin and Fishman, 1981, p. 123). These short family sequences, which we call *S1 interactions* (see Chapter Four) and which structural family therapists call *isomorphs,* are what many family therapists scan for in observing families, as well as what they use to construct their hypotheses about a family's structure.

Structuralists believe that they can quickly obtain a "biopsy" of the family. The family interactions elicited by their probes are seen as distillations of the family's history. They believe that they can obtain, from one small sequence, an understanding of the family's structure. For example, if a mother speaks for her son in response to a question from the therapist, it is assumed that this sequence may be isomorphic of an overprotective or enmeshed mother-son relationship and, possibly, of an enmeshed family. This belief in isomorphism—the power of small, short family transactions to represent and to change the larger family structure—justifies many aspects of structural family therapy, including relative lack of interest in the family's history, since it is assumed that all the clues one needs to understand a family's structure exist in the isomorphs that are demonstrated throughout family sessions. Isomorphism has also allowed therapists to intervene quickly and directly, often in the first session, rather than spend time assessing a family before intervening more actively. It is assumed that if one challenges an isomorphic sequence, one is beginning to challenge the family's dysfunctional structure. Finally, isomorphism contributes to the belief that what one sees in a family session is connected to the family's real and static structure, rather than to the therapist-family interaction, the artificial context of therapy, or to the family's current crisis. Isomorphism, then, has enabled structural family therapists to ignore some temporal or contextual aspects of a family's in-session behavior and thereby to intervene aggressively in that behavior, in the belief that when these small pieces of the structure change, the larger structure must also change.

Years ago, after repeated clinical disappointments based on the principle of isomorphism, we expanded our assumptions about in-session sequences. We now believe that these S1 interactions may be reflective of the family's structural organization, but we also see that structure as evolving over time and across contexts, rather than as static, and we entertain other explanations for family behavior, including the effects of our interactions with the family or of the therapy context itself. As we became more sensitive to these issues, we became more reluctant to plunge immediately into an aggressively interventive mode from the position of expert. Instead, we adopted a more collaborative position.

With these changes has come increased appreciation of the temporal dimension of therapy. As we discuss in Chapters Seven and Eight, we have become highly interested in the patterns of a family's structural evolution over time and across cultural contexts. We ask questions that help family members consider not only aspects of their current family structure and how well it fits with their cultural context but also how that structure evolved over the family's life cycle or over generations and across cultures, and how future events may affect the structure, and how they may want to change in preparation for these events. Thus, while we are still interested in a family's structure, our view of structure has become more elastic and contextual and, as a result, more complex.

This increased complexity would be a problem if the stance we take as therapists had not shifted. When we saw it as our job to quickly diagnose and challenge a family's structure, we needed simple maps, so that we could make quick hypotheses and action plans. Now that we view ourselves as collaborators with family members, we do not have to make quick, simple, standardized structural assessments on which to base interventions. Instead, family members examine their history, values, current polarizations, and context with us and decide with us on a course of change. In this process, we are examining not only the S1 interactions that take place in the office but also the S2 interactions and the S3 and S4 patterns that reflect this evolutionary perspective (see Chapter Four). The understandings that we reach about the family can be quite complex and idiosyncratic without overwhelming us, because we are no longer solely responsible for generating the assessment and the change, and because we are not restricted to one framework for understanding families. We can select from among a number of metaframeworks.

Internal Process

Structural family therapy's need for simplicity also played a role in discouraging the exploration of the inner workings of individual family members and of how internal processes affected the family's structure. It was assumed that an individual's external, family context was so powerful that his or her inner world would improve in response to the external structural improvements, and that focusing on this internal level of the system would obscure the more important family level.

As we said in Chapter Three, we have found that including an internal perspective, one based on precisely the same organizational principles as those that underlie the external, family perspective outlined in this chapter, enriches our therapy immensely. Here again, complexity is much less an issue from the collaborative therapist's position. In fact, many problems are made simpler and more workable by the addition of this perspective. For example, instead of trying to convince parents that their acting-out son is being disrespectful, in an effort to mobilize the parents to discipline him, the therapist can ask questions of the boy that will elicit descriptions of his rebellious part, his self-critical part, his hurt part, and so on, and of how these parts of him react to various parts of his parents. This is a far more complex understanding of the son's behavior than the idea that all of him is disrespectful, and yet his parents are left with a simple understanding of how to help him. They need to find ways to help him calm down or control his rebellious part, and they can discuss with his Self the best way to do that.

Function of the Symptom

Conceptions of family organization have been strongly influenced by functionalism and cybernetics (see Chapter Two). Just as functionalists in sociology and anthropology have tried to understand the functions that certain customs or kinds of deviance serve for the larger social system, family therapists have come up with various hypotheses about how the symptoms of one family member may be serving a function for the whole family. The cybernetic idea of homeostasis, moreover, implies that families will go to great lengths to preserve their rules, and that symptoms can be seen as serving such a homeostatic function.

The functionalist or homeostatic view of the function of symptoms has many negative consequences. First, implicit in the idea that the symptom serves a function is the belief that family members want or need the symptom bearer to suffer for the sake of homeostasis. This implication has made many family members feel guilty and defensive, and it has made patients and therapists angry or suspicious. Once a therapist believes that any parent is selfish or scared enough to knowingly allow or even encourage a child's symptoms, it becomes difficult to collaborate with him or her. Family members are also likely to sense this view of them in the therapist's interactions, and to become "resistant." In other words, this view of symptoms has often increased the polarization in which a symptom is embedded.

Second, the homeostatic view also implies that therapy is never complete until the hypothesized family flaw, which is creating the need for the symptom, is fixed. This assumption turns family therapists into pathology detectives, who disregard any improvements that occur before the putative flaw has been found (much as psychoanalysts have dismissed such improvements as "flights into health"). This assumption makes therapists gloss over or undervalue changes that instead could be accentuated or built on.

Third, recognition of the protective function of symptoms was such a revelation that the field reached extreme conclusions about it: that all symptoms serve protective functions in families; that the function a symptom serves in a family is the only or primary factor maintaining it; that the symptomatic family member's sole or primary intention is to protect others in the family; and that the family's need for a distraction is the sole or primary cause of the symptom. In other words, the supposed function of the symptom for the family came to overshadow all other factors and kept the focus of therapy exclusively on the family level.

These negative consequences of functionalism arose from the way it was applied (the view of problems as singly determined, and the single-level focus), which in turn was justified by the belief that a person has one mind and consequently has only one primary intention for his or her behavior. Multiplicity, by contrast (see

Chapter Three), attributes many different motives for problematic behavior (one of which may sometimes be to distract or protect others). In some cases, some parts of some family members may be so afraid of change, or so miserable in the current predicament, that they feel the *need for a distraction* and may focus on another's symptom for that purpose. In taking that simple position, we eliminate all the unidetermined and unilevel problems that accompany the function-of-the-symptom factors, as well as the implication that families *want* their symptomatic members to suffer.

We make a key distinction between the need or desire for a *distraction* versus the need or desire for the *symptom*. Polarizations between holons create the need for a distraction; and, out of the misery or fear that accompanies polarizations, people will seize anything available for that purpose. Since a child's symptoms are there, are available, parents may use those symptoms, along with any number of other distractions. We believe that, in most cases, desperate family members do not make the connection between their use of the symptom and its maintenance or exacerbation.

The Effect of Problems

As we hope we have made clear, family therapy has focused primarily on the effect of family process on the symptoms or problems of family members, and it has downplayed the effect of the problems on the family's structure. Recently, however, this trend has begun to reverse. White (1989) has discussed at length how people adapt to a problem, often slowly and imperceptibly, so that eventually it becomes a life-style. Rolland (1987, 1988) has described the stages that families go through in trying to cope with chronic illness. Anderson, Reiss, and Hogarty (1986) emphasize the devastating effect of schizophrenia on family patterns. The effect that a problem has on a family will vary according to the many family factors that predate the problem, such as preexisting polarizations, the family's developmental stage (see Chapter Six), and the clarity of family boundaries (see also Rolland, 1988). Regardless of these preexisting conditions, problems inevitably will disrupt the family's balance, at least in terms of family members' access to resources, and possibly also in terms of their access to influence. Whether these imbalances are temporary or generate continuing polarizations will depend on various qualities of the problem and on the family's or helping system's beliefs about and reactions to it.

Schwartz (forthcoming) has outlined some of these factors in detail elsewhere; we will summarize them here. A family's reaction to a problem will depend on the following:

- How socially acceptable the problem is
- How much it disrupts the family's routine or takes extra resources
- How much family members may be implicated in its onset
- How much they believe the patient can or should be able to control it
- How dangerous or damaging they believe it is
- How much hope they have that experts can solve it
- Whether they believe they can help solve it and know what to do
- Whether they are clear about what the patient must do to solve it
- Whether they can know, with some confidence, when it is solved.

Given these considerations, the kind of problem least likely to provoke family polarizations would be socially acceptable, not very disruptive or draining of resources, of clear etiology that was external to the family or patient, out of the patient's control, not very dangerous or damaging, and treatable through expert intervention, with clear roles for family members and for the patient. Any number of acute medical illnesses fit this description and generally do not create lasting distress within the family system. Problems that stray from this description on any of these factors have greater potential to generate the polarizations that can maintain or exacerbate problems.

Unfortunately, most psychiatric problems stray from this ideal description, on many of those factors. Take bulimia, for example. It is a highly embarrassing, potentially dangerous syndrome with unclear etiology and prognosis. A range of family or parental characteristics have been suggested as contributing to its onset, and it is the kind of problem that also makes the patient's will power highly suspect. Since there is no consensus on an approach to treatment that has clearly delineated roles for everyone involved, there is great potential for divisiveness on the direction or type of treatment and on the role of family members or of the patient. Bingeing can deplete stores of food, and the vomiting is repulsive and messy. Thus, family routines and resources are disrupted. The potential physical consequences of bulimia are devastating, making family members worry constantly, but without a clue about the best way to help. Because of the fuzziness surrounding the etiology of bulimia, family members wonder whether they themselves or other family members are the cause, or whether the patient is engaging in it for some selfish or vindictive motive. The patient may feel guilty and weak for not being able to control herself, and/or she may be angry with her family for making her bulimic.

These conditions of the syndrome, as well as the belief system around it, make polarizations between and within family members inevitable. The polarizations often revolve around efforts to coerce or shame the patient into stopping, versus efforts to protect the patient from those who are trying to coerce change, and around denying or distracting from the problem, versus overemphasizing the severity and importance of it. These polarizations may characterize the relationship between two family members, between two alliances of family members, between family members and helpers, or between two internal parts of family members.

The point here is that certain problems in and of themselves can have a tremendously disruptive influence on a family. Many of the patterns of enmeshment, cross-generational coalition, rigidity, and overprotectiveness that family therapists have observed, and which they have considered to be flaws in the family's structure that created or helped to maintain the problem, are actually often artifacts of living with and organizing around the problem. It is often true, however, that problem-generated polarizations do maintain the problem or create new ones. Since the polarizations can be attributed to the problem, however, rather than to family members, they are easier to explore without evoking guilt or recriminations. This is what White (1986) has discovered with his technique of "externalizing" the problem—that is, giving it a life of its own, separate from the person who suffers from it, and separate from the family.

Therapy

The general goal of therapy with respect to the principles presented in this chapter can be summarized as follows: *to remove the constraints impeding the balance and harmony of the family and the individuals within it.* To achieve this goal, the therapist collaborates with family members in improving leadership and boundaries and eliminating polarizations, at whatever levels of the total system seem most constraining.

We no longer hold up an idealized model or map of family structure and try to fit a family into it. We now believe that the normative map developed by structural family therapy, with its clear boundaries separating one generation from another and its emphasis on individual autonomy, does happen to fit well with our extremely mobile, capitalist, individualistic American culture. It does not fit as well, however, with many other cultural or economic contexts, where the primary alliances in the family may be cross-generational or with other members of the same sex and generation. Rather than try to fit families into preconceived notions of family structure, we now try to help them consider the cultural and historical origins of the current structure and how well that structure fits with the current context (Schwartz, forthcoming).

This is not to imply that we take a value-free, relativistic approach to therapy. Rather than a normative map, we bring to therapy a set of assumptions about how healthy human systems operate (see Chapter Two). We believe that any number of structures can be healthy, as long as they foster balance, harmony, and effective leadership.

Theory of Change

The therapist's collaborative (rather than antagonistic) stance is also facilitated by a different view of how people and families change. Structural therapists traditionally have seen themselves as bearers of the feedback that would allow a family to change. They have believed that dysfunctional families are likely to distort or deny such feedback, unless it is given to them in ways that prever t distortion or denial. Minuchin and Fishman (1981, p. 116) allude to an old joke in describing this process: A farmer had a donkey that would do anything it was asked to do. The farmer sold the donkey, and the donkey would no longer perform. The new owner asked the farmer why the donkey would not obey. The farmer picked up a two-by-four and walloped the donkey. "He obeys," the farmer explained, "but first you have to get his attention."

Structural family therapists have used a variety of ways to get a family's attention—to exceed the family's "threshold of deafness"—ways that frequently involve "two-by-four" techniques of dramatically and repetitively pointing out and challenging observed structural flaws. Structural family therapists have sometimes been oblivious to the possibility that a family's high threshold of "deafness" may be related to such "two-by-four" attitudes and approaches.

Moreover, because structuralists have been so enchanted with the power of external context (the family structure) to change individual family members, they have focused on action as both the instrument and the index of change; that is, the goal became one of producing behavioral changes in how family members related to one another. Such interactional changes were expected to produce new awarenesses and to activate new "self segments" of family members. As Minuchin and Fishman (1981, p. 118) have said, "The goal is to make the family experience the how of their interactions as the beginning of a process of change."

Changes in meaning were not seen as primary therapeutic targets. Instead, one could try to create a "workable reality" in the service of achieving behavioral change. In general, though, the structural attitude toward trying to change meaning can be summarized as follows: "Cognitive constructions per se are rarely powerful enough to spark family change" (Minuchin and Fishman, 1981, p. 117). This belief has also precluded a collaborative therapeutic position, because the therapist was put in the director's chair. He or she was the authority who must direct behavioral changes.

Finally, structuralists have believed that change comes through conflict escalation and crisis induction: "When a family comes to treatment, it is in difficulty because it is stuck in the homeostasis phase. . . . One of the goals of therapy, therefore, is to move the family to a stage of creative turmoil, where what was given must be replaced by a search for new ways. . . . Therapy is the process of taking a family who are stuck along the developmental spiral and creating a crisis that will push the family in the direction of their own evolution" (Minuchin and Fishman, 1981, pp. 26, 27).

Crisis induction is a logical conclusion of the homeostasis model of families. If one believes that families resist change because they are "in the homeostatic phase," it follows that one must try to break them forcefully out of this phase. But if one believes, as we do, that families resist change because they are caught in a web of polarizations that constrain them from exercising their resources for effective leadership, then the goal of therapy becomes to depolarize the system and release those resources. Therefore, rather than confront or challenge family members with what we believe to be their flaws, or force them into crisis by siding with one member against another, we explore with them the constraints to effective leadership, balance, and harmony, and we help them remove the constraints.

At least on one level, we find that constraints are products of extreme and polarized parts of each family member (intrapersonal polarization), which make them behave and think in extreme ways and obscure their Selves (see Chapter Three). At another level, the constraints often result from alliances and coalitions (intrafamily polarizations) among family members. At still another level, constraints may result from polarizations between family members and such nonfamily agents as school personnel and mental health professionals (extrafamilial polarization), or from the polarizing effects of elements within the family's context, such as poverty, racism, sexism, and individualistic American values (intracultural polarization).

Our goal becomes to join with each family member as quickly as possible, so that, as a group, we can all collaborate in exploring and clearing constraints. We find that authoritatively confronting, siding against, or pushing family members often makes their fearful and protective parts more extreme and gives us less access to their Selves. We may take a directive role at times, but usually only after the family has identified constraints and agreed that our leadership may temporarily be needed. We expect sometimes to encounter parts of family members (and, consequently, forces in the family) that fear change for a variety of reasons, particularly in highly polarized systems. Instead of fighting fear, we try to create an atmosphere in which family members feel safe enough to discuss and evaluate their ambivalence toward change, thereby calming their fears and releasing resources for change.

This is not to suggest that we actively avoid conflict or crisis; on the contrary. We often find that, once the fearful parts of the family are deactivated, long-standing conflicts surface, and crises ensue. This seems to be a common aspect of the balancing and harmonizing process of any system and can often be embraced as evidence of change. The difference is that we do not try to *force* the family into conflict or crisis, nor do we believe that conflict or crisis is always a necessary aspect of change.

When they do arise, however, crises offer valuable opportunities for change and self-reflection, because it becomes undeniably apparent to the system's members that the current structure is not working. A crisis can open a door through which feedback from the system's environment, or from within the system's structure, can finally be received without distortion and can thereby activate the system's previously constrained resources for change.

Joining Reexamined

Structural family therapy did the field of family therapy a great service by emphasizing what Minuchin called "joining"—that is, by emphasizing the importance of forming a relationship with each family member, in which they all feel that the therapist understands and respects them. It is easy to see why joining was so important to structuralists. One cannot confront and challenge family members forcefully and expect them to remain in treatment unless one has developed a solid relationship with each member.

For the therapist to join successfully, he or she must sincerely like or feel compassion for family members. In order to find things to like about some clients, structural family therapists had to resort to mental gymnastics. For example, discussing how to find a way to feel less antipathy for the parents of an abused child, Minuchin and Fishman (1981, p. 41) write, "It behooves the therapist to look

carefully at the role that the injured member plays in the maintenance of the system as a whole."

When the internal family systems model guides our view of
people, we do not have to struggle to find ways to like family
members, even those who have committed vile acts. We assume that
it is just a small part of a person that has perpetrated an extreme
act, and that the part itself did not want to do it, but that the
extremes of the part were activated by external and/or internal polarizations that escalated out of control. We also know that, no
matter how extreme and polarized a person's parts, he or she has a
Self to which we can relate, and which can begin to take responsibility for his or her system. With this view of people, joining
comes naturally. This is particularly true when the therapist can
lead with his or her own Self. As Minuchin and Fishman (1981,
p. 32) state poetically, "Somewhere inside, [the therapist] has reson-
ating chords that can respond to any human frequency." We find
that therapists who have worked on themselves to the point where
the Self is in the lead can resonate to most other human frequencies
and encounter far less "resistance" than therapists whose parts are
activated by one kind of person or another. Simply conveying this
view of people to a family, overtly or covertly, helps them feel less
blamed or ashamed and helps them see each other less pathologi-
cally. In this sense, then, joining is not a technique used to permit
the therapist to get away with forcefully provoking the family. Instead, it is a natural artifact of the therapist's assumptions and presence. From this perspective, the stance of the therapist is no longer
that of an authority who sees and challenges the family's or an
individual's flaws. Our assumptions about people and about how
they are organized allow us to relate to a family as the members'
collaborators, as partners who respect their ability to change themselves and help them scan their internal and external contexts for
constraints on their exercising of these abilities.

To illustrate these principles clinically, let us consider this
case example:

> Tom, a fifteen-year-old high school sophomore has
> Tourette's syndrome and consequently has uncontrol-
> lable facial tics and makes barking noises. In the past

year, Tom's condition has deteriorated, and he is on
the verge of being excluded from school. He is a
friendly, likable boy, but is also self-conscious and
nervous. In the first session, he talks openly about the
embarrassment he suffers at school and the loneliness
he feels. As Tom talks, his mother is obviously moved
to tears, but his father states coldly that he is tired of
hearing about how hard life is for Tom.

From this short sequence (S1), the therapist senses a polarization between the mother and the father over how to deal with
Tom's problems and remembers that problems like Tom's, in and
of themselves, have a polarizing effect on families. The therapist
tells this to the parents and asks where they believe the greatest
polarizations exist.

Tom's mother reports that her husband is alway pick-
ing on Tom because he believes that Tom can control
himself more than he does. She says that her husband
frequently compares Tom to his older brother, Bill,
who left for college a year ago and was the apple of
his father's eye. Her husband agrees that he cannot
stand Tom's whiny approach to life, or his lack of
productivity. He thinks that Tom uses his Tourette's
syndrome as an excuse for laziness, or as a way to bug
him. He thinks that his wife is easily conned by Tom
and lets him get away with murder.

The therapist empathizes verbally with the predicament of
each family member but also emphasizes the importance of the
parents' finding a way to work together to help Tom. As the therapist asks about the constraints they face to achieving this kind of
cooperation, a number of imbalances at different levels of the system
emerge.

Tom and his mother complain that the father is unappreciated at his stressful job and consequently
brings his frustration home to them. The father says

that there may be some truth in that but he feels unappreciated at home, too, where he says his wife nags about picky issues all the time. This comment angers his wife, who reports that several years ago, at her husband's urging, she went back to work, on the promise that he would help more at home. He has reneged on that promise. He comes home and sits in front of the TV while she cooks and cleans for everyone. Her husband retorts that he tried to help more at first, but that her standards for cleanliness are so high that he finally gave up.

While his parents argue, Tom becomes increasingly anxious, bouncing his leg and muttering under his breath. When the therapist asks what he says to himself when his parents fight, Tom says that he worries that his father may hit his mother (although the father never has) because his mother keeps pushing, despite her husband's increasing impatience with her. Tom admits that there are occasions when he uses his symptoms to distract his parents, because their fights are so upsetting to him, but he insists that he usually cannot help the tics and noises.

The therapist asks Tom, "If you were able to calm the part of you that worries so much about your parents and were able to take care of the part of you that's so sensitive to your father's disapproval, then would you have less trouble controlling your symptoms?" Tom says that he thinks so but that he will have trouble not worrying as long as his parents fight. The therapist asks the parents whether they would be interested in demonstrating to Tom that they can handle their disputes without hurting each other, so that Tom can worry less and consequently tic less.

At this point, the therapist is considering the apparent imbalances and constraining polarizations at several levels of the system and is trying to decide where to focus among the levels. The imbalances at the father's job contribute to the polarizations at

home by activating his angry or hurt parts and draining his time
and energy, which creates imbalances in the allocation of his resources to the family. The parental holon is imbalanced in terms
of responsibility and influence, with the mother working full-time
at her job as well as at home while the father works only on the job
and ultimately makes the decisions about who does what. The sibling holon is also imbalanced. Bill gets the father's praise and time.
As a result, Bill acts more like an adult and is given more responsibility and influence. Tom gets the father's wrath and the mother's
sympathy, acts more childlike, and gets little responsibility or direct
influence.

There is also evidence that the internal system of each family
member is imbalanced. The father seems dominated by his striving
and by his angry parts, which dislike weakness or lack of discipline
in those around him. He probably gives little access or influence to
his intimacy parts. The mother seems to lead either with her nurturer or with her angry parts; it depends on whom she is dealing
with. Tom shows mostly his childlike, insecure, or sensitive parts,
which, of course, are hated by the father's striver. In each person,
it appears certain parts are given too much influence, responsibility,
or attention, while others are given too little.

These imbalances create polarizations, both within each level
of the system and between levels. Within levels, the father is polarized with his co-workers, and the father and the mother are polarized on household duties, on dealing with Tom, and on a number
of other battlegrounds. Tom and Bill are in a complementary polarization: Bill is extremely serious, mature, and competent, while
Tom acts young, silly, and incompetent. To mention but a few of
the likely internal polarizations, the father's internal striver opposes
his childlike parts, the mother's nurturer opposes her angry parts,
and Tom's needy, childlike parts oppose his critical striver.
Between-level polarizations include the mother versus the father's
job, the father versus Tom, and the father's striver versus both the
mother and Tom's needy parts.

These polarizations also create the need for coalitions, en-
meshments, and distractions within and between levels. The most
noticeable coalition is between the mother and Tom. The most
obvious distraction is Tom's admitted use of his symptoms when

his parents fight. We do not have space here to go into detail about the likely coalitions and distractions within each person's internal system, but these are likely to parallel some of the external patterns. The therapist is aware that evidence could be found for many other imbalances and polarizations at these and other levels. For example, polarizations could probably be found in a history of the extended family of each parent (S4 patterns) or in a more detailed history of the relationships within the nuclear family (S3 patterns). We find, however, that if we begin work with the polarizations that the family identifies as the most constraining, other relevant constraints often emerge during that work.

The therapist discusses with the family members some of the polarizations that they have identified. Together, they decide to focus initially on the conflict between Tom and his father. From the multilevel perspective, the initial focus may be a relatively arbitrary starting point, although it is often the polarization that the family feels least threatened or most distressed by. By asking questions about constraints at other levels even while focusing on one level, a therapist can keep the multilevel perspective in the family's and in his or her own mind. This perspective conveys to the family that there is no one person or situation to blame for the problem, because there are many constraining factors.

The therapist asks Tom and his father to talk to each other with their Selves in the lead, rather than allowing their protective parts to do the talking for them. While her husband and her son talk, Tom's mother is asked to try to calm the part of her that worries and wants to protect Tom. In this process, the family is improving the boundaries around the father/son holon while each family member is improving his or her own internal leadership and boundaries. Tom and his father are able, at least temporarily, to relate in a different way and negotiate some time together.

> Tom complains that his father treats him as younger than his age, by contrast with the way he treats Bill. The father agrees to change his style of punishing Tom. The mother successfully restrains herself from actively interfering in this enactment, but she weeps silently while her son and her husband interact. Her

weeping seems incongruous, because the other two seem to be doing better, and Tom is acting much stronger and expressing himself more directly. [At this point, a therapist whose work is organized by the function-of-the-symptom idea might conclude that the mother's sadness reflects her distress over the possibility of not having Tom's problems as a distraction, or no longer being permitted to see her husband as a heartless ogre.]

After the father and the son complete their interaction, the mother says that she felt an overwhelming, confusing sadness while she struggled to keep her protective parts in check. The therapist asks her to focus on her sad part and ask it why it is so sad. After a pause, she says that it told her how lonely it has been feeling ever since the dispute between herself and her husband over housework. Her husband jumps to his own defense, and Tom gets agitated. The therapist asks if the parents would like to focus on the distractive sequence that just occurred and, with the family's permission, has the parents discuss their differences, with their Selves in the lead, while Tom works with the part of him that worries so much about them.

In this way, as polarization at one level of the system or within one holon decreases, issues at other levels or within other holons emerge, and the focus of therapy shifts. Over the course of therapy, the additional issues of focus included the father's negative reactions to weakness and vulnerability in his wife or his son, his sense of entitlement around housework, his stressful job, the mother's and Tom's fear of his disapproval and anger, Tom's issues with Bill, Tom's embarrassment among his peers, and the fear and loneliness that both parents felt as the boys grew up and away. These issues were approached from both the internal and external levels and included work with a variety of holons. After three months, Tom's symptoms of Tourette's syndrome abated, and they flared up only rarely during the remaining year of treatment. A follow-up session one year after the end of therapy showed Tom doing well in school. He had many friends and had been asymptomatic for over a year.

In this kind of therapy, the therapist's job is to explore with the family the constraints to their goals and the polarizations that create those constraints. Next, by improving boundaries around and leadership within polarized holons, the therapist helps family members negotiate new balances of influence, resources, or responsibilities. In the process, other polarizations emerge and are similarly addressed. Imbalanced, polarized, leaderless systems thus become balanced and harmonious, with effective leadership.

SIX

Beyond
the One-Dimensional Life Cycle:
The Development Metaframework

The concept of development did not enter the family therapy field until the early 1970s (Haley, 1973; Solomon, 1973). This oversight can be accounted for in large measure by the application of the presupposition of mechanism to human systems. As long as families were viewed as machines consisting of interacting and unchanging parts, whose present functioning provided the necessary and sufficient explanation of the system, reference to development was unnecessary. Not until an organismic presupposition began to replace the mechanistic one did development begin to receive consideration.

Family therapy's first recognition of the importance of development came with the concept of the family life cycle (FLC). Drawn from family sociology, the concept of the family life cycle involved the notion that, over time, a family must traverse a series of predictable stages, which are separated by predictable transitions, each one marked by some change in family membership (birth, death, leaving home, and so on). This so-called stage-transition model of the

Note: Extensive portions of this chapter are adapted and reprinted, with permission, from Douglas C. Breunlin, "Oscillation Theory and Family Development," in C. Falicov (ed.), *Family Transitions: Continuity and Change over the Life Cycle* (New York: Guilford Press, 1988). A secondary source is Douglas C. Breunlin, "Clinical Implications of Oscillation Theory: Family Development and the Process of Change," in C. N. Ramsey (ed.), *Family Systems in Medicine* (New York: Guilford Press, 1989).

life cycle, which we will summarize, not only brought a component of development into family therapy but was also helpful, because it freed family therapy from pathology- and deficit-based views of families, replacing their views with the idea that problems in families are products of failed transitions. The latter view has also proved more useful clinically.

Family development, however, entails far more than can be represented by the stages and transitions of the life cycle (Falicov, 1988a,1988b, 1988c). Families develop in many ways. To understand this, let us turn to the multilevel biopsychosocial model and recognize development at five levels: biological, individual, subsystemic (relational), familial, and societal. Family therapy's reduction of development to the life cycle was yet another reflection of its preoccupation with the family level, to the unfortunate exclusion of other levels. What is most obvious is that individual family members are also constantly developing biologically and psychologically, and those areas of development are affected by and affect family development. Between the family and the individual are relational subsystems (holons), each of which develops over time. Relational development is often subsumed under the rubric of the life cycle, but we conceive of it as a vital and distinct aspect of family development. Moreover, family therapy has ignored, until recently, the larger system in which the family is embedded; therefore, it has failed to include the impact on family development of evolving societal definitions of the family, with the concomitant values, norms, and beliefs about development. Family development, therefore, must be seen as including both the development across each of the levels of a biopsychosocial system and the interaction among those levels.

How a well-adjusted family successfully develops at all levels appears deceptively simple because development at each level nurtures and supports development at all the other levels. This synchronization of developmental levels acts synergistically, so that the net effect to family development is greater than the sum of its parts. We believe that such synchrony across levels is not easily achieved, however, because the odds are much greater that a disruption of development at one level will also recursively affect development at other levels, thereby imposing constraints that keep the family from pursuing and accomplishing its functions. Needs and goals are not met, and family members become psychologically constrained. Over time, the effect can be paralyzing and mystifying, both to the family and to the therapist. Nevertheless, the interlocking nature of the levels of family development also allows for a developmental surge at one level to free development at other levels.

Consider, for example, a family in which there exists a fifteen-year age difference between the parents, who married when the father was thirty-two and the mother was seventeen. The marital relationship was originally defined as being like that of a father and a daughter, and over the years it did not develop. The couple have children, and as the eldest daughter enters adolescence, the mother, now in her late twenties, begins to realize that she is still treated like a child by her husband and has not had a chance to grow up. With envy, she witnesses her daughter's struggle for autonomy and permits enough freedom that her daughter can be promiscuous. The father compensates by restricting normal adolescent activities, perhaps fearing that his daughter will run off with an older man. The daughter's development, then, is constrained by swings between adultlike and childlike behavior. The marriage has not developed in a manner that allows the couple to solve the problems of adolescence, and their conflicts further weaken the marriage. This family is in great pain, but its members cannot trace their pain to one source: a failed marriage, a bad child, a life-cycle transition. Rather, the source is in the multilevel constraints of development.

Unfortunately, information about development, with respect to the various levels, is not easily assembled. It is scattered throughout the literature of several fields, including psychology, psychiatry, social work, family therapy, human development, and sociology. Each field has captured a part of the picture; but, with few exceptions (Minuchin, 1974, 1985; Falicov, 1988a, 1988b, 1988c; McGoldrick and Carter, 1980), little crossover and/or synthesizing has occurred. As a result, there does exist a wealth of information about development, but most of it is rarely found and used by family therapists, most of whom still see the life cycle as the only relevant developmental framework.

To pull this information together, we offer another metaframework, one that transcends the family life cycle and the limited views of development at other levels. Nothing else in the literature depicts such a metaframework, notwithstanding Falicov's excellent book (1988b), which points in that direction. This new metaframework addresses developmental issues at each level, and it explains the interaction of development across levels. It also explains how development can impose constraints on a system and thus contribute to the emergence and maintenance of problems. Finally, it implies clinically relevant ways of addressing and removing constraints to development.

We will begin by commenting on the societal level, because changes in societal expectations about individual, relational, and family development directly influence development at all these other levels. We will then shift to the level of the family and to a discussion of the family life cycle, because it represents family therapy's first and most popular effort to incorporate development into its theory and clinical practice.

Society and Family Development

Appropriate development at all levels is defined by societal values and beliefs, which provide the norms by which families bring up children, individuals develop, and relationships flourish. The rapidity with which societal values and beliefs have been evolving, however, has eroded traditional norms for development, so that the parents of one generation cannot look to the previous generation for assured guidance on how development should occur. Therefore, many parents cannot articulate a model for appropriate development. They hesitate in their support of (or demand too much of) each developmental increment. Parents now experience their children's development as being so different from their own that they often cannot comprehend or condone what they see. Sometimes they even blame themselves for being bad parents, without realizing that they are in the grip of societal forces that transcend the immediate influence of the family.

Perhaps the greatest society shift has occurred in our culture's expectations of individual autonomy and freedom. The children of this generation are expected to achieve competence in many areas far sooner than their parents did. In school, for example, children learn mathematical concepts two to three grades before their parents did. Electronic media provide children with information about human nature and relationships, at a much earlier age than ever before. The onset of puberty also occurs a year earlier with each generation. Because children are encouraged to express themselves and be individuals, they are outspoken at an age when their parents would have been "seen and not heard." Parents often read such expressions as evidence of disrespect, and they initiate sequences of control that are ineffective, since the message to be expressive is part of the larger culture.

At the same time, children today are growing up in an era of greater danger. It is no longer an age of innocence. Children are confronting major social ills: drugs, AIDS, crime, the nuclear threat. Parents understandably wish to protect their children and are reluctant to grant them free rein. Economic realities have made leaving home more difficult: young adults now require more years of education to be successful, and many either are not leaving home or are returning home.

Each developmental increment of childhood leaves parents asking, "Should we go along with this or not?" With few straightforward answers, parents may easily oscillate between permissiveness and excessive control, with the oscillation itself constraining family development. Likewise, disagreement between parents, or between parents and grandparents, over proper development can cause rifts in families, unless there is a recognition that such disagreements often stem from different applications of evolving beliefs about development.

The definition of the family is also changing (McGoldrick and Carter, 1980). Half of today's families experience divorce as a major transition in the FLC, followed by the stages of single parenthood and remarriage. We are just beginning to depathologize these stages and have yet to establish norms for family development during these stages and transitions. Likewise, the entry of more women into the workplace has made the traditional single-breadwinner family a rarity. Families today are struggling to define developmental expectations for dual-income living. The template of our parents' marriages, formed by the ideal of a deepening commitment based on male domination and female devotion, has been erased by the women's movement. Today, most couples cannot describe the direction in which they believe their marriage should develop.

In summary, the rapid social evolution of the past two generations has confused the developmental picture at all levels, introducing constraints of anxiety and uncertainty into many families. When we see a family, we address this societal flux, and we ascertain whether the family's expectations about development are in disarray as a result of it.

The Family Life Cycle

Family therapists first became interested in family development through the sociological model of the family life cycle, which is most easily represented by the pie diagram shown in Figure 6.1 (Haley, 1973; Solomon, 1973). This diagram depicts a stage-transition model of the FLC, where the pieces of pie represent the stages and the lines separating them represent the transitions. The model, which is still largely based on the traditional nuclear family, is based on the assumption that, for each stage, families must master a set of tasks specific to that stage. A transition signals the need for change, which enables the family to leave a previous stage and begin negotiating the tasks of the next one. Transitions involve not only such changes in family composition as birth, marriage, leaving home, and death but also such major shifts in autonomy as going to school, entering adolescence, and retirement. Henceforth, we will refer to such transitions as *nodal transitions*.

As originally conceived, the FLC is predicated on the notion that only one transition occurs at a time, and that transitions occur in an orderly fashion. Neither assumption applies universally, however. Most families experience multiple transitions, and the "correct" order is not always rigidly followed (Falicov, 1984). Other important modifications to the FLC have been made, first by Carter and McGoldrick, who recognized the stages and transitions of nontraditional families and made a distinction between stresses of FLC transitions in the current generation (called *horizontal stressors*) and those emanating from previous generations (called *vertical*

**Figure 6.1. Pie Diagram Depicting the Stage-Transition Model
of the Family Life Cycle.**

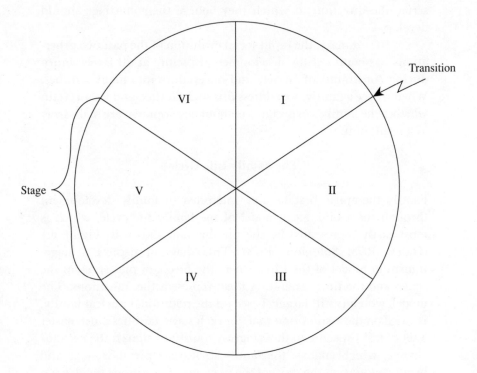

Source: Breunlin, 1988, p. 135. Reprinted with permission.

stressors) (Carter and McGoldrick, 1980; McGoldrick and Carter,
1980). Combrinck-Graham (1985) recognizes that the FLC is like a
spiral: from generation to generation, a family naturally oscillates
between periods of closeness (centrifugal force) and periods of distance (centripetal force).

Transitions are stressful for a family because they require
significant changes. Families that have trouble making transitions
often develop problems, and the problems in turn can serve the
function of keeping the family from making the feared transition.
In fact, studies have shown that mental health problems do tend to
cluster around the transitions of the FLC (Hadley, Jacob, Milliones,
Caplan, and Spitz, 1974). For example, Haley's (1980) leaving-home

model is based on the hypothesis that young adults with psychiatric problems are unable to leave home because the family cannot make the transition to the empty-nest stage, where the parents must learn to live with each other, without the young adult's acting as a buffer.

We can appreciate the clinical significance of the FLC if we cut the pie diagram, "unwind" it, and express the FLC graphically as a function of time (see Figure 6.2). This graph enables us to raise two questions. First, what aspects of a family change over time? Second, what is the shape of the curve that emerges when the FLC is plotted as a function of time? The FLC literature has been vague about what actually changes when a family passes through a transition. The answer is most often posed from the perspective of the family therapy models. Hence, the structural therapist would say that the structure changes (Minuchin, 1974; Minuchin and Fishman, 1981). The MRI therapist would say that the rules change (Watzlawick, Weakland, and Fisch, 1974). A Bowen therapist might say that the level of anxiety changes (Carter and McGoldrick, 1980).

The FLC itself does not contain a hypothesis about the shape of the curve, although it does derive from the argument that a

Figure 6.2. Development as a Function of Time.

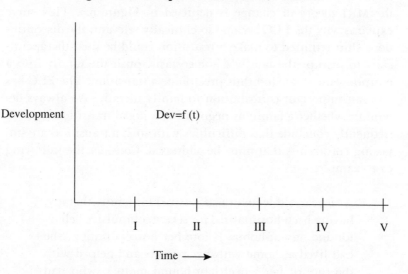

Source: Breunlin, 1988, p. 137. Reprinted with permission.

change that occurs in one stage, when specific tasks are being mastered, is different from a change that occurs during a transition. The shape of the curve was first hypothesized by Weeks and Wright (1977) and by Hughes, Berger, and Wright (1978), when they applied the theory of change proposed by the MRI group (Watzlawick, Weakland, and Fisch, 1974) to the FLC. The MRI group argued that there are two types of change: first-order change (that is, gradual, quantitative, and continuous change, within the current rules of a system) and second-order change (that is, qualitative, abrupt, and discontinuous change that entails changes in the system's rules). Take the example of making a car move. Pushing the accelerator makes the car go faster, which is a quantitative and continuous change. Shifting gears, however, actually changes the rules of operation of the engine, in a qualitative and discontinuous fashion (Watzlawick, Weakland, and Fisch, 1974).

The marriage between the MRI concept of change and the FLC seemed ideal. Hughes, Berger, and Wright (1978) argued that during any given stage, when specific tasks are being mastered, first-order change is involved. A transition requires fundamental change in the family (in terms of rules, organization patterns, and so on) and is a second-order change. The shape of the curve derived from the MRI theory of change is depicted in Figure 6.3. This curve explains why the FLC became so clinically relevant: the discontinuous shift required to make a transition could be used therapeutically to disrupt the family's homeostasis, push the family into a morphogenic state, and thus precipitate a transition. The FLC has been an important contribution to family therapy. We always determine whether a family is negotiating a nodal transition, and we frequently conclude that difficulties with such a transition are imposing constraints that must be addressed. Consider the following case example:

> A 30-year-old woman was referred for family therapy, having been hospitalized for severe compulsive behavior and agoraphobia. Before her hospitalization, she had lived at home with her parents and helped with the care of her wheelchair-bound mother, who had developed multiple sclerosis when the patient was

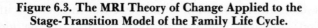

**Figure 6.3. The MRI Theory of Change Applied to the
Stage-Transition Model of the Family Life Cycle.**

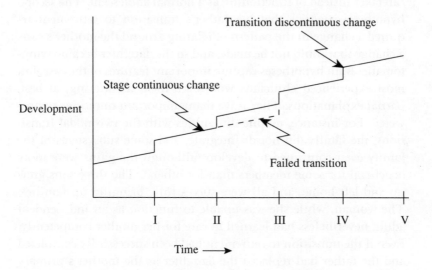

Source: Breunlin, 1988, p. 139. Reprinted with permission.

fourteen. Her three older brothers had all grown up
and left home, while the patient had become progres-
sively more isolated, dropping out of school and losing all her friends. As an adolescent, she had been
described as immature and unable to meet the demands of school. At the same time, however, she had
provided daily care for her mother and run the household. Her symptoms intensified when her father, who
had always worked at two jobs, retired and began to
help with the mother's care. The patient, now freer to
consider her own life, would stand for hours at the
front door, swinging it open and then shut, metaphorically leaving but not leaving.

The FLC offers hypotheses about two transitions, the one to
adolescence and the one to retirement. The first hypothesis suggests
that the onset of the mother's chronic illness, which occurred dur-

ing the daughter's transition to adolescence, interfered with that transition, and the daughter accepted the role of the mother's caretaker instead of functioning as a normal adolescent. The second hypothesis suggests that her father's transition to retirement required a change in the pattern of relating around the mother's care, a change that could not be made, and so the daughter became symptomatic. Both hypotheses capture important features of the case, but most experienced clinicians would see them as offering, at best, partial explanations. They leave many important questions unanswered. For instance, despite difficulties with the two nodal transitions, the family did not disintegrate, and some subsystems of the family even continued to develop (although the gains were more beneficial for some members than for others). The three sons grew up and left home, and all were successfully bringing up families. The woman, while she was unable to function as an independent adult, nevertheless had learned to care for her mother competently. Even if the transition to retirement had been successfully completed and the father had replaced the daughter as the mother's primary caretaker, it is unlikely that the woman would have experienced a sudden, discontinuous leap and begun to function as a competent thirty-year-old woman. To understand how development affects the predicament of this family, it is necessary to consider development within other levels of the system.

Individual Development

In the foregoing case example, the woman's individual development had not been arrested at adolescence. She grew up. She was functioning well in some areas of her life and poorly in others. Families cannot arrest development; they can only accommodate to it more or less successfully. After all, an individual's development is more than the product of a family's interaction around the infrequent nodal transitions of the FLC. It is also the product of individual development, which includes psychological maturation and an internal blueprint that dictates such frequent biological changes as physical growth, increase in mental capacity, and hormonal changes. When individual development is supported by family interaction, both family and individual development prosper. When it is not, each constrains the other.

The Clinical Relevance of Normal Development

Individual development can be expressed as a function of the mastery of competence in the domains of social, relational, emotional, cognitive, and behavioral performance. Competence is a function of age. The competent individual performs in an age-appropriate manner. Children who act younger or older than their age have problems related to competence, which are often expressed as behavioral, emotional, or physical symptoms (Breunlin, 1988, 1989). Of course, competence per se cannot be measured in isolation; the definition of age-appropriate competence must always be tied to one's innate abilities, and a child with exceptional intelligence will read several grade levels above a child with average intelligence. Cultural expectations also define competence. For example, in middle-class American society, young adults are expected to leave home by their early twenties, and their failure to do so is often associated with mental health problems. In other cultures, young adults do not leave home until they are ready to marry, which may not be until they are well into their thirties.

To know what is age-appropriate, therapists must have knowledge of individual development. Unfortunately, however, this is an area greatly neglected by family therapy. One could read the literature, but we believe that observing the manifestations of development in daily living would be more useful to family therapists. This experience can be gained through parenthood, to create what Schwartz (1982) has called the "familied therapist." Access to children can also be gained in other ways: through relationships with younger siblings, nieces, nephews, and neighborhood children, through children's literature, and through paying careful attention to children in therapy.

Knowledge about child development helps therapists understand a child's life and defines what is appropriate and possible in therapy sessions (Garbarino and Stott, 1989). To begin with, therapists who are knowledgeable about development adjust the level of their language to the ages of the children involved. They ask young children simple rather than complex questions. They also take the cognitive abilities of children into account and, accordingly, rely more or less heavily on action in therapy.

Relating development to competence also helps therapists determine whether behavior is problematic. For example, take the common referral problem of aggression in boys. Without some understanding of development, a therapist may define any report of aggression as a legitimate presenting problem. But aggression exists throughout the life cycle and means different things at different ages. The two-year-old who kicks is manifesting a different type of aggression from that of the adolescent who maims an animal. It is also important to know what parental responses to aggression have been. Parents who allow their children to have tantrums will struggle with their children's aggression more than parents who teach their children to substitute language for action. Aggression also occurs in a social context that includes peers. For example, boys between the ages of eight and ten are often referred because of their aggressive behavior at home or at school. Therapists who understand the peer relationships of this age group will be careful not to define the aggression automatically as a problem. Boys at this age are emerging from early childhood and are beginning to learn how to survive in a male-dominated world defined by competitive values. Watch any group of boys playing, and you will notice an intensely competitive atmosphere, around which hover constant acts of verbal if not physical aggression as the boys jockey to establish themselves in the pecking order of the group. A boy who cannot be aggressive in this context quickly loses status and is labeled a nerd. Many boys do opt out of these group dynamics, with damaged egos. Those who choose to tough it out experience an initiation by fire. The barrage of insults that they must endure may constantly hurt their feelings, but in no way can they acknowledge the hurt. At that age, they are just beginning to learn how to compartmentalize their feelings, and sometimes they fail, taking their anger home or into the classroom, where it gets discharged and taken for aggression. Many a parent of a boy between eight and ten has been the victim of that child's pent-up emotions. Therefore, the clinical assessment of the seriousness of aggression in any boy of this age must include the parents' response to it and the context in which it occurs. Sometimes the solution involves normalizing the aggressive behavior and providing a safer family environment for the boy to ventilate his pent-up anger. Sometimes the boy has to learn how to deal with his peers more effectively. At other times, however, the boy has been allowed to express aggression without limits, in which case it may indeed be a problem. To change the norms about male aggression for a boy of this age would require changes in the socially defined values of male behavior; feminists rightly question whether the social sanctioning of aggression contributes to the values of adult male dominance. Moreover, in some subcultures, aggression is seen not only as normal but also as necesary for survival. For example, Afro-American parents who are bringing children up in the inner city know very well that a male child who cannot defend himself is a prime target of random or gang-related violence, and so they toughen their boys, to prepare them for the dangerous world in which they must live.

The Microtransitions of Individual Development

A recursive relationship exists among individual, family, and relational development. As each family member develops, his or her potential for competence increases, and this new competence in turn can increase the flexibility and complexity of the family, which in turn can then foster further individual competence. (Ask any parent whose last child has just been toilet trained what it means not to have to haul around diapering paraphernalia whenever the family leaves the house.) For this potential to be reached, however, individuals must be challenged to use their competence, and the family must accommodate to and nurture that competence. Hence, a family must constantly change in order to respond to and encourage the age-appropriate development of its members while still maintaining an overall stability that enables it to preserve its identity.

Returning to Figure 6.2, we can ask once more what the nature of change is over a life cycle that now includes individual development. We hypothesize that each increment in individual development necessitates a significant and related change in the family. We call such changes *microtransitions* and distinguish them from the nodal transitions of the FLC. Terkelson (1980) notes that "even very small incremental developments can produce surprisingly widespread perturbations in family structure" (p. 35). For example, if a small child learns to be apart from a parent when the parent leaves the child for increasingly long periods of time, this allows the parents more time to relate to each other and do other things. Microtransitions involve both increments in existing competence (such as language development) and the acquisition of new competence (such as walking or bowel control). Since individual development moves relentlessly forward, significant microtransitions are always taking place. Families cannot *not* respond to microtransitions; they can only accommodate them more or less successfully. We believe that families negotiate microtransitions not in the step-function manner shown in Figure 6.3 but rather through a process that Breunlin (1988, 1989) has called an *oscillation*, as depicted in Figure 6.4.

To understand how oscillations emerge, we must briefly return to the sequences metaframework and recall that behaviors are always embedded in one or more classes of sequences. These sequences are not stable, however. Family members can never grow completely accustomed to the ways in which they deal with one another: just when they get used to one way of responding, a developmental increment necessitates a change. Therefore, each developmental increment, dictated by biology or by the demands of socialization necessitates a change in the associated sequences, so that the family is challenged to respond to the potential for new competence.

The change and the response to it, however, do not occur instantaneously; rather the old sequence and the old behavior exist concurrently with the new for some time. A microtransition, then, is a period when both sequences and their associated levels of competence exist simultaneously, so that a normal oscillation exists between the two sequences and the two levels of competence until the new gradually replaces the old. For instance, when a child first walks, walking does not abruptly replace crawling, in a discontinuous fashion; rather, sometimes the child walks (and frequently falls), and sometimes the child crawls, and during the microtransition the family sequences associated with both crawling and walking exist simultaneously. Sometimes the parents offer a hand or encourage and praise the child for walking; at other times, it is more convenient for the parents if the child crawls. The oscillation persists until the sequences that regulate walking predominate, and

Figure 6.4. An Oscillation in the Developmental Process.

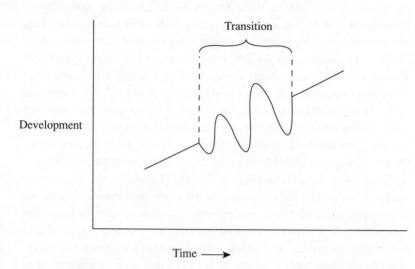

Source: Breunlin, 1988, p. 140. Reprinted with permission.

crawling is abandoned. This process of a microtransition is quite similar to the three phases of developmental change described by Terkelson (1980). Oscillations represent the family's attempt to accommodate to individual development while remaining stable. In normal families, oscillations appear and then dampen—that is, gradually disappear—with each oscillation producing both an increment in developmental competence for the individual and additional flexibility for the family.

In oscillation theory, the distinction between a stage and a transition becomes meaningless: there are only transitions. Some are nodal transitions; others are microtransitions. The difference between the two has to do with the magnitude of the change. Nodal transitions involve more change, partly because the impact of gains and losses in family membership is greater, and partly because the number of microtransitions that must be negotiated is greater during such times.

Oscillations and the Emergence of Symptoms

Symptomatic families cannot figure out how to dampen the oscillations associated with microtransitions and, therefore, how to foster emerging competence. They are not "on time." They seem either too slow or too fast in their responses to emerging competence (Neugarten, 1968). For a given age, they either fail to encourage and allow enough competence or allow and require too much. As a child grows older, his or her competence with respect to safety should become increasingly complex. For a small child, who has little such competence, the parents rightly make all the decisions, to the point of childproofing the house. A seven-year-old, who has more competence, should be allowed more decisions and may, for instance, be allowed to decide when it is safe to cross the street. Older adolescents should have the competence to make decisions in such complex social situations as dating. If the parents continue to make all the decisions about safety for a seven-year-old, the micro-transitions around safety will produce behavior that is less than competent. If the parents allow or require the seven-year-old to enter into situations in which an adolescent's competence is required, the outcome is likely to be behavior that is greater than competent for the child's age.

Oscillation theory hypothesizes that as the majority of oscillations dampen to age-appropriate increments in competence, family members will develop normally, and each one will possess a strong sense of self based on age-appropriate competence. Likewise, the family will have a good sense of each person and therefore will know how to accommodate to further developmental increments. When the family becomes inconsistent in its responses, sometimes accommodating appropriately but at other times allowing too little or too much competence, the individual's development may begin to oscillate, and he or she will sometimes act younger and sometimes older than his or her age. That person, not knowing what is age-appropriate, loses a clear sense of self and must face the humiliation of sometimes acting young, as well as the anxiety of sometimes acting older without having the maturity to support that behavior. As the oscillation in competence persists, other family members vacillate still more in their responses, becoming less and less certain about what is age-appropriate. We call this pattern a *stable oscillation.*

When a stable oscillation becomes part of the family's pattern of interaction, further increments of development are made in the context of the oscillation. These microtransitions are liable to intensify rather than dampen the oscillation. Although the family is still changing, the accommodation between individual and family development fails to work well. The oscillation limits rather than increases flexibility, because the family cannot rely on the oscillating member to perform in an age-appropriate way. In this context, the identified patient's behavior oscillates between competence that is less than and greater than expected. The oscillation then becomes a part of the family belief system: "Our son is two going on twenty-two, and we don't know what to do about it."

Symptoms and problems can be viewed as logical outcomes of a stable oscillation. A problematic behavior may be a manifestation of a child's acting too young or too old. For example, parents may object to a teenager's promiscuous behavior, and her appearance may be suggestive of an adult's. At the same time, her failure at school may be another problem, and her inability to attend to homework may be inappropriately young. The combination of these and other behaviors produces the oscillation. Symptoms are often metaphorical expressions of an oscillation: a child may be enuretic but also verbally precocious. Symptoms and problems recursively interact with and further stabilize the oscillation. For example, in the case example of the thirty-year-old woman, her agoraphobia existed as the product of an oscillation that had allowed years of behavior that was less than competent, and it metaphorically signaled her fear of growing up. In turn, however, the agoraphobia further constrained her life and limited her access to age-appropriate contexts.

We say that behavior is *less than competent* or *greater than competent* because these phrases are neutral and do not reflect a deficit-based view of behavior. Such terms as *immature, developmentally delayed,* and *regressed* suggest but are not synonymous with behavior that is less than competent. They generally refer to a presentation of self that is pervasive and not easily changed; our terminology refers to a context-specific behavior associated with younger or older parts, whereby an individual at a given age behaves as if he or she were less or greater than competent because such behavior is the logical outcome of heeding younger or older parts and passing through the relevant sequences.

It is easy to see how behavior that is less than competent can adversely affect development. But how is behavior that is greater than competent problematic? Is it possible to have too much competence? In symptomatic families, we have found that the identified patient almost always exhibits some behaviors that are too competent for his or her age. For example, a six-year-old latchkey child, who lets himself or herself into the house after school and thereby allow a single parent to work longer hours, is behaving in a way that is greater than competent. In the field of family therapy, a number of concepts describe such behavior.

The term *incongruous hierarchy* (Madanes, 1981) suggests that, at one level, a child is higher in the hierarchy than the parents are. The violation of a generational boundary (Minuchin, 1974) suggests that a child is allowed to share inappropriately in the world of adults. The term *parental child* (Minuchin, 1974) suggests that a child, by acting as a parent, is behaving in a manner that is greater than competent. Finally, the function-of-the-symptom notion implies that a behavior somehow serves to protect the family. We suggest that when a child behaves in a symptomatic way in order to protect his or her family, that child's behavior is greater than competent, even when the symptoms themselves may involve behavior that is less than competent.

In any pattern of oscillation, of course, appropriate levels of competence also exist, but they often go unrecognized. These behaviors are important because they signal the family's potential ability to negotiate microtransitions in a manner that does not produce oscillations. Such areas of age-appropriate competence point toward individual and family strengths and often serve as starting points for efforts to dampen an oscillation.

Theoretically, it is possible that microtransitions merely cause sequences to regulate competence at one extreme or the other. Our clinical experience suggests that this rarely happens, however. Even when a child has an apparently pervasive set of behaviors that are less than competent, the family has usually organized itself around them in a way that produces an incongruous hierarchy or results in symptoms that serve a protective function. Hence, the behavior is greater than competent. Likewise, when microtransitions consistently produce behavior that is greater than competent, the individual often compensates with other behavior that is less than competent, or the person may exhibit a symptom that metaphorically expresses such behavior. For example, an adolescent who acts much older than her age may be enuretic.

The following case example shows a typical oscillation between extremes of less- and greater-than-competent behavior (the alert reader will recognize this family as one discussed in Chapter Two, in a somewhat different context):

> A six-year-old girl was referred for enuresis and encopresis. Her status as a first grader, and the correspondence of the symptom onset with the birth of the two-year-old sister, served as strong evidence that the symptoms were related to at least two nodal transitions. A sequence observed in the first interview enabled the therapist to hypothesize how behavior that was less than competent had emerged from microtransitions associated with the birth of the sister. While the mother held the sister on her lap, the six-year-old sat alone and somewhat separate. At one point, the girl moved closer to her sister and, in an age-appropriate way, began to play pat-a-cake with her. Then she attempted to take the sister off her mother's lap. As she reached for her sister, the mother pushed the girl away and then gave a bottle to the sister. Simultaneously, the girl began to suck her thumb.

For the girl, the outcome of this sequence was behavior that was less than competent. One could hypothesize that the mother accommodated to the birth of the second child by becoming preoccupied with the baby. This excluded the girl, who felt neglected, and it activated young and needy parts, which encouraged her to act like a baby. The mother gave evidence of additional, confirming sequences. She never let the girl play outdoors and rarely expected her to help around the house. At one point she said, "At home, it's just me and the two babies." Later in the interview, the mother also described her efforts to secure employment. Each day, without success, she looked for work. She then returned home, frustrated, and engaged her daughter in conversations about her search for employment. This sequence required behavior from the girl that was greater than competent and resulted in the girl feeling somehow part of the mother's quest for work but unable to make any contribution. Indeed, she could not even help out by acting her age. An oscillation existed: the girl sucked her thumb, whined, and behaved less than competently in many ways, but she also functioned in an adultlike way with regard to her mother's job search. The symptoms of enuresis and encopresis could be viewed as metaphorical for her behavior that was less than competent but also as a stressful outcome of the behavior that was greater than competent.

We have found that microtransitions and stable oscillations enable us to connect individual and family development, thereby creating a rich pool of ideas from which to hypothesize. Moreover, we find that families are extremely receptive to hypotheses framed from the perspective of an oscillation. When we say to a parent, "Sometimes a young part of him takes over, and he acts five, and sometimes an adult part takes over, and he acts twenty-five," the parent usually nods. Parents are usually motivated by a treatment goal if it implies that when the child learns to act his or her age the problem will be solved.

Biological Development

Humans have an internal blueprint of biological development, which unfolds predictably. Humans also have temperaments, which are present from birth (Chess, Thomas, and Birch, 1972). A child's temperament is an enduring quality, to which parents must learn to find a fit. Family therapists who fail to acknowledge temperament and see behavior only as a function of interaction may encourage parents to interact with a problem child in a manner that exacerbates rather than improves a poor fit.

A major constraint exists when the biological blueprint unfolds in an irregular manner. The most obvious case involves developmental disability, where impaired mental functioning slows the developmental process. Children with less profound disabilities, such as learning disabilities or hyperactivity, also develop differently. Unfortunately, to avoid the trap of reductionism, family therapy has minimized the biological aspects of development, sometimes even suggesting that all developmental difficulties are simply responses to interaction. Such a position trivializes the complexity of the human condition and blinds us to the differences that exist among children. We can include biological development, without being reductionistic, as long as we continue to appreciate the recursiveness between the biological and other system levels.

Microtransitions are more likely to produce oscillations if biological development is not normal. For example, a child with a developmental disability (DD) cannot be expected to attain developmental milestones within the same time frame that a normal child would. Therefore, parents with a DD child must adjust their expectations and expect less, while still encouraging the child to live up to his or her potential. In such situations, getting the accommodation to work is much more difficult, and it is much easier to produce an oscillation. One common response is for the parents not to expect as much as they could from the DD child and thus to create sequences wherein the child acts younger than his or her age. Another response is for the parents to assume that the child can function at a normal level and thus to expect too much and create frustration for themselves and the child.

An even more common scenario involves attention deficit disorders (ADD). Many family therapists dismiss and trivialize ADD as a problem of not listening. We believe that ADD is, in some cases, a real biological condition that may have to be accommodated to by parents. They cannot expect the same degree of competence in some aspects of development, but they can in others. For example, ADD children are more impulsive and often do things without thinking. A normal four-year-old could play freely in a park while a parent observed from a distance; an ADD child in the same situation might suddenly run across the street. Therefore, the parent of an ADD child learns to stand nearby, ready to protect the child from the dangers of the street. It is more difficult for parents of ADD children to know how to give their children appropriate autonomy. ADD children do become less impulsive over time, and their parents, accustomed to anticipating and protecting them, are challenged to assess this change and to know when to back off.

Chronic illness, either in a parent or a child, also interferes with development and creates conditions ripe for an oscillation. Note that in the following case example, the oscillation is embedded within several S3 patterns:

A twelve-year-old boy who lived alone with his mother was referred for repeatedly running away from home. He would disappear for several days and would usually be returned home by the police, having been caught sleeping on a subway train. The mother suffered from multiple sclerosis. From the time he was six, she had taught her son to use public transportation, because she wanted him to be able to handle himself should anything ever happen to her. Other behaviors that were greater than competent also appeared whenever the mother experienced an exacerbation of her illness. At these times, the boy would run the house quite competently and would not run away. When the mother recovered, however, the boy would fall apart; his competence gave way to immaturity as he refused to help around the house, and he did very poorly in school. Frustrated by his collapse, his mother would attempt to control her son, and he would then run away again. The oscillation between behavior that was greater than and less than competent occurred in relationship to the mother's illness. To complicate matters, the boy had been born when the mother was only sixteen years old. Now, at age twenty-eight, she was attending nursing school, and she stated bluntly that she would not allow her son's behavior to interfere with her plans to have a career. The mother acted competently as a student but also incompetently in the context of the family, where she neglected her responsibilities as a parent. She oscillated between the extremes of wanting to be a teenager finishing school and an adult raising a family. By running away, the boy periodically tried to solve his

mother's dilemma, again making himself more competent than his years.

Relational Development

Family members experience the family at multiple levels: as individuals in the family; through a complex web of dyadic relationships; through triads and subsystems; and through the family as a
whole. Next to individual experience, relationships are felt most
immediately; consequently, members are most likely to describe the
family in terms of these relationships. For example, when a daughter reports that she and her dad are not close, she experiences distance in the dyad of father/daughter, but not the way her mother
may have interfered whenever father and daughter tried to relate. In
short, without training, family members are not systems thinkers.
Unfortunately, family therapists have avoided dyadic relationships
for the same reason that they have avoided the individual: out of
concern that focusing on a dyad, rather than on the whole family,
would be reductionistic. As long as we retain a multilevel systems
perspective, however, we can address the relational level and its
developmental qualities, without becoming reductionistic.

Family relationships last a lifetime. They must serve the
needs of the individuals in them, and of the family as a whole, over
a wide range of changing circumstances. For relationships to succeed under changing demands and circumstances, they too must
develop. In the family therapy literature, relational development is
often subsumed under the topic of family development, but this is
a limited view. It ignores the fact that relational development has
its own autonomous, inner logic that unfolds, at least in part, independently of individual or family development (Wynne, 1984).

The Processes of Relational Development

What is relational development? When we speak of relationships
that mature, deepen, and become more solid, we imply that relationships evolve and become more complex over time. What does
this mean, and how does it happen? To answer that question, we
will build on the work of Wynne (1984, 1988), who has proposed

a model of relational development involving the sequential mastery of four processes: *attachment/caregiving,* defined as complementary affectional bonding; *communicating,* defined as the development of shared communicational codes; *joint problem solving,* defined as the ability to work together on mastering and accomplishing complex tasks; and *mutuality,* defined as the ability to renegotiate a relationship. Wynne has also proposed *intimacy* as a fifth process, which may grow out of mutuality, but he does not consider it as a necessary or ultimate ideal of relational development.

Wynne's sequencing of relational processes is easiest to see in parent/child relationships, where attachment/caregiving emerges during infancy, communicating parallels language development, and mutuality emerges in adolescence and young adulthood. This sequence is more difficult to see in adult/adult relationships, such as marriage, where each adult brings to the relationship preexisting styles of attachment/caregiving, communicating, and problem solving.

Relational Development and the Epigenetic View

Wynne proposes that relational development is epigenetic—that is, subsequent processes necessarily build on the successful accomplishment of previous processes. Hence, relationships optimally develop toward mutuality, with attachment/caregiving, communicating, and joint problem solving as the necessary antecedent and sequential processes. Wynne believes that if a relationship fails to master any one of these processes, the subsequent processes will be constrained. For example, a shared meaning is difficult to achieve in the absence of attachment/caregiving; joint problem solving is impaired if there is no shared meaning; mutuality, which is a form of relational problem solving, cannot exist without communication and the security of attachment/caregiving.

Epigenetic theories are linear and therefore conflict with systems theory, which is recursive. Wynne does acknowledge some recursion among the processes—for example, he says that sustained efforts at joint problem solving can engender attachment. For our part, we believe that the mastery of processes as proposed by Wynne would be desirable, but we also believe that there is recursion among the processes, particularly in adult relationships. Therefore, we believe that relationships are not necessarily handicapped if the processes are not mastered in the prescribed order; any of the processes can be mastered at any time, if the relevant constraints are lifted.

Relational Development: A Metaframeworks Perspective

Our own model of relational development describes six relational processes, some of which overlap with those proposed by Wynne. They are *attraction, liking, nurturing, coordinating meaning, setting rules,* and *making metarules.* As Wynne does, we acknowledge intimacy as a process, and we too see it as an ideal, rather than as the ultimate outcome of relational development. We will describe the processes sequentially, but we urge the reader to keep in mind the recursion among them. Each of the processes is highly complex. Space limitations prevent us from making many of the subtle distinctions that pertain to each process and to the relationships among them; our intent is to provide the reader with a sense of the importance and relevance of relational development.

Attraction and liking bear some similarity to the attachment component of Wynne's attachment/caregiving, but we believe that they are distinct processes. Attraction is the experience of being drawn to another person. It is probably biological in part. For a mother, it involves maternal feelings; for adults, "chemistry" is often invoked to explain an initial attraction. As the initial fuel of a relationship, attraction is important, but very few relationships founded on "love at first sight" can be sustained on attraction alone.

Liking, while it is sometimes a function of attraction, is also different, because it involves an appreciation and valuing of the other person's attributes. Liking can beget attraction, and it usually endures well beyond attraction. Ideally, two people who form a relationship each contribute complementary attributes that create and maintain liking. A common source of relational distress is attraction without liking.

Nurturing is similar to Wynne's concept of caregiving. It is the capacity to give and receive care. Nurturing creates security in a relationship because it provides assurance that the other person will be there in times of need. If nurturing exists in a relationship, the parties can show vulnerability and need, knowing that the response will be nurturance. Nurturing should be balanced, reciprocal, and given without obligation. Some people can nurture without liking or attraction. Conversely, two people may be attracted to and like each other but not be able to nurture.

We prefer the term *coordinating meaning* to Wynne's *communicating*, because the latter term is too general and ambiguous. A relationship has coordinated meaning when both parties attribute similar meaning to the speech acts and episodes in which they jointly participate (Pearce and Cronen, 1980). This creates a consensual reality in the relationship, which then constitutes a common basis for communication. Further, when shared meaning is missing from an episode, its absence is recognized, and the conversation shifts to the metacommunicative level (that is, to a discussion of the discrepant meanings given to the episode). With sufficient motivation and maturity, people (for example, supervisor and subordinate) can coordinate meaning in the absence of liking and nurturing. In an intense need-meeting relationship, such as marriage, the absence of liking and nurturing may impair efforts to coordinate meaning.

Setting rules is the process by which the rules that define and operate the relationship are established. It is the "This is who I am in relationship to you" and the "quid pro quo" of the relationship (Lederer and Jackson, 1968). We define it here more broadly than Wynne's joint problem solving, because it creates the means for joint problem solving to be effective: if a relationship has functional rules, it will be able to solve problems. Rules can be set implicitly and may emerge as products of interaction. Rules are established from the outset of a relationship and are often prescribed by role expectations. As a sustained relational process, however, setting rules involves actively negotiating how the relationship will work. For example, a dual-career couple with children must be able to work out functional rules that enable multiple demands to be met. In the absence of coordinated meaning, the setting of rules is constrained, because the parties do not share the consensual reality that must form the basis of their negotiations.

Finally, every successful, enduring relationship operates by metarules—that is, rules for changing the rules of the relationship as it encounters new demands. Such demands arise in response to the development of the individuals in the relationship and to transitions in the family life cycle. For example, when children leave home, the "empty nest" couple must redefine the relationship as one that does not involve intense parenting. Unfortunately, many marriages fail at this time. Metarules are the active ingredient of Wynne's process of mutuality. Relational impasses, such as parent/child cutoffs or infidelity, often signal the lack of metarules in a relationship.

Wynne, in excluding intimacy from his relational model, sees it as an ideal and as difficult to achieve, given the life-styles and cultural values of many people, particularly males. He defines intimacy as "the sharing of personal feelings, fantasies, and affectively meaningful experience associated with each of the stages . . . that connotes an acceptance of the listener, who could betray or exploit the speaker but who is trusted not to do so" (Wynne, 1988, p. 95). In some form, intimacy can be expressed throughout a relationship. People are often attracted to each other initially because frank self-disclosure creates a sense of intimacy. The capacity for intimacy is predicated on absolute trust, so that each person comes to believe in and experience the relationship as completely safe. Trust may be eroded over time, as the parties in a long-standing relationship disappoint and sometimes betray one another; therefore, intimacy is sometimes impossible. At the same time, intimacy involves risk and vulnerability and may easily become threatening. Consequently, many couples with stable and successful relationships never become truly intimate. For this reason, we agree with Wynne that intimacy should not be seen as the ultimate goal of relationship therapy.

Recursion of Relational Processes

The six relational processes enable a relationship to thrive and have continuity over a long period. Attraction and liking are enough at first to draw the parties toward each other. They learn to nurture each other, and coordinated meanings produce a consensual reality for their relationship. The rule-setting process produces flexible relational definitions and enables problem solving to take place.

When the relationship requires renegotiation, metarules can be activated to redefine it.

The six relational processes can be described sequentially: attraction begets liking, which begets nurturing, and so on. To some extent, this is accurate, but all the processes are also present from the outset and function throughout the relationship. Perhaps there is a figure/ground distinction: at certain times, one relational process assumes prominence as the figure, while the other processes recede to the ground. Again, unlike Wynne, we do not believe that failure to master the processes in a certain order necessarily handicaps the future of a relationship. We maintain that recursion exists among them. Recursion implies that any of the processes can affect any of the others. For example, nurturing (and being nurtured) can engender liking, rule setting and negotiating can engender nurturing, and so on. To understand a relationship, it is important to know how it has developed and to grasp which processes have been mastered and which have not. When a relationship successfully masters all six relational processes, each one recursively strengthens the others. Such a strong relationship is symbolized as a stable star relationship in Figure 6.5.

Action and Meaning in Relational Development

Each relational process has dimensions of action and meaning; that is, the parties *do* something as part of the process, but they also attribute *meaning* to the relationship in relation to that process. For example, nurturing involves acts of caregiving. For those acts to be experienced as nurturant, however, the recipient must attribute a meaning of caring to them. The invoking of metarules involves intense discussion, but the new rules redefine the relationship, giving it new meaning. Therefore, the therapist can address any of the processes at the levels of action and meaning.

Relational Development and the Internal Family System

The development of each relational process is mediated by the respective parts of each party. For example, consider nurturing. Being nurtured activates protective parts, which both desire and fear

Figure 6.5. The Recursion of Relational Processes.

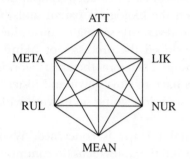

Note: The abbreviations stand for (clockwise, from top) *attraction, liking, nurturing, coordinating meaning, rule setting,* and *metarules.*

vulnerability and are ambivalent about entrusting childlike parts to another person. Caretaker parts want to nurture others. In a culture of individuality, assertive parts value autonomy and are fearful that nurturing may lead to exploitation. Striver parts fear that caregiving is too time-consuming. Hence, nurturing between adults can be achieved only to the extent that the self of each person exercises leadership and keeps his or her parts from becoming extreme or polarized.

Implications for Therapy

When we juxtapose relational development with the macrotransitions of the family life cycle, we note that the macrotransitions are not all identical processes, because the quality of the relationship may differ considerably at the time of given transitions. For example, the transition to school differs from that to adolescence. In the former, the parent/child relationship has not developed the capacity for mutual rule setting; in the latter, it has. Any macrotransition will be constrained if the parental relationship that is providing the leadership for the transition lacks metarules and so cannot make the necessary changes in family rules.

The concept of relational development also implies an impor-

ing complaint in blended families is conflict between a child and a stepparent. Therapists often tackle such complaints as difficulties in rule setting between the biological parent and the stepparent. In blended families, however, rule setting is constrained when relationships have not developed the processes of liking, nurturing, and coordinating meaning. Therefore, therapists working with blended families sometimes have to slow down and foster the development of relational processes before going on to work with the structure of the blended family.

Where marital therapy is concerned, Wynne (1984, 1988) notes that some marital therapies focus on communication, without regard for liking or nurturing. Others are problem-centered and apparently presuppose that meaning is already coordinated. Therefore, an important part of marital therapy is assessment of relational development, in recognition of the fact that, in some marriages, communication training or problem solving may be doomed if such essential relational processes as nurturing and coordinating meaning are not already operating.

Developmental Constraints and Synchrony

We have argued that family development involves development at the biological, individual, relational, and family levels in a manner consistent with societal values and beliefs about development. When a family is working well, development at each level fosters development at other levels—that is, synchrony exists among levels. The macrotransitions of the family life cycle are facilitated by appropriate levels of relational development, and microtransitions create new levels of competence and associated sequences that make the macrotransitions possible. Microtransitions create new contexts for relational development; relational development in turn creates the conditions for successful microtransitions (to dampen without oscillation).

When synchrony exists, development across levels creates a synergistic effect, so that the net benefit to the family's development is greater. This is one reason why healthy families appear to be so well adjusted: they accommodate to the many developmental demands in a manner that increases the competence of members and the flexibility of the system. Achieving synchrony is an enormous challenge, however. Family life is constantly changing in response to development, and to shift gears at all levels in the face of a developmental increment at one or more levels requires considerable flexibility of holons. Levels can easily get out of synchrony, and the developmental process is thereby disrupted.

It is possible for developmental constraints to exist at only one level. More often, however, disrupted development at one level will also disrupt development at others. The resulting interaction effect creates a negative synergy: disruptions at several levels amplify one another, so that the total constraint on each level and on the family as a whole is greater.

Nevertheless, it is important not to become pessimistic about development, because it also constantly creates new opportunities. We respect the plasticity of families, and we apply concepts of embeddedness (see Chapter Four) to assess the severity of developmental constraints. If the embeddedness of developmental constraints is not extreme, then a shift at one level will trigger shifts at other levels and create significant change. If developmental constraints are deeply embedded, however, then therapy must address several levels simultaneously, and significant change will not occur until developmental changes are made at each of these levels.

The development metaframework has many clinical implications, summarized in Table 6.1. In that table, we list the levels separately, but it is important to remember that a recursive relation-

Table 6.1. Clinical Implications of the Development Metaframework.

Level	Developmental Issue	Constraint	Clinical Implication
Family	Nodal transition	Stuck in wrong stage	Move family to appropriate stage of FLC
Individual	Microtransition	Oscillation	Dampen oscillation so individual acts age-appropriately
Biological	Uneven maturation	Restricted competence	Achieve a fit that adjusts expectations to potential
Relational	Six processes	Missing or partial process	Develop process

ship exists among them and to avoid the tendency to identify a single developmental constraint and focus on it alone.

As in using any of the other metaframeworks, in using this one we can draw on any of the relevant psychotherapy literature to plan treatment of any of the developmental constraints. The specific clinical approach may be drawn from many sources, provided that it is consistent with our presuppositions of systemic therapy. Approaches originally designed to focus exclusively on one level may have to be modified, to account for the recursive relationships of that level with other levels. This is particularly true in biological interventions, where awareness of the recursion among the individual, biological, relational, and family levels may preclude the exclusive use of medication. Let us consider a final case example:

> An adolescent daughter was referred for dabbling in drugs. At home, she demands complete freedom, throwing tantrums when her parents attempt to limit her activities. She has a history of learning disabilities, is failing at school, and rarely does homework. Her mother covers for her at school and hides the difficulties from the father who constantly criticizes the daughter. He is furious about her 20-year-old boyfriend, but he often buys her clothes suitable for a young adult.
>
> The parents are middle aged. The father is facing a midlife career crisis. He is depressed and resentful about losing a promotion. He recently bought a sports car and is having an affair. The mother, believing that her role as mother is nearly finished, attends college and often borrows her daughter's clothes. She is rarely at home, and her husband resents the fact that he often has to prepare his own meals.
>
> The marriage is in crisis. The mother is increasingly disenchanted with the traditional nature of her marriage. Husband and wife now have little in common and spend most of their time together in silence. The wife tries to tell her husband that the

marriage has to change, but he acts hurt, and she slowly recognizes that she and her husband have never learned to talk. The daughter, bitter because her younger brother is the parents' favorite, constantly criticizes him, and he tattles whenever he can.

The father's mother, a widow, lives alone but has severe arthritis. She requires care but is hostile whenever her son or two daughters come to help. The three adult siblings rarely talk, and no plans have been made to care for their mother when she can no longer live on her own.

Table 6.2 summarizes the developmental problems faced by this family. Problems at one level exacerbate those at other levels. The parents' waning marriage cannot be renegotiated because it lacks metarules. The parents cannot set rules about their marriage or their daughter. The daughter's oscillation polarizes the parents, who disagree about what is age-appropriate for her, and this conflict further jeopardizes their marriage. The daughter gains no support from her brother, because that relationship has not developed beyond sibling rivalry. The father and the mother have become preoccupied with their own development, giving little attention to their marriage or to their daughter. Moreover, the parents have never accommodated to the additional demands created by the daughter's learning disabilities. These sequences of neglect constrain the daughter's limited potential, but they also enable her in acting older than her age. The father is depressed, both over his career and over his own mother. He is unable to relate to his adult sisters or to his wife, carries his burden in isolation, and has an affair for consolation. His frustration and anger spill over into punitive actions toward his daughter.

Developmental synchrony, which could have allowed this family to address the many challenges it faces, has been supplanted by a web of developmental constraints, which make it difficult for the individuals, the relationships, and the family itself to develop. Without this complex view of development, a therapist could naïvely assume that the only relevant goal is to help the family make the transition into the stage of the daughter's adolescence.

Table 6.2. Summary of Developmental Problems Faced by Family.

Developmental Problem	Assessment
FLC Nodal Transitions	
Transition to adolescence	Family has not reorganized to deal with adolescence
Transition to old age	Family has not reorganized to allow adult siblings to care for aging parent
Individual Developmental Microtransitions	
Daughter oscillating	Acting 20 years old with clothes and boyfriend, but acting 7 by not doing homework and 2 by having tantrums
Mother oscillating	Wants job of parenting to be over when it is not; wants to be a college kid again
Father oscillating	Giving up on career when he should be entering his prime; acting like an adolescent, with car and girlfriend
Biological development	Learning disabilities have disrupted normal education
Relational development	Most relationships have not developed important relational processes

This macrotransition is certainly an issue, but we would also assess all the developmental constraints and evaluate their degree of embeddedness. The relational problems, the many oscillations, and the impact of the daughter's learning disability seem to be interacting and creating a negative synergy. Therefore, we would proceed with caution, respecting the family's position and addressing each of the relevant developmental constraints.

Like all the other metaframeworks, this one enriches our appreciation of systems by providing a complex, hopeful, yet also sobering view of family development. We are challenged, but also find that our clinical applications of this metaframework have made our therapy more effective, since we have been more able to identify developmental constraints, as well as opportunities.

SEVEN

Unifying Diverse Parameters:
The Multicultural Metaframework

Among the many definitions of heaven and hell, there seem to be some that fit particular cultural preconceptions, as in the following popular joke:

> Heaven is a society where the policemen are English, the chefs are French, the engineers are German, the bankers are Swiss, and the lovers are Italian. In hell, the English are the chefs, the French are engineers, the Germans are policemen, the Italians are bankers, and the Swiss are lovers.

These common preconceptions about culture are derived from casual encounters with given cultures. The scenarios described in this joke may ring true, but they represent only a partial view of culture and its impact on behavior. Cultural explanations (theories) also need to consider other experiences that result from the evolution and interaction, over time, of intracultural, intercultural, and universal beliefs and behaviors.

Intracultural literally means "within culture" and refers to easily recognizable sociocultural groups. Intracultural groups provide a sense of continuity to the society by generating and maintaining culture-specific values and beliefs. Culture-specific values are always being influenced by historical and political (internal and external) events. Culture-specific values continually interact with intercultural and universal values.

Intercultural, or between-culture, beliefs and behaviors are those that exist across several cultural groups because of commonalities of experience. Such commonalities may develop because of similar economic, geographical, historical, or political experiences. In multicultural societies, commonalities also develop through the contributions that the various waves of immigrant groups bring to their host culture.

Universal beliefs connect the similar with the dissimilar and provide a sense of commonality among all the nations of the world. These beliefs result from such human experiences as birth, joy, maturation, and death. They also involve the shared meaning attributed, for example, to motherhood, babies, nationality, and heroes. Universals, clearly articulated in music and the arts, reach us all in similar ways.

The contribution of culture-specific, intercultural, and universal beliefs to the evolution of values is a recursive process of mutual influence between levels of a system. For example, families influence not only their members but also their communities, and communities influence both families and institutions. The degree of influence that each social level exerts depends on the organization of the society. In autocratic societies, the leaders in power allow few opportunities for participation by members. In democratic societies, all groups supposedly contribute to the evolution of their society. The degree to which this happens in our society is questionable. Many minority groups experience marginality and have few opportunities to participate in the evolution of values.

Food seems to be a metaphor for how values penetrate mainstream society. Take, for example, the many ways chicken is prepared. There is chicken cacciatore, chicken cordon bleu, southern-fried chicken, chicken in mole, chicken with cashews, chicken tandori, chicken shishkabob, chicken with rice, chicken soup, and so on. What seems to connect us all is the chicken, a universal common denominator that we share; what varies is how we prepare it or the flavor that we prefer (culture-specific). One trend toward multiculturality in the United States is reflected in the increasing number of combinations of dishes that vary or mix sauces and condiments from different cuisines.

Discussions of culture are usually about what is culture-specific. For example, in discussing chicken mole, we usually talk about the history, preparation, and way of eating chicken mole. It is less common to talk about the chicken itself (universal) or about how the mole sauce has been altered over time by the contributions of other groups (intercultural).

In this chapter, we adopt a broad definition of culture. We do not view culture as synonymous with ethnicity but rather as a larger category that includes ethnicity, as well as other sociocultural contexts (for example, race, gender, education, and economics). Culture is the class of sociocultural contexts; ethnicity, race, education, gender, and economics are some of the sociocultural contexts of membership. From the multicultural perspective assumed in this chapter, there is a multiplicity of sociocultural contexts, which influence values over time. These values influence all levels of systems: individuals, families, communities, and institutions. From the multicultural perspective, families and therapists share similarities (specific sociocultural contexts) as well as differences, and each sociocultural context triggers opportunities as well as constraints.

From the multicultural perspective, diversity is a valuable resource for the growth and enrichment of all societies. This perspective is multidimensional because it incorporates the many contextual dimensions that contribute to cultural values. It takes account of the values of the therapist in complementarity with those of the family—that is, it includes the recursive context of the family's values in relation to the therapist's values, minorities in relation to the majority, and distinctions made in relation to those making the distinctions (Karrer, 1989).

This chapter reviews the impact of the multiple meanings of culture on our views. It then presents a rationale for the multicultural metaframework, and it discusses the presuppositions that guide our cultural thinking. It also considers those sociocultural contexts that contribute to value formation, discusses the opportunities and constraints that sociocultural contexts provide, and offers guidelines for family therapy practice.

What Is Culture?

Because cultural beliefs come in as many varieties as there are human beings, it is difficult to address the totality of the meanings of culture by focusing on only one definition of culture. Therefore, we review several definitions of culture, which may be applied to a variety of contexts. Kluckhohn (cited in Geertz, 1973, pp. 4–5) listed the following definitions: "the total way of life of a people"; "a way for people to change adaptively in pace with their time, and to learn and contribute to their generation"; "the social legacy the individual acquires from his group"; "a way of thinking, feeling, believing"; "an abstraction from behavior"; "a theory on the part of the anthropologist about the way in which a group of people in fact behave"; "a storehouse of pooled learning"; "a set of standardized orientations to recurrent problems"; "learned behavior"; and "a mechanism for the normative regulation of behavior."

The definition referring to culture as "a theory on the part of the anthropologist" is particularly appealing because it fits our presupposition of perspectivism. According to this definition, the observer (the anthropologist) is a part of the culture that she or he is defining. This is an interactional definition that reminds us of our own role in the creation of social realities.

The definition that refers to "a way for people to change adaptively in pace with their time, and to learn and contribute to their generation" is attractive because it suggests accommodation to a given historical period and highlights the contributions of the members of each generation to their historical context. It is a reciprocal, interactive definition that emphasizes adaptation.

"The total way of life of people" is also an intriguing definition because it emphasizes both complexity and variation. It does not presuppose a particular way of life. Rather, it stresses a total way of life, which implies the sum of many different ways. This definition is not quite systemic, however, in that it does not reflect the holistic idea of the system's being greater than the sum of its parts.

The definitions referring to learned behaviors do not acknowledge the attribution of meaning to those behaviors. Because we consider meaning pivotal to all metaframeworks, we include Weber's definition of culture as "a web of significance spun by man himself" (cited in Geertz, 1973, p. 5).

Each of these definitions adds a dimension to our understanding of cultural values. Each alone represents a partial view.

Falicov (1988c, p. 336) has offered perhaps the best systemic definition of culture, as shared world-views and adaptive behaviors derived from simultaneous location in a variety of contexts. Karrer
(1989) has expanded on this definition by describing the sociocultural contexts that contribute to the multiplicity of values in our
society and by addressing the role of the observer in the social construction of these contexts. (These sociocultural contexts are one of
the cornerstones of our multicultural perspective and will be discussed later in this chapter.)

Rationale for a Multicultural Metaframework

A multicultural perspective validates the variety of ways that culture
teaches us to be human. Culture provides a blueprint for how to act
and behave in communities, institutions and society. The family
therapy field has legitimized the sociocultural context as an essential focus of attention. Moreover, many authors have questioned
monolithic explanations of culture (Falicov, 1983; Karrer, 1987,
1989; McGoldrick, Pearce, and Giordano, 1982; Montalvo and Gutierrez, 1983, 1989; Saba and Rodgers, 1989; Sluzki, 1979a, 1979b,
1982; Schwartzman, 1983). Nevertheless, no multicultural perspective has yet had the impact on the theories and practice of family
therapy that it deserves.

To clarify the difference between our multicultural perspective and the evolution of views of multiculturality in the United
States, we will briefly summarize how multiculturality has been
understood over time. The "melting pot" ideology was prevalent
for the first part of this century (up to World War II). This ideology
viewed acculturation as a one-way process toward assimilation (that
is, total absorption of the immigrant's cultural identity by the mainstream American values prevailing at that historical time). With the
continued influx of immigrant groups throughout this century,
cultural pluralism was a reality before it became a theory. (The
correctness of this assessment depends, of course, on one's definition
of pluralism.) Stent, Hazard, and Rivlin (1973) define cultural pluralism as "a state of equity, mutual respect, and interdependence
among several populations that form a single society" (p. 22). In

terms of this definition, it would perhaps be too optimistic to say that the United States is pluralistic. Berry, Kalin, and Taylor (1977), however, distinguish between *pluralistic* and *multicultural* societies. Pluralistic societies contain diverse cultural groups, which retain their cultural identities while contributing their values to the mainstream of their society. In a multicultural American society, by contrast, each cultural group not only would maintain its original identity and contribute its values to the mainstream society but also would be perceived as American. The difference is that pluralism, while emphasizing everyone's views, does not address the question of belongingness.

Obviously, we have reached neither a multicultural nor a pluralistic stage of evolution. Many immigrant and Native American groups are neither seen as equal in nor respected by the dominant society. African-Americans, despite their presence for many generations in this country, have had fewer opportunities for participation in the mainstream and are not respected by the dominant group. Native Americans, the original inhabitants of this continent, have been marginalized for many generations. We recognize that our multicultural perspective rests on an ideal that is far from reality, but we also believe that it is valid to view reality from a perspective that encourages us to be better than we are now and the best that we can be.

Statistics provide a compelling reason for adopting a multicultural perspective in family therapy. Data from the 1980 census suggest that cultural diversity is and will become an even more salient issue in the United States in the 1990s. Census figures reflect a dramatic increase in the minority population (one person in five in the United States is a member of minority group). The population changes have been and will be most dramatic in certain locations. By the year 2000, 46 percent of the population of California will consist of individuals of Latin American descent.* By the year

---

*The question of whether we can use the term *Hispanic* as an ethnic and/ or racial referent to describe populations from Latin America is a controversial one. The term itself is a misnomer, since it refers to groups of Spanish descent (that is, people from Spain), whereas Hispanic groups are only one of the many ethnic groups that have immigrated to Latin Amer-

2010, this future will have increased to 55 percent. By the year 2020, one in three children in the United States will be a member of a minority group. Minorities (including women) will be the majority entering the work force (U.S. Bureau of the Census, 1989). Diverse cultural groups are already prevalent in large metropolitan areas (for example, Miami already has so many groups of Latin American descent that English, not Spanish, is the secondary language). Therapists working in such areas have bilingual, bicultural caseloads.

The Multicultural Metaframework

The multicultural metaframework consists of a set of presuppositions (beliefs) about the importance of a multicultural perspective in the treatment of families; a matrix, which considers the many sociocultural contexts of membership that contribute to value formation and their interaction with the therapist's values; ways to utilize these contexts of membership in an assessment of the opportunities and constraints that each sociocultural dimension may present; and therapeutic guidelines that consider the family's as well as the therapist's multicultural background.

The multicultural metaframework operates from the same presuppositions as all the other metaframeworks. First, systems are conceptualized as multileveled. The values of any society are generated from a multiplicity of minds, as they interact with many institutions within diverse sociocultural contexts. Consequently,

---

ica. The term is particularly inappropriate because it leaves out the indigenous groups that were the original inhabitants of these regions, as well as African-Americans, other Europeans, and Asians, all groups that have immigrated to Latin America. Moreover, the term *Hispanic* is inappropriate as a racial descriptor, since Latin Americans belong to all races and represent combinations of races. We prefer the term *Latin American* in this chapter because it is a geographical descriptor, similar to those we use for other groups (Europeans, Asians, Africans, and so on). This term has the advantage of grouping all Latin Americans together for purposes of political discussion. The best descriptors of Latin Americans, however, are nationality-based (Mexican, Puerto Rican, Argentinian, Chilean, and so on).

there are multileveled explanations of what is meaningful at all levels of society. All levels of social systems (the individual, the family, the community, institutions, and society) are at their best when harmoniously balanced. Societies provide opportunities for balance when they allow equal access to institutional resources, when they offer equality of responsibility and influence in the society, and when all groups truly belong to the society.

Ludwig von Bertalanffy (cited in Davidson, 1983, pp. 211–212) defined perspectivism in two ways: as the "many flavors of truth" and, more formally, as "a viewpoint that the validity of knowledge depends on the perspective from which that knowledge is perceived." The first definition speaks about the many views of reality and the dangers of emphasizing one view at the expense of others. It calls our attention to how rich the "many flavors of truth" become in combination—when they are multicultural. The second definition calls our attention to how perceptions are not necessarily reflections of "real" things but rather cocreations between the observer and the observed. From the multicultural perspective, this is particularly relevant in addressing the majority-constructed view (which is likely to include the perspective of therapists), as it defines the truth, and considering its complementarity with the "many flavors of truth" found among minority groups in our society.

Multicultural Contexts

The sociocultural contexts that we will be describing were developed in our conversations with families from a variety of ethnic groups. In numerous clinical and research interviews, families were asked to describe what was important to them and what organized their behavior and expectations. As we talked with the families, they frequently described religious beliefs, economic opportunities or constraints, educational aspirations, and beliefs associated with age, life-cycle stage, and racial, ethnic, and regional background. Men and women alike described how their gender constrained, as well as enhanced, their relationships and affected their views on everyday events. Immigrants frequently reported how their beliefs had changed or were in the process of changing as a result of cultural transition. Most families also referred to the predominant historical themes of their generation and to how "in time" or "out of time" they felt with these themes. Their descriptions (language, which we view as a "window" into beliefs) involved not just one but many sociocultural contexts. In this way, it became clear to us that, in order to consider the complexity of cultural beliefs and their impact on people's behavior and expectations, we had to adopt a multicultural perspective, one that would give emphasis to the many sociocultural contexts of membership that contribute to value formation. Each context provides a range of variation by contributing both unique (culture-specific) and similar (intercultural and universal) meanings about rules, roles, and expectations for the people in it. Each context to be described here represents potential similarities and/or differences between the family and the therapist. Figure 7.1 illustrates various sociocultural contexts.

Two levels of sociocultural context contribute to diversity. The first, cultural transition, has two temporal dimensions: historical/generational sequences (cultural evolution), and immigration/acculturation. Historical/generational sequences and immigration/acculturation evolve over time, as a result of changing ideologies or circumstances that influence the second level of sociocultural contexts: economics, education, ethnicity, religion, gender, age, race, minority/majority status, and regional background. Interrelatedness between these contexts of membership results either in fit or lack of fit between majority and minority groups, the immigrant and the host society, and the family and the therapist. Cultural fit is the degree of congruence that each group experiences in interaction with the other.

Cultural Transition

Historical/generational sequences constitute the setting for all sociocultural contexts. They represent the cultural themes held in common by those who contribute to cultural evolution and by the institutions they represent. Immigration and acculturation have to do with immigrant families, their descendants, and the experiences they have over many generations. Families who have been in this country for several generations may also experience migration

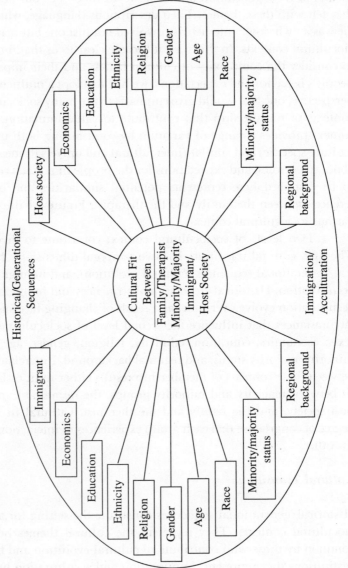

Figure 7.1. The Multicultural Metaframework.

(moving from one region to another). This process resembles immigration because it involves similar adaptive tasks (reestablishing support networks, leaving friends and possessions behind, and learning about the resources of the new hometown), but it lacks the stress of moving to a foreign country.

Historical/Generational Sequences. The British historian Arnold Toynbee (Capra, 1982), discussing cultural evolution, stated that civilizations grow through a dynamic interplay between stability and change. This pattern of interaction results from environmental demands, which come both from within the society and from other societies that share geographical, historical, or political commonalities with the given society. Toynbee saw this fluctuation as both a challenge and a response to environmental demands; we view it as a historical/generational sequence (S5) (see Chapter Four).

This pattern of ongoing redefinition of beliefs, which unfolds during cultural evolution and defines the generational sequence, has a spiral pattern. As the Mayans did, we conceptualize temporal patterns as cycling simultaneously backwards and forward: people draw on experiences from the past, considering the way they fit the present, and use them to plan for the future. This view allows us to value all temporal positions—those that maintain stability, and those that are in the process of transformation.

The everyday impact of historical/generational sequences is more visible now than ever before, because of the rapid dissemination of information. The media, particularly television, have a great impact on how different countries perceive one another. The media also inform us about our own cultural evolution. These historical/generational sequences evolve over time, through consensus about and individual participation in the creation of predominant beliefs for each generation. Some of these sequences can be traced through decades; others, through generations. Ehrenreich (1983) has reviewed in great detail the most visible American historical/generational sequences in the last several decades. Her comprehensive review provides us with excellent examples of the impact of these historical/generational sequences on family life. We will briefly summarize some of these themes, beginning with the "Gray Flannel generation" (1950s). She describes this group's priorities as working hard, buying a house in the suburbs, marrying young, and having children early. This sequence brought about a countercultural challenge that involved gender roles and expectations. Betty Friedan is famous among these dissidents. *The Feminine Mystique* (Friedan, 1963) challenged traditional roles and had a strong impact on the evolution of cultural beliefs for generations to come. Hugh Hefner and *Playboy* magazine expressed another form of dissidence, validating men's sexual needs while devaluing marriage. The Beat Generation emerged from this polarization, objecting to both marriage and work, and supporting machismo. The human potential movement triggered another historical/generational sequence, which validated doing one's own thing and taking care of one's own growth. During this historical/generational sequence (1960s and 1970s), almost every belief previously held in this society was challenged, bringing to the fore a series of social issues: civil rights, women's rights, the antiwar movement, and the hippie generation. This group emphasized adrogyny and challenged consumerism, introducing an era of hedonism and drug consumption. Inevitably, the pendulum swings once more, back to a generation that embodied materialism and consumerism. Male liberation became an important focus at this time as seen in the popularity of *The Liberated Man* (Farrell, 1975), which advised men on how to benefit from the feminist movement. This time also saw the beginning of a movement toward legitimizing gay rights, which is still going on. The last decade (1980s) found the women's movement struggling with the Equal Rights Amendment and the polarization between feminists (both men and women) and traditional groups (both women and men). A recent book by Strauss (1991) raises some compelling dilemmas that our society (and the world) will have to face in the future. This outstanding book not only focuses on past historical/generational sequences but anticipates the challenges that the next generations will face.

As we enter the 1990s, there are clear historical challenges ahead. We view this challenge optimistically and hope that this generation will be awed by the historical significance of living in the last decade of this century and of this millenium, and so redirect resources toward alleviating the plight of minority and poor families, challenging gender imbalance (sanctioning both men and women's liberation), and responsibly addressing the diminishing economic and ecological resources that we globally face.

Embedded within these historical/generational sequences are the meanings that particular beliefs and behaviors have for each generation. Therapists and families are part of this historical context and are therefore influenced by these meanings. Sometimes therapists and families share meanings, and sometimes they do not. Generations have different contextual markers, which bring particular meanings to the fore: "Where were you when President Kennedy was assassinated?" "Where were you the day Martin Luther King was killed?" "Do you remember the evacuation from Saigon?" Contextual markers reflect the degree of temporal synchrony (or lack of synchrony) that people experience with their peers, the community, and the rest of society. Such markers reflect one's sense of belonging to one's own time, as well as one's position in time with respect to cultural evolution. Most important, changing beliefs are part of the context of each individual and family, and successful therapy must reckon with them. The following list includes questions relevant to assessing the historical/generation sequences that the family and the therapist share or do not share:

Historical/Generational Sequences

- What is the salience of this context for the family at present? For example, what are the family's beliefs regarding the prevailing cultural themes of the time?
- Are family members respectful of their generational differences?
- What is the fit between the therapist and the family regarding these sequences?
- Is there potential for expansion of beliefs through the understanding of generational historical sequences?
- Can the therapist use current historical metaphors to expand family members' perceptions of the problem? of one another?
- Are all family members familiar with the prevalent historical themes for their generation?
- If so, can the therapist strengthen the interconnections? If not, can the therapist bridge the differences?

Immigration and Acculturation. The decision to move from one country to another (immigration) begins a process of cultural transition that lasts several generations (acculturation). Acculturation is an accommodation process that occurs when groups from two distinct cultures are in contact over a sustained period of time (Berry, 1980). Karrer (1987) describes acculturation as a transactional process during which the immigrant's experience with the host culture is either facilitated or impeded, according to the degree of reciprocity (fit) and/or conflict experienced in interaction.

In the United States, immigrants contribute to the evolution of their host society by incorporating into their everyday lives some of the beliefs and practices from their native lands while simultaneously accommodating to the beliefs and practices of their host society. In theory, acculturation is mutual and reciprocal. Typically, however, one group (the majority) dominates and exerts greater influence over the values that the immigrant and the society will retain (Berry, 1980).

Sluzki (1979a, 1979b) and Karrer (1987) have both suggested that the phases of immigration and acculturation are predictable, irrespective of specific ethnic background. A pilot study conducted by Karrer and Burgoyne (forthcoming), which examined families from Europe, Asia, the Middle East, and Latin America, supported this hypothesis and found similarities across various phases of immigration and acculturation, irrespective of country of origin. For example, all families in the study experienced conflict related to losing family members, friends, and peer groups who had served as support networks in their cultures of origin. They also experienced difficulties in rebuilding networks, establishing friendships, and learning a new language, as well as in understanding and negotiating proximity and distance (the appropriateness of spatial considerations in relationships) and differences in meaning attributed to child-rearing attitudes and practices. Data from this study suggested that immigration and acculturation also appear to affect younger and older persons, and women and men, differently. Children attempting to fit into peer groups acculturated at a faster pace and frequently reported serving a buffer function between their families and their communities. At times, this special position in the family allowed them to interpret the beliefs of the host society to their advantage (for example, by prematurely demanding more autonomy and freedom from their parents, on the basis of its being the "American" thing to do). For some families, this split had the effect of polarizing the generations (and thus introducing the double stressor of generational and cultural polarization), with one or more children promoting an "American" value system and one or more parents maintaining the value system from the country of origin.

Szapocznik and Kurtines (1980) support this finding. They examined the negative effects of intergenerational polarization by acculturation level on the emotional well-being of family members who reported on adolescents and parents experiencing increased conflict about developmental issues.

There are some clinical indications that women may acculturate faster than men (Karrer and Burgoyne, forthcoming; Montalvo and Gutierrez, 1983), particularly women who find jobs in this country and are able to keep them. Their upward mobility facilitates their acculturation. As they acculturate, they begin to incorporate more contemporary views about the quality of their marital relationships and become more aware of gender imbalance in their families. These realizations can skew their relationships and bring the families into treatment.

Immigrants love to recount their stories, particularly about how they planned and resolved immigration tasks. These stories can serve as valuable resources for the therapist. What distinguishes immigrants from nonimmigrants is that immigrants have already demonstrated the ability to change. They have taken a radical step toward change by relocating across regions and across cultures. We do make a distinction between immigrants and refugees. While immigrants often describe the experience as a crisis, with stresses and opportunities, refugees refer to the decision to immigrate as a trauma that takes many years to overcome. Other significant differences between immigrants and refugees are that immigrants have a planning stage, whereas refugees have to leave suddenly (frequently in fear for their lives), and that immigrants retain the hope of returning to their countries of origin while immigration seems to be an irrevocable decision for refugees.

Therapists often have people in their families or social network who have immigrated, and they can benefit from the recency of their associates' experience. A therapist whose family has been in this country for several generations, and whose family, in the wish to acculturate, has lost touch with its country of origin, needs to recreate this context by asking relatives and friends about their experiences of cultural transition. The closest direct experience that a therapist may share with a family in cultural transition is his or her own move from one region of the country to another. The following questions suggest some ways for therapists to assess the relevance and salience of this sociocultural context:

Immigration and Acculturation

- How salient is this sociocultural context for the members of the family?
- What is the fit between the family and the therapist regarding this sociocultural context?
- Are some of the members more comfortable with their immigration?
- Was the family able to plan its immigration?
- If so, who was in favor of coming? Who was against it?
- Who was left behind? Whom did the family bring?
- Do some of the members experience themselves as "frozen in time," experiencing confusion about the beliefs of their country of origin and those of the adoptive country?
- How successful was the family in the country of origin? Did the family experience some economic loss?
- What did family members expect of their adoptive country when they first came?
- How much did they know about the United States when they came?
- Are the members of the family at all phases of acculturation?
- If so, are there polarizations within the family along the "old country/new country" dimension?
- Do some of the family members always defend the old country's values?

- Do some of the family members always defend the new country's values?
- Has the family been able to mourn the loss of family and friends?
- What is the ethnic allegiance of the members of the family? Are there some who keep their identity and loyalty with the old country? some with the new country?
- How much can family members discuss these differences among them?
- Has the therapist experienced relocation recently (across countries, regions, or city areas)?
- Are there commonalities between these experiences that can be built on? if there are differences, can they be bridged?
- Does the family recognize the advantages of the old values? of the new values?
- Can the therapist examine with family members the opportunities in the new country?
- Can the therapist examine the constraints in the new country?
- Do some members of the family experience biculturality as an opportunity?
- How much overall maneuverability does the therapist have in this sociocultural context?

The case example that follows illustrates how a family's different phases of acculturation can contribute to its members' various perceptions of the meaning of a problem and its potential solutions:

> Rick was referred by his school because of aggressive fighting with peers. The Balenciaga family, racially mixed (Native Mexican Indian and white), consisted of the mother, a second-generation American of Mexican descent raised in an inner-city community in Chicago; the father, a recent immigrant from a small rural town in northern Mexico; and their three children, Rick, fourteen, Norma, twelve, and Estela, ten. The

parents explained that they did not see eye to eye on how to bring up their children.

The father's family of origin had brought him up in the traditional belief that men protect the women in their families. For the mother, however, protection had a different meaning: in the inner-city context where she was brought up, men and women had to be equally strong and able to protect themselves. Having been abused by her father from a very young age (a situation that obviously undermined the notion of men as protectors), the mother had learned to protect herself by being absent from home and spending time with friends in the neighborhood. Eventually, she left home, at the age of fourteen.

The parents' different levels of acculturation (the father was a Mexican in America, and the mother was an American of Mexican descent) influenced their explanations about protection and limit setting. By the time they came to therapy, these views had polarized them. The more the father tried to teach protection to his son, the more extreme his expectations became as he used explanations that belonged to a rural, traditional Mexican setting of a generation ago. The mother's attempts to teach nonviolence to her children were leaving unaddressed the serious risks that they all faced in their community.

Rick was caught between the different meanings that protection had for his parents. To fulfill his role in accordance with his father's expectations, he had to prove that he could protect his sisters. This was particularly difficult because the family lived in an area where feuding gangs are common. Rick had recently become a gang member, in an attempt to protect himself. The degree of "strength" that protecting his sisters required from him in this context was significantly different from what he would have needed in a small rural town in Mexico a generation before.

Rick's involvement with the gang raised a series of ethical dilemmas. According to gang rules, as a "protector," he needed to be ruthless, but this would set him against his mother and corroborated the (intergenerational) meaning she attributed to men and violence. When Rick showed his protective part at home, it was usually in an extreme manner. For example, if his sister Norma reported that an opposing gang member had threatened her in school, Rick would became "protective." Either he challenged the opposing gang member (accommodating his father's expectations, but directly opposing his mother's) or he "protected" his sister by challenging her attitudes: "You stupid. You got to fight, get with it, or you will not grow up to see your next birthdate. I cannot be in all places at once." Norma would break into tears (which corroborated Rick's belief that she would not survive without his protection) and accuse him of abusing her. It was clear that Rick felt overwhelmed by the enormity of the responsibility to be a "protector" to his sisters, as well as caught between the different meanings that protection had for his family and his community.

The family's dilemma raised many hypotheses, which included all the metaframeworks. The therapist could have focused on the complementarity of the parents' organization, thus focusing on the structure of the family. She could have focused on the developmental issues pertaining to Rick's entering adolescence, as well as on the demands on him to function as if he were older than his actual age (both in the community as a gang member, and at home as protector) while still abusing his sisters in a younger-than-age manner. She could have focused on the sequences of interaction in the family at the action level only: the frequent "protective abusive" sequences (S2), and the intergenerational sequences that touched on the mother's experiences with violence as a small girl (S4). She could have focused on how Rick's extreme protector and abuser parts interacted with the members of his family, as well as on the gender imbalance between Rick and his sisters and on the different meanings that protection held for the husband and the wife. She actually did consider and use all these metaframeworks at various points in the treatment, in conjunction with the multicultural perspective. It became clear that the constraints family members experienced had to do with living in a poor neighborhood infested with gangs. Moreover, protection and violence had different meanings for them because of their different acculturation levels.

Externalizing their dilemma, in terms of cultural transition and the nature of their neighborhood, depolarized their positions. The opportunity to face these constraints together, rather than push and pull in opposing directions, seemed useful to them. Out of this dialogue new meanings emerged and opened up opportunities for continued discussion of the many other internal and external constraints the family experienced.

Economics

Economics is a sociocultural context that has a dramatic impact on everyday life. In this context, distinctions (say, among the life-styles of the poor, the middle class, and the very rich) typically have greater impacts than differences in other contexts. There are more similarities between the poor in Chicago and the poor in other parts of the world than between the poor and the rich in Chicago.

Working-class families report experiencing the greatest burden at times of economic change (whether in a recession, an inflation, or a robust economic period). These families also experience a sense of disenfranchisement, because they frequently do not fit the requirements for supportive social programs. Middle-class families experience themselves as being overtaxed and underserved. At the same time, their high degree of conformity to the consumer ethic of our society ends up constraining the quality of their lives.

The economic context is embedded in a political context, and the poor are increasingly losing out. Of the 33 million poor people in this country, 13 million are children, and 500,000 of those children are homeless. At the beginning of this century, this nation stood for principles that made no distinction between the class a child was born into and his or her opportunity. This tradition has been disappearing with every new generation of poor families. In a special edition of *Newsweek,* Kozol (1990) examines how the American dream is failing. Immigrants flocked to this country to provide educational opportunities for their children. Now, there is a chasm between the dream and the reality. Kozol gives us a powerful indictment of the role of economics in today's society: "Today it is not law but economics that condemns the children of the very poor to the implacable inheritance of a diminished destiny" (p. 53). He emphasizes his point by quoting a superintendent of a Chicago public school: "No matter what they [the poor] do, their lot has been determined" (p. 53).

Poverty is such a powerful and prevalent sociocultural influence that therapists must develop a new repertoire of responses. Poor families are frequently overwhelmed by the demands that many agencies place on them. If we expect to have some impact on the mental health of poor families, then a larger systems approach is essential. A strong partnership among the family, the therapist, and community agencies that advocate for the rights of poor families and provide supportive services is an integral part of treatment.

Working-class families and middle-class families are also experiencing diminished resources and fears of losing their hard-earned economic standing. These families need to examine the trade-offs among their economic reality, family life, and their aspirations. Middle-class families also need to be challenged when they adhere to a self-imposed extreme consumerism. The following questions suggest some ways for therapists to assess the relevance and salience of this sociocultural context:

Economics

- What is the fit between the family and the therapist regarding economic background?
- If similar, how can they build on this shared experience?
- If different, can the therapist advocate with the family for better economic resources?

- What do the members of this family think about their current economic state?
- What are the economic constraints and opportunities of the family?
- If the family is poor, what are the costs of poverty for this family?
- How can the therapist empower this family in the struggle against classism?
- What larger systems does the family interact with?
- How can the therapist help the family understand and utilize these systems more efficiently?
- Has the family's economic status changed recently? Has it improved? worsened?
- How do family members perceive the quality of their life?
- Are they overworking at the expense of the family's stability?
- Are they expecting too much of themselves economically?
- Are they caught in cycles of consumerism?
- How much maneuverability does the therapist experience within this sociocultural context?

Education

Economics and education are now more interelated than ever. Therefore, we need to view the educational-sociocultural context in combination with economics and minority status.

It is possible to view education from a variety of perspectives. One form of education is the acquisition of knowledge through schooling and professional specialization, with each area adding specific information and a new set of rules and expectations. Each profession has its own language, which reflects the beliefs and expectations of the field. Doctors talk in terms of illness and health. Lawyers talk in terms of legal and illegal behavior. Teachers consider the abilities and motivations of their students, as well as how families support educational aspirations. Engineers talk about stress, structure, and bridges in very different ways from the ways in which mental health practitioners do.

Education can also mean the breadth of knowledge that people have (as opposed to specialization). Another view of education concerns the interests that people have. For example, someone who spends considerable time on sports will gain specific information and develop a specific language that will differ from that of someone interested in collecting stamps. Interests balance our lives and expand our perspectives in many such ways.

Traditionally, education has been the sanctioned gateway through which poor immigrants could pass to improve their economic status. In today's world of competing ideologies and diminishing resources, however, education (basic schooling) is facing its most acute challenge. This problem is reflected in the double standard in our political institutions, expressed in our language when we speak about "training" the poor and "educating" the rich (Kozol, 1990, p. 53).

Therapists must accommodate to families at all educational levels, and such accommodation takes place through language. It is important to address the specialized meanings that language has for families from varied educational backgrounds, as well as to translate therapeutic jargon into the everyday experiences of families at various educational levels. It is also important that therapists advocate, in collaboration with families, for better educational opportunities for all family members. The following questions suggest some ways for therapists to assess the relevance and salience of this sociocultural context:

Education

- What is the fit between the therapist and the family regarding this sociocultural context?
- What kind of education (formal or informal) does each member bring to the family?
- What areas of specialization does each member in the family have?
- What interests does each member of the family have?
- Are members valued (recognized) by other members because of education? profession? interests?
- Does the therapist share any professional or educational background and/or interests with the family?
- If so how can she or he build on these commonalities?

- If not, how can he or she bridge these differences?
- What are the educational aspirations of the members of the family?
- Can their educational strengths help the therapist expand their beliefs?
- Do all members of the family have the same opportunities for education? for a profession? to pursue their interests?
- How can the therapist help the family explore more educational opportunities?
- Are some members of the family sacrificing their education for others?
- How can the therapist help family members balance their educational aspirations?
- Are some members of the family too focused on achievement?
- How much maneuverability does the therapist experience within this sociocultural context?

Ethnicity

Definitions of ethnicity have sometimes confounded ethnicity with economics. At other times, ethnicity has been seen as synonymous with race or culture. We define *ethnicity* as the national origin of the parents in the family. Most Americans have mixed ethnic backgrounds, which stem from the national origins of their parents and their parents' parents. Observations about ethnic behavior have tended to focus on culture-specific aspects and have minimized intercultural and universal beliefs that cut across all ethnic backgrounds. Ethnic beliefs consist of subtle, multiple creations of meanings that influence the rules the family has about relationships (for example, proximity and distance dimensions) and the timing of transitions (for example, expectations about life-cycle stages). They also influence roles in the family (traditional, egalitarian) and expectations about how rules and roles can and cannot change.

Falicov and Brudner-White (1983), focusing on the work of Hsu (1972), examine how the centrally emphasized relationship in a family system (dominant dyad) varies across ethnic groups. They note that in the mainstream American sociocultural context, the dominant dyad is mother and father. In other ethnic groups, however, the most influential dyad is father and son (as in the Chinese and Middle Eastern societies). In still others it is mother and son (as in traditional Hindu society), mother and daughter, or brother and brother (as in some African societies). They observe that rules about inclusiveness and exclusiveness, proximity and distance, are present in all ethnic groups; what varies is their relative emphasis. They warn therapists about assuming ethnocentric norms—as when, for example, a therapist expects the dominant dyad of a family to be similar to that of his or her own.

Ethnic background also influences the definition of who is included in a family. The nuclear family organization is a relatively recent historical development, which resulted from the upward mobility that this nation experienced after World War II. Given the many economic opportunities that the postwar generation had, it was adaptive for families to be able to leave extended family members behind, in order to maximize economic growth. It seems that there is currently a trend toward reincorporating the nuclear family into an extended family organization. Perhaps a change in historical/generational pattern (S5) is in the making.

The separation from the extended family has left the nuclear family without much support, especially during family formation and the empty-nest years. The extended family traditionally provided support and nurturance when parents needed relief from caring for young children, or when they experienced the loss of their children as the children left home. We wonder whether the increase in child abuse and neglect reflects in some measure, the isolation of nuclear families. While the extended family does provide support to families, it can also be constraining. At times, the help that the extended family provides to the parents can be too intrusive, and it may be a source of role confusion or undermine parental authority.

Ethnic differences offer an opportunity for expansion of perspectives, both for families and for therapists. In today's multicultural society, families and therapists alike tend to have mixed ethnic backgrounds. Ethnic content is very useful in using a variety of rituals, tasks, stories, and metaphors, which tap ethnic background and can open opportunities for change. With the Balenciaga family, for example, the therapist and the family discussed not only the different acculturation levels of the parents but also their ethnic affiliations. Their different views about protection were coded by ethnic affiliation. The father expressed his perceptions of Mexican values, and the mother expressed her perceptions of American values. This position limited the mother's examination of her Mexican background and the father's opportunities for biculturalism. Their ethnic perceptions constrained both of them unnecessarily. The following questions suggest ways for therapists to assess the relevance and salience of this sociocultural context.

Ethnicity

- What is the fit between the family and the therapist regarding this sociocultural context?
- What are the ethnic affiliations of the various members of the family?
- What is their ethnic diversity?
- What ethnic loyalties do they share?
- What is the ethnic affiliation, diversity, and loyalty of the therapist?
- What are some of the ethnic themes that family members utilize in support of their own beliefs?
- Who in the family shares these beliefs, and who does not?
- Are these beliefs constraining them unnecessarily? For example, do they maintain outdated views of what a specific ethnic behavior is or is not?
- Is ethnic affiliation to the native country constraining the family's ability to adapt to the adoptive country?
- How can the therapist both expand and challenge constraining ethnic beliefs?
- How can the therapist utilize his or her ethnic diversity to expand his or her own beliefs?
- Has the family experienced ethnocentric oppression?
- If so, how can the therapist empower family members in their struggle against ethnocentricsm?
- Are there some ethnic metaphors that the therapist can use to increase options in therapy?
- How much maneuverability does the therapist experience within this sociocultural context?

Religion

Religion can be one of the most powerful organizers of belief systems. Religious beliefs have many common principles. Jews, Catholics, Protestants, and Muslims all support the belief in one benevolent, compassionate, transcendent God. These principles translate into common expectations for the appropriateness of the behaviors and practices interpreted by each religious institution. Within the institutional domain, territorial skirmishes take place that highlight differences between principles and practices, deemphasizing the commonalities between them. It is also frequently forgotten that religious prophets were radical thinkers. Their beliefs sanctioned change and challenged the prevailing doctrines of their time.

Religious beliefs have the potential to expand the family's and the therapist's beliefs. To expand the meaning of a given religious description provided by the family, therapists can refer the members of the family to themes that will sanction change. They can approach this task with a sense of respect for the family's religious beliefs, as well as with the certainty that all religious scriptures have a wide range of themes that sanction change.

The following example illustrates how both the therapist and family expanded their views as a result of a religious analogy. An Iranian Muslim family was having difficulty attending to its everyday conflicts because the parents interpreted these conflicts as God-given tests. The therapist remembered a New Testament injunction that states that one renders to God what belongs to God and to Caesar what belongs to Caesar. She asked the family whether the Muslim religion contained a similar injunction. The father immediately offered the following analogy: "The Koran says that when you go to Mosque, you should make sure that your camel is tied to a post, so that when you come out you still have your camel." This analogy provided an opportunity to begin discussing how family members could attend both to God and to pragmatic everyday concerns.

Religious beliefs may also be constraining. For example, there is now polarization about Islam. The West tends to view this religion as a rigid doctrine with extreme practices and dangerous implications for those who do not adhere to it. The Muslim nations view the practices and beliefs of the West as satanic. These differences overshadow the ethical principles that these religions share, and they make communication between Muslims and Westerners difficult.

When the therapist and the family have different religious beliefs, the therapist needs to connect with the universal principles of all religions and to learn about specific practices from the family. With religious fundamentalists, amplification of such themes is particularly difficult, and it may be necessary to choose another sociocultural context as a point of entry. A few years ago, we had a trainee, herself a fundamentalist Baptist, who specialized in treating families of similar religious persuasion. She used to start each session asking the Lord's blessing, so that the work of the session could move in the right direction. This style reflected her own religious beliefs and allowed her to question constraints, as well as clarify the opportunities that this sociocultural context offered. Obviously, this option was available to this therapist because she and the family shared religious beliefs. The following questions suggest ways for therapists to assess the relevance and salience of this sociocultural context.

Religion

- What is the fit between the family and the therapist regarding this sociocultural context?
- How do the religious beliefs enrich the family?
- How do they constrain the family (for example, in fundamentalist religions or religions that object to treatment)?
- What is the value of religiosity within the family?
- Do all the members of the family hold the same beliefs, or are there differences between them?
- If there are differences, are these recognized and respected within the family?
- Does the therapist share some of these religious beliefs? If so, how can she or he build on them? If not, can the therapist bridge these differences?

- When necessary, how can the therapist elicit family members' cooperation, to expand their religious beliefs?
- Have any members of the family experienced religious persecution?
- How can the therapist help family members clarify and defend their beliefs in a balanced manner?
- How can the therapist utilize religious themes in the service of change in the family?
- How much maneuverability does the therapist experience within this sociocultural context?

Gender

Although feminism has been evolving through many generations, gender awareness has not yet had a thorough impact on societies. It is possible that a move toward attaining gender balance will be one of the generational/historical patterns of the 1990s (see Chapter Eight). The following questions suggest ways for therapists to assess the relevance and salience of this sociocultural context.

Gender

- What is the salience of this context for the women in the family?
- What is the salience of this context for the therapist?
- What meaning do members of the family attribute to being a woman? a man?
- Is there gender imbalance between the spouses and/or the siblings?
- Who is in control of the relationship?
- Do men and women in this family validate one another's gender-related experiences?
- What are the losses and gains experienced by the women and men in the family?
- How can the therapist connect with both men and women regarding gender issues in treatment?
- How can the therapist support the family's evolution toward gender balance?
- Are the members of the family in synchrony with their time?

- Are the parents preparing their children for evolving gender roles?
- How can the therapist support any member of the family's struggle against sexism?

Age

Each society provides different experiences for old and young. The young of the world share experiences that transcend culture-specific beliefs, a commonality symbolized by blue jeans, rock and roll, and so on. Nevertheless, there are also significant differences among the young across cultures. Senior citizens, too, have many contexts of commonality. They share a wealth of experiences that can be tapped as a resource for the family and for themselves. They share a more flexible view of history than the younger members of the family do. At the same time, they have special needs, whether physical or psychological, that frequently distance them from the rest of the family. The old in this society are not valued enough. Their experience and wisdom ought to be considered by the therapist as a potential resource. The rest of the family, however, may need to be educated about these possibilities.

Similarities and differences in age between a therapist and some member of the family will always exist. The challenge is for the therapist to relate to all ages and to create a context in which young and old have opportunities in the family to contribute to its evolution and growth. Some families are too adult-oriented; some are too child-oriented. The therapist must balance the family by validating every member's age-appropriate needs, aspirations, and strengths.

Life-cycle expectations, as they are related to chronological age, change with different economic, educational, and ethnic groups and vary between rural and urban groups as well. Therapists must consider these variations across all sociocultural contexts and help families explore the life-cycle expectations that fit their sociocultural backgrounds.

Young therapists may face credibility issues with some families, particularly if they are at different stages of the life cycle irrespective of age. For example, in the Balenciaga case, the therapist and the parents were in their thirties. The similarity ended with their age, however. While the therapist was single, the parents had each been married, divorced, and remarried. The therapist was childless and the parents had a blended family; Mrs. Balenciaga had two children from a previous marriage, and Mr. Balenciaga had two children from his first marriage with whom he had no contact. Mr. and Mrs. Balenciaga also had two of their own children. Obviously, the fact that the therapist and the couple were close in age only served to highlight the different life-cycle experiences between them. This difference offered one opportunity: discussing how the parents very different life experiences introduced complexity into the treatment, and a perspective that the therapist alone did not have. The following questions suggest ways for therapists to assess the relevance and salience of this sociocultural context.

Age

- What is the salience of this sociocultural context for the therapist?
- What meaning does the family have for different generations within the family?
- What meaning does the therapist have for the different generations in his or her own family and in the families he or she works with?
- Does the family experience its life-cycle stages as an opportunity? as a constraint?
- Do family members respect one another's age? life-cycle stage?
- Are members of the family sharing with one another the difficulties of being a certain age?
- Is the family stuck at some developmental stage?
- Are some members of the family acting younger than their ages? older than their ages?
- Are some members of the family excluded from participating in the family because of age?
- How does the therapist's age and life cycle facilitate the treatment?
- Does the therapist validate all age groups in the family?
- How much maneuverability does the therapist have with all the

different age groups in the family? with all the different life-cycle stages?

Race

Racial definitions need to consider the majority-constructed view of who belongs to a particular racial group and who does not. For example, the majority-constructed view tends to group people as either "black" or "white." In all heterogeneous societies, however, there are many racial variations. Some are both black and white. Some are neither black nor white. Some are Indian (both Native American Indians and Eastern Indians, who differ significantly in values). Some are Asian. Some belong to the indigenous races of Australia and New Zealand.

Because there seems to be a deficit orientation toward black families, Boyd-Franklin (1989) has raised a clear, persuasive voice in the attempt to redress years of such prejudice. To this end, she lists five strengths that black families have: the bond of the extended family, the adaptability of family roles, a strong religious orientation, a belief in the value of education and the work ethic, and the ability to adapt to economic hardship. To these strengths, we would add the ability to adapt to racism. She has also made a case for variations in black families that have to do with the contexts in which they live, variations determined by membership in different economic, educational, regional, ethnic, gender, and age groups. When therapists focus on the universal experiences that all humans share and validate race-specific experiences, racial differences between therapists and families may become enriching. Because most heterogeneous societies are polarized with respect to racial attitudes, it is necessary to discuss racial constraints in relation to minority status. Therefore, the reader should consider the following section as a continuation of the discussion of the racial context.

Minority/Majority Status

The term *minority* has embedded in its meaning both prejudice and discrimination (Mayers, 1984). Rodriguez, (1987, p. 130) defines discrimination as "those acts or institutional procedures that help create or perpetuate sets of advantages or privileges for the majority group, and exclusion or deprivation for the minority group." Minority status is also a political definition, because white groups are a numerical minority when we take a global perspective.

We believe that therapists need to consider both the differences and the similarities that they have with families across all sociocultural contexts. Hardy (1989) shares this belief and says that when we focus on the differences between minority and nonminority families, we tend to perpetuate an either/or attitude. The most appropriate way to look at this question, Hardy says, is to ask how minority and nonminority families are different *and* similar.

Minority status is related not only to the racial sociocultural context but also to economics, education, gender, and age. The figures for poverty, education, and minorities are consistent. There are more poor dark women and men than poor white women and men. Minority children are twice as likely to die in infancy, as compared with nonminority children. Minority children are twice as often seen as having neurological impairment, retardation, and conduct disorders, and 40 percent of all minority children do not graduate from high school (Kozol, 1990).

Therapists who work with minority families must provide opportunities to discuss racial oppression, if it is experienced by the family, and must help family members in their struggle against racism. They also must provide a context in which the family can explore its own racial definition (particularly a biracial or multiracial family). Therapists who are from the majority group must constantly remind themselves not to impose their majority-constructed perspective on families. The following questions suggest ways for therapists to assess the relevance and salience of the racial and minority/majority sociocultural contexts (the two sets of questions are listed together).

Race

- What is the fit between the family and the therapist regarding race?
- Is any member of the family experiencing racial oppression?

- If so, how can the therapist empower him or her in the struggle against oppression?
- How do the members of the family describe and understand their racial identity?
- Are some members of the family valued or devalued because of their relative darkness or lightness?
- Is the family biracial? multiracial? If so, do members acknowledge all their racial identities?
- What is the family's experience with multiracial groups?
- What is the therapist's experience with multiracial groups?
- Can the therapist openly acknowledge racial differences while validating all racial groups?

Minority/Majority Status

- What is the family's world-view on minority/majority status?
- How do members translate this world-view into action? Do they have friends from diverse racial and/or ethnic backgrounds?
- If the family is minority, do members experience racism and/or ethnocentricism?
- If the family is majority, do members have a sense of social consciousness and responsibility regarding their majority status?
- Is the therapist minority or majority? What meaning does he or she attribute to being majority? minority?
- What meaning do the members of the family attribute to their being minority? majority?
- What meaning do the members of the family attribute to the therapist's race?
- How much therapeutic maneuverability does the therapist experience regarding minority/majority status?

Regional Background

There is wide variation within cultures across geographical regions, rural versus urban settings, and climate. These differences are especially visible in regional orientations to time and in the accepted space that is tolerated or desired in relationships. People from rural environments, for example, organize their time very differently from those from urban settings. In warm climates, people have adapted by developing a slower pace than what is found in cold climates. Cities differ from suburbs, and both cities and suburbs differ from inner-city neighborhoods.

The threshold for proximity/distance also varies across geographical regions. For example, New York has been described as a city of disconnected individuals, whereas people in Los Angeles tend to be physically closer (hugging, kissing, and showing more affection). Of course, the Hollywood culture influences these attitudes; nevertheless, in other California cities, as contrasted with New York, there also seems to be a more proximal way of relating between people.

Rural/urban differences can also influence people's values in important ways. For example, a rural town in Illinois is likely to have more commonalities with a small town in Indiana, in Iowa, or even in the East, the South, or the West than with the city of Chicago. At the same time, while commonalities do exist between rural and urban areas, there are also variations that have to do with specific historical and political events that have taken place in particular regions.

Families love to talk about the characteristics of their native regions, warmly referring to their hometowns and describing a favorite lake, mountain, river, ocean, desert, or plain. These memories offer many opportunities for the therapist to connect with the family by sharing hometown stories and regional metaphors. There are also invaluable possibilities for therapeutic planning, such as transitional rituals that incorporate the various meanings that the family attributes to its hometown.

For example, a Cambodian single man was extremely depressed soon after he arrived in Chicago. He spoke English with great difficulty and was isolated from other Cambodians. When interviewed, he expressed his loss by talking about how much he missed the mountains back home. The therapist had also originally come from a mountainous region and could share the meaning of his loss. In addition to connecting him with an agency that had support groups for recent immigrants, the therapist planned some rituals that could transfer the meaning that mountains had for him to Lake Michigan. In collaboration with the therapist, the man made several visits to Lake Michigan and wondered about the differences and similarities between lakes and mountains. Over time, he became a discriminating observer of the many colors and shapes of the lake, contrasting them with those of mountains. In this symbolic way, he began the process of transferring his attachment from Cambodia to Chicago. The following questions suggest some ways for therapists to assess the relevance and salience of this sociocultural context.

Regional Background

- What is the fit between the family and the therapist regarding this sociocultural context?
- Have any members of the family moved from one region of the country to another?
- If so, have they reestablished their networks of family? friends? contact with services?
- Do any members of the family identify themselves as from the North? South? East? West?
- What meaning do they attribute to the different regions of the United States?
- Are the members of the family from an urban, rural, or suburban area?
- Is the current context very similar or dissimilar to their hometown?
- Have they experienced loss regarding their hometown?
- Are the members of the family from the same regional background?
- If not, do they value or devalue one another's backgrounds?
- Have members of the family been able to share this loss with other members of the family? with the therapist?
- Has the therapist experienced changes in regional background or in size or type of hometown?
- How much maneuverability does the therapist experience within this sociocultural context?

Because one's rural or urban background is rarely seen as a powerful organizer of one's beliefs and practices, we include the following case example, in which a couple is caught in a conflictual cycle attributed to their differences in regional background:

> Ted and Sylvia came to therapy because they were planning to get married and found themselves fighting about many things. "We don't have similar values. We don't agree about anything that is meaningful," Sylvia explained.
>
> Ted was thirty-eight years old and Sylvia was thirty-five. She was particularly worried because she sensed her biological clock ticking away, and this increased her motivation to change her relationship with Ted. In the first session, she said, "I won't have a family with Ted if we are going to disagree about such basic issues."
>
> As they began talking about their specific disagreements, they said that each of them experienced the other as very different. Sylvia had grown up in Chicago, and Ted had been brought up on a farm near Grand Rapids, Michigan.
>
> Ted had few childhood memories of visits with friends. There were neighbors and social events, but usually people stayed to themselves. They remained in their own houses, working on their farms and minding their own business. Ted recalled that his family usually spent time together around meals, talking about everyday events but rarely discussing family relationships. Sylvia's family spent many hours together. She had a large extended family. Relatives would visit frequently, help the family with child care, and allow the parents and children to spend time enjoying each other and discussing their relationships.
>
> Ted's memories of family life seemed to center on his relationship with his father, who had died when Ted was twelve and had left him a legacy of hard work. He had not wanted Ted to be a farmer; he had expected him to go to college, do well, go to the city, and make money, and this was exactly what Ted had

been doing. After Ted's father's death, the family sold the farm but remained in the vicinity.

Sylvia's family had also had a strong achievement orientation. Her parents had expected Sylvia to go to college, but they also talked about enjoying leisure time with each other.

These differences between Ted and Sylvia were played out in the way they organized and used their time. Sylvia wanted to have friends, visit, and go out. Ted wanted to come home and work on the house or on office projects. At home, Ted preferred to be quiet, but Sylvia loved to talk about everything, particularly about family stories, and to make plans to go on vacations and visit friends.

The couple's conflict had escalated to such a point that it had become difficult for them to visit their prospective in-laws. Sylvia hated to visit Ted's mother because, according to her, Ted's mother was not talkative, was rather simple, and did not dress well. Ted was uncomfortable visiting Syvlia's parents because they were too effusive, talkative, and meddlesome.

Although this couple shared many sociocultural contexts (generational/historical sequences, age, education, economics), they seemed to focus initially on their respective backgrounds as the main problem in their relationship. These differences constrained their perceptions of each other. As soon as the meanings they attributed to their upbringing began to accommodate other sociocultural contexts, a more balanced view of each other became possible.

Interrelatedness of
Sociocultural Contexts: Cultural Fit

It is undoubtedly more difficult, in all societies, to be a poor, dark, rural, uneducated older Catholic female and member of a minority or ethnic group than it is to be a rich, white, urban, educated younger man and member of the dominant Anglo-Saxon Protestant majority. *Goodness of fit* is congruence of sociocultural background between the minority and the majority family, between the immigrant and the nonimmigrant family, and between the family and the therapist. Families that share membership in the majority group will experience a better fit and are likely to experience less conflict in interactions with members of the host society. Families without education, by contrast, who are poor and of a different race (the majority of new immigrants to the United States) typically experience lack of fit. This is mediated by the port-of-entry community. Frequently, immigrants who experience lack of fit with the larger society find communities that resemble the ones they came from and that allow them to experience a better fit.

For immigrants, level of acculturation, economics, and education are also interelated. Middle-class immigrants will have a better fit with mainstream society and will tend, therefore, to experience less acculturative stress (Berry, Kalin, and Taylor, 1977). The more formal education immigrants have, and the more they know about American mainstream norms, institutions, and values, the more likely they are to find better jobs. When they do, they feel better about having immigrated and are more receptive to acculturation.

The interrelatedness of the various sociocultural contexts may not be visible to a therapist who is first seeing a family but it will appear in a later phase of therapy. For example, in Ted and Sylvia's case, the religious beliefs of their families (Jewish and Catholic) did not seem to be constraining them when they entered therapy. They both were believers, but neither attended church or temple services regularly. It was clear, however, that as they prepared to raise a family, the religious context might attain more saliency for them and so had to become part of the therapeutic planning.

There is also interelatedness between the sociocultural contexts of the family and the therapist. Similarities facilitate connectedness between them and provide a sense of sharing common experiences. At the same time, however, similarities may be entrapping, if the therapist feels too similar to the family. Differences will serve to expand the family's and the therapist's views. When differences are not viewed as enriching, however, they may trigger mutual stereotyping between the family and the therapist, as well as lack of collaboration. The following questions suggest ways for therapists to assess the relevance and salience of the family's fit with their own.

Fit

- What is the goodness of fit of each member of the family with mainstream society? with the therapist?
- What are the costs for each member of fitting? of not fitting?
- How similar or dissimilar are where the family came from and where the family lives now?
- How similar or dissimilar was the family's organization in the country of origin? extended family? kin?
- Did the family have a traditional role structure?
- Does the family's current community support the family's beliefs?
- Did the family experience upward or downward mobility recently?
- Is the family's education similar or dissimilar to that of the community?
- Is the family experiencing pressure to acculturate (to become American)?
- Are family members pressured into maintaining contact with their own ethnic group?
- Is there an opportunity in the community to maintain ethnic and racial identity?
- Are there role models in the family's network who support bi-culturality and/or racial or ethnic affiliation?
- Did family members have a choice in selecting their community?

Assessing Opportunities and Constraints

Each of the preceding discussions of sociocultural contexts serves to delineate the beliefs and practices that families and therapists share. Each context provides opportunities for expansion but also constrains the meanings that we attribute to experiences. Whatever road we take prevents us from taking other roads, at least for the present. Over time, there will be many opportunities to expand, revise, and redefine beliefs and practices.

The point at which families seek therapy is also inherently constraining. For some time before entering therapy, families have been attempting to expand their views and change their behaviors but have found themselves caught up in behavioral sequences and in cycles of hopelessness, unable to find alternative solutions to their problems. Minuchin and Fishman (1981) have aptly described this as underutilization of resources. The narrowing of options that families in pain experience not only has an impact on how they perceive their own resources but also affects their perceptions about the opportunities that each sociocultural context offers them. For example, poor families may tend to focus excessively on their poverty, ethnic families may go back to outdated ethnic beliefs, religious families may tend to be more traditional in interpreting their religiosity and so on.

Montalvo and Gutierrez (1983) have also described the tendency for families in conflict to focus on their ethnic constraints, as a "parody of ethnic blueprints." They explain this tendency as a use of "cultural masks." Their suggestion to therapists is to adopt a flexible view of ethnic groups, rather than merely develop specific sensitivities to any given sociocultural context.

We suggest that therapists focus on what the family perceives as constraining, in order to validate its experience, as well as on unexplored opportunities within the family's various sociocultural contexts. Individuals and families are seldom totally absorbed by the beliefs of one sociocultural context, to the exclusion of all others. The potential for expanding beliefs, for both the family and the therapist, lies in participation in all contexts.

Therapeutic Guidelines

It is difficult to translate the multicultural metaframework into therapeutic guidelines, because we do not want to construe them as simple "steps" in the therapeutic process. Given the complexity of the task, we believe that it is best to raise questions with the family that will help in evaluating the opportunities and constraints of each sociocultural context. To this end, we find it useful to ask ourselves the following questions: What are the sociocultural contexts of this family? What are our own? Where do they differ? How are they the same? What are the generational/historical themes of the family and the therapist? How can we elicit family members' cooperation in the examination and expansion of their beliefs? How can we examine and expand our own beliefs? The following guidelines address these questions.

Scanning the Sociocultural Contexts of the Family

By systematically scanning the multicultural contexts of the family, the therapist can think multiculturally, utilize the multicultural matrix for assessment (hypothesizing), and plan interventions with the family that consider its complex and evolving circumstances. (See all the lists of questions previously presented in this chapter.)

Examining the Sociocultural Contexts of the Therapist

It has been common to describe therapists as not having specific cultural backgrounds. Most therapists, however, belong to mainstream society by virtue of their education and training. Therefore, they have all the constraints and opportunities of middle-class, educated groups. The literature on cultural issues makes it appear that only ethnic and racial minorities have cultural backgrounds, but therapists have the same sociocultural contexts as families do, and some of these contexts overlap with those of the family. When they do, there is connection at the level of experience, which increases proximity. When they differ, opportunities arise for mutual expansion of views.

Expanding Our Own Cultural Views

Because we conceptualize therapy as an opportunity to expand the family's and the therapist's views, it is important to enter the therapeutic domain with an open, fluid view of all sociocultural contexts. Therapists who view constraints and opportunities as recursive descriptors of a system will enter the therapeutic context with curiosity, rather than with preconceptions that limit therapeutic maneuverability. Curiosity about the family's sociocultural experiences, their descriptions (the language they use), and their explanations (their theories) is the best tool therapists have for working with families from various sociocultural backgrounds. Curiosity translates into validation of everyone's point of view (Cecchin, 1987). Therapists must also systematically examine their own presuppositions about cultural beliefs. The following questions suggest ways for therapists to examine their own beliefs.

Beliefs	*Questions*
Diversity	How do we view the increasingly diverse population of the United States?
	Is our culture enriched by the variety of ethnic and racial groups that have recently come to this nation?
	How can we validate diversity?
	Do we explore commonalities in sociocultural background with families?
	Do we believe that contact with diverse families enriches us?
	Do we believe that our views also need expanding?
Balance	What is the impact of our practice?
	Are our interventions detrimental to the members of the family?
	Are we condoning racism? sexism? classism? ethnocentrism?
Constraints/ Opportunities	Do we consider the constraints as well as the opportunities in each sociocultural context?
	Do we believe that all sociocultural contexts offer opportunities for change as well as constraints?
Leadership	Are we utilizing our leadership in a collaborative manner?
	Do we explain our personal beliefs?
	Do we view therapy as a political context, where mutual influence is not only possible but also necessary?
	Are we accountable to the family for our own beliefs?

As we faced the task of explaining the multicultural perspective, we struggled with the impossibility of escaping the "tyranny of language" (Selvini-Palazzoli, Cecchin, Prata, and Boscolo, 1978). Language is basically sequential and, consequently, linear. Fortunately, thinking processes are of a different nature. They are not necessarily sequential, particularly when we allow them to flow and follow their own stream of consciousness. Therapists experience this fluidity; they have been thinking on their feet in a fluid way for many therapeutic hours.

Perhaps the best way to conclude this chapter is to leave the reader with an analogical image to express the complexity of the multicultural perspective. The image that comes to mind is a hologram, which shows all the levels of a system's embeddedness, plus their interaction. A holographic image represents more than the sum of its parts, but each holon contains both the whole and the part (although not at the same level of resolution). The image even shows a characteristic "flicker" (fluidity) between figure and ground, which aptly reflects the changing characteristics of living systems.

EIGHT

Reweaving Feminism and Systems: The Gender Metaframework

Over the past twelve years, the feminist perspective on family therapy has raised questions about the legitimacy of our theories, concepts, and techniques. By challenging our presuppositions, it has offered to the theory and practice of family therapy an alternative perspective that more accurately reflects the sociopolitical dilemmas that families face.

We have learned from the feminist critique of family therapy that we must change our view of the family as a benevolent unit of socialization. We cannot believe that every individual in the family has the same options, the same opportunities, and the same influence. We cannot view therapy as apolitical or see the therapist as neutral. We must not remain silent when presented with an unbalanced relationship between men and women or wait until the right opportunity arises to challenge this value or organization. We must think of ourselves as intervening within and beyond the family sphere. We cannot forget the sociopolitical inequalities that make women more financially and emotionally dependent than men. Finally, we cannot utilize the familiar paths for change.

Is the gender metaframework proposed in this book synonymous with the feminist perspective? Although we agree with many of the ideas that the feminist perspective has brought forth, we believe that the field of family therapy has reached the stage where it can integrate the systems view and the feminist perspective

237

without trivializing, subsuming, or corrupting either ideology for the sake of the other.

A brief review of both the organismic, systems view and the feminist perspective reveals internal consistency along several pivotal concepts. For example, both conceptualize the world in terms of interrelatedness, holism, pattern, and organization. Although some systems concepts have suffered from narrow interpretation by purists, we need not throw the baby out with the bath water and start again from scratch. The feminist perspective adds a neglected ideology to the organismic, systems view.

The purpose of this chapter is threefold. First, we will review briefly the impact of feminism on our modern culture by focusing on feminist ideology and its potential for cultural transformation. Second, we will examine the feminist critique of the family therapy field, as well as its contribution to the development of gender-sensitive approaches to family therapy. Third, we will discuss our own gender metaframework, which derives from the feminist perspective, from systems theory, and from the previously discussed metaframeworks.

The Impact of Feminism on Modern Society

Historically, feminists have played a part in the weaving of the tapestry of Western Culture, but until now they have not had sufficient influence to change all levels of society. Capra (1982), perhaps optimistically, foresaw our current historical period as being at the threshold of a cultural transformation. He attributed this ideological shift to three global transitions: the decline of patriarchy, the decline of the fossil-fuel age, and the advent of systems theory. Whether or not patriarchy will imminently and inevitably decline remains an open question; it is generally agreed, however, that it has only slowly declined (over three thousand years).

Eisler (1987) also views the current historical period as one of opportunity for cultural transformation. In her excellent analysis of feminism and its historical impact, she describes the different periods when our society oscillated between what she metaphorically refers to as the "chalice" and the "blade." The chalice symbolizes periods when society moves toward cooperative values (partnership societies). The blade symbolizes periods of competition, when society moves toward domination. As Capra does, Eisler views the current ideological shift as a move toward the harmonious integration of female and male characteristics, or yin and yang. Eisler, referring to this harmonious interaction between female and male characteristics, uses the word *gylany* (taken from the Greek words *gyne*, woman, and *andros*, man) in order to distinguish it from andocracy, which she views as characterized by historical periods in which domination and technology have prevailed. Her historical overview raises some compelling questions about partnership societies, their role throughout civilization, and the potential for this type of society to reemerge.

On the pessimistic side, there are other voices warning us that we are running out of time, and that unless we adopt a more ecological ideology with respect to our planet, our survival as a species is questionable (Ehrlich and Ehrlich, 1990; Rifkin, 1989; Manes, 1990). For a cultural transformation of the type hypothesized by Capra (1982) and Eisler (1987), a significant change in patriarchal roles, rules, and expectations must take place. Despite all the indications that many groups of women and men are liberating themselves from constraining roles and expectations, the fact is that most beliefs held by the majority (whether silent or verbal) are still predominantly in support of the patriarchal family. Our collective optimistic parts, however, agree with Capra (1982) and Eisler (1987) and view the coming decade as a time of opportunity, with many ideologies converging, which may have the potential for a cultural transformation toward unprecedented growth in our society.

The Feminist Perspective and Family Therapy

During the 1950s in this country, the historical/generational roles sanctioned for middle-class society were typically traditional. Men and women took on complementary roles: men were trained to be breadwinners; women, homemakers. In this historical context, the originators of the field of family therapy predictably developed theories, concepts, and techniques that reflected conventional sociopolitical views on the family.

A brief examination of that decade reveals that the "great

originals" (Hoffman, 1981), family therapy's pioneers, were mostly
men who accepted their generation's predominant values. Virginia
Satir, unquestionably another of the "great originals" and a force
in her own right, was a controversial figure. The only woman
among men, and a social worker among psychiatrists, she excelled
because of her great clinical strengths and her charisma. Her theoretical contributions have been criticized, however, because her
model has not had the same following as others in the United States
and has not generated as many publications as the structural, strategic, MRI, and Milan models have (Luepnitz, 1988). This is interesting, when we consider that Satir's ideas are easily teachable, and
that her therapeutic model has had worldwide impact—unquestionably more than any of the other models have. It is possible to
assume that her model is not sufficiently valued because it is relational, and that the lack of recognition given to her role in the field
of family therapy is isomorphic of the scant recognition given to
women's roles in society.

     It is ironic that the field of family therapy, having emerged
as an alternative to traditional psychotherapeutic theories and practices, ended up supporting traditional social beliefs about families.
It is also ironic that a movement that began by legitimizing the
external context, and by taking a strong position against reductionism, ended up with a reductionistic definition of external context
(as the domain of family interactions only), ignoring the sociocultural contexts in which the family is embedded.

The Feminist Critique of the Family Therapy Field

It is amazing that it took so long for the feminist perspective to
emerge in the field of family therapy. The first paper that addressed
feminism and family therapy appeared in the 1970s (Humphrey,
1975) and addressed the changing role of women, as well as the
implications that women's changing roles had for treatment. That
paper went basically unreported and unexamined, and so it has had
no visible impact on the field. When Hare-Mustin's historical article on feminism appeared (1978), it opened up a heated dialogue,
which at times threatened to split the entire field. The feminist
critique undoubtedly has created opportunities to examine the con-

straints of our theoretical presuppositions and their applications. Several important books have contributed recently to the examination of the feminist perspective in family therapy (Braverman, 1988; Goodrich, Rampage, Ellman, and Halstead, 1988; Luepnitz, 1988; McGoldrick, Anderson, and Walsh, 1989; Walters, Carter, Papp, and Silverstein, 1988). For a comprehensive view of the feminist perspective on family therapy, we refer you to these sources.

The Challenge to Theoretical Concepts

What Is a Family?

Hare-Mustin's article (1978) challenged not only the theories of family therapy but the very concept of the family itself. She showed how families systematically use women as objects of gratification, at the expense of women's own development. The notion that families are healthier for men than for women has received additional attention from Goldner (1985), Luepnitz (1988), and Walters, Carter, Papp, and Silverstein (1988).

Luepnitz (1988) raises pertinent questions about how uncritically clinicians have accepted research on women in families. She utilizes the Timberlawn study (Lewis, Beavers, Gossett, and Phillips, 1976) as an example of this type of androcentric research. The Timberlawn study found that, within the "normal" family population, women reported significantly more symptoms and dissatisfactions than other family members did. That study's interpretation of this finding, however, was that the families in that population were doing *well*. Clearly, this biased interpretation disregarded the fact that women were reporting more symptoms and dissatisfactions.

Eichler (1988) has identified four problems that research like the Timberlawn study is likely to have: androcentricity, overgeneralization, gender insensitivity, and double standards. The Timberlawn study exhibited three of these problems (androcentricity, gender insensitivity, and double standards). It is clear that a change in the androcentric beliefs of scientists must occur before we can embark on a balanced study of women and of the relationships between the sexes.

Restricting one's focus to the family as the primary level of observation is reductionist. Families derive their beliefs through their embeddedness in a variety of sociocultural contexts, and they contribute to the expansion of such beliefs in their communities and in society. For example, when men abuse their wives and children, they behave in accordance with two beliefs: that to be the "head of the household," a man must put women and children in their place, and that any man should be given respect (whether he deserves it or not). Such beliefs have helped minimize the significance of wife battering and child abuse.

The elevation of the family's needs above the individual's (Taggart, 1985; Luepnitz, 1988; Hare-Mustin, 1978) stems from functionalism (Parsons and Bales, 1955), a sociological theory that considers the individual's needs in relation to the family's, just as the family's needs are considered in relation to the community's and society's. Luepnitz (1988) and Goldner (1988) have criticized functionalism because it views the family through an organismic metaphor, unnecessarily restricting the therapist's focus and predisposing the therapist to consider the part as largely in service to the whole. As a result, family therapy minimizes the individual's experience, and particularly women's experience. The systems notion of interdependence between the family and the individual should not keep us from examining women's needs, experience, and history.

Ignoring History

Because the field has ignored history, family therapy has not been able to consider the intergenerational patterns within the family that maintain its patriarchal organization. At the same time, it has also ignored those historical/generational sequences (see Chapter Seven) that reflect, for each generation, predominant themes concerning women's and men's roles and expectations. This failure to focus on history has also prevented examination of the sociocultural presuppositions from which therapists approach gender.

Circular Causality

James and MacIntyre (1983) and Taggart (1985) have raised a relevant question about the concept of circularity: Has the systems view retarded gender equality in family therapy? We believe that the systems view, and certain purists' conceptions of circular causality, have unquestionably retarded the development of holistic, historical views, such as the feminist perspective. Goldner (1988) has shown how ludicrous it is to associate circularity with equality. She explains that nobody would question whether the relationship between master and slave is interdependent, but that it takes a big leap in logic to assume that such interdependence means equal participation in the maintenance of a master-slave relationship. What systems purists have failed to consider is that the victimizer and the victim do not have the same options (influence) for changing the relationship (Taggart, 1985).

Therapy as Political

The advent of cybernetics into the field made it possible to examine the observer as a participant in the therapeutic system (Keeney, 1983). This focus on the observer as a coparticipant in the creation of observable phenomena has raised the question of whether family therapists can address political issues in the therapeutic context. The Women's Project in Family Therapy (Walters, Carter, Papp, and Silverstein, 1988) has been at the vanguard in challenging the notion that therapy is apolitical. These women have taken a clear position, using the language of the 1960s to emphasize that "taking no action is taking action." When therapists do not challenge the views of the family, they are in collusion with any values that support established views.

The Women's Project's influence on family therapy, although now recognized as pioneering, suffered at times from being labeled political. In a recent book, these clinicians have described how their struggle found a sympathetic echo in the many grassroots groups that were also examining their own presuppositions and practices. Among many other contributions, their definition of the feminist perspective in family therapy stands out: a humanistic world-view "concerned with the trade-offs that both women and men experience when limiting their roles, and accepting narrow rules and expectations" (Walters, Carter, Papp, and Silverstein, 1988).

The political impact of therapists' values has been contested, but the question has not been laid to rest. Trainees who are beginning to struggle with the dilemma of balancing the systems view and the feminist perspective frequently ask, "Do we have the right to impose our own values on the families we treat?" This question presumes that therapists somehow do keep their own world-views in check when they enter the therapeutic arena, and that therapy itself is value-free. In our opinion, therapists are continually attempting to influence families, and they do so from their own perspective. The more relevant question is "How do we influence families? Do we do so irrespective of their beliefs, language, and behavior, or do we develop therapeutic themes that take into consideration both their perspectives and ours?"

Position of Neutrality

The term *neutrality*, proposed by the Milan group (Selvini-Palazzoli, Cecchin, Prata, and Boscolo, 1980), assumes that therapists need to remain nonaligned. The concept of neutrality in family therapy implies value-free therapy. James and MacKinnon (1986) have challenged the notion of value-free therapy. One "cannot not have values," just as one "cannot not communicate" (Watzlawick, Beavin, and Jackson, 1967). Therapists may be unaware, however, of how their values affect their theories and their actions in therapy. For example, a therapist who attempts to maintain neutrality toward sexist behavior implicitly condones sexism. More recently, Cecchin (1987) has redefined the term *neutrality* as *curiosity*, a more apt term if we wish to convey the intention of maintaining an open mind about the family's and our own presuppositions. Nevertheless, the Milan group itself needs to show more "curiosity" about the lack of balance between the sexes in families. Other concepts that become suspect when examined from a feminist perspective are power, hierarchy, and enmeshment.

Power

The Batesonian notion that power is an illusion has been the focus of many controversies. The view of power as an illusion ignores women's experience in a society where men unquestionably have more influence than women do in all sociopolitical areas. The presupposition that belief in power is a form of "chopping the ecology" (Bateson, 1972) is the intellectual construct of a white, middle-class man who can easily afford this way of thinking. Bateson's notions reflect the history of his privileged life; the everyday lives of many women are hardly congruent with his experience.

When controversies have arisen, the term *linear thinking* has been used in the field to indicate what is unacceptable. It is no accident that this concept also comes from Bateson, an anthropologist who abhorred intervening in any system. In actuality, however, any intervention is a linear punctuation of the family's complex behavioral repertoire, regardless of whether the feminist perspective informs it.

Hierarchy

At its worst, this controversial concept has been defined so as to help social systems abuse power and oppress those considered to be of lesser rank. At its best, it has reflected an organizational arrangement that functions to facilitate the performance of tasks and the clarification of roles. The first kind of definition assumes that some persons have the right, by virtue of sex, race, ethnicity, or socioeconomic background, to more influence in society. This outdated, unethical, and unhelpful definition of hierarchy presupposes the existence of an efficient way to organize the world. But influence ought to be earned by virtue of knowledge and experience and their effective application. We question the abuse of influence, as well as the irrational idea that influence is a given. We prefer the term *leadership* (see Chapter Four). This term reflects different degrees of influence, and it is useful way of conceptualizing the pragmatics of everyday life. For example, there is no question that parents, on the basis of their experience and knowledge, ought to have more influence on their children than therapists do. We also believe that therapists, by virtue of their training, experience, and social mandate, ought to have more influence in the therapeutic context than families do. We see collaboration as the best way to exercise leadership.

Enmeshment

This concept—frequently used, for convenience' sake, as the pre-dominant explanation of the organizational problems of women in families—is conceptually and politically archaic. It is true that mothers frequently assume a central role in their families. That role has been sanctioned for many generations, and throughout many societies, by patriarchal beliefs, which have given women few alternative roles. Some related techniques of family therapy, such as unbalancing and reframing, have also been questioned.

Unbalancing

Clinicians have used structural family therapy's unbalancing technique excessively, to decentralize women from their mothering role and minimize the peripherality of fathers (James and MacKinnon, 1986). (In unbalancing, the therapist purposely forms a temporary coalition with one member of the family and opposes another.) James and MacKinnon have also questioned the uncritical and exclusive tendency of structural therapists to unbalance by siding with men because women can be depended on to remain in treatment. This technique not only is unfair to women but also embodies a belief that men should be treated with kid gloves. It implies a male fragility that men do not necessarily suffer from.

   As therapists and trainers, we have tended to depend on women to use their influence with their families. It is quite true that many women have great influence in the family, influence that they have earned with time and their own labor. It is also true that women's influence is often the type that is not publicly acknowledged: the sort of underground influence typically found among oppressed groups, which should not be confused with the sort of influence that is valued by society and openly acknowledged in the family.

The Not-So-Gentle Art of Reframing

One hallmark of the strategic model has been criticized as one of the most political techniques in the field of family therapy, because it is frequently associated with therapists who adopt a position of power. There is no question that reframing can be a useful way for attempting to influence the meaning that families construct about themselves, their problems, and the process of therapy. For example, one can point out that the glass is half full instead of half empty. This is a useful reframing. It challenges the family's pessimism, has the potential to instill hope, motivates the family to change, and presents the opportunity for all members to experience themselves as more in charge of their own solutions and destinies. It is important not to use reframing indiscriminately, however. Some reframing techniques end up as caricatures of the family or of some family members. At times, they have been used to connote a father's peripherality positively, by framing his failure to spend time with his children as his preoccupation with the outside world. This reframing excuses him from the fathering role and perpetuates the mother's centrality. Other forms of reframing amount to giving disinformation. For example, a therapist may attempt to alter the meaning that a family gives to its experience by changing the family's explanation in ways that do not validate the experience, the description, or the explanation that the family provides.

In summary, the feminist critique of family therapy has provided significant opportunities to the field. The feminist critique has opened a healthy dialogue among theoreticians, clinicians, and researchers. This dialogue is still in process, and its impact seems well accepted at the public level of discourse. At the private level, however, therapists continue to question the pragmatic consequences of adopting such a perspective.

The Gender Metaframework

The gender metaframework has been evolving for the past ten years. The first step in this evolution began with awareness of outdated systems principles and their impact on our theories and practice. Introduction of the gender metaframework into teaching and supervision was the second step in developing this approach. Teaching gender-sensitive ways to hypothesize about and plan with families in therapy has allowed us to explore the experiences of a varied group of trainees (from those who are gender-aware to those who have not thought about gender imbalances before training). This training context not only has enabled us to question our gender presuppositions but also has forced us to clarify related theoretical concepts and their implementation. There have been many suggestions made by those we teach, from whom we also learn.

The gender metaframework is always present and organizes the way we conceptualize the individual's internal struggle, the relational experiences of the family, and the sociocultural context in which family members live. The choice of one metaframework as a point of entry, or of one in combination with another, depends not only on the therapist's explanations (theories) but also on the family's descriptions and explanations. For example, some family members say, "A side of me feels unjustly treated, while another side of me feels hurt" (internal process). Others talk about how certain problems tend to occur periodically in the family (sequences). Some families talk openly about how some beliefs are more important than others (culture). Others describe their experiences in terms of losing control of the children (organization) and/or in terms of seeing the children as immature or as too responsible (development).

In our discussion of the gender metaframework, we will describe our presuppositions and connect them to a model both for assessing the family's position along gender evolution and for planning therapeutic objectives and the treatment of gender imbalance. (The model is illustrated by two case examples.) Finally, we will discuss the therapist's beliefs and position with respect to gender balance.

Presuppositions

Balance. In keeping with the preceding discussion, we believe that societies, families, and individuals need to attain balance and harmony in order to grow. We view patriarchal beliefs as oppressive for some members of the family and therefore as too costly for the growth of an individual, a family, and society. Families attain balance through collaboration. For a family to experience balance, the mother and the father need equal opportunities to influence family decisions, share family responsibilities, and have access to familial and social resources.

Ecofeminism. This holistic concept derives from the ideal of a balanced and harmonious relationship among humans, animals, plants, and the rest of the environment. At the social level, collaboration and global interdependence are emphasized. Ecofeminism challenges not only sexism but also other oppressive ideologies in our society, such as racism, classism, and ethnocentrism. Ecofeminism is ideologically consonant with the organismic systems view. It is also perspectivistic, equally concerned with every level of the organism's integrity. Collaboration between the sexes, as well as between the individual and the larger sociocultural context, is stressed. By adopting an ecofeminist perspective, we can more aptly organize our hypothesizing, planning, and treatment with families.

Positions in the Evolution of Gender Balance

Families enter treatment at different points in their evolution, and with different levels of gender balance. For example, each parent/ spouse is experiencing the meaning of gender differently from the way she or he might have a decade ago. Gender evolution in our society has succeeded in recontextualizing the interrelated levels of meaning that we have about gender. Women experience more dissatisfaction with narrow gender roles and expectations. Men are increasingly recognizing trade-offs of being breadwinners at the expense of their caregiver roles and are attempting to expand their own repertoire of gender roles. We have observed five transitional positions along this cultural evolution, which can be described as *traditional, gender-aware, polarized, in transition,* and *balanced.* (See Table 8.1.)

Traditional. In this phase families tend to have a patriarchal organization that views men as primary breadwinners and women as caregivers. The decision-making process occurs along narrowly assigned parental roles (for example, relational and instrumental), and the children have roles and expectations that conform to parental beliefs replicating the gender-role complementarity of the parents. If women work, they still assume most of the household responsibilities. Most important, the types of work they do, and the income they derive from their jobs, are not considered as essential

Table 8.1. Positions in the Evolution of Gender Balance.

Gender Evolution Positions	Characteristics
Traditional	**Organizational** Complementary roles (women as caretakers, men as breadwinners). If women work, they still assume most of the home responsibilities. **Internal** Women may experience some oppressed and angry parts. Men may experience guilty parts. **External** Descriptions and explanations about problems are not given in terms of gender. Experience support from dominant norms in community and society.
Gender-aware	**Organizational** Questioning complementarity of roles. Beginning to experience gender roles as constraining. Fluctuation between struggle to amplify roles and resignation. **Internal** Women may experience angry parts. Men may fear loss of nurturance. **External** Beginning to question patriarchal roles and expectations in community and society. Still experience support from dominant norms in community and society.
Polarized	**Organizational** Openly challenging gender roles and expectations. Open conflict between spouses. Splits and coalitions with respect to gender. **Internal** Extreme angry parts in women (long lists of injuries); worried and fearful parts activated. In men, extreme defensive parts; guilty parts that fluctuate with worried and angry parts. **External** Gender oppression experienced in socialization of roles, but may be described in personal ways. Experience support from minority groups and are in conflict with dominant norms in community and society.
In transition	**Organizational** Toward mutuality and supporting flexible fa-

Table 8.1. Positions in the Evolution of Gender Balance, Cont'd.

Gender Evolution Positions	Characteristics
	milial roles and expectations. Moving toward egalitarian roles and mutual participation in decision making.
	Internal
	Angry and fearful parts less extreme. At times, old flare-ups occur. Parts more aware of temporary setbacks.
	External
	Less organized by narrow gender roles. More apt to challenge socialization of roles and expectations. Fluctuate between experiencing support from dominant norms in the community and experiencing conflict with dominant norms in the community and society.
Balanced	Organizational
	Egalitarian organization. Mutual participation in decision making. Vigilance about gender constraints.
	Internal
	Each spouse has attained more balance internally, allowing more collaboration between parts.
	External
	Likely to be politically active, attempting to change narrow social roles and expectations. Experiencing minority status when contrasted with dominant norms and expectations in society.

as the father/husband's job and income. The men tend to associate with male groups, as in an "old boys' network", and the women have primary relationships with "old girls' networks." Traditional families experience themselves as balanced through complementarity and do not describe any conflict between their gender roles and/or expectations. Externally, they view the feminist ideology as a misguided system of beliefs likely to bring dislocation to society.

Internally, members of this family may have some parts that are feeling oppressive or oppressed, guilty, worried, and/or angry.

These feelings translate into experiences of inequity that are neither described nor explained in terms of gender. The women in these families may report doing more chores than the men, being undervalued, and even being oppressed by men. The men may sometimes refer to parts of themselves that are guilty, worried, or experiencing loss of contact with their children, wives, and friends, but they justify their descriptions and explanations in terms of socially acceptable roles and expectations. In other words, social sanctions help to maintain the invisibility of pain related to gender roles.

A woman in the traditional position is likely to have parts that are angered by the imbalance but kept from her awareness by other parts, which may tell her that she must think only of others, or that she will be abandoned if she challenges things. A traditional man also has parts that may feel guilty about the inequity, as well as other parts that are unhappy with the lack of intimacy built in to gender-imbalanced relationships. These parts, however, are kept from his awareness by other parts, which feel entitled to hold on to traditional justifications for such imbalance and may fear abandonment by the wife as the man gets in touch with their anger.

Gender-Aware. These families are at varying stages in their awareness of gender inequity but are beginning to experience discomfort regarding traditional gender roles and expectations. The women in these families usually experience more discomfort than the men. They report feeling less validated within the family. They are in the process of questioning male-oriented views. They usually report being overutilized and undervalued. Although their experiences may be painful, they appear unsure about how to describe them. Their explanations, or the meanings they attribute to these experiences, tend to be ambiguous and at times contradictory. One moment, they justifying their beliefs as results of their socialization; the next moment, they attack these views as excessively constraining.

Gender-aware families may also include men who are questioning the social justification for their roles and expectations, more commonly among younger male members of the family. Internally, these men have parts that feel guilty and that also yearn for more intimacy between family and friends. At the same time, they may have parts that worry about loss of nurturance from their spouses.

Externally, they express confusion if gender roles and expectations change too rapidly, but they also fear the psychological and physical costs of rigid male proscriptions. The gender-aware position usually begins when the wife's angry parts gain a little more access to her awareness. In constant internal turmoil, her angry parts battle the alliance of parts that have been keeping her anger down. Her anger does not flow openly, and there is growing tension in the marriage.

Polarized. These families are experiencing open conflict over gender issues. Men and women alike find themselves frequently fighting about role definitions, blaming each other, and demanding changes in beliefs and actions. Their experiences are acutely painful, and each member is pulling in a different direction. There are many descriptions of experiences (usually extreme), but there seems to be no sense of how to resolve gender imbalance in the family. The meaning that family members attribute to these experiences is consonant with their behavioral descriptions. Externally, they may explain their experiences in terms of historical, political, and familial contexts, but their tendency is to do so in a blaming, accusatory way.

Internally, family members experience angry, critical, and unyielding parts. Because these parts are so extreme, it is difficult at first to access the vulnerable parts that experience worry and loss. Families become polarized around gender most often when the wife's angry parts (strengthened by a culture that increasingly challenges traditional gender roles) break through her fear or denial and take over. As her anger increases, the husband is likely to resort to the strategies that used to control her (buying her things, trying to intimidate her, threatening to separate, and so on). If these strategies do not work, he will become sullen and defensive, and both spouses will exist in a state of "cold war," with flashes of active combat between their negative, angry parts.

Externally, these families replicate the polarization in sex roles prevalent in our society, and spouses use social descriptions and explanations to justify their beliefs and oppose those of their partners. Polarized families may have members at all levels of cultural evolution: some traditional or gender-aware, all frequently drawn into the conflict and expected to form alliances or coalitions along gender beliefs.

In Transition. These families, although still in conflict, are hopeful about their ability to evolve toward gender balance. Their gender roles and expectations are in the process of expansion. Although there is a clear sense of transition in these families, they are still experimenting with new roles. The new roles are tried on for size, but the fit is still in question. There is an increasing sense of mutuality and sharing in the decision-making processes over a wide range of family tasks. Family members seem to be pulling in the same direction. There is validation of the roles that women and men have in the family. Although there is fluctuation between the old beliefs and the new, these families verbally explore the gains and losses they experience when roles change. Externally, these families are less likely to be organized by society's roles and more apt to challenge narrow gender definitions.

Internally, the spouses have been able to acknowledge some of the imbalances, and so their angry parts are less extreme and they are more comfortable with each other. While they may oscillate between old and new roles, they share an awareness of the previous imbalance and a commitment to improving it. Each part will debate how much and what kind of change is needed, and there may be flare-ups when parts find themselves in old patterns. Generally, however, they are less conflicted as they strive for more internal and external balance.

Balanced. This transition requires ongoing awareness of the subtle ways in which we fall prey to our gender conditioning. It also requires constant vigilance and willingness to negotiate relationships in a variety of ways. For example, it presupposes that families can develop mutuality (equal access to decision making) and collaboration at all levels of interaction, from the internal family system (IFS) to interactions between husband and wife, mother and son, mother and daughter, father and daughter, and father and son. Balance may also be attained in interactions with colleagues at work, in friendships, and in community activities.

In balanced couples, each spouse has achieved a better and

more stable internal balance, which permits more collaboration in the relationship. It may be that the wife's angry part has relinquished its domination but has not returned to internal exile. Instead, there has been a negotiation and reconciliation with the past and former oppressors. Similarly, the husband's parts that felt entitled to the imbalance have lost their dominant position and are reconciled to the need for balance. His parts that feared abandonment have also been reassured. Increasing gender balance brings increasing intimacy in negotiation of gender issues. Therefore, each spouse can keep the Self in the lead, to resolve issues quickly.

Externally, what is lacking during this transition is a sociocultural infrastructure to support this kind of evolution. A cultural transformation toward a partnership society would serve to nurture gender-balanced groups but has yet to occur. What seems clear, however, is that these transitions cannot continue to evolve without social changes, particularly because society is at the polarized stage. There are large segments of society in direct conflict with each other, mutually blaming each other for the dire social consequences of our time and accusing each other of having "bad attitudes." (An example of this polarization is the gap between the prochoice and antichoice factions in the controversy over abortion.) As for society's polarization, what about families in the process of transformation? Being a social pioneer entails opportunities, responsibilities, and costs, which may prove too disorganizing for some families to bear in unsupportive contexts.

Contexts That Influence Gender Evolution

Life-cycle changes prompt an examination of values and may result in taking a new position. There is considerable fluctuation of values throughout the different life-cycle transitions. Sometimes family members who have been becoming more gender-aware choose to return to a more traditional kind of organization when experiencing a life-cycle change. For example, a childless couple may have attained a balanced position regarding gender roles and expectations, but having a child throws everything up for grabs. The experience of sharing in the raising of a child may sound attractive to these couples, and the meanings they attribute to shared parenthood may seem balanced, but the lack of social support may lead

them to question the practicality of such an arrangement. As a
consequence of the lack of social support, women may decide to stay
home and assume the more traditional Eurocentric role of caretaker,
thereby postponing career objectives. These families experience a
loss in their sense of ideological evolution, which at times brings
them into therapy.

Marriage is also influential in changing values. As new
spouses accommodate to each other's beliefs, a change toward tra-
ditionality or toward transition may take place. Reaching middle
age may prompt some to recount their life stories and either move
toward gender awareness or nostalgically reenact more traditional
ways of thinking and behaving.

Other dimensions of culture also affect gender values. For
example, a family in the process of transformation and living in a
diversely populated city may move to a small town, where family
members find little support for their ideas and experiences, and this
lack of support may influence their beliefs. As they accommodate
to their new community, they may reconsider traditional beliefs and
find that they fit best in the current context.

Religious conversion may also prompt a reexamination of
traditional values, as may the upward or downward mobility of the
family. Upwardly mobile families may become more protective of
their economic status and may reexamine traditional beliefs from
the new vantage point, or their economic improvement may free
them to think differently about their values. Likewise, poor people
have little time to struggle with ideologies that have no direct bear-
ing on their survival, and so they examine values as they pertain to
the everyday experiences of meeting basic needs. Because there are
more poor women than poor men in our society, it is predictable
that women will experience polarization toward men and society.
Ethnicity also influences gender values. The sociocultural beliefs of
our ancestors persist through the generations. Ethnic themes are
more or less salient according to the degree of cultural transition
that the family experiences, as well as the family's ethnic identity.

Internal struggles influence gender values as well. Individuals who are experiencing changes in internal balance translate their
views into relationships with friends, spouses, and children. It is not
uncommon to see individuals who are in therapy, or who are in

the midst of life-cycle changes, questioning their level of gender awareness.

Planning

The overall objective of using the gender metaframework is to create an awareness in families of the gender-related constraints that everyone experiences. Gender imbalance has a serious impact on the family's everyday life and threatens its development, integrity, and viability as a social unit.

Planning about gender-sensitive issues with families starts at the beginning of treatment, when therapists begin sharing hypotheses with the family. In our experience, planning of treatment objectives is best when treatment is discussed openly with the family and evolves as the therapeutic process unfolds. To discuss the constraints of gender imbalance with a family, an experienced therapist needs to find ways of questioning the family's beliefs without being disrespectful. Like most other therapists who have thought seriously about gender issues, we accept the responsibility of raising these issues while keeping the family in treatment. This is not easy. It is helpful to view individuals and families as containing many parts and having many more options than they utilize. It is also helpful to view families as culturally evolving and adapting to their changing circumstances, and one changing circumstance is the evolution of values regarding gender.

We believe that introducing a discussion of the constraints of gender imbalance is not unlike discussing the family's perceptions of the problem, members' perceptions of one another, and the meaning of therapy. One of our objectives is to introduce complexity into the system, and the gender metaframework provides us with an opportunity to do so. Nevertheless, planning therapeutic objectives that address gender imbalance in families raises a question: Do the goals belong to the family or to the therapist? We believe that it is the therapist's responsibility to plan objectives that will help the family attain balance and harmony. Ultimately, however, if the therapist does not include the family as a partner in planning and fails to consider how well gender-sensitive goals fit the family, the family will let her or him know. Ideally, the therapist will be able to hear the family's feedback and readjust his or her expectations.

Specific goals vary with each family type, according to where the family is in the evolution of its awareness. Each transitional position in the evolutionary process presents different dilemmas and different opportunities.

With traditional families, the therapist's plan is to promote awareness of gender imbalance. During this transition, the therapist has opportunities to expand experiences and promote descriptions and explanations of gender inequality. Traditional families have members at different levels of evolution, and so the therapist must explore each member's position and promote dialogue among members of the family.

With gender-aware families, the therapist must discuss ways to amplify these experiences, raising questions about potential accommodation to or negotiation about change. During this transition, it is important to validate everyone's experience while expanding descriptions and explanations.

With polarized families, the therapeutic task is to decrease polarization while validating each member's experience. Within these families, there is considerable fluctuation between blaming and negotiating. The therapist must expect such fluctuation and, with the family, plan a context where family members can experience not only their polarization but also the possibilities for solutions.

With families in transition, whose members are striving to find a sense of balance and mutuality, the therapist must amplify questions before new descriptions and explanations can emerge. The therapist's role is to lead by following the family's initiative, in order to facilitate its move toward balanced relationships. Families in transition experience some degree of lack of fit with society. Consequently, the therapist must address the costs, to all members of the family, of being out of synchrony with the rest of society.

With balanced families, the therapeutic planning focuses on consolidating this balance and facilitating its transfer to the internal, interactional, and social areas of the family's life. These families also experience lack of fit with the rest of society. Many problems arise when families listen to a different drummer and are out of synchrony with their time. For families to have a good fit with their cultural context, they need the support of an evolving society.

Treatment

The treatment of gender imbalance consists of validating experiences and of expanding descriptions as well as explanations of female/male interaction. This process begins in the first session of treatment and is an ongoing concern. It is implemented through statements, questions, and directives. Statements are unobtrusive ways of presenting the therapist's beliefs, normalizing beliefs, and expanding descriptions in families, particularly when universal statements are made. Universal statements are well suited to planting the idea of the importance of balance and the consequences of gender imbalance in families. For example, simply saying, "It is painful when family members experience limitations" will open up discussion about the meaning of limitations and about how women and men experience them.

Questions actively reflect the therapist's concern about gender imbalances and are particularly helpful because they support the expectation that there is another view, equally valid and worth examining. We find that using circular questions (Selvini-Palazzoli, Cecchin, Prata, and Boscolo, 1978; Tomm, 1987b) is an excellent way to explore gender differences. Circular questions create a context in which family members can compare and contrast beliefs and think interactionally.

Directives are most useful as tools to seal changes, stop redundant sequences, and promote changes in action. Directives, although often viewed as supporting patriarchal and authoritarian positions, need not be authoritarian, but they are appropriate only when the therapist plans and assigns tasks in collaboration with the family. A collaborative therapist elicits the family's cooperation in setting up the task, as well as in ascertaining the best timing for the task. In addition, the therapist reads the family's feedback and openly discusses whether a task has been helpful and should be elaborated or has not been helpful. Statements and questions are most useful when we wish to increase awareness, expand meaning, or amplify options. Directives are most helpful when the family is ready to collaborate and try changes of action or meaning. All three modes of intervention increase therapeutic flexibility.

Making universal statements and then asking questions is useful with families at all transitional points but particularly appropriate for traditional and gender-aware families, because they are beginning the process of cultural evolution: "Parents worry about their children's potential. How do the two of you worry about your daughter's future?" "Parents are concerned about providing guidance to their children. How do you view your child's chances for developing responsibility in this family?" "Parents worry about their children's opportunities. Who has more opportunities in your family?" "Families encourage growth in their children. How do you do it with your daughters? your sons? each other?"

With traditional families, it is possible to be overt about our own beliefs and say, "I think you can both help each other and make joint decisions about your family." This statement can then be followed by a question: "What does each of you think about the way responsibilities and decisions are shared in your home?" Although this issue can be raised from the beginning, it need not be the immediate focus of continued discussion if family members' feedback clearly indicates that they do not wish to talk about sharing responsibilities or decisions at this time. Traditional families usually do not consider these issues important, or they consider them too fraught with conflict and do not wish to open the proverbial can of worms.

Because the therapist must validate the family's experiences, he or she must address the presenting complaint while simultaneously finding ways to expand the family's descriptions and explanations (beliefs) of how the problem developed. "Later, I would like us to consider the consequences to your family of your wife's being so fatigued by two jobs." "I hope you will let me discuss with both of you, later on, the consequences to your children's growth when your daughter is in charge of all the housework." Discussion of these questions can wait, but the therapist still has to raise them periodically, in order to plant ideas that increase the family's awareness of how gender imbalance can constrain everyday functioning. The family's feedback may indicate that the therapist should not continue pushing for gender awareness at that time, but the process of questioning beliefs has begun, and the therapist has clarified her or his position regarding sexist roles.

Therapists can use questions at all levels of transition. For example, with traditional and gender-aware families, the therapist can ask, "Who in the family is most worried about finances?" This information can be readily connected with power and influence: "Is this the same person who is most influential in this family?" At times, a more direct question is necessary: "Who pays the bills?" "Who decides what needs to be purchased for the family?"

Questions about gender awareness require answers from all the members of the family. We cannot assume that all family members have similar views on gender. Contrasting these differences begins a process of dialogue and provides a respectful context for discussing beliefs. Quite often, elicitation of this dialogue will itself increase the family's awareness of gender imbalance and begin the family's process of expansion regarding gender roles and expectations.

In traditional families, one of the parents (most likely the father) will often make a statement like "I alone decide what happens in my family." If the therapist is in the middle of working with the family about what to do about the son's school problems, it is difficult to respond to this statement in a way that would connect it with its impact on all the members of the family. It is possible, however, to say, "I hope you will let me come back to your statement later and examine the consequences for you and your family when you make decisions without their participation."

With polarized families, questions must validate all family members' experiences, expand descriptions, and provide an opportunity for recontextualizing explanations. Helping family members see that the anger, resentment, worry, and confusion of changing their roles and expectations are only reactions of parts of themselves allows family members to hear each other better and feel more hopeful about change. For example, the IFS model (see Chapter Three) can be used with polarized families whose members are in conflict: "Your wife is questioning whether you value what she does. A part of her is angry, another part is worried about what you will do, and still another part is worried about what will happen to your rela-

tionship if she does not take care of these things for the family."
This statement can address the complexity of the wife's emotions,
partialize her experiences, and connect them to the husband/wife
relationship.

With traditional families directives can be given at the meaning level: "Would the two of you think about how you prepare your
daughters for adulthood in the 1990s?" "Will you all think about
what would happen to your family if your mother stopped working
so hard?" With gender-aware and polarized families, one between-
sessions directive that is often helpful is to ask family members to
think about how their views of gender organize their everyday lives,
constrain their relationships, impede their communication, and
maintain their imbalance. In our experience, these tasks are helpful
in examining gender imbalance and frequently generate ideas in the
family about how to start the process of transformation toward
balance.

Polarized families experience anger, conflict, and frustration
in a painful manner, and so family members need to have their
experiences validated. At the same time, they need to reexamine
their descriptions and explanations. The therapist must be prepared
to deal with anger and resentment, which the members of the family
often direct toward each other but also toward the therapist. At
times, a polarization needs to "hold" for change to occur—for example, when the wife's experience is so painful that she remembers
a long list of injuries and begins to recite it in each session. At this
juncture, regardless of how unprepared the husband is to listen, the
wife needs to go through the list of grievances as a healing, cleans-
ing ritual. Cutting off polarization prematurely may keep the couple polarized at an underground level, through unacknowledged
resentment. In these cases, the spouses need to be told that they are
in transition, and that each transition has its own unique timing:
"For your wife to be able to hear from you that you are interested
in helping her, she needs to talk about the part of her that has
accumulated anger for a long time." Such a statement can communicate the nature of the transition. It is helpful to introduce families
to the idea that there are many parts to everyone, and that the anger,
resentment, worry, and confusion are actually polarized parts in
conflict.

Another way to contextualize experiences is to examine intergenerational explanations. Frequently, the younger generation has not understood what the parents were taught about gender and may be critical of the parents' beliefs. It is also useful to examine historical generational sequences and how families have adapted to them. When everyone examines these beliefs from a familial and sociocultural point of view (when beliefs are contextualized), the beliefs usually begin to lose their "sting," and the members of the family tend to become depolarized.

A particularly helpful directive with polarized families is to reassign an "odds-even task" developed by Selvini-Palazzoli, Cecchin, Prata, and Boscolo (1978). With respect to gender roles, for example, the wife can be asked to assume some of the family's instrumental tasks while her husband assumes the relational tasks. Responsibility for these tasks is then alternated between the two parents. When both spouses agree to explore the underutilized parts of themselves, they frequently have powerful experiences with each other's roles and discover new talents of their own. Rituals are also useful and have the advantage of working metaphorically (at many levels of meaning). Each member of the family derives her or his own meaning and possibilities for action from this analogical task. A comprehensive discussion of rituals in therapy is beyond the scope of this chapter. Because they are particularly helpful with gender issues, however, we refer you to a recent book about rituals (Imber-Black, Roberts, and Whiting, 1988).

With families in transition and/or balanced, directives that explore either the beliefs or the actions contained in the family's personal, professional, and community roles can be helpful. For example, the therapist can assign the task of having each person in the family discuss her or his world-view at work, at school, in a community forum, or in a group of friends. In the political arena, it is important for adults to find out how their representatives vote on gender issues and to write letters. Parents can also discuss their views with their children and involve them in the political process, so that the children can grow up in an informed, balanced home.

As change begins to take place, it is important for therapists to prepare families for the consequences of change. Because change implies both gains and losses, the therapist must anticipate these consequences and legitimize the experience by reviewing the present in light of the past and projecting the future dilemmas that change will bring. Questions about hypothetical events can be helpful at this time: "What do you think will be the repercussions of your children being raised with your level of gender awareness?" "What kinds of dilemmas will you encounter as your children get older?" "How do you foresee the impact of your community on your family's beliefs?" See Table 8.2 for a summary of planning and treatment objectives.

Two Case Examples

The following section presents two case examples, illustrating families at different points in the evolution of gender views. The first case illustrates treatment with a traditional family whose members came to adopt a gender-aware perspective. The second case discusses a couple who came into therapy polarized and left at the beginning of a transition toward balance.

A Traditional/Gender-Aware Family

This case began in an atypical way. In most cases in which our help is sought, a woman makes the initial contact, and she usually presents a child as the problem. Mr. Aldama called to request services for himself and his wife. He stated that his wife frequently threatened to leave him, and that he wanted to save their marriage.

The Aldamas were immigrants of Mexican descent. Although they had lived in Chicago for eight years, they did not speak English. This was not surprising, because they lived in a Mexican port-of-entry community, and they were part of a large extended Spanish-speaking family, which was their primary social network. Mr. Aldama had been laid off recently. At work, he had communicated through a Spanish-speaking foreman. Both spouses came from a small rural town in the north of Mexico. The family was poor and lived in an inner-city community.

The Aldamas were experiencing several transitions. They were acculturating to a new society. They were adapting from being a family with young children to being a family with adolescent

Table 8.2. Summary of Planning and Treatment:
From Gender Imbalance Toward Balance.

Gender Evaluation Positions	Planning	Treatment
Traditional	Promote gender awareness	Question narrow gender roles and expectations Expand descriptions through universal statements Question explanations that justify patriarchy Validate internal struggles Discuss cultural evolution through historical and familial themes
Gender-aware	Amplify experiences of gender imbalance Clarify descriptions and explanations	Support increasing awareness Question constraints when family adheres to narrow gender definitions Discuss opportunities and exploration of new roles Raise possibilities for new accommodations Access the internal struggle through parts language Discuss cultural evolution through historical and familial themes
Polarized	Decrease polarization and encourage negotiation of balanced gender roles	Validate individual's experience Allow long lists of injuries to be recited and heard Question extreme descriptions, coalitions, and splits Give directives that allow experience of the other's gender role Encourage balancing among extreme parts Validate aspirations toward change in each family member Discuss cultural evolution through historical and familial themes

**Table 8.2. Summary of Planning and Treatment:
From Gender Imbalance Toward Balance, Cont'd.**

Gender Evaluation Positions	Planning	Treatment
In transition	Amplify changes toward egalitarian roles	Support and validate beliefs Discuss consequences of change in all family members Predict fluctuations in beliefs Validate internal struggles Clarify new roles Discuss lack of social support
Balanced	Support egalitarian roles Increase vigilance about narrow social roles Expand changes into other social areas	Discuss trade-offs and consequences of beliefs Examine potential social traps Examine consistency of beliefs and actions Support mutual decision making Increase potential for intimacy Discuss impact of lack of social support Expand roles to all members, particularly children and adolescents

children. They were changing from a working-class family to a poor family, because of the frequency and duration of unemployment. They were also changing from a traditional family to a gender-aware family.

The initial hypothesis was that this couple had been thrown into a reexamination of values because of the many transitions. This hypothesis was shared with the couple, and it prompted a discussion about the many losses entailed in the cultural transition. As the spouses discussed these losses, Mr. Aldama commented that in the past they had experienced most transitions together, but now he was afraid that his wife wanted to leave him. Because his wife was indeed saying that she wanted to leave, we asked her to describe what she would need from her husband in order to consider staying in the marriage. She said that she wanted her husband to view her as a partner, which would require him to spend more time with her and discuss many of the decisions they were facing about child rearing and their relationship to the extended family, as well as their decision of whether to go back to Mexico or stay in Chicago. Mr. Aldama attempted to convince his wife that he too wanted to change many of these things, in the same way. It was obvious that he was afraid he was losing his wife and did not know how to convince her of his commitment to change. We asked his wife to think about whether she wanted to be convinced of his intentions and, if so, how much time she would need.

At the second session, we noticed considerable relief on the part of both spouses. They reported that they had spent more time together between sessions and had seen their in-laws less often. Mr. Aldama was still very concerned about his wife's leaving, but Mrs. Aldama said that she would give him (and us) a month. For the next two consecutive sessions, we maintained this focus, helping the spouses negotiate with each other about what kind of couple they wanted to become. They discussed all ranges of options, from decision making to going out together without the children. The therapist helped keep the wife on track (predictably, she was oscillating between clearly articulating her needs and disqualifying herself). The therapist also helped keep the husband on track (given his fears about losing the nurturance of his wife, he was too quick in promising to change). This in-session pattern (S1) was so persistent that we encapsulated it in a cultural metaphor, referring to it in terms of a regional Mexican folk dance that has a series of elaborate steps but always returns to a circular formation. This cultural code allowed us to help the couple short-circuit this sequence and remain focused on the "new steps." At the same time, we were able to validate the stability that the couple experienced in returning to the "circle."

Since the couple had described a fluctuation between hopefulness and hopelessness, it was easy to introduce the IFS metaframework. We combined parts language with the dance metaphor and asked both husband and wife to describe the part(s) that wanted to learn the new steps, as well as the part(s) that were worried about what these changes would bring. The parts language gave us the opportunity to delineate feelings of separation and togetherness, and of hopelessness and hopefulness, as mere parts within each individual. Both spouses agreed with our description: that there was a part of the wife that wanted separation, while another part was hopeful and wanted to take time for things to change. At the same time, there was a part of the husband that wanted to change, as well as another part that was fearful of losing his wife's nurturance and not having enough time for both of them to change. The wife's hopeless part activated the husband's compliant part, which then activated the wife's hopeful part (S1). At that point, the husband's angry part would come in and express frustration at not being able to "do it all at once," which would trigger the wife's hopeless part. Whenever the wife's hopeless part took over, she would think of only one way to alleviate her anguish: separation. The husband would then activate his compliant part and promise many things that he had not had time to explore or was not fully confident that he could do.

The spouses came to the fourth session expressing only their hopeless parts, which in turn spurred the therapist and the team into hopefulness. It was time to go back to the drawing board and plan how to extricate ourselves from this sequence. We did so by changing directions and presenting the Aldamas with our dilemma. We suggested the possibility of focusing on the meaning that a separation might have for them, as a couple and as a family. We did not strategically adopt this position as a restraining tactic (in other words, we were not hoping that the couple would oppose us by moving toward a hopeful position); this change in direction was a direct reflection of the couple's own experience. Conceptually, it stemmed from respect for the complementarity of change and stability, as well as from the need to balance the system by validating both hopelessness and hopefulness. We had already explored hopefulness, and now it was time to explore hopelessness.

We asked the Aldamas if they would continue thinking about their hopeless parts, but if they would do so separately. They were asked to make lists of what would happen to each of them if they continued to feel hopeless about each other and to explain what meaning it had for each of them and how hopelessness helped and hindered them. We explained that we thought it would be better if they made their lists separately. We were concerned that if they performed this ritual together, their hopelessness would overwhelm them. As it turned out, however, our fears were confirmed, and the hopeless feelings did prove too powerful.

As we began to discuss the ritual, both spouses said that perhaps it would be better to separate. It was then possible to suggest that they think about the meaning of separation and add it to their lists.

The couple was late for the next session. The team was concerned about whether the Aldamas' hopelessness had increased and about whether they could discuss separation, even at the meaning level. Once again, we were in for a surprise. When we were notified that they had arrived, the therapist went to the reception area and met the wife, who was unrecognizable. In the previous sessions, this woman had worn a simple dress, kept her coat half on and half off (explaining that she was cold), and worn her hair pulled back. This time, she was "dressed to the hilt." She had a new hairstyle and looked strikingly younger. She explained that she and her husband had been looking for a parking spot for the past twenty minutes. They were going to a party afterward and doubted that there was time enough for a whole session. Both she and her husband wanted to let us know that they were doing very well, however, and that they wanted another appointment.

When they returned to therapy, they explained that they had made a list of all the reasons why they should not separate. They were writing their lists separately, but Mr. Aldama asked his wife to look at his, which had only two reasons: "losing you, and losing the children." She was not able to complete her own list, and they spent time crying and planning how to stay together. They said that they had come to a decision to work hard at improving their relationship.

In the following session, they explored the meaning that separation had for their extended family. They said that no one in either family of origin had ever separated, let alone divorced (S4). In addition, they talked about their experience in their native town, where divorce was unacceptable (S5). Not only their internal struggle (the fearful, hopeful, and hopeless parts) but also these cultural and familial patterns gave them renewed motivation to stay together. As we explored the frequency of their hopeful/hopeless sequence, they reported considerable oscillation (internally and externally) approximately every three or four months (S3). This pattern regulated proximity between them (working together toward saving their marriage) and distance (expressing hopelessness that things could ever change).

At this point, the therapist presented the team's reflections. It seemed to us that for the couple to experience mutuality in their relationship, they had to consider the possibility of separation. Mutuality had to be a choice, both internally, in terms of the fearful and hopeless parts, and externally, in terms of their families of origin and the social meaning that marriage had. We also expressed our concern that when both spouses experienced the distance between them, they resorted to separation (the wife would activate her hopeless part), only to be pushed in the direction of togetherness (the husband would fear the loss of his family and promise to change). The only possible way to break this pattern was for both of them to make a decision, by seriously considering separation or by deciding to give therapy a chance and not discuss separation for a while. The wife then said that she would not discuss separation, giving the husband an opportunity to consider seriously whether he wanted to change his behavior toward her.

In the next session, the spouses began to talk again about mutual decision making, but they did so in a significantly different way. There was more reciprocity in their interaction. The hopeless/hopeful cycle seemed to abate temporarily, and they worked hard and consistently on redefining their relationship. Over the next two sessions, they reported a stronger wish to stay together. They also began to discuss what to do about raising their children, how to respond to the extended family's demands, and whether or not to stay in the United States. The latter theme emerged when the husband got another job, and the prospect of staying in this country became more attractive to the family. The therapist wondered aloud whether the wish to go back to Mexico might reappear if he lost his job once more.

After three more sessions, in which the spouses continued to discuss these issues, they decided to terminate. At this point, we still do not know whether they will continue their evolution. Upon follow-up, however, (two months later), they said that they were spending more time together and less time with the extended family. They were discussing things together more openly, particularly how to raise the children. They also had made a joint decision to stay in this country. They both specifically stated that there was more mutual support between them. Mrs. Aldama said that Mr. Aldama was supporting her both as a wife and as a mother. Mr. Aldama described his relief after his wife stopped threatening to separate from him. He was not very sure of how they were going to end up, but he felt confident that the two of them could work things out.

The gains that this couple experienced were possible because they were already in transition toward gender awareness when they came to therapy. The therapist was able to read their feedback and to lead by following the clear direction that they provided. We coded many of the interventions in cultural descriptions (the regional dance, as well as metaphors about life in the country that referred to their rural upbringing). Thus, we used the cultural metaframework in combination with the gender metaframework. Discussions of the hopeless/hopeful and proximity/distance themes stemmed from the sequences and internal process metaframeworks.

It was also clear that the therapeutic team was open to adopting the gender metaframework, even with a presumably "macho" Mexican-American man and a "traditional" Mexican-American woman. We listened to their experiences, rather than imposing hypotheses of how Mexican, rural, traditional, lower-class families "should" behave.

A Polarized/In Transition Couple

Joan and Tom came to therapy at the point of separation. Each partner was highly polarized and had a long list of complaints about the other's lack of sensitivity. They had been married for twenty years and had two children, ages ten and eight. Joan was a second-generation American of Irish descent. Tom was a third-generation American of Polish descent. The family was in the upper-median economic range.

During the first ten years of their marriage, Tom had been

addicted to alcohol and cocaine. On his own, he had stopped drinking and using cocaine five years before they came to therapy. Joan had been very supportive throughout this time and had complete confidence in Tom's ability to change whatever he wanted to change. Tom saw himself as a goal-directed high achiever (he was a very successful businessman). He agreed with Joan (although this was the only thing they did agree about) that he could stop any behavior when he wanted to. Tom's complaint was that Joan was not giving him enough attention. She was more of a mother than a wife. In the early years of their marriage, they had not had children, and they had enjoyed their freedom. He had also appreciated the support that Joan gave him while he was struggling with his addictions. Now, however, she no longer seemed interested in him.

Joan experienced Tom as too demanding. She described his demands as excessively focused on her appearance. "He wants me to be his doll," she said. "I always have to be dressed in my best clothes, perfectly groomed, with perfect nails and hair." To this, Tom would answer, "I need to be stimulated sexually. I want an attractive wife. I want to come home after a tough day at work and find her ready to seduce me. I want her to make romantic love to me, and to surprise me." Joan would respond, "I have two young children to raise. My job is very demanding [she was an English instructor at a local university]. I am exhausted and cannot always be ready to perform, emotionally or sexually." The lists went on—endlessly, it seemed.

The therapy focused initially on each spouse's list. As Tom's list shrank, however, Joan's lengthened. She reported several years of having experienced herself as both taken for granted and over-utilized. She was particularly upset about Tom's lack of commitment to the children. He had not wanted to have children and was leaving the parenting tasks almost exclusively in her hands. She also was tired of being a caretaker for Tom, and she needed to think about herself for a change. At this stage, Joan became more unavailable to Tom emotionally and sexually, and they decided to separate. It seemed to us that separation was the only possible way for these spouses to redefine their own roles and their expectations of each other. They had reached such a level of polarization that there seemed to be no opportunities for mutual accommodation.

In our experience, it is frequently true that as couples separate physically, they can begin to consider the possibility of examining whether they can recommit themselves to their marriage. Both spouses worked with their internal systems in individual therapy for six months. Joan felt considerable pain when Tom left and initially had difficulty not "watching over him." She imagined that he would go back to drinking and/or using cocaine, and she was concerned about his mental health. She also missed his presence and his friendship. Initially relieved, Tom continued to work very hard, in his characteristically intense manner, and began dating many women at the same time. He also became genuinely interested in his children and spent more time being a father than he ever had before. Tom and Joan attempted to date each other, and they had good experiences. Some romantic rekindling developed, but it did not last very long, because Joan became increasingly angry over Tom's many women friends.

From the beginning, treatment had focused on the examination of gender roles and expectations. Both spouses had come into treatment saying that their complementary roles constrained them. Tom expected a "baby-doll wife," and Joan expected an "absent provider" who would give her time to be a mother. After their separation, and once their anger had subsided, they both were able to view their marriage from a different vantage point. The most helpful intervention at this time was for us to explore the constraints that each one experienced and the opportunities they could discover while they were separated. Tom recognized his dependence on Joan and how much she had kept him from addictive behavior. Joan recognized how much she needed Tom's economic support. They had divided their tasks along traditional lines, with Joan taking care of the family's emotional needs and Tom assuming the economic burdens. Their separation allowed each to explore the other's emotional nature. Joan found out that she could fix things in the house and that she could pay bills and be self-sufficient. She also had time to focus on her own goals and her own future. After a few months, she gave up her watchful role with Tom and began trusting him to take care of himself. Tom underwent a period of depression. Therapy continued to focus on raising questions about his vulnerability, on the differences he experienced as a single man, a father, and a lover, and on the loss of Joan.

At this point, they began talking about getting back together again. Individual therapy continued, but we included marital sessions once a month. The focus now became intergenerational sequences. Both experienced strong legacies from their families of origin. Tom worried that Joan was too much like his mother. Joan experienced Tom as being too much like her father. Their gender socialization was a very strong organizing factor in their relationship and was one of their blocks to commitment. A new list began to develop, but this one did not have the emotional intensity of the first. They had survived each other's lists, and they knew how to move on to solutions. They had reached the point in their evolution of wanting to be a more balanced couple, and they began to explore together the meanings that a more balanced relationship would have, the consequences of getting back together, the effects of being different with each other and of trying to have broader expectations, and the results of exploring more opportunities of showing their potential. Therapy terminated three months after the couple had started living together again.

The Therapist's Gender

Our gender affects not only the way we view the world but also the way family members view us. Gender sensitizes us to imbalance and places us in potential gender-related traps (for example, becoming rescuers of our sex, or overcompensating in the opposite direction). Clients may perceive either male or female therapists as intimidating or as siding with their own gender, regardless of therapists' intentions.

One of the main dilemmas that therapists encounter in using a gender-sensitive approach is facing issues of power and control. To the extent that we use power and control in therapy, we will unbalance the therapeutic relationship. We tend to use power when we are attached to specific therapeutic outcomes, irrespective of the family's beliefs and experiences, and when we do not elicit a context where collaboration with the family is possible. Collaboration translates directly into validating the views of each member of the family, as well as our own.

Our views of leadership emphasize the therapist's responsibility for directing the process toward change, through collaboration with each member of the family. We view the therapist as a leader—a guide who has the best interests of the family in mind. The distinguishing feature of this view of leadership, therefore, is that it sees leadership as best expressed through collaboration.

In the practice of family therapy, part of our collaboration is to make our values clear to the family, whether they have to do with gender issues or with any other beliefs we hold. We frequently tell families, "This is how we think about that." Naturally, the language we use is congruent with the language of the family and with the specific issue under discussion. When differences in beliefs are evident, we ask the family's permission to enter into a conversation about the differences. We take care to explain that we need family members' participation in developing a collaborative view, one that feels comfortable to them and to us. This process may include their realizing that therapy involves our influencing them toward a specific direction, and that we will be doing so openly.

Collaboration also implies accountability for our actions. We frequently ask families to join us in the struggle to balance our beliefs and their best interests. To this end, it helps when we assess our own positions on gender evolution and examine whether we ourselves are traditional, gender-aware, polarized, in transition, or balanced. We have found three areas of evolution that therapists need to examine: the personal (our beliefs about gender balance with respect to our families of procreation and our families of origin), the political (whether we take a position on the advancement of gender balance at the sociocultural level), and the professional (whether we take a clear position against gender oppression with colleagues and trainees, as well as with the families we treat).

Male and female therapists alike may experience particular constraints and opportunities with same-gender clients. It may be more difficult for male therapists to utilize their "feminine" parts, and they may be constrained by thinking that they will lose some of their credibility, which they have by virtue of being male, if they appear "too soft." It may also be difficult for women therapists to utilize their "tough" parts and be seen as credible in androcentric terms. There are times in therapy when we need to share these dilemmas with the family and elicit the family's cooperation in transcending our gender: "How could I say this in such a way that you would not *only* hear it as a woman saying it?" "How can I say this without your thinking that I am siding with your husband?" At other times, what we need is precisely a different-gender therapist. For example, a woman who has been abused by the males in her family may find it especially significant that a male therapist is nurturant and supportive. If a man has experienced himself as too controlled by his mother, it may be especially important for a woman therapist to be collaborative. What seems necessary is that therapists remind families that when we speak, we are going to be heard as either female or male therapists. At times, we need to ask, "How did you hear what I just said? Is it stronger by virtue of my being male? Is it more credible?" "If I were a male therapist, could I reach you better? What would I need to understand better?" Questions like these create opportunities for gender perceptions to be brought into the open. Most important, they trigger possibilities for each member of the family to enter into a collaborative relationship with the therapist.

Implications for Using the Gender Metaframework

What are the implications for us as therapists when we practice from a gender-sensitive perspective? The gender metaframework provides us with opportunities to continue our personal growth, because it helps us take a position against oppression at all levels of social organization. It increases our ability to formulate collaborative hypotheses and engage in planning, by helping us share our thinking with families. It also allows us to share responsibility with families as we invite them to participate in the development of the therapeutic process. Finally, it frees us to use those political aspects of our thinking that will help us, as well as the families we serve, influence the evolution toward a partnership-based society.

As we experience the excitement of a new era of personal and professional growth, we must remember our history and our previous experience of transformation. The first transformation was a move from the internal to the external context, from the individual to the family. As we evolved from first to second cybernetics, we raised our conceptual awareness and allowed ourselves to include the therapist as part of the observing system. Finally, the feminist critique of family therapy has affected our thinking irreversibly. It is present in all the other metaframeworks, but it most specifically influences those presuppositions, theories, and techniques uniquely concerned with gender values. These transformations have specific implications: movement from being neutral toward being curious, from being experts to being collaborators, and from being apolitical to taking positions that openly oppose oppression and imbalance, from focusing on this or that model to transcending the models through conceptual metaframeworks.

PART 3

From Theory
to Practice

NINE

A Blueprint for Therapy

The metaframeworks perspective has four building blocks: the systemic view, a set of presuppositions, the metaframeworks themselves, and the blueprint for therapy. The blueprint is nothing more than a set of guidelines for operationalizing the metaframeworks perspective in the actual conduct of therapy.

Our presuppositions lead to a holistic view of human systems as multilevel entities, wherein each level influences and is influenced by the others and problems arise from the constraints imposed at one or more levels. We see change occurring through a collaborative effort between the therapist and the family to remove constraints. We aspire to a multiplicity view of the mind, informed by perspectivism, which is neither radical constructivism nor naïve realism. We accept power as a variable in human systems, although we approach it not through the concepts of hierarchy and control but rather through leadership, balance and harmony. We are inclusive of whatever has proved valuable in the field of family therapy, seeking both/and rather than either/or positions. Therefore, we believe that therapy should encounter the domains of experience, description, and explanation and that change occurs through action as well as meaning.

For heuristic purposes, the preceding six chapters presented each metaframework as a discrete cluster of ideas about human systems. In fact, however, the metaframeworks are a recursive set of ideas that interact with and complement one another. For example, in any human system, all members have their own internal family systems, which inevitably contribute to how the larger system is patterned, organized, and developed. The sequences metaframework, which describes the patterns of a system, also provides information about the patterns of organization and development. Likewise, the IFS of each family member involves internal interactions that use the same classes of sequences. Development, patterning, and organization are always embedded within gender- and culture-based norms and values.

To understand a system, we often draw on more than one metaframework, and what emerges as a hypothesis, is often a hybrid taken from the ideas of several metaframeworks. For example, we might hypothesize that a child with a school problem is caught in an oscillation (development) that fails to dampen because leadership in the family (organization) is compromised by parents with polarized parts (internal process) and gender imbalances (gender). Remove any of the metaframeworks, and the hypothesis is weakened. The points of entry for therapy are also limited.

The metaframeworks provide a wealth of information about how human systems function. What is more pertinent to therapy, however, is that they also tell us where to look for and identify the constraints that limit functioning and maintain problems. Some families seem to have only one constraint, which involves only one metaframework. More often, however, there are multiple constraints that, to be understood, must be approached through several metaframeworks. Inherent in each of the metaframeworks are pathways for eliminating the constraints. For example, the IFS model implies that an individual functions best when led by his or her Self, and that parts should not be extreme or polarized. Each of the four classes of sequences can impose constraints; changing sequences lifts constraints. A system's organization should have effective leadership that provides balance and harmony for its members; families must develop, negotiate transitions, and provide a context wherein all members function in an age-appropriate manner. Developmental oscillations impose constraints that can be lifted through dampening of the oscillations. Individuals and families exist within a culture; cultural differences and conflicts between any two levels can impose constraints, and families that cannot find a niche in the larger culture will feel oppressed and constrained by it. Helping the family to fit better with its culture can go a long way toward lifting cultural constraints. Finally, men and women must find ways to live in partnership, whereby both genders have equal influence and access to resources, with neither gender oppressing the other.

The goal of therapy is always to remove constraints. The process of therapy varies, however, according to the number of constraints and how they interact. In straightforward cases, only one constraint is involved. For example, a toddler may have severe temper tantrums because the parents have failed to exercise leadership. This hypothesis may invoke organization, sequence, internal process, and development concepts, but the goal would be to help the family establish more effective leadership, with the expectation that it would eliminate the tantrums, and any of the metaframeworks just mentioned could provide an avenue for achieving that change. In more difficult cases, several constraints must be addressed. Typically, therapy follows one of three approaches: the miracle, the crisis, and the systematic approach.

Every competent therapist has experienced "miracles," and famous family therapists love to present them in their books and workshops. In these cases, the family appears hopeless but is quickly cured. We believe in miracles, but experience has taught us that they cannot be achieved in all difficult cases. Rather, miracles occur when the therapist skillfully locates a nodal point, where several significant constraints converge, and then successfully shifts the constraints around that point. The effect is like opening a bag of charcoal that is sealed with a braided string: pull the string in the right spot, and it unravels easily; miss it, and the string becomes a hopeless knot. Sometimes miracles last, and the family truly changes. At other times, the so-called miracle has not addressed other relevant constraints, which slowly erode the change and even lead to the reimposition of the constraints that had been lifted.

Families often enter therapy when constraints produce a systems escalation evidenced by some impending crisis, such as the threat to hospitalize someone. The crisis shifts the constraints, but often the escalation begins again as an ebb and flow (S3). In these cases, therapy uses the momentum of the crisis to alter the constraints, so that the S3 pattern is interrupted. While much of family therapy is based on crisis induction, we prefer to see ourselves not as causing the crisis but as helping the family use the crisis to develop a different approach to constraints. For example, a young adult female cocaine addict came to therapy with her parents while she was in the middle of a relapse. Within three sessions, she relapsed again. Her parents made her leave home. She hit bottom and entered another treatment program. The therapy facilitated the crisis, addressing the constraints of the oppressive addiction, the family's overinvolvement, and the parents' conflict, so that when the woman came out of the treatment program, she and her family were better prepared.

By far the most common pattern of therapy with difficult cases is the systematic altering of several constraints over a period of time. The length of time varies according to the number of constraints and how they interact, but we have become comfortable with therapy that lasts from six months to a year, recognizing that it often takes this long to identify and address the relevant constraints. For example, in a family presenting with a child's school problem, we often find that all the metaframeworks need to be evoked. Typically, we address sequences and organization early in therapy, to shore up family functioning around the school problem. But the school problem may have worsened to the point where the child needs special education, in which case the child usually has some developmental difficulties, which take longer to address. In addition, the therapy may uncover gender imbalances, which the parents may choose to address in marital therapy. The final outcome is not merely the solution of a specific school problem but rather a child who approaches development in an age-appropriate way, and parents who are better equipped to handle their family and their marriage.

Regardless of the number of constraints, we believe that families do feel oppressed by them and do hope to rid themselves of the difficulties that bring them to therapy. Our view of therapy, then, is straightforward: collaborate with families to help them remove the constraints that limit their functioning. Both how families deal with their constraints and the therapeutic pathway for alleviating them will be, in our view, highly variable. Therapy must be uniquely adapted to each family and to the constraints that the family confronts. We do not aspire to outline a theory complete with a manual for how therapy should be conducted. Sometimes the same therapeutic plan can be used for two families with similar constraints; at other times, two families with the same constraint may require very different plans.

Blueprint

We offer our guidelines in the form of a blueprint. We intend it to help therapists organize the complex process of therapy around the metaframeworks perspective. In introducing the blueprint, it will be useful to distinguish between an approach based on adherence to a particular model of therapy and one based on the metaframeworks perspective.

A model dictates most clinical decisions: what clinical data to look for, what the data mean, how change takes place, the conduct of therapy, and when to end. Model purity greatly simplifies therapy but also imposes the constraint of narrowness, which renders any pure model ineffective in some situations.

With the metaframeworks perspective, we hope to transcend the models' narrowness while retaining their advantages. In doing so, we lose the rigor and certainty afforded by any particular model's essentialism, and we encounter both the risks and the benefits of greater complexity (Schwartz, 1985). The risks involve possible confusion over ideas to select and practices to follow. Specific techniques are no longer coupled tightly with specific theories, and so therapists do have greater range but must also avoid the pitfalls of fuzzy eclecticism. The benefits of such complexity are access to more points of entry and the ability to handle a wide range of clinical dilemmas.

With our blueprint for therapy, we do eliminate the specificity and security of the models but also the constraints imposed by their inevitable limitations. Such a blueprint must enable therapists to consider all components of therapy and to move fluidly among them. It must afford sufficient complexity to relate the metaframeworks to theory and practice, but it must not overwhelm therapists.

It must allow therapists to draw on the best of the models without imposing constraints of its own.

Our blueprint is not an integration of models, as has been proposed by some (Stanton, 1981; Pinsof, 1983; Lebow, 1984) and rejected by others (Fraser, 1982). Model integration requires both an in-depth understanding of each of the models and a set of guidelines for combining them in a systematic way. It is a complex and sometimes tedious enterprise to retain the models' integrity but still manage the contradictions inherent in them. What we have proposed throughout this book is an approach that transcends the models in a way that minimizes or eliminates contradictions.

In our experience, the metaframeworks perspective does not confuse family members. Since all of the metaframeworks are predicated on the same presuppositions, they are interrelated and represent different views of the same phenomenon, any one view being the product of the therapist's perspectivism. A couple with marital conflict, for example, can appreciate that the conflict is related to the interaction of their respective parts, sequences, the organization and developmental stage of their marriage, and their cultural and gender differences. They do not become confused when the therapist shifts from one metaframework to another, as long as conceptual bridges are constructed among the metaframeworks.

Since the therapy is a collaborative endeavor that matches treatment to one or more metaframeworks, rather than to a model, interventions drawn from a number of different models can be used. For example, we can ask circular questions to elicit information about the metaframeworks and, with that information, use many of the interventions associated with the models. In a family therapy session with parents and two precocious children, the parents complained that the children frequently refused to do what they were asked. The mother stated that she knew the children loved them, but their behavior often suggested otherwise. At this point, the therapist first suggested that the noncompliance could be viewed as a lack of respect. When the parents acknowledged this, he asked, "If you could only have one, respect or love, which would you choose?" Both parents immediately said love, and the therapist responded with a statement: "Most parents would say that, but in some families respect is more important than love. In still others, members are kicked out because they don't show proper respect." The father acknowledged that this in fact had occurred in his own family of origin (possibly an S4 pattern). A discussion about what had happened then took the form of an enactment, in which the whole family interacted around the distinction between love and respect.

The metaframeworks perspective is actually close to what we believe most experienced therapists do. Even if they intend to use a particular model, they soon learn its limitations and how to transcend them. They create their own styles of therapy, which work for them and can be modified for the particular families they encounter. The metaframeworks perspective and its blueprint provide a more systematic yet flexible way to pursue this quest for a personal style of therapy.

Components of the Blueprint

We identify four interrelated components that constitute the process of therapy: hypothesizing, planning, conversing, and reading feedback (Aponte and VanDeusen, 1981; Tomm, 1987a). The four components are recursively related, so that therapists are constantly checking one against the others, as illustrated in Figure 9.1. We define *hypothesizing* as selecting a set of ideas drawn from one or more metaframeworks, which organizes and makes understandable specific feedback offered by the system. *Planning* is selecting a course of action for conducting therapy at any point. *Conversing* is deciding what to say to the family on a moment-by-moment basis. *Reading feedback* is observing and attributing meaning to the family's utterances and interactions in the context of therapy.

Figure 9.1. The Basic Blueprint.

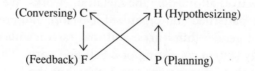

Because our therapy is a collaborative endeavor with families, it would be more correct to place the prefix *co-* before each of the components (*cohypothesizing,* and so on). This implies that hypothesizing, planning, conversing, and reading feedback are not the sole responsibilities of the therapist but evolve through collaboration. Because prefixes become cumbersome, we do not use them, but we alert the reader to keep the collaborative nature of therapy in mind.

Therapists must attend simultaneously to all components of the blueprint. Obviously, at times one component moves into the figure, while the others fade to the ground, but recursiveness constantly forces therapists to check each against the others. At one moment, a hypothesis may suggest a question, which elicits feedback on which the therapist plans. Or the feedback may suggest a different hypothesis, which changes the plan and alters the nature of the conversation.

Hypothesizing

Broadly defined, hypothesizing is the conceptual piece of therapy, but it has had many different meanings (Aponte and VanDeusen, 1981; Selvini-Palazzoli, Cecchin, Prata, and Boscolo, 1980). To establish our definition and distinguish it from others, it is necessary to return first to our presupposition about reality. In Chapter Two, we noted that the naïve realists believe in a knowable reality; for them, therefore, hypothesizing is an exercise in discovering the truth about a family. Radical constructivists, believing only in a constructed reality, see hypothesizing as the way therapists construct their own meanings about families. As perspectivists, we accept that knowing is always subjective, but we hold that there *is* a reality out there. That reality can be approximated with the multiple perspectives afforded by the metaframeworks. We believe that families are patterned and organized, develop, and are affected by cultural and gender differences, and that each member has an internal family system consisting of a Self and parts. Therapists can never know these dimensions absolutely, but the knowledge provided by the metaframeworks enables a dialogue with the family that represents a useful approximation of them. From this position, hypothesizing is a conceptual exercise between therapist and family, which enables us to select metaframeworks that have some connection to reality and may be helpful to therapy.

Families in distress come for therapy expecting help from their therapists. Consequently, we believe that therapists should exercise leadership regarding all aspects of therapy, including hypothesizing. The therapist involves the family and uses its feedback, but ultimately the therapist must take responsibility for the direction of the conversation, which is nevertheless propelled by his or her ideas and the feedback of the family. Knowing that information relevant to all metaframeworks is immanent in all human systems, and that any of this information potentially provides useful avenues of inquiry, therapists must still begin somewhere. Even if a session begins with an open-ended question, the response of the family will take on meaning with regard to one or more metaframeworks. The therapist then asks further questions, each of which draws a distinction that severs the conceptual universe of the family and constrains its members to respond at a particular moment to one idea, rather than to all other possible ideas (Keeney, 1983). In this sense, therapy evokes and highlights some aspects of the family and, by neglect, conceals others. For example, if the therapist is interested in pathology, the family will discuss its pathology and thus appear pathological, but its strengths will remain hidden. Or a therapist may draw distinctions about the family's structure, and the family will reveal something about its subsystems, boundaries, and leadership while revealing less about its beliefs, culture, or development. How the therapist selects and orders areas of interest and then asks questions influences what is learned about the family and thus what the family becomes for the therapist.

Encouraging therapists to hypothesize gives them confidence and provides direction for the sessions. Commenting on the usefulness of a hypothesis, Hoffman (1981, p. 394) notes, "It not only offers a rough scaffolding on which to hang the masses of information thrown out by a family, but can give the therapist a thread to follow in conducting an interview, thus blocking out the meaningless chatter that consumes so much of the usual session." Some argue that any hypothesis constrains therapists from hearing and understanding the story of the family (Anderson and Goolishian,

1988; Whitaker, 1976). We agree that there is a danger that any hypothesis, even one not assumed to be the truth, imposes such constraints. Even greater constraints, however, are imposed when therapists simply have no useful ideas and/or do not know what to do with the information given to them. Our experience in training therapists has taught us the importance of providing young therapists with schemes of ideas (that is, the metaframeworks) to guide their thinking. Access not to one but to six conceptual schemes provides both richness of thinking and direction. In the face of new data, therapists can shift from one hypothesis to another and engage the family in the hypothesizing process. As a therapist gains experience, the metaframeworks blend and serve as templates for mapping the information and feedback provided by the family into a complex whole.

The challenge of the metaframeworks approach is deciding which metaframework to employ at a given moment. Here, the recursiveness among the metaframeworks themselves and between the therapist's distinctions and the family's feedback become crucial. We liken a therapist's mind to a computer screen containing several documents, each of which is a metaframework. Early in the therapy, the therapist moves from document to document, opening one and then another in an effort to make sense of what the family is saying. Whichever metaframework is open and on the "screen" guides the inquiry and hence the distinctions of the therapist. At some point, however, feedback from the family may dictate that another metaframework be opened, particularly as the family shares its views about the emerging hypotheses. Eventually, the metaframeworks will coalesce into a hypothesis or a set of hypotheses that suggest an appropriate direction for the therapy.

For example, a common problem in marital therapy is a complaint lodged by the wife: that the husband is irresponsible. This problem can be grossly oversimplified as a sequence wherein "men screw up and women notice." But why do men act irresponsibly? The internal process metaframework might suggest that some men have irresponsible parts, but the gender and culture metaframeworks also suggest that many men have a sense of entitlement, which dictates that they do not have to notice the things their wives complain about. If they forget to pick the kids up at school, they do not feel the same degree of worry that their wives do. Moreover, when wives do notice, the men accuse them of nagging, and so the husbands often do not respond. The sequences metaframework might expand the original sequence to one of "nag and withdraw" but, again, the gender and culture metaframeworks would add that men are socialized to believe that they are in charge of their families and do not have to take the complaints of a subordinate member seriously. This creates a paradox for the couple because the wife, who functions as the more competent partner, cannot influence the husband, who is less competent. Overburdened and without influence, many women become very angry. Their anger is often futile, however, because they cannot easily change the patriarchal underpinnings of the paradox. Over time, then, the anger simmers, and parts of them become very resentful. Husbands could reduce their wives' resentment by addressing their own areas of incompetence, but this would constitute a concession, and so husbands often continue on the same path, activating stubborn parts that tell them not to respond to their wives' complaints. These resentful and stubborn parts compromise relational development as the couple finds it difficult to communicate and solve problems. As the years pass and macrotransitions arrive, without metarules, the partners handle the transitions poorly, which further constrains their relationship. This scenario can be made ever more complex, of course, but the point here is that each of the metaframeworks mentioned in the example (internal process, sequences, culture, gender, and development) enriches the hypothesis and provides many possible directions for the therapy.

Hypothesizing is closely connected to feedback, since it always represents a fit between the ideas of the therapist and the utterances and interactions of the family. To hypothesize with the metaframeworks, the therapist must maintain an attitude of curiosity, which Cecchin (1987) defines as passionate interest in an idea together with the willingness to see its claims refuted. Without such curiosity, therapy lacks the edge that gives it momentum, and it becomes a passive conversation. Cecchin has also noted that it is impossible for us to be curious if we believe our hypotheses, because then we become "true believers," destined to see our beliefs fulfilled. Each of the metaframeworks gives us direction, but we escape the narrowness of any one metaframework because we always have the others to complement it.

Planning

What therapists do in therapy has dominated the family therapy field to the point where, until recently, family therapy has been described as a technique in search of a theory. Therapists' activity has been called *intervening, using technique, giving directives,* and *strategizing.* These terms all imply that the therapist must do something to the family to make it better. By naming therapists' activity *planning,* we are attempting to move away from a view of the therapist as expert or fixer to a view of the therapist as collaborator. For us, therapy is still an activity that involves planning, but the plans are defined through mutual exploration between family and therapist. We adopt this position for two reasons.

First, we no longer view families with problems as resistant to change and therefore needing to be tricked or challenged. We no longer have to figure out how to outwit the family homeostasis but rather must find ways to encourage healthier ways of changing. We see families as constrained from changing. We assume that, once they know the constraints, they will be as motivated as we are to seek ways of removing or alleviating them. Difficulty in succeeding is not a sign that the family is not trying.

Second, because we now have access to our own internal process and that of family members, we are not constrained to focus only on patterns of interaction or to use interventions that target the family as a machine consisting only of interacting pieces. We still value change in action as a way to remove constraints, but we can also have a dialogue around the constraints imposed by extreme parts that adopt constraining and limiting meanings, values, and beliefs.

Planning can still include what family therapy has called *techniques* or *interventions,* but with the family's participation. Planning does sometimes require strategic thinking, but the family will usually share our strategizing. For example, a couple's therapy may be going poorly, and the therapist may conclude that the impasse could be broken if each partner were seen alone. The therapist has strategized about the sequence of sessions and may strategize more about how to present the idea of separate sessions to the couple, but the plan will be implemented through collaboration with the couple, so that they will know why the therapist is asking for the individual sessions.

Our views of therapy have evolved over the past fifteen years and, as trainers, we are familiar with most of the interventions associated with family therapy. At different times in our history, we have accepted and applied many of these interventions as originally conceived. We still find some of them useful but have modified them, to make them consistent with our current presuppositions. The point here is that an intervention does not have to be abandoned if one's view of therapy changes; rather, the intervention has to grow with the therapist. Therefore, we encourage young therapists to read the literature and familiarize themselves with the range of interventions available and then apply them in a manner consistent with their own approaches. Planning is a complex endeavor that requires considerable mental agility, because therapists must attend simultaneously to three issues: relating, staging, and creating events.

Relating. For several decades the mechanistic view of family therapy minimized the importance of the therapeutic relationship by postulating that well-planned interventions alone were sufficient to produce change. We are now appreciating once more the importance of the therapeutic relationship. Therefore, we see establishing a collaborative relationship with a family as the primary goal of relating, and it should always remain a part of planning. Once this relationship has been achieved, the therapist is respected as a leader because he or she brings special experience and knowledge to therapy. But the therapist does not act as an authority who imposes solutions on the family; rather, as a leader, the therapist evokes the positive qualities and strengths of each family member, which are then harnessed to remove the constraints. The collaborative therapist believes in the inherent capacity of the family to change itself.

Achieving and maintaining a collaborative relationship can be challenging, however. Families enter treatment with their own beliefs about and experiences with seeking help in general and therapy in particular. One cannot assume that each family member seeks a collaborative relationship, or that all family members know how to establish and share one with a therapist. Previous experience with helping professionals may have been authoritarian and even punitive. Some members may have parts that are activated by the context of therapy, which requests self-disclosure, honesty, and caring. The internal process, sequences, organization, and culture of the family may not be geared to the kind of relationship that the therapist wants to offer. Some members may believe that the therapist is not able to collaborate with everyone. For example, an acting-out adolescent may enter therapy convinced that the therapist will side with the parents. Not surprisingly, he or she will then initially view the therapist with suspicion. In the beginning, therefore, therapists must read the feedback regarding the definition of the relationship expected and sought by each family member. Openly defining the kind of relationship that the therapist hopes to establish with each member helps, but clients with protective and/or vulnerable parts cannot always respond immediately.

It is also likely that, at points in therapy, the collaborative nature of the therapy will be jeopardized by key events and decisions. For example, if therapy helps the parents exercise leadership over an out-of-control child, the autonomous parts of that child will initially rebel angrily against the therapist. A therapist may challenge a husband to reexamine his attitudes about gender; he may initially feel threatened and may respond with hostility or withdraw temporarily from therapy. In yet more difficult situations, a couple may decide to divorce, and one spouse may initially blame the therapy for the collapse of the marriage. In all these instances, the therapist must strive to remain connected to each family member, not necessarily remaining neutral about the decisions but always trying to understand all positions.

Staging. Most therapists would acknowledge that therapy occurs in stages, but few have articulated a view of staging that goes beyond beginning, middle, and end. While such macrostaging ideas are important to therapy (Breunlin, 1985a, 1985b), we have come to view the staging of therapy as a far more subtle affair. By *staging*, we mean the ability of therapists to know where they are in therapy at all times. To do so, therapists must mark several discrete and simultaneously occurring therapeutic processes. Planning must take each of these processes into account and include decision making about which ones to prioritize.

An analogy to tennis can help clarify what we mean. In tennis, people hit a tennis ball back and forth. Tennis is also divided into points, games, sets, and the match: points determine a game, games a set, and sets a match. In this way, each moment of a tennis match simultaneously involves the ball at some spot on the court when a given point is scored, which is part of a given game, which is part of a given set, which occurs at some time in the match. Throughout the match, the process of hitting the ball remains the same. Clearly, however, not all points, games, and sets mean the same thing. A point that decides a game is important, but a point that decides a set is more important, and a point that decides the match is of greatest importance. Tennis hinges not only on the physical abilities and skill levels of the players but also on the psychology of each player and of the game, which ebbs and flows throughout the match.

Hitting the ball is analogous to a therapeutic conversation, the point to an event in the session (perhaps an enactment), the game to the session, the set to a discrete stage, and the match to the whole course of therapy. Just as a tennis player attends to where the ball is placed with respect to the other player, so does the therapist attend carefully to how the therapeutic conversation takes place. Just as it is important at times to stay at the baseline and at others to come to the net, so does the therapist decide on the nature of the conversation: whether to listen, question, or challenge. Just as most skilled tennis players perform masterful strokes without conscious thought, so do most senior therapists converse freely. Upon careful analysis, however, it becomes obvious that their therapy consists of sophisticated uses of the conversation. (Novice therapists, by contrast, have to give a great deal of thought to the mechanics of the conversation; not surprisingly, they can attend less to other dimensions of therapy.)

The point in tennis is analogous to the event in a therapeutic session. There is a buildup of energy, with some partial resolution before the next event occurs. Therapists punctuate these events with transitions. Sometimes the transitions are quite overt, such as when children leave the session and the parents meet alone with the therapist, or when an enactment is constructed. At other times, the transitions are more subtle, as therapy shifts from one topic to another. At still other times, a serendipitous moment in the session may call for a new event. For example, if the event is a discussion of a child's misbehavior, and if the child begins to misbehave in the room, the therapist must choose whether to continue the discussion or focus on the misbehavior. Such opportunities occur throughout a session. Shifting focus without attention to planning creates a disjointed session, but the failure to shift can also mean a lost opportunity. A good therapy session appears to be one continuous event. In fact, however, it is a series of connected events, just as points make up a game in tennis.

A point takes place in the context of a game, and the game is analogous to a therapeutic session. Like the game, the session has an end, and so the therapist must be aware at all times where in the hour he or she is. Beginners often pack the meat of the session into the last five minutes or forget to plan a task until the last minute, and then they must do so in an incomplete way. The session must have closure, and so new events must not be planned if they cannot be resolved adequately. Because we involve the family in planning, the pace of our therapy is slower, since we must allow for input from family members.

A game takes place in the context of a set, and the set is analogous to a demarcated stage of therapy. In therapy, sessions are not isolated events but should be viewed as building on one another in some manner that reflects planning. In this sense, therapists should spend time before a session contemplating the previous sessions and questioning how the coming session will advance the current stage. Between-session events are useful in creating a logical progression of sessions; an assignment can be reviewed at the outset of the subsequent session, as a way of tying the sessions together. In therapy, several sessions often constitute one stage. That stage may be defined by the resolution of one of the presenting problems or by a shifting from one unit of therapy to another, such as from the whole family to the marital relationship. The idea of a stage reminds the therapist that therapy should not drift endlessly. If it appears to be doing so, it is time to take stock of what is being accomplished.

A common referral is that of a married woman who requests help for mental distress, such as depression, anxiety, or fatigue. The question is, Who should attend the initial session, and with whom should the initial stage of therapy be conducted? The decision is often predicated on the viability of the marriage: Has the woman decided to divorce? Is she ambivalent about divorce? Is she willing to try to make the marriage work? More often, we engage in a discussion with the woman about the benefits of involving her husband in the initial interview. In the initial interview, we explore with the couple the extent to which both partners agree that the distress is constraining the marriage. Sometimes the initial stage focuses on the marriage. At other times, we work with the woman alone in the initial stage, with an agreement that the husband will periodically attend sessions. Couple therapy then becomes the second stage.

In tennis, sets are played in the context of the match, to which the whole of therapy is analogous. Here the analogy breaks down, however, because the rules of tennis dictate when the match is complete, but in therapy, except for time-limited contracts, the end is not clearly specified. At all times, therapists must guess where they are in therapy and anticipate possible issues of termination. Like all other aspects of our therapy, the decision to terminate should be made collaboratively. Match point is a crucial moment in tennis; likewise, therapists must recognize when they are at "match point" in therapy. Sometimes this is obvious, as when the disgruntled parents of an acting-out adolescent enter the session and declare that they wish to hospitalize their child. Often, however, the match point is more subtle, as when one spouse obliquely expresses dissatisfaction with the progress of therapy. Such dissatisfaction, if not attended to, can lead to dropout or to an unexpected shift in marital status (such as a request for separation).

Our analogy suggests several guidelines for staging. First, like the tennis player, the therapist must always know where he or she is with respect to all components of the therapy: the moment in the conversation, the session event, the session, the stage, and the whole of therapy. At the same time, priorities must be established

for determining where to focus. Good therapists constantly notice
things: "I need to begin winding this session up." "If I don't attend
to the mother's angry look, I don't think she's going to come back."
"I think it might be useful to see the adolescent alone next time, so
I should create an event to discuss that option." This level of flexibility comes with experience, but it is also something that must be
practiced before it can be mastered. Second, just as in tennis all
points are relevant but some are critical, so also in therapy all moments are relevant but some contain the essence of change. Therefore, it behooves therapists to distinguish those moments that hve
the maximum therapeutic potential. Skilled therapists can recognize when a moment is pregnant with potential. At such times, their
critical faculties go on alert, and they do their best therapy. Third,
like tennis, therapy cannot be controlled; rather, the therapist must
adapt what is possible to the therapeutic conditions, which include
the context of therapy and the clients. Sometimes the entire therapeutic "court" is open; at other times, it can narrow dramatically,
leaving the therapist with very little maneuverability. For this reason, we believe that therapists should possess a range of abilities,
which they can call on in different circumstances. Finally, like tennis, therapy can be very unpredictable. Things can take sudden
turns for the better or for the worse; but, as in tennis, they can go
poorly for a long time and there will still be a possibility for a
favorable outcome.

Creating Events. We believe that therapy is more than a conversation. It is a series of events, wherein the family and the therapist collaborate and sometimes struggle together to remove the
constraints limiting the family's functioning. In the literature, such
terms as *interventions, techniques, directives,* and *strategies* have
been used to name such events. All of these terms evoke a relationship whereby the therapist does something to the family. We prefer
simply to use the term *event,* which implies that something significant is happening, but that it is an agreed-upon activity derived
through collaboration.

Many of family therapy's best-known events have originated
from particular models: enactment, from structural family therapy
(Minuchin and Fishman, 1981); paradoxical interventions, from

strategic therapy (Watzlawick, Weakland, and Fisch, 1974); circular questioning, from systemic therapy (Selvini-Palazzoli, Cecchin, Prata, and Boscolo, 1980); genograms, from Bowen's therapy (Bowen, 1978). These interventions are congruent with the presuppositions of particular models, and we contend that, as long as they remain consistent with our own presuppositions, we can also use them, without having to aspire to the purity of the models from which they were derived. The key is to be clear about our own presuppositions.

Our therapy events are both action- and meaning-oriented. We often stimulate action in or between sessions, knowing that important meaning changes may grow out of such action. For example, a woman contemplating divorce said that she could imagine the future only as one in which she was either unhappily married or bitterly divorced. She could see value in her marriage in the present, but that value disappeared in her vision of the future. Because the woman liked to write, the therapist discussed with her the idea of her writing a short story, set in the future, in which she was contentedly married. She agreed and tried, but she could not write the story. She returned and admitted that if she had no future orientation toward her marriage, she was defeating what was valuable about it in the present. This writing event had given her new meaning.

In another case, a recently divorced woman, whose former husband wanted no contact with her, reported having had disturbing dreams. She was understandably preoccupied by a desire to communicate with him at least once more, to let him know that she bore him no ill will. She addressed this concern for several sessions but was unable to bring herself to contact him directly, or even through his relatives. In a later session, the therapist provided paper and pen and asked the woman to try writing the letter right then. She could not. The therapist took the paper, wrote the salutation, and handed the paper back to the woman, and she burst into tears. She still could not write the letter. Putting the unfinished letter into an envelope, the therapist asked her to take it home and not to finish it unless she felt so inclined, stressing that parts of her would want to write but other parts would not. By the next session, the disturbing dreams had vanished, and she no longer felt she needed to contact her ex-husband.

Action in a session can take the form of an enactment. By contrast with structural family therapy, where enactments are indispensable, action is encouraged in our therapy for specific reasons. Most often, we stimulate action to focus on problematic S1 interactions, hoping that a new style of interaction will facilitate better use of therapy. These S1 interactions constrain the system by preventing effective family problem solving and meeting of needs through face-to-face interaction. We recognize, however, that S1 interactions are influenced by many variables, including longer sequences, the beliefs of extreme or polarized parts, gender issues, and problems of development. Therefore, an enactment may begin from the perspective of the sequences metaframework and as an attempt to address face-to-face interaction, but it may also become the plan for addressing issues through the other metaframeworks. In this sense, the enactment is nothing more than a dialogue among family members, which is monitored by the therapist both for opportunities to alter the nature of the S1 interaction and for clues regarding other relevant constraints. The therapist must feel free to intrude when the content of the dialogue reveals other constraints (extreme or polarized parts, beliefs, and so forth) that are handicapping the dialogue.

Therapy events can also take the form of tasks, when therapist and family agree that something should be done between sessions. It may be an action or simply thinking about something. We present our tasks as experiments, which are optional. Feedback will be useful whether the experiment is conducted or not. Again, tasks are devised with the active participation of the family, and family members can suggest their own tasks or veto the suggestions of the therapist, particularly if parts of some members are not ready to deal with a task.

The distinction between direct and paradoxical tasks, so prevalent in the family therapy literature, loses its meaning when we recognize that all people have parts that want to comply and others that do not or are afraid to. Accordingly, we first identify the parts that have an opinion about the task, and we discuss with them why they favor or oppose the task. We then decide with the person's

Self whether those fears are extreme and should be calmed or over-ridden or are realistic and should be respected for the moment, in which case we may restrain the person from acting. This restraint is not paradoxical, however, because we are not trying to trick the person into compliance.

Likewise, at the level of the family system, a family may be heavily constrained and virtually unable to act. In such a case, we may agree with the family that no action should be taken for the moment. For example, a couple may recognize that separation would be best for them, but they may be unable to separate because of financial and domestic constraints. A paradoxical phenomenon can occur, however, when a context for change (that is, therapy) supports no change (Haley, 1963). Nevertheless, we do not believe that it is useful to exploit such a phenomenon as a paradoxical technique; instead, we see it as the depolarization of a person's fearful or protective parts, once they are no longer being pushed to change.

We have moved away from schemes that dichotomize tasks along dimensions, because such schemes impose an either/or logic on the therapist, and we are always looking for both/and logic (Rohrbaugh, Tennen, Press, and White, 1981; Brown-Standridge, 1989). We have found, for example, that while a task may appear to target behavior (an action task), it may in fact have the effect of changing meanings, and vice versa. We are never surprised when we ask people to do something and they return having thought about it differently, or when we ask them to think about something and they return having done something differently. For example, a mother and her nine-year-old daughter entered therapy because of the daughter's poor social development, which was caused, in part, by her craniofacial disfigurement. The disfigurement and other congenital anomalies had required periodic surgeries throughout the child's life. The S3 pattern associated with the surgeries in-volved an oscillation of competence; with each surgery, the girl would act younger than her age. Together, the family and the ther-apist devised a task called "illness training," whereby for ten min-utes each day the girl was to pretend that she was ill and the mother was to acknowledge her illness but not treat her as younger than her age. The mother and the daughter did the task, and the interaction began to change. The mother reported, however, that for her the change was more the result of her coming to believe that she could not afford to let her daughter's development be arrested by the multiple surgeries.

Tasks require planning; hence, in staging an interview, therapists must allow time to devise tasks with the family. Time must also be allotted at the outset of the next session to review a task (Breunlin and Cimmarusti, 1983). Poorly conceived tasks that are not adequately understood can lead to failure, but they are sometimes assigned by young therapists who feel compelled, without careful thought, to throw an intervention at the family.

Metaframeworks, Planning, and Levels. Planning must always include decisions about which level of the biopsychosocial continuum to include at any given moment in therapy. Therapists must choose among the biological, individual, subsystem, family, and larger systems levels, and sessions or parts of sessions must be orchestrated to include the selected levels. To make these decisions, we use metaframeworks to examine the constraints, and then we judge which level would best facilitate removal of the most important constraint (see Chapter Five).

A common question is the relative importance of constraints associated with the internal family system of one or more family members and the constraints associated with the family. Here, therapists must decide whether to work with parts of family members while other members observe or to see one person individually and focus on his or her IFS. When one family member has extremely polarized parts that constrain him or her from working productively in family sessions, it is useful to meet alone with that person, to help the person's Self calm those parts down. If the whole family is polarized, however, individual work with one family member's parts is unlikely to have a lasting impact. In that case, it is preferable to work with the whole family first, or to do so while working with the individual.

Conversing

Therapy is a special kind of conversation wherein people in need solicit the assistance of a therapist whom they believe can be helpful. How help is defined colors the nature of the conversation. When help is defined as treatment for a pathological condition, the conversation becomes a dialogue between expert and patient. When it is defined as a strategic game between adversaries, the language of help will sound like that of a "cold war"—for example, "taking a one-down position" (Fisch, Weakland, and Segal, 1982) or "creating reactance" (Rohrbaugh, Tennen, Press, and White, 1981).

Since we define therapy as a collaborative effort between therapist and family to locate and remove the constraints that prevent a family's successful functioning, the conversation is contextualized by metaphors of mutual exchange, shared exploration, and so forth. Therefore, it is more peerlike and open, but with the recognition that the therapist must sometimes exercise leadership. We are interested in having clients and families act *with* rather than *against* us. We may take a one-down position at times—not because the client is an adversary, but because the immediate moment in therapy calls for it. For example, if a parent enters therapy with a learning-disabled child and comes armed with a wealth of knowledge and information about learning disabilities, the therapist, if he or she knows less than the parent, acknowledges that the parent is indeed the expert of the group around these specific items of information.

Because therapy has often been defined as a struggle between a resistant family and a therapist, much attention has been directed toward what therapists should or should not say and how they should or should not say it. We read about the importance of "creating a 'yes set' with the customer" (Fisch, Weakland, and Segal, 1982), reframing the problem (Watzlawick, Weakland, and Fisch, 1974), giving directives (Haley, 1976), and using circular questions properly (Cecchin, 1987; Penn, 1982, 1984; Tomm, 1987b). Within the logic of the homeostatic view of families and the precepts of particular models, each piece of advice is correct.

But what if the family is not resistant? In our view, what therapists have called families' "resistance" may be nothing more than their confusion, misunderstanding of therapy in general or of what therapy requires at a particular moment, fear of the unknown, or protection of some vulnerable part or family member. It may also be healthy resistance to a therapist who does not know what he or she is getting into. When these experiences are acknowledged and made part of the context of conversing, we find that family members seldom seem resistant. Freed from the language of resistance, we are no longer constrained by the narrow logic of any model's preferred style of conversing in the face of resistance. Instead, we can use the full range of a therapeutic conversation.

Questions, Statements, and Directives. Any conversation is constrained by the grammar of our language, which contains only three types of sentences: questions, statements, and directives. In the context of therapy, we define a question as any sentence intended to elicit a response that will generate new or existing information. A statement is a declarative sentence in which the therapist offers new or existing information to the system. A directive is an imperative sentence in which the therapist directs the system to do something.

Therapy relies on all three sentence forms, but the models differ considerably in their emphasis on one form over another. For example, the hallmark of the structural and strategic models is the use of directives, whether they are used to set up and conduct enactments or to give tasks. Cognitive and educative therapies rely on the use of statements. The systemic model is noted for its sophisticated use of questions, particularly circular questions.

Unfortunately, a controversy has arisen: the proponents of the systemic model caution against the use of statements and directives (Tomm, 1987a, 1987b). Statements are eschewed because they are thought to limit a therapist's maneuverability by committing him or her to a certain position; directives, because they constrain the family to act in a certain manner and therefore inhibit the family's freedom to choose. It is virtually impossible, however, to carry on an extended conversation without using all three sentence forms. Moreover, analysis of the transcripts of therapists who advocate one kind of sentence form has revealed that all three are actually used (Pinsof, 1986). Therefore, we believe that it is important to free therapists from the constraining effects of *rules* regarding the use of questions, statements, and directives in therapy. We have found that if therapists work with families in a genuinely collaborative manner, they need not be guarded about what they say, for fear of jeopardizing therapy. We find that the most effective therapy employs a blend of questions, statements, and directives in a manner consistent with a therapist's personal style of relating.

Language as Context. Language contextualizes itself. The MRI group first popularized this notion, proposing that language contains *report* and *command* levels, whereby the command level specifies (that is, contextualizes) how a particular communication is to be understood. For the MRI group, the command component is conveyed paralinguistically—that is, through tone of voice or kinesic movement (Watzlawick, Beavin, and Jackson, 1967). For example, in a session a husband may say that he is open to hearing about his wife's distress, but he simultaneously sighs and looks out the window, indicating that he does not fully mean what he says. Sentences themselves can contextualize one another, particularly when they are juxtaposed. In this way, one sentence acts as a context for another, with the first sentence giving the message: "Take the next sentence in this way." Hence, if the therapist wants to ask a difficult question or make a potentially controversial statement, it is useful first to make a contextualizing statement that will make it easier for the family to hear the question or statement. Family members can hear and respond to powerful language, properly contextualized, without protective parts being activated; consequently, the conversation's collaborative nature is preserved. For example, if two parents disagree on how to deal with their teenage daughter, and if the therapist wants to support the mother's actions but knows that the father will object, the therapist can contextualize the supportive statement with another statement: "I know it is going to sound to you like I am siding with your wife on this issue, and I hope I don't upset you, but I'm willing to take that risk because I think both of you want to solve the problem. I have to admit that I think your wife used good judgment when she didn't come down hard on your daughter last night." This sentence contains four statements, the first three of which contextualize the statement supporting the mother. The father hears the statement about the mother's good judgment in the context of statements that support him, and so he can hear it more readily than if it had been made alone. The point here is that the therapist did constrain herself by making the statement, but she retained her maneuverability by contextual-

izing the statement in a way that anticipated the constraint from the
father's protective part. Conversing becomes a matter of
juxtaposing questions, statements, and directives, so that some sentences contextualize others in a manner that enhances the collaborative nature of therapy.

The Language of Metaframeworks. Each of the metaframeworks, as it evolved, emerged with its own language, which we use
in conversing with families. We recognize that, by doing so, we are
creating distinctions that elicit feedback in terms of a particular
metaframework; thus, for that moment, we constrain the family. We
are also willing, however, to shift to another metaframework, if its
language seems appropriate or if feedback from the family suggests
that a particular metaframework is inappropriate.

From the outset of therapy, we use the language of the IFS
model, planting the idea of the mind's multiplicity. Consider the
following example:

Mother: I get so angry with him, I just don't know what to do.

Therapist: So a part of you becomes very frustrated. What does
that part say you should do?

Mother: I don't know. Part of me says I should punish him, but
another part feels he's hurting because of our divorce.

By responding in the language of the IFS model, the mother implicitly accepts a hypothesis that includes polarized parts. We recognize,
of course, that when we call attention to parts, we contribute to
making parts central to therapy.

We use the language of the other metaframeworks (particularly development and gender) to highlight a process. For example,
we may ask a husband, "Is your wife modern or traditional?" His
response to this question will suggest his beliefs about gender roles.
We may make a statement to normalize a developmental process
that is defined by the family as problematic: "I've seen a lot of
twelve-year-old girls, and most of them are concerned about their
appearance."

Reading Feedback

The utterances and interactions of a family take place in the context of therapy, and they constitute a form of feedback that must be read by the therapist and used to guide the progress of therapy. Again, as in hypothesizing, when we read feedback, we apply our presupposition of perspectivism. Therefore, reading feedback is not a question of grasping the reality of the family but rather of understanding our own attributions of meaning to the family's responses, which meanings must then be checked with the family. Only when a consensus of meaning is reached between therapist and family can the feedback be incorporated into hypothesizing and planning. To *see* feedback, therapists need keen observational skills; otherwise, the subtlety of interaction is lost. But to *read* feedback, therapists must use a conceptual scheme, through which they give the feedback meaning. We invoke one or more metaframeworks, recognizing that the same behavior can take on different meanings when different metaframeworks are invoked.

Three Case Examples

A therapist is meeting with a biological father and his three sons, who were placed in foster care because of neglect: the biological mother abandoned the family, and the father failed to provide adequate care for the boys. The goal of the therapy is to work toward family reunification. During the interview, the sons constantly disrupt the session by fighting with one another and repeatedly defying and provoking the father, whose anger toward them hovers just below the surface. The eldest, thirteen-year-old Adam, defiantly leans his chair against the wall, despite requests from his father to move forward and participate in the session. The therapist reads all this feedback as the sons' rejection of the father's leadership but also hypothesizes that the boys may well be directing all their anger toward the father because they cannot express it to the missing mother. With the boys, the therapist speculates that they behave as if they are angry with the father and do not seem to want him to succeed. The therapist asks whether they know who they are really most angry with, the father or the mother. For the first time, Adam sits forward and confirms the hypothesis by saying that they cannot be angry with the mother because she is not around.

In the next session, the boys arrive before the father, and so the therapist meets with them to address their disruptiveness. To his surprise, the boys are calm and cooperative. This feedback is read as a change. Acting puzzled, the therapist asks why the boys seem motivated to behave. Adam answers that he has decided to give the father a chance. He says that those who want the father to succeed will behave, and those who do not will continue to "screw around." At this point, Joe, the six-year-old, who has been sitting away from his two brothers, walks over and sits next to them. Invoking the concept of the sibling holon, the therapist reads this feedback as a sign that Joe has "voted with his feet" to be part of the holon that is willing to give the father a chance. Adam, accepting leadership for this sibling holon, again leans his chair against the wall, and his brothers immediately try to imitate him. The therapist reads this behavior, not as another act of defiance but rather as one of "cool" leadership. He begins to talk with Adam about how the brothers can form a team to help the father succeed, with Adam taking a leadership role.

As in the stages of planning, the family's interactions and feedback can be responses to any number of levels of the therapeutic context, and responses may include all of the following: family members' immediate reactions to particular questions, statements, or directives that are part of the therapeutic conversation; spontaneous behaviors, occurring in the flow of the session, which are part of the family's pattern or organization; reactions to a session event; reactions to the nature of the therapeutic relationship; reactions to the nature of therapy itself; and reactions that reflect changes in the family, which occur in relation to the overall progress of therapy or specifically in relation to tasks that are undertaken between sessions.

> A therapist is meeting for the fifth time with a mother and her ten-year-old daughter, Ann, and her seven-year-old son, Billy, regarding Billy's behavior problems, both at home and at school. Billy is a small child, well below the 5th percentile in height and weight, who presents as hyperactive. In the first four sessions, Billy has communicated only reluctantly with the therapist, giving hostile one-word answers, and has constantly disrupted the sessions by misbehaving. The therapist has repeatedly invoked the organizational metaframework and has used enactments to encourage the mother's leadership in setting limits on Billy's behavior. The mother has responded in the sessions and has reported some improvements at home and at school. Billy has been less disruptive, but he is still unwilling to communicate.
>
> During the fifth session, Billy spontaneously locates an undersized child's chair, conspicuously places it in front of the therapist, and says, "This chair is just the right size for me."

How is the therapist to read this feedback? Is this behavior more of the same—just another of Billy's disruptions, requiring that the mother again settle him? Or does it signal a change, and if so, what does the change mean? It may mean a shift in the way Billy sees the therapy and the therapist, or it may mean that a change has occurred in the family, making it possible for Billy to open up. The therapist reads the chair as a metaphor for Billy's concerns about his size, and he hypothesizes that Billy now feels secure enough to talk about this issue.

Having read this feedback, the therapist has to shift to planning and decide how to address this issue with the family. He can ask Billy whether he wants to talk about his size. Knowing the developmental level of a seven-year-old, however, and that Billy still has an easily activated oppositional part, the therapist decides instead simply to facilitate the opening.

> The therapist admires the chair and asks Billy to describe in detail why the chair is just right for him. Billy responds and confirms the appropriateness of the therapist's move. The mother quickly gets into the conversation, which shifts to Billy's chair at school and ultimately to his feeling of being teased for being so small. Throughout this interaction, Billy remains focused and does not disrupt the session.

Because feedback is ubiquitous, therapists must distinguish between what is useful and what is not. This is not a qualitative decision but rather a judgment, based on the perspective of the therapist, which includes the particular metaframework being invoked at the time and the planning at that moment in the session. Therapists can elect to respond to, ignore, or store for later use any feedback that they read. For example, if one parent subtly criticizes another during an initial interview in which a child is presented as the problem, the therapist may note but choose to ignore this feedback because it will prematurely make the marital conflict overt and jeopardize the family's engagement in therapy.

The reading of feedback takes place throughout therapy. It is most challenging at the outset, because all information is novel and potentially relevant to all the metaframeworks. The therapist may begin with a tentative hypothesis based on intake information, but he or she should remain open to all metaframeworks. Each utterance and interaction of the family is then checked against the relevant metaframeworks, to determine its usefulness. Consider the following response of a mother who has been asked a circular question regarding the presenting problem, Johnny's refusal to do homework:

Therapist: Who in the family is most upset that Johnny doesn't do his homework?

Mother: That's hard to say. You see, my husband works long hours, so I spend more time with Johnny, and I have to hassle over the homework every night and still deal with the baby. But then my husband comes home and yells if the homework isn't done, and we end up fighting. He says that Johnny manipulates me, and he's right. My son loves to talk. Adults are always impressed with his maturity. So he does con me into these conversations, and before I know it, it's late and the homework isn't finished. Everyone says I should crack down on him, but with the move and his illness, he's been through a lot, and I just don't know if that's the right thing to do.

Sequences: Possible S2, wherein the family has no effective evening routine for Johnny's homework

Organization: Possible problem with leadership

Development: Possible oscillation, whereby Johnny acts younger by not doing homework but older by talking to adults

Internal Process: Possible guilty part that tells the mother that she has caused the problem

This single response is rich with feedback, which can be read with at least four of the metaframeworks. Questions about gender and culture can also be raised, because the mother appears to accept, without question, the father's long work hours. The next response of the therapist will be based on the momentary priority given to a particular metaframework. Any of the following questions or statements could be used:

> *Sequences (S1 or S2):* Tell me more about how the evening goes.
> *Organization (problem with leadership):* What happens when you and your husband disagree about the homework?
> *Development:* When he doesn't do his homework, he acts very young, but then he also acts much older when he talks to you like an adult.
> *Internal Process:* It sounds as if part of you believes you

should be hard on him, but part of you disagrees with that
stand.

Internal Process and Development: Johnny, when you don't
do your homework, it sounds like a young part of you
takes over.

As a session unfolds, feedback accumulates, and one or more
of the metaframeworks will begin to capture the essence of the family's dilemma most effectively. This metaframework will move into
the figure, while the others move into the ground. A tentative hypothesis can also emerge, one based on a blend of components of
the relevant metaframeworks.

Diane, a twelve-year-old African-American girl, is
brought to therapy because she is openly defiant at
home and obeys neither her mother nor her father. In
the first interview, the family reports that the mother
suffers from arthritis, which makes it difficult for her
to "whup" Diane when she is defiant, and that the
father, who is reported to have a drinking problem,
believes that if everyone left Diane alone she would be
fine.

This feedback evokes the organization metaframework and
suggests that the defiance is maintained by ineffective leadership,
fueled by parental disagreement and the father's coalition with Diane. It is also possible that Diane's defiance distracts from parental
discord related to the father's drinking or the mother's chronic illness. If therapy were planned only in terms of the organization
metaframework, the issue of leadership would become prominent.

Diane is the youngest of seven children. Another
daughter, seventeen-year-old Mary, helps the mother
compensate for her arthritis, but she is going away to
college, and Diane is expected to take her place. The
development metaframework leads to a hypothesis
that the family is going through a nodal transition
and that Diane is having difficulty assuming the role

of the mother's caretaker. Further information, increases the complexity of the developmental picture, however. Several older daughters, who work and have moved out of the house, bring six of their children over to be cared for by the mother. Diane's defiance often begins with disagreements that she has with her nieces and nephews and ends when she hits one of them. It is not clear whether Diane is seen as part of the holon of young children or as their caretaker. The dilemma may be creating an oscillation, whereby Diane is expected to act sometimes like a child and sometimes like a young adult. There appears to be no niche where she can act consistently like a twelve-year-old.

Throughout the session, Diane behaves as if she feels misunderstood, rather than defiant, and she becomes most animated when the subject of child care is raised. Perhaps Diane's defiance signals an imbalance in the family: the older daughters need their mother for child care but should not be relying on her. The mother, lacking access to her assertive parts, does not speak up about much of anything, including feeling overburdened by her grandchildren or her husband's drinking; Diane, the youngest, is saddled with the job—both caretaking and speaking out (although through acting out). Therefore, her defiance is less a problem of impudence than a comment about arrangements that allow some members to prosper at the expense of others. Culturally, it is congruent for a grandmother to care for her daughters' children. In this case, however, the mother's chronic illness makes it impossible for her to do so without help from Mary or Diane. Balance, for this family, would require everyone to participate in a different way.

We can also invoke the gender metaframework here and hypothesize that the mother and the father do not have a partnership relationship, and that the father should offer more assistance to his wife, thereby freeing the daughters. In this case, however, the culture metaframework suggests that in Afro-American families in general, and in this case in particular (because of the number of influential daughters who side with the mother), the women may already have more influence than the father. To start off by challenging the father may only lower his status even more and jeopardize the therapy.

The initial goal is to find a resolution to the dilemma and thereby free Diane from the constraints that keep her from acting her age. Simply getting the parents to work together to exercise consistent control over Diane seems unlikely to resolve the dilemma; the development framework, with its language of transition and oscillation, seems to capture it more accurately. This framework is shared with the family, and all members agree with this view. As therapy progresses, Diane's attitude and behavior begin to improve. These changes probably will not maintained, however, unless the constraints that involve the marital relationship and the drinking are also addressed.

Using the Blueprint

We have now described each of the four components of the blueprint. The final step is to construct a format for using it in therapy. Ideally, therapists would think about all the components simultaneously. But since therapists can actively entertain only a few ideas at a time while still attending to the events of a session, they must find ways to move between and among the components of the blueprint. To aid this process, we use a simple 3×5 card, as shown in Figure 9.2. This figure depicts the metaframeworks perspective. It contains the components of the blueprint and the categories of each component—that is, the six metaframeworks for *hypothesizing,* the three categories of *planning* (relating, staging and creating events), the sentence forms of *conversing* (questions, statements, and directives), and *reading feedback.* It also reminds us to check our ideas against our presuppositions and to recall the action-versus-meaning distinction and the domains of experience, description, and explanation.

We keep such cards in our appointment books and, before each session, review them as a form of planning. During a session,

Figure 9.2. A Blueprint for Therapy.

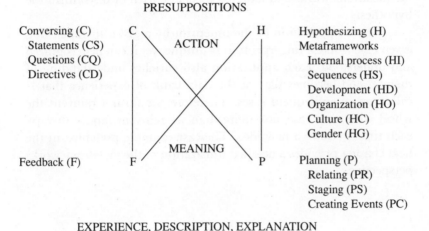

PRESUPPOSITIONS

Conversing (C)
  Statements (CS)
  Questions (CQ)
  Directives (CD)

ACTION

Hypothesizing (H)
Metaframeworks
  Internal process (HI)
  Sequences (HS)
  Development (HD)
  Organization (HO)
  Culture (HC)
  Gender (HG)

MEANING

Feedback (F)

Planning (P)
  Relating (PR)
  Staging (PS)
  Creating Events (PC)

EXPERIENCE, DESCRIPTION, EXPLANATION

our mental images of our cards enable us to prioritize our thinking and guide our decision making. There is no one way to use the blueprint, and each therapist will develop a style to fit his or her own way of thinking about cases. We have developed a few guidelines, however.

First, focus on all the components. Even in the beginning, when hypothesizing is so critical, the other components should not be neglected. For example, if a family presents with an acting-out adolescent who is attending the session reluctantly, the therapist must also plan how to bind that adolescent into a commitment to therapy. According to how the therapist handles the first encounter with the adolescent, he or she may succeed or fail within the first few minutes of the session.

Second, do not remain focused on one component for too long. Have a mental alarm clock, which signals the times to return to the blueprint. A therapist may become fascinated by a session event and forget to hypothesize about the feedback that is generating. Or, in the heat of the moment, the language of conversation may be neglected, and the therapist may become careless about how ideas are articulated.

Third, even when a hypothesis proves helpful, do not be-

come too attached to it. Instead, constantly read feedback against all
the metaframeworks and look for ways to enrich or disconfirm the
hypothesis.

   Each application of the blueprint by a given therapist to a
given case is like a fingerprint: it is unique, yet it can be recognized
and understood. Each application also enriches understanding of
therapy and becomes part of the data bank of experience that is
called on in subsequent cases. Therefore, we do not reinvent the
wheel with each case, any more than we reinvent family therapy
each time we have a new idea. The case example presented in the
next chapter provides a detailed illustration of the metaframeworks
perspective.

TEN

A Case in Point

To illustrate the use of the blueprint presented in Chapter Nine, we present the following case example. This case material should be seen as only one possible application of the blueprint. The way the therapist in this case hypothesized, planned, conversed, and read feedback is unique to her personality and style of therapy; another therapist would have perceived and combined the material differently. For heuristic reasons and because of space limitations, we have condensed a number of events and eliminated some material that appeared, in hindsight, to be less important. Therefore, the reader, should not infer that all therapy can have such an impact. Our therapy, like that of all other therapists, has slow moments, when the therapist is lost, is marking time, or is just willing to enjoy a slower pace with the family. These aspects of therapy also contribute to its success.

The therapist used the blueprint presented in Chapter Nine and shown in Figure 9.2. Each aspect of the blueprint is abbreviated here, as in the figure, and these abbreviations are inserted into the narration, to guide the reader and highlight how the blueprint is applied throughout the therapy. The presentation includes a description of events, a reconstruction of dialogue, and the thoughts of the therapist at key moments.

The Selvino Family

The Selvino family was referred to Ann, a family therapist, by a pediatrician who believed that the parents should seek counseling for their nine-year-old daughter, Sandra, whose persistent eyebrow plucking he viewed as a sign of serious emotional disturbance. Curiously, the pediatrician had followed Sandra from birth and diagnosed her as having attention deficit disorder (ADD) without hyperactivity, but the parents had never sought treatment for this condition. They did, however, follow the Feingold diet and reported it to be helpful. In the initial phone conversation with the mother, Judy, a medical technician, Ann also learned that Sandra was having serious problems at school, both with schoolwork and with classmates. Judy also said that Sandra was very uncooperative and angry at home.

In addition to Sandra and Judy, the family consisted of the father, Tony, who was an insurance salesman, and two younger siblings, seven-year-old Kate and four-year-old Billy. The family lived in a middle-class suburb, and the children attended excellent public schools. The family routine made it difficult to negotiate the time for the first appointment. Ann learned that Judy worked part-time but organized her work schedule into twelve-hour shifts two to three days in a row. Tony's work schedule was flexible, and so he was responsible for getting the children off to school in the morning and for child care on Judy's long work days.

Ann enjoyed hypothesizing about cases on the basis of the intake information. She knew that her ideas were totally speculative, but the exercise always helped her apply each metaframework and make comparisons with cases that had similar profiles. She usually began by musing on the presenting problem and then trying to relate it to the metaframeworks.

(H) It was curious that Judy had sought help for the eyebrow plucking but not for ADD. Did the parents agree with the diagnosis of ADD? Did Sandra fit this profile?

(HD) Ann accepted that Sandra's biology might contribute to some of her behavior, but she did not want her initial hypothesizing to be organized by the ADD diagnosis. She believed that the prognosis was unduly pessimistic and that the diagnosis did not sufficiently recognize the contributions that other levels of the system might be making to the problem. Other problems also existed, both at home and at school. How might the problems interact? How might one problem constrain another? Eyebrow plucking was an interesting symptom. It might be a metaphor for stubbornness, anxiety, or hyperactivity. It might be a statement of difference. It could also prove to be a very difficult problem to eliminate.

In scanning the metaframeworks, Ann used the computer-screen analogy, clicking open metaframeworks as she made associations. (*HI*) Ann's first association touched on internal process. What sorts of parts might encourage Sandra to pluck her eyebrows? Many people with similar compulsive habits have an internal system that includes parts that are hypercritical of them, parts that feel young, lonely, and guilty, and parts that rebel against the internal criticism.

(*HO*) The organization metaframework suggested that the parents must have tried, without success, to get Sandra to stop the plucking. Did this suggest a problem with leadership? Moreover, if Sandra had the typical behavioral profile of a child with ADD, then these problems would oppress the family.

(*HD*) The development metaframework suggested that the constellation of problems must also have interacted in the family in a manner that constrained Sandra's development. There was already a clear indication that she was not acting in an age-appropriate manner in school, and other oscillations probably existed as well.

(*HS*) The sequences metaframework alerted Ann to be aware of the many sequences in which the problems were embedded. Ann was particularly curious about the family routine, which was very tightly scheduled.

(*HC*) Ann knew that, except in cases where there are obvious ethnic or acculturation issues, cultural constraints are difficult to spot in intake information. This family had an Italian name, and Ann wondered at what point the Selvinos had "made it" to the suburbs. She also wondered whether Judy had an Italian background.

(*HG*) Gender imbalances could be anywhere. There were no overt reports of marital disharmony reported at intake, but Ann knew that it might exist. That Tony, an Italian male, shared child care with Judy was impressive, but Ann was curious about whether he did so willingly.

The First Session

(*H*) Initial impressions may be valuable or irrelevant. Regardless of their ultimate use, they provide the feedback (*F*) that initially orients the session.

(*HD*) Sandra presented as an awkward and active but verbally precocious child. She participated well in the session but seemed easily distracted and often sullen. She was also very clumsy, dropping paper and crayons and tripping over the chairs. Although not unattractive, Sandra somehow managed to create an appearance that minimized her physical assets. Her clothing did not match, her hair was messy, and the absence of eyebrows accentuated the prominent features of her face. She was the sort of child who would not be classified as pretty by her peers. But if it were addressed appropriately, her appearance also would not have been attacked. Knowing the importance of peer approval intensifies by the fourth grade and that appearance correlates with popularity among girls, Ann hypothesized that Sandra's appearance made her a sitting duck for peer teasing. It was as if she were saying to herself, "If I can't compete at the top, I'll do my best to make sure I end up at the bottom." Such messages from pessimistic or critical parts would be very constraining.

(*HC, HD*) Judy and Tony presented as an attractive, upwardly mobile couple dedicated to the work ethic and to the American ideal of material well-being. They appeared to have a solid marriage, communicating well and successfully solving problems. Ann hypothesized that their relationship had developed well. Both took pleasure in having a family. Tony seemed relaxed and open, but Judy was tense and short with Ann. She seemed unaware of the frown on her face, and Ann wondered how often Sandra, too, had confronted the same look.

(*HC*) Ann inquired about the family name and learned that the Selvinos had come from Italy after World War I. Tony's parents and grandparents still lived in the "old neighborhood," and Tony and Judy had lived near them until they purchased their current home in the suburb where Judy had grown up. This move had been made just before Sandra started first grade. Tony quipped that they could just afford the smallest house in the community. Judy's family owned a bank. Both of her parents traced their ancestors to the Revolutionary War. Judy smiled when she said that Tony and her father did not talk about money or politics. Ann wondered whether Sandra's problems in school were related to the family's migration to the suburbs and/or to differences that Tony and Judy might have over achievement.

(*HG*) Ann matter-of-factly asked Judy whether she had the same last name. Judy blushed and said she now used her maiden name as her middle name; as she said this, Tony appeared to frown. (*PR, F*) This feedback seemed significant, but Ann chose not to address it at that moment, knowing that her primary task was to engage the family. On the journey toward becoming gender-balanced, Judy and Tony certainly were not traditional, but neither were they polarized.

(*HO*) Throughout the interview, the three children were very restless. The parents reacted when the noise level rose unacceptably, but they set no limits on any of the children, each of whom created many distractions. They appeared more reactive than proactive, and when they said, "Don't do that," they were most often speaking to Sandra.

(*PC*) At one point, to structure the children's activity, Ann provided drawing materials, and the children worked separately with paper and markers. (*HO, F*) When Ann asked to see their work, Sandra told Ann to look at Kate's because it was better, and indeed it was. (*HD*) The writing on Sandra's was well below age level, making Ann wonder whether Sandra did have a problem with fine-motor coordination. When Ann pointed out that each child's work of art was special, (*HI, HO*) Sandra responded that Kate could do everything better than she could, and she refused to accept any praise for her work. Noting the artwork, Judy commented that Sandra had trouble completing assignments in school, and so she often brought them home, in addition to a normal amount of homework. What could have been half an hour of homework often became a three- or four-hour ordeal, and the parents had to coerce her to finish.

(*HS*) Not far into the interview, a striking S1 interaction occurred. Without warning, Sandra reached into Judy's purse and pulled out a roll of film. Judy reacted instantaneously. She snatched the film back and snapped at Sandra not to go into her purse. Sandra recoiled and returned to her chair, with a sullen look on her face.

(*H, P*) As the interview progressed, Ann used the feedback to formulate hypotheses. She also shifted to planning, to decide how to proceed with the case. (The descriptions provided here summarize her thought process; obviously, during the session, she engaged in a stream-of-consciousness thought process that moved back and forth.) The initial interview was drawing to a close, but the interactions and discussions had already provided Ann with a rich source of data for hypothesizing. In no special order, she drew on the metaframeworks in the following manner.

(*HO*) The eyebrow plucking could be just one of many behaviors that the parents did not control effectively. As such, it might have reflected a problem with leadership. On the discipline side of leadership, the parents appeared competent and caring and were usually able to agree on how to deal with the children. Their frequent failure to set consistent limits could be accounted for by their exhaustion and burnout, or by the difficulty of knowing how to treat a child whose behaviors are not consistently age-appropriate (*HD*). Sandra's many problems were of a nature that oppresses families (see Chapter Six). On the nurturant side of leadership, it was too early to tell what kind of nurturance Sandra was receiving or had received in the past.

(*HS*) Ann hypothesized that the parents' attempted solutions to such problems as impulsivity, poor judgment, clumsiness, forgetfulness, and poor attention might have resulted in many nonproductive sequences, particularly S1 interactions in which the parents ended up being over- or undercontrolling of Sandra. (*HD*) Ann also hypothesized that the parents had learned, through thousands of transactions, always to be vigilant and half a step ahead of Sandra, lest she hurt herself or do damage. (*HS, HD*) In the incident involving the film, Judy must have feared that Sandra would pull it from its casing and ruin it. Her solution was to get the film back from Sandra before that could happen, but, as a result, Sandra felt bad and lost an opportunity to show competence. Such sequences, while adaptive for small children, would lead to microtransitions that would encouarge behavior that was less than competent. Sandra's verbal abilities, by contrast, enabled her to carry on adultlike conversations, which she preferred to playing with friends. Therefore, she also acted older than her age. Ann speculated that an oscillation existed, generated partly by biological constraints on Sandra's development and partly by a series of microtransitions that encouraged age-inappropriate behavior.

(*HS*) Ann also wondered about the family's routine. What happened at home in the morning, before school, and in the afternoon, when homework was to be done? (*HG*) How had Tony and Judy worked out the routine? Was it fair and balanced?

(*HI*) Sandra must have had some polarized parts. Every comparison she made between herself and her sister or her classmates was unfavorable to herself. A critical part appeared to tell her that she could do nothing right, but a perfectionistic, achievement-oriented part also seemed to say that nothing but the best was acceptable. Judy seemed to have similar parts. She was a successful adult, but she seemed to expect criticism from Ann. (*HC*) Achievement seemed to be a major concern in the family, and Ann wondered whether the parents' two cultures entailed different values, which in some way confused Sandra. Both parents appeared to have worked hard to accept Sandra as she was, but Ann wondered whether Sandra had still come to believe that her parents were very disappointed in her. (*HG*) Ann had a mixed read on gender: ostensibly, the couple seemed gender-balanced, but the uneasy response that both gave to the question of Judy's name suggested that some gender issues might still be unresolved.

(*H*) Ann was satisfied with a tentative hypothesis that connected the eyebrow plucking and other problems to a multilevel system that included a set of recursive constraints involving the metaframeworks. One statement of the hypothesis—which could be articulated in several ways, according to the prioritizing of the metaframeworks—is that a cluster of problems (eyebrow plucking, school problems, behavior problems at home) oppressed the family. Their attempted solutions exacerbated rather than solved the problems. Sequences involving these solutions activated polarized parts in Sandra that were critical, pessimistic, and stubborn, and which constrained Sandra from using her Self to find solutions with her family. The quality of leadership was constrained by burnout and frustration. Individual development was constrained for Sandra, possibly by biology and microtransitions, and the relational development of the sibling holon was also constrained. The foregoing constraints could also be compounded by a cultural constraint that was imposed when the family moved to the suburbs and Sandra had to fit into a middle-class peer group. Gender, too, was certainly on the table as Tony and Judy actively struggled to achieve gender balance in the family. The family had become an oppressive place for both Sandra and her parents. The atmosphere at home was one of constant tension and conflict, which exacerbated helplessness and disappointment in both Sandra and her parents.

(*PR*) Ann knew that her task was to join with the family and develop a collaborative relationship, which would allow the family to address and remove the constraints. (*PS*) The problems, however, were embedded in a multilevel system, and so the sessions ultimately might have to focus not only on the whole family but also on the sibling holon, Sandra's and the parents' internal systems, and the school. Decisions about the sequencing of sessions represented a larger staging issue, which Ann could address between sessions. (*PC*) Her immediate concern was how to use the initial session and then bring it to successful closure. Therefore, she asked herself whether she could plan any useful session events.

(*PC*) Ann was very tempted to initiate an enactment that would allow her to see whether the parents could exercise leadership and set limits on the children. She recognized, however, that the parents' leadership attempts had already created struggles that activated a stubborn part in Sandra. To initiate such an enactment now might only expose that polarization and set an uncollaborative tone.

(*PR, PS*) Ann also recognized that the parents, particularly Judy, were most interested in solving the problem of eyebrow plucking and were pressing her for an immediate explanation and solution. They admitted that Sandra had other problems, but they had not previously sought therapy for them, nor did they see, at this point, any connections among the problems. An enactment might jeopardize the potential for revealing the relationships among problems, and so Ann decided to spend time making connections and not attempting to provoke an event that could shed light on the plucking:

Judy: So what do we do about the plucking?

Ann: (CS) I know you would like to take action to solve the problem, but I need to tell you that this problem of plucking eyebrows is very tricky. It could be connected to many things, and they are all related. A problem like plucking is usually fueled by anxiety, which is produced by worry, and parts of Sandra could be worried about many things. We already know that a part of her is worried about not having friends and doing poorly in her schoolwork. Once it starts and becomes a mannerism, like any habit, the plucking can be hard to stop. Then, when adults try to be helpful, the help can turn into a struggle. In the end, everyone is frustrated, and no one can see a way out.

Tony: That's us.

(PR) Ann then talked to Sandra about the plucking and learned that Sandra wished to get over the problem but could not make herself stop. (PC) At the end of the session, Ann decided that a simple monitoring task would preserve a focus on the plucking and provide useful information about the sequences surrounding it and the thoughts that family members had about it:

Ann: (CS) To begin our work on this problem, I would like you to do something that will really help me. (CD) I would like each of you to pay attention to what is going on when the plucking occurs, and what you say to yourself when it happens.

(PR) Ann knew that, early in therapy, the primary task of relating is to create a collaborative atmosphere with all members of the family. Sandra's relaxed and open interaction made Ann feel quite joined with her. Ann was less sure about the parents. Judy seemed vulnerable and fearful of being blamed. The events of the session had not shown either parent in a good light. The younger siblings also related well, but their activity level created many distractions, which could have been addressed only through their be-

ing drawn into enactments or excluded. (*PR, PS*) Therefore, to establish a more apparent collaborative atmosphere, Ann suggested
that the parents come alone to the next session, so that they could
provide additional background information.

The Second Session

(*PR*) Before the second session, Ann reviewed the case. She decided
that she could best address her own concerns about relating if she
simply asked Judy and Tony to fill in background information
about the family. If she could establish a collaborative atmosphere,
it would be much easier to address the multilevel nature of all the
problems.

Ann began the session by acknowledging that Sandra might
be a real challenge to her parents. She said that it would be helpful
if Judy and Tony could begin with Sandra's birth and tell their
story about raising her. Both parents visibly relaxed and proceeded
to tell one horror story after another about their difficulties with
Sandra. Their sleep was disturbed until Sandra was three. She constantly injured herself, and until recently they literally had not let
her out of their sight. She often did dangerous things, and sometimes she involved her siblings in play activities that could produce
injuries. Ann sympathized and wondered how it affected the parents' view of Sandra:

Ann: (*CQ*) Do you see Sandra as a normal child who just needs
to learn to behave differently? Or is she different in some ways,
which forces you to fit differently with her?

Tony: It's not so much a problem for me that Sandra is different.
I had a brother like that, but it seems to really matter to Judy.

Ann: (*CQ*) Do you agree with Tony, that you work harder to see
Sandra as normal?

Judy said that, despite Sandra's many difficult behaviors, she
did not want her daughter labeled. Therefore, she had advocated for
Sandra at school but did not want special education for her. Until

the parents had sought therapy, the entire burden of understanding and dealing with Sandra's behavior had fallen on their shoulders.

Ann then asked about the school situation. The parents were unhappy with the teacher, whom they saw as unwilling to accommodate Sandra. Many of his assignments required considerable writing, and Sandra seemed never to get them done. Ann wondered whether the school, the parents, and Sandra had fallen into a bind: the parents wanted Sandra to be seen as a normal child, but they also expected the teacher to behave in a manner that accommodated Sandra's limitations. In a regular classroom, the teacher was constrained to treat Sandra like the other children. Caught in the bind of having to seem like a normal child, but not feeling and behaving like one, Sandra understandably became very frustrated and anxious. The eyebrow plucking began to make more sense.

Ann talked about the importance of finding the right fit between Sandra and her parents and between Sandra and the school. The fit was not working now because Sandra had many problems, and both she and her parents felt oppressed by them. The parents' efforts had turned into power struggles with Sandra, and the eyebrow plucking was a symptom. Ann suggested that if Sandra, the parents, and the school could form a team and collaborate, in an effort to find a better fit for Sandra, she would become less anxious and stubborn and would handle her problems better, and the plucking might abate. Judy, validating Ann for the first time, asked how that could be done. (PS) Ann replied that the first step was to ensure that everyone wanted to be part of the team. The parents affirmed their commitment to therapy. Ann therefore suggested that a meeting with school officials be held immediately. She also suggested that, because Sandra seemed embarrassed by her problems, it might help for Ann to spend some time alone with Sandra.

The School Conference

School conferences are political mine fields, where a therapist has to take both sides, respecting the expertise of the school professionals while still advocating for the family and the child. When Ann contacted the school to set up a conference, she learned that the school professionals knew of the parents' frustrations about Sandra.

At the same time, they believed that they were on top of the situation. The conference itself made it clear that school officials thought Sandra could succeed without special education. They acknowledged her eyebrow plucking, and the teacher admitted that he probably drew attention to Sandra by reminding her not to do it. (P) It was agreed that the plucking would become a therapy issue and would be ignored at school. Sandra did have only a few friends, but the majority of the children left her alone, and by no means was she seen as the class scapegoat. As for the written assignments, the teacher admitted that he was not aware of Sandra's difficulty with handwriting. He could not make exceptions for Sandra, and he had to require the same amount of work from her, but it was agreed that she could tape or type her assignments at home. It was also agreed that the school's special education teacher would watch Sandra write and determine whether handwriting exercises might help. Ann left the conference feeling very positive about the school and more hopeful for Sandra.

The Third Session

By agreement, Judy brought Sandra to this session. Ann met first with Judy, to talk about the school conference. Unlike Ann, Judy felt that the conference had gone poorly: the school seemed unwilling to get involved in Sandra's problems. Ann told Judy that she was puzzled, because she thought that Judy did not want Sandra to be labeled. (HI) Further discussion clarified that one part of Judy did not want Sandra to be labeled, but another part felt very protective toward Sandra and believed that the school had not done enough. Ann replied that the part that wanted Sandra to be normal should be pleased with the conference, because it had verified that Sandra was doing all right, and the teacher was willing to accommodate her handwriting difficulties. Judy reluctantly agreed to give the school a chance, as long as Ann agreed to go on with contacting the school. (P) Ann agreed, and later she established weekly contact with the school's social worker.

(PS) Ann then talked alone with Sandra, who was embarrassed by and unwilling to talk about the eyebrow plucking. She seemed more concerned about her lack of friends and said repeatedly that only the "dorks" would pay attention to her, and that any nice girl risked losing her reputation by being seen with her. Using information from the school conference, Ann challenged this perception, but Sandra was adamant. (*HI*) Ann commented that a part of Sandra certainly did think things were hopeless when it came to making and keeping friends. Sandra agreed. (*HC*) Knowing that Sandra probably would not shift her beliefs about friends easily, Ann decided to address the issue through action. She asked Sandra to make three lists of kids: one of her friends, one of her enemies, and one of kids who were neither but whom she might like to get to know. She gave Sandra construction paper and asked her to pick a color for each group. Of course, her enemies got black. Sandra worked diligently on the lists. While she originally maintained that she had only two friends and many enemies, she repeatedly moved kids from the enemies list to the friends list as the lists developed. Ann was careful not to comment on this trend, suspecting that if she did so, Sandra's negative part would object. (*HC*) When Ann asked Sandra what the kids on the enemies list were like, Sandra replied that they were all the kids who lived in the big houses on the other side of town. Ann speculated that, in a status-conscious suburb, the children from the wealthier families might well discriminate against Sandra who had lived in the city and still had a slight urban accent. (*PC*) Ann then asked Sandra to cut the lists into small squares, with a child's name on each square, and to store the squares in three envelopes. Sandra spontaneously sealed the envelope of enemies, stating that that way none of them could bother her. Ann was pleased, and so she also asked Sandra to do something with the squares between sessions: Sandra was to pick one name from the envelope of potential friends and do one tiny thing (like say hello) to initiate a friendship with that person.

When Ann asked about the eyebrow plucking, Sandra said that she wanted to stop. Ann asked how she would manage to do that, since it appeared to have become a bad habit. Sandra replied that her mother had promised her a horse-riding outing if the eyebrows began to grow back in, and that she really wanted to go. Ann understood that Sandra was a determined child, and she supported Sandra's new commitment, but she also pointed out that Sandra should not feel bad if she had a few setbacks in the first few days.

The Fourth Session

Sandra and her parents attended the fourth session. At the outset, Ann commented on how rapidly Sandra's eyebrows were growing back. Judy added that not only were the eyebrows growing in, Sandra had suddenly decided to do her homework, and that things at home were generally much better. Sandra, of course, frowned at the good news and refused to take any credit for the improvement.

Recalling her days as a strategic therapist, Ann momentarily wanted to lay claim to a miracle cure. She already had a title for the case study: "Go Ahead, Raise Your Eyebrows." Since she had begun using the metaframeworks, however, Ann had learned to view such changes more soberly. She knew that she could not point to one intervention that alone had precipitated the change. In fact, she had done very little. True, she had convened the family and worked hard to establish a collaborative relationship with everyone of importance. She had convened a school conference, listened to the parents, and engaged Sandra in a game of lists. But how could any of this create change? (HO) Ann hypothesized that her efforts had enabled the system to be less polarized and more balanced. Everyone had responded positively to opportunities. It was correct to be hopeful. Nevertheless, many of the constraints that had originally contributed to the polarization still existed. They could easily coalesce again, and the problems could return.

As Ann listened to the positive reports, she also hypothesized and planned. (HI) She knew that Sandra still had a very negative part that would not allow her to feel good. (HD) She knew that the oscillation had not dampened, and that the parents were often inconsistent. The parents' belief about Sandra and the fit they adopted for her developmental needs were not fully worked out. (PS) To buy time while she hypothesized, and to include the family, she juxtaposed a statement with a question and listened to the feedback:

Ann: (CS) These changes are all very encouraging, but I am wondering, (CQ) can you think of things that might keep the changes from lasting?

Judy: I don't know, but you just saw it now. Sandra is still so negative about everything. Sure, she can be a pleasant child, but I worry that she can't be positive about things.

Tony: Yeah, that's one thing, and another thing is, we still have to watch her like a hawk. Things could go along just fine, then she'll do something that really upsets us.

Judy: It would be nice if we could just count on her once in a while.

Ann: (*CS*) Sandra, you're getting older now. (*CQ*) Do you think your parents can count on you more?

Sandra: They never will. They trust my sister to do things, but they won't let me. She can even ride her bike to the store, and I can't.

Tony: Why is that, Sandra?

Sandra: I don't know.

Judy: We've told you. We can count on Kate coming back. The last time you rode your bike, you fell off six blocks away, and we were called by a stranger who came out of her house to help. We'd let you do those things if we thought you'd use good judgment.

Tony: There are still times when we tell you not to do something, and you go ahead and do it, like you didn't even hear—like yesterday, when I told you not to open that can of pop in the car, and you did, and it went all over, and who had to clean it up?

(*F*) As she listened to and read the feedback, Ann continued to hear constraints that involved at least three metaframeworks. (*HI*) Parts of Sandra still encouraged her to be pessimistic and stubborn, and parts of each parent still reacted to her in extreme ways. (*HD*) She was still oscillating between behavior that was less than and greater than competent. (*HO*) She seemed intensely sensitive to the apparent reversal of status with her sister. Ann knew that she could respond to this feedback through any of these metaframeworks. She decided that the developmental metaframework could also capture both parts (the pessimistic and stubborn parts that made Sandra act young) and the organizational issues (a problem in relational development between Sandra and Kate) that created the reversal in sibling leadership:

Ann: (*CS*) I want to ask you a difficult question, Sandra. (*CQ*) How old do you think your parents think you are?

Sandra: Five, or—wait, no—*two,* most of the time.

Judy: But you often act that way.

Ann: (*CS*) So Sandra, you have a two-year-old part that sometimes takes over. (*CQ*) But do you always act that way?

Sandra: No. Lots of times I act my age, but they never notice. Like the time Billy fell, and you were across the street, and I called the doctor myself.

Ann: (*CQ*) How do you feel when your parents treat you as if that two-year-old part was all of you?

Sandra: It makes me mad, and I don't want to do what they say.

Ann: (*CS*) So it provokes that stubborn part of you. (*CQ*) But do you sometimes appreciate it when they look out for you?

Sandra: Yeah, I want them to be two steps ahead of me, but not three.

(*F*) Ann read the feedback and realized that Sandra had provided a perfect metaphor for the persisting oscillation. (*HD*) Parents do have to be three steps ahead of toddlers, but perhaps only one or two steps ahead of a nine-year-old. Over the years, Judy and Tony had learned to be three and often four steps ahead of Sandra, and in some instances they still needed to be farther ahead than the parents of a completely normal nine-year-old. But they had not learned that sometimes it would now be just fine to be only two steps ahead.

Ann: (*CQ*) Would you be more willing to show your parents that you can act your age if you knew that they were going to treat you your age?

Sandra: But they never will. They just treat Kate her age.

Ann: *(CS)* I think you and your parents are on to something. *(CD)* Could you ask that pessimistic part not to interfere for a moment, so I can discuss with you how they can recognize when you act your age?

(PC) The parents and Sandra next worked on a list of all the ways in which Sandra used good judgment and acted her age. At the end of the session, an agreement was reached: Sandra would try harder to act her age, and the parents would comment whenever they saw evidence of this. Of course, Sandra had to convince her pessimistic part that she could accept the compliment. *(HS)* Not coincidentally, during the discussion on good judgment, Sandra again opened her mother's purse and casually examined her lipstick. After a few moments, she replaced it. This time, Judy did not jump on her. When asked about this S1 interaction, Judy admitted that Sandra had used good judgment, but that it was very difficult not to snatch the lipstick from her.

(HI, PS) After the session, Ann realized that Sandra's negative part was indeed constraining her, and she resolved to work on it during the next session. She also decided that Sandra's preoccupation with the accomplishments of her sister warranted some sessions with the siblings.

The Fifth Session

Judy and Tony had learned a lot between sessions. The family had gone on vacation, and Tony reported that it had been the best ever. Both parents noted many occasions on which Sandra had used good judgment. Again, Sandra declined the compliments. Ann then had a discussion with Sandra about her pessimistic part, which always told her that nothing would go right for her. *(PC)* When Ann was sure that Sandra understood her, she handed Sandra a bag of hand puppets and asked her to pick the one that most reminded her of her pessimist. Sandra selected a cloth dragon, which she quickly put over her hand. Ann asked Sandra if she would like to give the dragon a name, and Sandra named it Drako. Ann asked Drako why he told Sandra these negative things, and Drako said that he did not want Sandra to be disappointed. Ann asked whether there was another part, very hurt by disappointments, that Drako was protecting. Sandra saw her hurt part as a four-year-old girl, whom she called Baby.

Ann: (CS) We want to help Drako see that he doesn't have to protect you or Baby by making you not care or try. We want to help him find a different role inside you, so you can hear from other parts that have more confidence. We want to help him see that you can take care of Baby, so he doesn't have to. (CD) Let's continue with our conversation, but whenever Drako wants to be negative, I want you to hold up your hand and talk through the puppet. Okay, let's practice once. So, how is Sandra doing with her friends?

Judy: Much better. Remember, you asked her to make a list of five things she could do with a friend and to choose one of them. Well, she had a sleepover. She was really nervous, but I think it was a success. Usually Sandra has a hard time, but this time she and her friend played very nicely.

Sandra: Kate kept coming downstairs, and Kelly played with her more than me.

Ann: Sandra, who's telling you to say that?

Sandra: It's that dumb Drako.

(F) The same sequence occurred several more times, at which point Sandra jumped up and went into the closet, where she hid Drako. Ann struggled to read this feedback. Was Sandra embarrassed by the game? Was she really that ready to give up Drako? What should she do next? (PS) Her mind raced to staging: Did the therapy event hinge on Drako's presence? Should she have Sandra fetch Drako from the closet? If she did, would that engage Sandra's stubborn part and lead to a power struggle? Should she ignore the feedback and move on to something else? Ann decided that she would risk a question about Drako. If Sandra responded, Ann would pursue it; if she got nothing from Sandra, she would go on to the parents.

Ann: (*CS*) Drako has always had so much to say, Sandra. (*CQ*) Do you think he'll like having to be in the closet?

Sandra: Drako's gone, and I don't want him back.

Ann: You don't have to get rid of Drako. Drako only does that to protect you, and if you work with him and take care of Baby, then he can change and become helpful.

Sandra: I want to leave him in there until he can see that he doesn't have to protect me. Then he can come back.

Sandra left Drako in the closet, but she continued to participate. (*PS*) Toward the end of the session, Ann again thought about staging: What should happen to Drako? After discussion with everyone, it was decided that Ann would keep Drako at the office for now. Drako later became a fixture of the sessions, but Sandra ceased being pervasively negative. Sandra was also able to form an image of Baby and, in imagination, hold and comfort Baby on a regular basis.

(*PS*) Another staging issue had to do with Sandra's progress. Her eyebrows had grown back in. The school and the parents confirmed that she was doing better with friends and schoolwork. Ann considered opening the subject of termination, but it was only four weeks until summer vacation, and Ann had seen too many school problems blow up in her face when she terminated at the first signs of progress. Therefore, she decided to discuss the parents' willingness to shift the focus a bit and include Kate and Billy in the next session.

The Sixth Session

(*HD*) From the outset of the therapy, Ann had hypothesized constraints in the relational development of the sister holon. The constraints involved a reversal in leadership, which was maintained by Judy's preference for making requests of Kate more than of Sandra, because of Sandra's impulsiveness and gross-motor problems; Sandra's messy schoolwork, versus Kate's neat and tidy assignments; and Kate's attractiveness and popularity at school, and her many friends. This situation fueled Drako, who saw the injustice of Sandra's predicament and encouraged her to be pessimistic and stubborn. Unable to see herself as the elder sister, Sandra was obsessed with sibling rivalry, which Ann thought would persist indefinitely. (HO) This rivalry also limited the family's flexibility: it consumed energy and precluded the sister holon's functioning as a resource for the family.

(HS) In planning, Ann considered three openings for working with the sister holon. First, she knew that Kate herself was no angel. The parents were so preoccupied with Sandra that they simply did not notice when Kate set Sandra up. Second, while Kate flaunted her status, Ann believed that she also missed the benefits of having an elder sister. Third, Kate's acting older than Sandra created an oscillation for Kate. (PC) To establish a focus on the sister holon, Ann first wrote the names of all three children on a piece of paper and then addressed Kate:

Ann: (CS) (*Showing Kate the paper with the names*) Kate, you are in the middle. You have an older sister and a younger brother. (CQ) Do you feel more like one of the older kids (*drawing a circle around Sandra and Kate*) or more like one of the younger kids (*drawing a circle around Kate and Billy*)?

Kate: (*Pointing to the circle with her and Sandra*) This one.

Having drawn a boundary around the sisters, Ann proceeded to talk about being sisters, first trying to focus on the positive elements of the relationship. Sandra refused and became quite agitated, saying that it was awful to have a sister. (HI, PC) Ann pulled out Drako, and Sandra complained bitterly about how Kate would tease her behind their parents' backs and then Sandra would get into trouble, and she said that whenever she, Sandra, had a friend over, Kate always stole the friend. Ann decided to create a session event, with Sandra talking to the parents.

As the conversation unfolded, Judy admitted that she had been blind about Kate. She admitted that Kate did tease Sandra, and she promised that Kate would have to stay away when Sandra was playing with her friends. As the parents validated Sandra's complaints, Sandra, rather than appearing pleased, became more agitated. She moved about the room, gesticulating wildly with her hands. (*F*) Ann could not make sense of this feedback. Why would Sandra come unglued when she was being validated? (*HI*) Some polarized part must have been activated. Ann had little time to hypothesize, however, for the session was quickly spinning out of control. Before Ann could act, Sandra had left the room. She returned with a glass of water and refused to return to her seat. The parents began to become critical.

(*HS*) Ann knew that she had to act, and so she asked the parents to get Sandra's attention. Tony told Sandra to sit down. Instead, Sandra held the cup over Kate's head, threatening to spill it. Both parents admonished her not to. Sandra hesitated and then dumped the water on Kate, who burst into tears. Judy simply muttered, "Now look what you've done!"

Realizing that she had not been able to read the feedback and plan anything useful with it, Ann felt defeated, but she knew that she had to pick up the pieces of this disjointed session. She hypothesized briefly. Sandra's behavior was surely viewed by the parents as yet another impulsive act, confirming their belief that she always used poor judgment. Ann, however, was convinced that the incident involved premeditation. (*PC*) Shifting to planning, she asked herself how she could use the event to help the parents shift their beliefs about Sandra. She decided to see whether she could locate a part of Sandra that had become polarized during the interaction:

Ann: (*CS*) I'm really confused, Sandra, so maybe you can help me. We were talking about being the older sister, and your parents were listening to your concerns, and then you did something that got you into trouble. (*CQ*) What were you saying to yourself when you had the water?

Sandra: I didn't care.

Ann: What part was it that told you not to care?

Sandra: It was that stubborn part. It had decided to spill it on Kate.

Judy: See? How can we lighten up on you, Sandra, when right in the middle of a counseling session you're still capable of such bad judgment?

Ann's mind was racing. Her question to Sandra had interrupted the escalation and produced collaborative responses from Sandra and Judy. She had a moment to hypothesize, and so she tried again to read the feedback. (*HI*) A stubborn part of Sandra had seemed to propel her to act inappropriately. (*HI, HD*) The parents were certainly in a bind: How could they dampen the oscillation if they rightly feared that Sandra would use five-year-old judgment when nine-year-old judgment was called for? (*HS*) But the water sequence (an S1 interaction) also revealed something about the way the parents handled episodes of bad judgment. (*HO*) When Sandra threatened to spill the water, the parents told her not to, but they did not indicate that there would be any consequences if she did. And, indeed, once the water was spilled, the only response was exasperation. Ann asked the parents why they had not told Sandra what would happen if she poured water on Kate.

Judy: It doesn't matter what we say. Sandra still does it.

Ann: (*CQ*) So you believe that what happened just now was an impulsive act, which you could not affect?

Judy: How could we? Her mind is in another place.

Ann: (*CS*) Yes, sometimes Sandra still lets an impulsive part take over, although I believe much less so. (*CS, Q*) But just now, was her mind really in another place, or did she just need help controlling that stubborn part that told her not to listen? (*CD*) (*To Sandra*) I'd like you to be honest now, Sandra. (*CQ*) Did you hear your parents tell you not to spill the water?

Sandra: I already said so.

Ann: (*CQ*) Do your parents make it clear to you what will happen if you listen to your stubborn part in a situation like that? Like they might have said, "Sandra if you spill that water, you won't go horseback riding."

Sandra: They almost never say that.

Tony: You know, that's right. We do a lot of threatening, but we aren't very good at being clear with Sandra that she has a choice and that, if she wants to listen to that stubborn part, she will have to pay a price.

(*PC*) Judy and Tony seemed to change their beliefs about Sandra's impulsivity, but Ann believed that some action would solidify the change, and so she and the parents collaboratively worked out a simple contingency point system to reward good judgment. Sandra would be reminded to use good judgment. She earned points when she did and lost them when she did not. Ann explained to Sandra that her stubborn part would cause trouble but that it needed to learn that, by using poor judgment, Sandra invited her parents to continue treating her as young, something that Sandra did not want.

(*PS*) Shifting to staging, Ann realized that the session was drawing to a close, and that the relational issues between Sandra and Kate had been lost. Ann knew that Sandra would have difficulty altering the meaning she gave to her position in the family as the incompetent daughter, and that it would take action and persistence for the meaning to shift. (*PC*) Ann had purchased a button for Sandra on which was written "Who's the big sister?" She gave it to Sandra and asked her to wear it. She then asked Sandra to make a list of the advantages of being the eldest. She asked her to bring the list to the next session and an album of family pictures taken before Kate was born.

The Seventh Session

(*PS*) Ann knew that the agenda for this session was complex. She had to look at the picture album, address feedback about the sister relationship, check in with the stubborn and negative parts, follow up on the contingency system, and expand it to the other children. (*HO*) Ann felt that the latter item was crucial. It was increasingly clear that the parents had difficulty with all three children, and their leadership style meant that they were constantly reacting to misbehavior, often by yelling. The adversarial atmosphere in the family and the energy drain on the parents constituted major constraints.

Moreover, of all the children, Billy was really the one most out of control.

Everyone in the family was in a good mood. The contingency system was working, and the parents reported that, to their surprise, many times Sandra did listen or use good judgment on her own, and they were increasingly seeing her as a nine-year-old. Sandra and Kate had gotten along better, and Judy admitted that Sandra had a lot to offer Kate. Everyone enjoyed looking at the picture album, and Sandra allowed herself to be the center of attention. Drako remained silent throughout.

(PS) Partway through the session, Ann read the feedback and shifted to staging. If she created another session event and addressed Billy's behavior, she would certainly do so with an enactment, which would probably end in tears because Billy would test limits until the parents succeeded in controlling him. And in the midst of all this, Sandra could get activated, as she had in the water incident. Ann decided that work on Billy could wait, and that it would be more beneficial for the family to enjoy this pleasant moment.

The Eighth Session

This session focused on Billy. Ann recognized that Billy was the baby of the family and was spoiled. Ann wondered what constrained the parents from "taming the monster" that Billy was fast becoming. She hypothesized that, for many years, they had been so preoccupied with Sandra that when Billy arrived, parts of them were burned out and just did not attend to him. They felt defeated and believed that little could be done to control his behavior. Every approach they tried failed. (PC) Ann decided that these beliefs would not change without some action to demonstrate that Billy could indeed listen. Such a demonstration would require an enactment: "seeing is believing."

(PC) Ann also planned to do something to keep Sandra from getting activated. She decided to begin the session by collaborating with Sandra to "keep cool" while her parents dealt with Billy. If Sandra could succeed, she would witness her little brother "getting what he deserved," and at the same time she would be praised for acting appropriately, as an elder sister.

Ann began by asking the parents how Sandra was doing. They had high praise for her. Together, Sandra and Ann made a list of improvements as Tony and Judy named Sandra's accomplishments. (PC) Ann then asked Sandra what she thought of Billy's behavior. Sandra reported that it was terrible and that her parents should do more to correct it. Ann commented that her parents had been so concerned about her, Sandra, that they had neglected to think about Billy. Now that Sandra was doing so much better, perhaps they could start "shaping up Billy." Sandra seemed pleased.

Ann: (CS) For your mom and dad to shape up Billy, they will need something from you.

Sandra: Like what?

Ann: (CQ, CD) Well, do you think you can continue to work on being nine? You know, like doing your homework, helping at home, using good judgment, so that Mom and Dad can pay attention to Billy?

Judy: That would really help.

Sandra and her parents then signed the list of improvements, making it a contract. Sandra settled back in her chair to watch the fireworks.

It was only a matter of moments before Billy was out of his seat and causing distractions. (PC) Knowing that it would trigger a power struggle, Ann asked the parents to get Billy to sit down. Of course, Billy refused. Drawing on her background in structural family therapy, Ann knew that she had to focus the enactment until the parents were successful. But it also seemed that some of the parents' parts were constraining them. Ann asked them both what they were saying to themselves as they tried to get Billy to behave. They both found frustrated and pessimistic parts of their own and got those parts to back off.

After a few more repetitions of the same transaction ("Billy, we want you to sit down and remain seated"), Billy began to look worried and finally began to whimper. He then sat down in his chair and presented the look of a child who finally understands that his parents do have the right to tell him what to do. Both parents were amazed but skeptical about whether they could do the same thing at home.

Ann: (*CQ*) So, what would keep this from happening at home?

Judy: Well, one thing that happened here is that we could count on Sandra not doing something to distract us.

Ann: (*CS*) That was great, Sandra. (*CD*) Can you keep that up at home for a few weeks?

Sandra: I can try.

Tony: You know, the more I think about it, we just don't do at home what we do here.

Judy: (*a bit defensively*) What do you mean?

Tony: It took almost ten minutes to get to this point. At home, we just never have that kind of time. We just let it drop because something else comes up. Like in the morning, when I'm trying to get them off to school. If I did this each time Billy caused a problem, they would never get to school.

Ann: (*CS*) So one constraint is lack of time. But if you don't convince Billy of your leadership, he will know he's free to do whatever he wants, and in the long run you burn even more energy.

After further discussion, the parents made a commitment to dropping whatever they were doing, to be sure that they followed through with Billy. (*HS*) Ann also wondered how other aspects of the family's routine might be imposing constraints, and she resolved to return to this subject in a later session.

The Ninth Session

Judy could not attend the next session, and so Tony came with Billy and Sandra. Tony reported that Billy had been better, but he realized just how difficult it was to find the time and energy to follow through. It was just easier to let him get away with things.

(*HS*) Tracking of the family routine confirmed that the schedule was indeed tight. Judy was often gone in the morning, and Tony had to get the kids off to school before he went to work. Even a five-minute delay could throw off the whole schedule. Tony said that he and Judy had hoped that as Sandra grew older, she would be more helpful, making lunches and watching Billy when necessary. Sandra had been unable to handle this responsibility and often made things worse, doing such things as spilling milk or setting the toast on fire. These acts brought criticism, which fueled her pessimistic and stubborn parts; in the end, she could not make a contribution to the family. Tony reported, however, that during the past week Sandra had been much more helpful, and that situation had freed the routine up a bit and enabled Tony to attend more to Billy. Sandra took pleasure in this report.

(*HS*) Ann then asked whether there were ways that the family could loosen the routine, so that they were not always short on time. Tony reported that Judy had many activities besides her work, and she always seemed to be on the go. He often got angry with her, but she rarely cut back on anything. He said that he would like to discuss that issue in the next session. (*HG*) Ann agreed, but she also recognized a gender issue. Was this a reasonable request, or was Tony attempting to define Judy's life?

As the session progressed, Billy became restless, of course, and got into mischief. Tony attempted to settle him, but Billy seemed even more determined to misbehave. (*F*) This feedback was interesting. Did it suggest that Judy could be more successful with Billy than Tony was? In the midst of Tony's futile attempts to settle Billy, Sandra suddenly flung herself to the floor and began to crawl on her hands and knees, making sounds like a horse. Tony, naturally, was horrified and yelled at her. This sequence highlighted the fragility of the changes. (*F*) Ann struggled to read this feedback. Had Sandra gone back on her agreement, or could this be an attempt to be helpful? Tony could still attribute very negative meanings to Sandra's behavior. As long as such episodes (S1 interactions) were contextualized by negative meanings, the family was prone to blame Sandra for being bad, and Sandra's pessimistic and stubborn parts would continue to be activated. Ann decided to find out what the episode had meant to Sandra:

Ann: (*CS*) (*to Sandra*) I'll bet your dad thinks that you just used bad judgment, but I'm not sure why you got down like that. (*CD*) Could you explain it to him?

Sandra: I can usually get Billy to play horsey with me, and then he stops doing the wrong thing.

Tony: (*with a tone of disbelief*) Is that why you did it now?

Sandra: Yes.

Ann: (*CQ*) So a part of you wants to keep Billy from getting into trouble?

Tony: That sure is a strange way to go about it.

Ann: (*CS*) You know, Sandra is very creative, and sometimes when she appears to use bad judgment, I wonder if it's something else. This time, it was her way of trying to be helpful.

Tony: (*to Sandra*) If Ann is right, Sandra, then you have to accept that it's our job to get Billy to behave.

Sandra: But you always smile when he's in trouble.

It was true. Billy was a cute kid, and he knew just how to elicit warmth rather than sternness. (*PC*) Ann asked Sandra whether her dad knew how to kill his smile, and Sandra said no, and so they worked out a deal whereby he would be reminded by Sandra to "kill the smile." If he did not, he owed her a nickel. The game provided a way for Sandra to be helpful without having to act protectively toward Billy and thereby undermine the parents.

The Tenth Session

Summer was approaching, and there would be only a few more sessions. Ann reviewed the case and wondered whether constraints still existed that would make it difficult for the family to maintain the gains it had made. (*HS*) She was concerned about the family routine. If this did not change, everyone could get overburdened again, and the old constraints could return. (*HG, PR*) Ann was glad that Tony wanted to talk about the routine, but she knew that she had to process the discussion through the gender metaframework. (*HC*) Differences of opinion over the routine might be related to the culture metaframework as well. (*PS*) Ann also decided to space out the remaining sessions, so that the family could get used to not coming to therapy.

Tony opened by commenting that, after the previous session, he had realized that he and Judy were just burned out, and that their life-style did not really allow them to recover their energy. How were they ever to get on top of the situation with Billy? He told Judy that it concerned him that she was always so busy and never seemed satisfied unless she was doing something:

Tony: (*to Judy*) Can't you give up some of the extracurricular activities?

Judy: (*flashing an angry look*) Look, buster, those are things that matter to me.

Tony: I know they're important, but you never seem to relax. We have to learn to take time to smell the roses.

Judy: You might have time to smell the roses, but I have things I want to do, and you're not going to tell me not to.

Tony: (*to Ann*) What's the use?

Ann hypothesized that she had arrived at the intersection of several metaframeworks. (*HS*) Sequences suggested that the family's routine (S2) was counterproductive: functions were not handled efficiently, and there was constant tension in the family. (*HI*) A strong achievement-oriented part drove Judy to overextend herself, and a part of Tony rebelled when she did. (*HG, HC*) The struggle over who controlled the routine could be a gender issue, or it might reflect differences in culture.

(*PR*) Before Ann could respond, however, she needed a moment of intense planning. While she agreed with Tony that the routine was a problem and that the problem was exacerbated by Judy's achievement-oriented part, she also knew that to side with him could heighten a gender imbalance. (*HG*) For years in patriarchal families, women had been sacrificing their own needs, so that men and children could succeed; now Judy was trying to succeed, and Tony was objecting. Yet if Ann, a female therapist, sided with Judy, Tony might feel attacked by "the women." (*HC*) It was also possible that unacknowledged cultural differences were constraining open discussion about the routine. (*PS*) The routine did weaken the family, but addressing it would require the use of several other metaframeworks besides sequences. The immediate issue for Ann was to select the metaframework from which to formulate her next remark. Ann knew that she must not impose her values on the family, but she also believed that the gender issue might get lost among the others and that this situation would unfairly place Judy at a disadvantage. Therefore, she decided to lead with a statement relating gender and routine and then to read the feedback:

Ann: (*CS*) Let's back up for just a moment. You know, in traditional families, mothers assume responsibility to make the family run smoothly. And, in doing so, they often sacrifice their own needs. Modern marriages balance the demands of family life and individual needs, for all members. You have a more modern marriage, and you are searching for a balance, but this discussion suggests that you are not there yet.

Tony: (*with an exasperated tone*) What more can I do? I take care of the kids as much as Judy does, and she does what she wants anyway.

Ann: (*CS*) You are doing a lot, but so is Judy, and the question is, (*CQ*) If the routine is too tight, and something has to give, then who and what should give?

Tony: I just never thought it would come down to our lives being so crazy. I never have a minute to relax, and neither does Judy.

Ann: (*CQ*) When did you start getting so busy?

Tony: It wasn't this bad before we moved. At least we'd sit around on Sunday with my parents.

Ann: (*CS*) It sounds like a part of you likes to relax and do nothing, and that now that part is saying you are never able to relax.

Tony: I work hard, but you're right, Ann, a part of me really resents that we are on this merry-go-round and we can't seem to get off, and *(to Judy)* I don't think that you really want to.

Ann: *(CS)* Judy, when Tony's relaxer tells him to shut down, *(CQ)* do you go along, or do you see him as being lazy?

Judy: *(smiling)* I never even saw my father read the newspaper. I guess I do see it as laziness, but this discussion helps me to appreciate that if I never relax, it's pretty hard for Tony to.

(*HS, HG, HC, HI*) It was becoming clear why the routine was such an issue. (*HI*) Judy's achiever drove her and made her view Tony as lazy when he wanted to relax. Tony's relaxer told him that his life had spun out of control and saw Judy as a workaholic. They appeared to interact in a way that polarized their respective achiever and relaxer parts even more and confirmed their beliefs about each other. If each could view the other as constrained by polarized parts, then they could work together to achieve a better balance between hard work and relaxation.

(*HC*) But Ann knew that it was important to recognize the role of culture. Judy's achiever had developed in an upper-middle-class culture of success, which permeated her family of origin. Hard work was expected and rewarded; to live otherwise was to be lazy. Tony's desire to relax had developed in a traditional Italian culture, where relaxation was highly valued for its own sake and as a reward for hard work. If they could recognize their cultural differences and how those contributed to their different parts and different expectations, then they could be less blaming and more open to finding a better routine.

(*HG*) Nevertheless, the relaxation that Tony had witnessed in his family of origin was possible because his mother did not work outside the house. Through her hard work at home, she buffered other family members, thus creating time for relaxation. In doing so, however, she sacrificed her individuality for the benefit of her husband and her children. The Selvinos of Tony's generation had drifted a long way from being traditionally Italian. They had moved away from the extended family and were constrained to make the family work with only the resources of the nuclear family. They had bought the American dream of material well-being, and both Judy and Tony wanted demanding careers. Relaxation evaporated in a sea of demands. Their frustration was felt by Sandra, as disapproval that she could not take up the slack, and by Billy, in the lack of consistent limits. Ann also wondered whether Sandra's difficulties with peers were related to the cultural changes that she had experienced upon moving to the suburbs. Her "odd" appearance could be seen as an abandonment of hope that she could ever be like the "rich" girls in her class.

(PS) Ann knew the therapy could be pursued through a focus on any of the relevant metaframeworks. (HI) It would be helpful to work on Tony's relaxer and Judy's achiever. (HG) It would also be necessary to focus on Judy's sense of felt responsibility for the whole routine, because she could never relax if she ultimately felt responsible for everything, even the areas where Tony performed the work. (HC) The couple also seemed to have little awareness of their cultural differences. Ann decided to summarize her understanding of the contributions made by the metaframeworks.

Ann: (CS) Look, this business about the routine is very complicated and important. If you don't stay on it, the routine could sneak up and constrain you from maintaining the excellent progress you've made with Sandra, Kate, and Billy. The issue has something to do with the way modern men and women share responsibility. But to get that right, you also have to take into account the fact that you two come from cultures that may appear to have many similarities but in fact have many differences. And as long as Judy's achiever and Tony's relaxer stay polarized, neither will allow you to discuss this issue rationally. It may sound like we're drifting away from the problems you came to solve, but I think all of this is territory we should cover, and it might take us a few sessions to do so. (CQ) Can I count on you hanging in there with me?

Judy and Tony both agreed, and for the remainder of the session the conversation collaboratively produced information and ideas that related the relevant metaframeworks to constraints on the routine.

The Eleventh Session

(PS, H) Ann knew that the session would continue to focus on the routine, but it could take many directions. She tried to evaluate how the constraints discussed in the last sessions should be addressed. They were all recursively connected, but focusing on them in some order would be necessary, in order to structure the session. She would begin by sharing her ideas with the family, but she was leaning toward the internal process metaframework. She believed that if Tony's relaxer and Judy's achiever could be calmed, the other discussions would be far more productive.

Tony and Judy had already discussed the previous session on several occasions and were eager to pursue the conversation. Judy had also spoken to Sandra, and she had learned that Sandra's eccentric choice of clothing combinations did reflect her ambivalence about becoming liked and accepted by the kids at school. Judy realized how much she wanted Sandra to be accepted, and the power struggle over clothes seemed to disappear when Judy backed off and Sandra began to make more appropriate choices. *(HC, F)* Ann saw this change as a result of the previous session's focus on culture.

Tony and Judy had also talked about Judy's sense of felt responsibility, and Tony had assured her that he would accept additional responsibility but did not want Judy to check up on him. This conversation created an opening to work on the parts. *(PS)* Ann decided to focus first on Judy's achiever and then on Tony's relaxer:

Ann: *(CS)* Let's say for a moment that you and Tony achieved a balanced division of domestic responsibility. *(CQ)* Would you continue to do all that you do?

Judy: Yes. You are what you accomplish, and that's all. There's no reason to take time to smell the roses.

Ann: *(CD)* Tell me more about that part that tells you that accomplishments are all that matters.

Judy: I get that from my parents. The only time we ever got praised was when we did something productive, so I was into everything as a kid, and I still am.

Ann: (*CQ*) What does that part tell you would be the consequences of not accomplishing a lot?

Judy: It tells me I wouldn't amount to anything if I didn't have accomplishments. I know what Tony means. We never do have any free time, but I don't know how to cut back.

Tony: Try saying no the next time you get asked to do something.

Ann: (*CS*) Tony, it sounds like this achievement part doesn't let Judy say no. You can't force Judy to cut back. Only she can decide whether she wants to calm down her achiever. (*CQ*) Judy, do you want to do some work with that part?

Judy: I don't want it to interfere so much, but I don't want it to stop getting me going, either.

(*PC*) Ann then had Judy do some imagery work. Judy focused on the achiever's voice, and she saw an image of her mother with a scornful look on her face. She asked that part why it pushed her so hard, and it responded that if it did not, Judy would not do anything because she was so lazy. Ann suspected that this achiever was polarized with another part, and she asked Judy to see if she could find a part that told her not to work so hard. Judy saw a teenager dressed in leather, who told her to get away from the family and do whatever she wanted. Initially, Judy felt angry and afraid of this teenager and didn't want to continue talking with it. Ann asked Judy to move her achiever into a room in her mind where it would not interfere. Once away from the achiever's influence, Judy felt sorry for this teenager. The teenager softened, too, and told Judy that it just wanted her to relax sometimes and try to enjoy her life. It said that all her parts were tired of being dominated by this extreme achiever. Judy returned to her scornful achiever, with more conviction that it had to let her lead and share time with the other parts. She had it talk directly with the teenager and with some others, and she set up agreements among them.

As she did this work, Tony looked excited. When she had

finished, Tony said that he would be thrilled if this change could stick. He wanted to know how he could help Judy with this, and they talked about his supporting any effort he saw her make to slow down but not criticizing her when she did not. Ann then asked Judy which part of her had been initially most attracted to Tony. Judy smiled and replied that, of course, it had been the teenager. But whenever the teenager wanted to listen to Tony, the achiever interfered, fearing that Judy would become lazy. Tony said that he was beginning to see how he could talk directly to Judy without always having to fight his way past her achiever.

Ann then shifted the focus to Tony's relaxer. Not surprisingly, she found a similar constellation of parts that had become polarized around relaxation and achievement.

Throughout this discussion, Sandra became very quiet and listened intently. All her polarized parts were calm, and she could be her Self. Ann pointed this out, and both parents remarked on how pleasant the session had been.

The Final Three Sessions

(F) Ann thought that Sandra was on her way. The presenting problems had been resolved, and her development now appeared to be progressing more normally. Certainly, she still struggled in some areas of her life, but the constraints that had exacerbated her limitations were largely gone. At the end of the school year, Sandra received her best report card ever, and her scores on the standard achievement tests were also by far her best. Judy and Tony were pleased, and Sandra accepted their praise.

(PS) The therapy could have ended after the eleventh session, but Ann wanted to stabilize the changes. She congratulated Sandra and said she would check in with her sometime shortly after the start of the next school year. The remaining sessions, with Tony and Judy, involved a collaborative discussion about gender and culture and their respective parts. (HG, F) Judy and Tony moved toward gender balance and acknowledged that there would be some struggles before they learned how to process their differences without polarizing their parts. (HS, F) Important aspects of the family routine changed. Tony came forward and assumed more responsibility, and Judy cut back on some of her activities. The quality of family life improved. Everyone seemed to be under less pressure. (*HC, F*) The couple began to appreciate their cultural differences and used them as a source of curiosity and discussion rather than blame and conflict. They were prepared to end therapy, and they thanked Ann for her help.

Follow-up

(*F*) Several months into the following school year, just as Ann had been planning to contact the family, Judy contacted Ann and reported that Sandra was having problems with her math homework, and that struggles over it were threatening to create the same atmosphere that originally had brought the family into therapy. Sandra had also briefly plucked her eyebrows but had now stopped. Judy reported that the summer had been wonderful and that Sandra had friends at school and excellent activities. Judy sounded confused and said that she did not know what to do. Part of her felt protective toward Sandra. She believed that Sandra could not understand the work and needed special consideration. Another part, however, had locked horns with Sandra's stubborn part.

(*PS*) Follow-up calls always posed a dilemma for Ann. She did not want to offer a session and thereby send the message that the family could solve problems only with therapy, but she also knew that the old constraints could reverse the family's progress, and that perhaps some constraints still had not been identified and addressed. Knowing that such transitions as the start of a new school year can be stressful, Ann suggested that the family come in to explore why Sandra appeared to be having trouble getting off to a good start in the new school year.

At the outset of the session, Ann said that having such a meeting did not mean the family had to come back to therapy, but that it was good to check in, particularly because Sandra seemed to be having difficulty getting the school year off to a good start. She stated that the family members had learned many ways to handle these situations, and that perhaps they had overlooked or misplaced them. This session would be an attempt to determine whether the family could pick up where they had successfully ended therapy or whether more sessions were indicated.

As the family described the situation, it became clear that Sandra's teacher expected organization and neatness at a level unfamiliar to Sandra (a common jump from fourth to fifth grade), and that her stubborn part had become polarized and told her that it was all right to do things her way. Her homework kept coming back with notes for her parents, who felt put on the spot by Sandra's performance. Judy and Tony were divided on how to handle the situation. Judy's achiever had been activated, and she did not want to be seen as a bad parent, and so she had become very intrusive with Sandra. Tony felt that the school was asking them to do its job. He was willing to help Sandra if she asked, but he did not want to be responsible for her homework. (*HO*) The disagreement had produced a crisis of leadership in the family, leaving Sandra with no clear expectations about her homework.

The bright spot was Sandra. She participated actively in the session without becoming distracted. She said she could do the work and that her parents were treating her like a baby, not only with the homework but also in the general amount of autonomy she was given.

(*H, PS*) Ann hypothesized and planned for a moment, and then she decided that if Sandra would take charge of the homework, and if the parents would agree on how they would help, then the issue could be resolved without another round of therapy. Ann asked Sandra whether she was committed to having a good year in the fifth grade. Sandra said yes, and so Ann asked whether Sandra's pessimistic and stubborn parts believed her. Sandra was adamant that they would not get in the way. Ann pointed out that the homework problem could be seen as evidence to the contrary. Sandra shot back that if people would just leave her alone, she would take care of it.

Judy and Tony talked, and they agreed that neither one of them should feel responsible for Sandra's homework. Both would offer help if asked. If a note came home, Sandra would have to deal with it, but the parents would not feel that it was a comment about them. A decision was made to try this for a few weeks. If it did not work, the parents would contact Ann again.

ELEVEN

Refining the
Metaframeworks Perspective

For the past five years, our application of the metaframeworks perspective—in our collaboration with colleagues, in our teaching and
supervision of students, and in our clinical work with clients–has generated significant refinements, which we present in this chapter.
These refinements have been spurred both by further work on the
perspective itself and by the larger challenge to address and incorporate new trends in mental health (Nichols and Schwartz, 1997).

The Six Metaframeworks Today

The six core metaframeworks continue to serve as the conceptual
core of our perspective. The *organization* metaframework and the
development metaframework remain essentially unchanged. The *sequences* metaframework has been expanded beyond the domain of
action alone to incorporate the recursive sequences of action, meaning, and emotion. The *internal family systems* (IFS) metaframework,
the *multicultural* metaframework, and the *gender* metaframework, like
the sequences metaframework, have all been enriched through successive applications in teaching and therapy.

Action, Meaning, and Emotion: The Sequences Metaframework Revisited

When we first described our therapy in *Metaframeworks*, we stressed
the importance of finding a balance between lifting constraints on

action and lifting constraints on meaning, rather than focusing exclusively on one or the other. It seems curious to us now that we did not specifically address constraints on emotion, since we were working with intense emotions at the time. Every time clients approached hurt or angry parts of themselves, they would experience strong feelings, and we were spending large portions of our therapeutic sessions helping clients deal with a variety of emotions. Looking back, we can see how we were still products of our socialization within the pure-systems track of family therapy, which was originally dedicated to changing action and later shifted to an exclusive focus on meaning (Breunlin, Rampage, and Eovaldi, 1995). The writings of pure-systems therapists rarely targeted emotion as a legitimate goal of treatment, and so even though our own therapy had become quite emotion-based, we had trouble recognizing that fact.

Extensive work with the internal family systems metaframework (or what we may now begin to call the mind metaframework) has sharpened our appreciation of how important emotion is. Unlike some other therapies, ours does not ask people how they feel just so that they can talk about and experience their emotions; instead, our therapy attempts to uncover and lift emotional constraints, since emotional constraints can keep people from taking the actions necessary to solve a problem or can prevent people from changing their beliefs or thinking clearly. For example, highly conflictual couples generally have intense face-to-face sequences that escalate out of control. Focusing on action alone, we might attempt to interrupt such sequences by introducing a new behavior. If that approach failed, we might ask what beliefs the couple has that may be fueling the conflict or keeping it from cooling off. What we recognize now is that such conflicts also often include emotional flooding, or what we would describe as angry or hurt parts taking over. Gottman (1994) suggests that emotional flooding, which powerfully affects each partner's physiology, keeps the couple from arguing effectively and must be addressed before conflict-resolution strategies can be pursued.

Action, meaning, and emotion are ubiquitous in human experience, and so any attempt to separate them only serves heuristic and pragmatic purposes. When we first conceived of the sequences metaframework (Breunlin and Schwartz, 1986), we were still thinking primarily as structural and strategic therapists. Consequently, we envisioned sequences exclusively as patterns of action. We now see sequences as much more complex, and as involving a subtle chore-ography of recursively related actions, meanings, and emotions, as illustrated in the following example from Douglas C. Breunlin's case-load:

> Joe and Sylvia are in therapy with their two daughters because Kate, the younger one, is fighting frequently at school. The family describes intense conflicts at home: two people will get into an argument with each other, and other family members then join in, until everyone ends up in a yelling match.

This pattern could be described purely in terms of a sequence of behaviors, but the parents' description of the sequence includes many references to out-of-control emotions. Emotional parts of family members are flooding them and making it impossible for them to engage in effective problem solving:

> When Breunlin asks what keeps family members from calming down so they can avoid senseless yelling, Joe reveals patriarchal gender beliefs. He says he thinks that a father should be able to gain control of his family by yelling. He admits that he has yelled so much that no one listens to him anymore. Breunlin asks Joe how the family can help him develop a different style of leadership. Joe says that Sylvia should walk away rather than escalate the yelling. The girls agree, stat-ing that Sylvia will follow them into their rooms to keep an argument going. Breunlin asks Sylvia what keeps her from walking away. She says that it drives her crazy when Joe walks away because it feels like he is ignoring her.
> Breunlin asks Sylvia if she grew up in a family of yellers. She reports that her parents were in a war for many years until one day her father just stopped fight-ing. Her mother continued the war, but he refused to fight. Sylvia fears that Joe will do the same thing, and

> her belief that walking away is a message of not caring
> keeps her from changing her behavior.

Thus we see that this simple sequence of yelling becomes far more complex when we untangle the subtle choreography of action, meaning, and emotion that keeps it in place.

We seek a clinical balance among the domains of action, meaning, and emotion, since we believe that all three can constrain a system. We also believe that it is possible to effect change through any one of these domains and, if the focus on one of them is not productive, to shift to another. For example, if the therapist and the family agree on a course of action for solving a problem, and this action does not work or cannot be implemented, we ask a constraint-oriented question: What kept you from carrying out this agreed-upon course of action? The answer to this question inevitably reveals constraints of meaning and emotion, which then must be addressed. With Joe and Sylvia, an action change might involve family members calling "time out" when the yelling starts to escalate. If the family returns and Sylvia has not been able to take time out, asking her what kept her from doing so could reveal constraints of meaning and emotion, as just described.

From Internal Family Systems to Mind

The name *internal family systems metaframework* creates a linguistic dilemma: the word *internal* points to intrapsychic phenomena exclusively, implying that the IFS metaframework is relevant only to the inner realm of human experience. To avoid this dilemma, we are considering renaming this framework the *mind metaframework*, in keeping with Bateson's assertion (1979) that mind or mental process is immanent throughout the biopsychosocial system—that is, characteristic patterns among subpersonalities ("parts") and the Self, as described by the IFS model, can be observed at all levels of human systems.

For example, we can track the "interpersonal mind" of a couple, and in their interactions we can recognize the same polarizations and imbalances that characterize each party's inner world. We can also notice how a whole family, community, or country seems to have a collective Self, with various members of each of these systems assuming rigid roles that correspond to the common roles of inner parts, and we can witness contagions of emotion through whole groups of people when parts activate other parts, as if the group were one big mind. Conversely, each of us also contains the collective cultural mind in the form of society's values, as internalized by certain of our parts, and the IFS model has moved in the direction of tracking parallel patterns among the levels of human systems. Schwartz (1995) includes chapters on examining families and culture through the IFS lens.

Further refining the ecological thinking about parts, Schwartz (Goulding and Schwartz, 1995) has also described three groups of roles that parts commonly assume after a person has been hurt:

1. The role of the Manager, who tries to control the inner and outer environment so that the person is not hurt again
2. The role of the Exile, who carries the pain and memories of trauma and is closeted away
3. The role of the Firefighter, who impulsively tries to douse or distract from the fire of feelings that is ignited when the exile is upset

This sort of ecological understanding of common inner relationships allows the therapist to help people enter their own inner worlds with respect and sensitivity. Entry is often gained through a sort of imagery process in which clients see or sense their parts while focusing on them internally. Once a client has viewed a part as a separate entity, he or she can begin to engage in dialogue with it.

For example, therapy may begin with a client's cautious, distrusting Manager and her explosive Firefighter. These two parts can be credited with protecting the system, and they can be asked about their fear of allowing the client anywhere near her exiled pain. The therapist waits for permission from these gatekeepers before encouraging the client to approach the vulnerable, delicate Exile. During this entry-earning period, the therapist is also helping the client differentiate her Self by detecting when her parts are blended with the Self and asking them to separate from it. As the parts separate, the client becomes increasingly compassionate toward all her parts and confident in her ability to deal with them. The client's compassionate Self, once given permission, can form a trusting relationship with the Exile. At that point, it is safe to ask this part to tell its story—to show the client scenes from the past that illustrate where the Exile got the extreme feelings or beliefs that it carries.

We have found that this compassionate witnessing of a part's story is often all that is needed for the part to unload its extreme beliefs and emotions, a process called *unburdening*. Once unburdened, parts are spontaneously and rapidly transformed. They are released from the rigid, polarizing roles into which they were forced, and they are free to find much preferred new roles. As their Exiles heal, clients find that they feel lighter, less easily hurt, and more solid. Because the whole system is no longer so vulnerable or delicate, Managers and Firefighters can now relax and release their own burdens. As this happens, what was a rigid three-role system becomes a harmonious inner family, with flexible roles and trusted leadership. Thus the IFS metaframework has evolved into a healing process with clear, teachable guidelines. As people harmonize internally, they are better able to harmonize externally; their relationships and families begin to reorganize (Schwartz, in press).

The preceding discussion does not by any means imply, however, that we have now become individual therapists. We still find that this process works in the other direction, too: harmonizing and balancing the outer aspects (biological, relational, family, community, and societal) of a person's system will help harmonize his or her internal family. Therefore, the therapist can move fluidly from internal to external and back again, as the collaborative search for constraints may dictate. Used along with the other metaframeworks, the IFS metaframework continues to offer an extraordinarily rich and broad perspective, even though it has itself become a comprehensive approach to therapy.

Making Multiculturalism Work

In keeping with the development of our original multicultural metaframework, we have continued to ask our students and families about the membership contexts that organize their beliefs and preferred ways of acting (Mac Kune-Karrer and Taylor, 1995). This questioning has given us information about other important contexts that were not originally specified in the multicultural metaframework. As a result, we now take account of minority/majority experiences that are attributable not only to ethnicity, race, economics, religion, gender, age, education, and regional background but also to sexual orientation, disability, and physical characteristics (being too tall or too short, being too thin or obese, wearing thick glasses, and so on). We will undoubtedly discover new contexts of minority/majority status as we continue to teach and practice the metaframeworks perspective.

Clients who are respectfully asked about their experiences as members of these groups inevitably give responses that reveal the oppression, prejudice, and discrimination associated with not fitting the dominant majority's "ideal." Conversely, the "goodness of fit" that majority-group members feel can produce in them a sense of privilege that may prevent them from recognizing, let alone changing, the oppressive nature of their privilege. The recognition of privilege and the willingness to relinquish it can alleviate the constraining effects of oppression, prejudice, and discrimination on members of minority groups.

Efforts to address all forms of discrimination must take place at all levels. For example, the oppressive and constraining effects of racism will not be eliminated until individual members of the dominant white group recognize and change the subtle and insidious effects of racism on their daily interactions, until communities root out the racist practices of their institutions, and until our society becomes more socially just. Therefore, planning directed toward addressing racism must also be multileveled and can include racial-sensitivity training, institutional change (for example, in schools), and political action.

Testing Assumptions About the Gender Metaframework

The gender metaframework has continued to undergo revision, primarily through research focused on developing a survey for empirically testing the validity of the gender metaframework's primary construct: the evolution of gender balance. (This work is the product of the Chicago Center for Gender Studies, whose members include Virginia Simons, Kathy Stathos, Cathy Weigel-Foy, Betty Mac Kune-Karrer, and Stan Starkman.)

To date, we have tested our survey's assumptions and developed construct validity for the tool as a whole. The survey has been completed by psychotherapists in training and has attempted to determine whether they develop gender awareness in the same sequence posited in the model. As a result of this research, we have revised our initial construct and now conceive the evolution of gender balance as comprising four positions rather than five. (We found that the categories In Transition and Balanced could not easily be discriminated, and so we collapsed them both into the Balanced category.) We are now entering the last phase of the research project and are increasing our sample so that we can reach an empirical conclusion about whether the survey has been effective in determining where our student psychotherapists stand in the evolution of gender balance.

Our work in couples therapy and our personal journeys have also continued to impress on us the many constraints on the achievement of true gender balance. We once believed we could work toward and achieve gender balance through couples therapy, but we increasingly recognize that gender balance is a multileveled issue. Men and women alike struggle to step out of deep-seated gender roles, which often restrict movement toward gender balance even when each member of the couple professes the desire to move in that direction, and sometimes individual work is needed. The institution of marriage itself, with its economic, role, and emotional constraints, can also inhibit the quest for gender balance, and a couple aspiring to gender balance may need to have a sobering and profound discussion about the viability of this institution.

The Question of Additional Metaframeworks

Although we are still comfortable with the flexibility afforded by the six metaframeworks, our colleagues and students have suggested that we also include other metaframeworks, particularly metaframeworks for biology and spirituality. These suggestions have prompted us to clarify our definition of what a metaframework is, and to establish a clear distinction between metaframeworks and levels. A *level* is a discrete unit of the biopsychosocial continuum. For example, it is possible to observe, hypothesize about, and plan treatment to address a particular level. A *metaframework*, by contrast, is a principle encompassing a whole domain of ideas about human systems, and it is isomorphic (that is, applicable) across all systems levels. For example, development is a metaframework because it is a principle of living systems, it encompasses a vast domain of ideas, and it is isomorphic across all levels.

Biology

In view of these distinctions, it seems to us that biology is a level rather than a metaframework. We can observe and hypothesize about biological processes, and we can plan treatment to address the constraints of biology. Viewing biology as a level, we can acknowledge and incorporate the huge contribution that recent biological research has made to our understanding of human systems. As family therapists, we were taught that biological theories were to be avoided because they were reductionistic rather than holistic. As seasoned clinicians, however, we have seen clearly that physiological systems exert powerful influences on individuals and families. We now always include the biological level in our assessment of a system's constraints, and when biological constraints are detected, they are simply understood as part of our hypothesis, just as we understand other constraints.

Each metaframework affects and is affected by biological processes. For example, the presence of sickle cell anemia among African-Americans, or the high incidence of diabetes among Native Americans, would constitute a cultural constraint at the level of biology. Organizational constraints can also exist at the level of biology. For example, a muscle condition called *fibromyalgia*, which causes aching and fatigue, constrained several women from functioning well as parents by producing imbalances in their families, imbalances that led to polarization and impaired leadership.

Accepting the impact of biological constraints has made us less reluctant to recommend the use of psychotropic medicine. If a client's depression or anxiety is not relieved by the release of constraints at other levels, we do not hesitate to recommend that the client be evaluated for medication. When medicine lifts a biological constraint, a client can more readily address other constraints.

The down side to using medication, of course, is that people may give the drug credit for improvements, and this attribution can decrease their trust in their Selves or their relationships. This is why we still try first to release other constraints. Fortunately, however, we find that a client's parts and his or her physiology are highly interrelated, so that by bringing harmony to inner systems we can often release biological constraints without using medication.

Spirituality

Interest in spirituality is increasing, both in society generally and in the practice of psychotherapy, and so it is incumbent on us to ascertain how spirituality can be incorporated into the metaframeworks perspective. Determining whether spirituality is a metaframework was a challenge, partly because it is difficult to define what spirituality is. It can be found at the levels of the person, the relationship, the family, the community, and the society, but we have been unable to define the biology of spirituality, and we also recognize that some aspects of spirituality transcend all levels. At the time of this writing, we are debating the appropriateness of a spirituality metaframework. Nevertheless, we have found multiple ways of incorporating spirituality into our work.

Aspects of spirituality, particularly the spiritual dimension of religious experience, can be addressed with the culture metaframework, but spirituality as currently understood in our culture transcends religion. It has been referred to as the fourth dimension of human experience, the dimension that addresses the yearning humans have to be connected with a larger power or divine being (Anderson and Worthen, 1997). For many people, spirituality gives meaning to life, whether spirituality means an individualized set of beliefs and practices, a shared passion that makes relationships cohesive, or a lifeline to a group of other people (the family, the community, the culture) who provide a sense of belonging and connectedness.

Because increasing numbers of our clients complain of feeling isolated and lacking meaning in their lives, spirituality has become an important theme in our therapy. The IFS model has also moved in a spiritual direction as our clients have found that the energy of the Self provides a path to spiritual experiences that give direction and comfort.

The Narrative Movement

Since we wrote the first edition of this book, postmodernism in general and social constructionism in particular have come to permeate psychotherapy. These two currents have promulgated the idea that reality is a social construction experienced by clients as a story or a narrative. With that assumption comes the proposition that clients' or family members' reality can be totally and lastingly transformed if they are helped to reauthor their personal narratives through the practice of narrative therapy (White and Epston, 1990). In metaframeworks language, narrative therapy lifts constraints of meaning through a plan of reauthoring.

We do believe that personal narratives can themselves be powerfully constraining, but we also find that new narratives emerge spontaneously as clients become less and less constrained in other ways. Rarely do we have to actively coauthor a new narrative or lead a client to a new, empowering story. Such stories already exist within clients; all we have to do is liberate these stories. Here lies an important difference between the metaframeworks perspective and narrative therapy: we remain convinced that people contain untapped resources, whereas social constructionism has led narrative therapists to discard this point of view and ascribe any credit for an improved perspective to interaction with others. For this reason, narrative therapists use a questioning process to lead clients to new, often heroic, stories about themselves and their lives.

The suggestion that all a client needs is a new story is unfortunate. Clients are often trapped in tangled webs of constraints that a new story will not change. A constraint that has been ignored can quickly unravel a new story unless the story is constantly buttressed by a therapist or a support group. For example, Richard C. Schwartz works with many female survivors of childhood sexual abuse (Goulding & Schwartz, 1995). It is quite possible to go over the history of a woman in this situation and, by pointing out times when she overcame her fears or pain, convince parts of her that she is heroic rather than dirty or defective. When Schwartz tried to work this way, however, he found that other parts of the client did not go along with this new story; in fact, these parts would try even harder to bring her down. There were parts that hated the client for having sexual feelings, and they were afraid that if she began to feel competent, she would act on her sexual feelings. Other parts carried the belief that if she began feeling good, she would be punished because that is what the abuser used to do. Still other parts carried a powerful loyalty to the abusive family and feared that if the client felt stronger she would cut off contact with her family. Schwartz found that things worked better if he and his client, instead of hearing these resistant voices as relics of the old story and trying to ignore or fight them, listened to these parts' fears and let them tell their stories. Once the client could witness and embrace these parts in a compassionate way, they no longer had to sabotage her progress.

When a narrative therapist becomes active as a coauthor with a client, the "selling" of the new story can turn it into an oppressive, dominant discourse within the person. The result can be the marginalizing of other inner stories that conflict with the new one. This may be one reason the narrative approach has come to rely so extensively on adjunctive supports (the creation of client "leagues," or the writing of letters). The implication is that some clients need constant reinforcement to maintain the internal hegemony of the new story and suppress the old.

In other cases, changing the stories does not alone solve the problem because the problem is embedded in constraints on action or emotion. Constraints at other levels (such as the level of biology or the level of the community) or within other metaframeworks (such as the organization metaframework or the development metaframework) might also exist. It may not be possible to lift these constraints by working exclusively from a narrative perspective. In order not to handicap therapists, we remain committed to the view that the narrative metaphor is useful so long as we can transcend the narrow precepts that dictate its exclusive use.

Toward a More Comprehensive Theory of Constraints

Over the years, as we have listened to clients, we have marveled increasingly at the incredible variety of ways in which people can become constrained. Constraints have popped up in unexpected places: what to other therapists might have sounded like excuses (if those therapists were searching for deficits) sounded to us more and more like legitimate constraints.

Our theory of constraints had to allow us to tap this variety fully without becoming overwhelmed by it. Even though the metaframeworks perspective proved very helpful in naming constraints, we increasingly found that we had to pay careful attention to where the constraints existed. Fortunately, biopsychosocial theory and its concept of levels continues to provide a framework for guiding us to constraints.

As family therapists, we still believe that having as many family members as possible participate in the therapy makes it easier to identify constraints. To read the feedback of family members, however, we often found ourselves moving away from the family level and listening instead with our attention on other levels less familiar to family therapists, particularly the levels of biology, the person, the community, and even the society. As we shifted from one level to another, it also became clearer that constraints related to a particular metaframework often surfaced at more than one level. This finding offered clinical confirmation of the concept of isomorphism. In our hypothesizing, we also found ourselves juxtaposing the language of levels and metaframeworks; we might speak of constraints of organization at, say, the individual, family, and community levels.

Understanding that the metaframeworks are isomorphic at all levels, and seeking a way to depict this set of relationships visually, we constructed Figure 11.1, which we named *the web of constraints*. This figure is a convenient device for anchoring clients' reports to the theory of constraints. Our recognition that many client systems are constrained by such webs created a recursive learning process: the more we listened to and were open to the evidence of such webs, the more clients were prepared to share them with us. We found it harder and harder to hold fast to a unidimensional understanding of client systems, as the models of therapy often purport to do.

The web of constraints evokes the image of a spiderweb and suggests that a problem, once trapped in the web, can be difficult to dislodge unless the constraints are changed. It also suggests that constraints can be interlocking: one thread of a spiderweb can carry little

Figure 11.1.   The Web of Constraints.

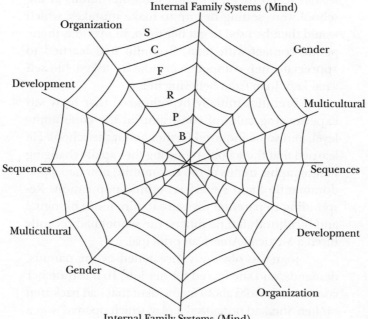

Internal Family Systems (Mind)

Organization

Gender

Development

Multicultural

Sequences

Sequences

Multicultural

Development

Gender

Organization

Internal Family Systems (Mind)

S
C
F
R
P
B

The letters in the figure stand for the levels of the biopsychosocial continuum: B = biology, P = person, R = relationship, F = family, C = community, and S = society.

weight, but the interlocking grid itself is very strong. The following example from a case treated by Breunlin illustrates the application of the web of constraints and highlights the importance of levels, the metaframeworks, and the concept of isomorphism.

> Joan, a forty-two-year-old single teacher, returned to therapy feeling anxious and depressed. Joan had grown up in a close-knit Lithuanian community in the suburbs of Chicago. The community where she lived and taught had undergone many demographic changes. As a result, many ethnic tensions had developed among the students, the parents, and the school staff.

Joan believed that her students were refusing to let her teach them, and that the other adults at the school were setting her up to make mistakes, which would then be used to get her fired. In previous therapeutic contact with Joan, Breunlin had learned to appreciate her competence; now he asked himself what kept Joan from believing in it.

Breunlin initially hypothesized that Joan was experiencing cultural constraints at the community level, and so he inquired further about the school. He learned that the school, reflecting the rapidly changing demographic trends of the community, now had a predominantly Latin American ethnic population. Responding to parental pressure to hire more bilingual and bicultural staff members, the school had recently hired a Mexican-American principal.

Joan was obviously threatened by the parents' demands, and she feared for her job. To illustrate her concerns, she told about an incident that had backfired on her. She had organized a play, which opened with a scene in which several Mexican-American students were waking up from a siesta. After the play, a Mexican-American teacher accused her of perpetuating stereotypes by using a scene that portrayed Mexicans as lazy.

Clearly, the fit between Joan and the community, and specifically between Joan and the school, had shifted. Undoubtedly this shift accounted for some of Joan's insecurity, but Breunlin wondered what kept her from being able to deal more effectively with these political tensions in the school. He hypothesized that she might have polarized parts.

When Breunlin asked Joan what she said to herself when she felt criticized by her colleagues, she identified two polarized parts. One she called Pushy Sister, an advocate and protector who often encouraged Joan to stand up for herself; Joan had begun to wonder whether her assertiveness was being viewed as hostile and aggressive by her colleagues. The other part, Sob

Sister, told Joan that she could not cope. This part often catastrophized and made Joan feel hopeless about the situation at school.

Fearful that Pushy Sister had made her say or do things that had alienated her colleagues, Joan would no longer listen to her, and so she was more and more at the mercy of Sob Sister's negativity. Joan's internal process was clearly replicating the ethnic polarization in the school. As a consequence, her internal process and the multicultural context had combined to create a web of constraints that accounted in part for Joan's increased fears and her seeming lack of competence.

Another change in Joan's context required Breunlin to shift to the level of the family. Joan's father had died several years earlier, after a long illness that had required Joan to miss many days of teaching. Her mother, with whom she had an ambivalent relationship, had just had a stroke.

Uncertainty about her mother's prognosis, as well as the looming demand for her future care, weighed heavily on Joan. She legitimately wondered how she could take care of her mother, meet the intense demands of her teaching position, and also contend with the politics of the job. Moreover, Joan felt that Pushy Sister had given her the courage to move out of her parents' home years before, and now she questioned whether this had been the right thing to do. She seemed to believe she was responsible for her mother's care, even if taking on that responsibility meant that she would have to quit her job and move into her mother's home to provide it.

Within a few sessions of entering therapy, Joan's fears about her job intensified, and she became more depressed. She began to ruminate about school, question her judgment, and lose sleep as the hospital planned to discharge her mother. Joan decided to quit her job, believing she had become so ineffectual that she was actually harming her students. At times she was suicidal, and it seemed that only her concern about her mother's health was keeping her from killing herself. Her acute stress was the product of a web of constraints that existed at the levels of biology, person, family, and community and involved the metaframeworks of mind and culture.

Unable to calm Joan's polarized parts, Breunlin shifted to the level of biology and suggested to Joan that her high levels of anxiety and depression might be keeping her from thinking clearly about her complex situation. He referred her to a psychiatrist to be evaluated for the appropriateness of medication. Breunlin and Joan also discussed the option of her taking a medical leave of absence to reduce her high levels of stress. Joan refused, claiming that her taking the leave would hurt the children further.

The benefits to be had from medication were a few weeks away, and Joan's parts continued to be polarized, so Breunlin shifted again to the community level. He secured Joan's permission to speak to her principal, hoping to gain a better understanding of the school constraints.

In the telephone conversation with Breunlin, the principal praised Joan and offered his assurance that she was in no danger of losing her job. Initially Joan was relieved, but soon she dismissed this information, explaining that the principal would not be honest. Her mistrust in the Latin American community seemed to be growing.

Breunlin decided to explore her cultural and family background further. Joan was proud of her ethnicity and often spoke of her family, which included a younger sister and many aunts and uncles. In one session, she mentioned that her foster sister, Rosa, had visited her mother in the hospital. Having never heard about this foster sister before, Breunlin inquired about her. Pieces of the puzzle fell into place when Joan volunteered that Rosa was of Mexican descent. The connection between the foster sister and her polarized parts, Pushy Sister and Sob Sister, became clear as Breunlin and Joan discussed how a child of Mexican descent had been received in her family and in the community.

In time Joan began to explore the ambivalence she felt about her foster sister. She remembered that Rosa was often ill and required much attention from her mother, and how Rosa often got into trouble in school. Eventually Rosa's troubles ushered in a tumultuous time for the family, with Joan feeling very neglected. No wonder Joan had ambivalence about Mexican-Americans! A part of her had been drawn to the Latin American community, just as her parents had been toward Rosa, but another part of her was ambivalent about the impact of Mexican people on her life, both in her family and in her career.

To increase the complexity still further, Joan began talking about her relationships with Latin American men. None of these relationships had become serious, because her family could not tolerate Joan marrying outside her ethnic group. Her involvement with Latin American men became an added constraint that made it difficult for her to find a partner. Joan eventually stopped dating and concentrated instead on teaching Latin American children.

When the political balance in the school shifted, Joan's long-denied ambivalent connections with Latin American people—at the personal, relational, family, and community levels—came to the surface. To address her symptoms of anxiety and depression, and to make a decision about her job, Joan had to address her web of constraints and learn to balance the tension between her polarized parts, the demands of the school, and the care of her mother.

The Metaframeworks Perspective and Managed Care

The metaframeworks perspective can be readily adapted to the system of managed care, which entails a focus on specific problems and time limits. The therapy based on the metaframeworks perspective begins with a clear definition of the presenting problem and the articulation of a web of constraints related only to that problem (Pinsof, 1995). Once the web is defined, the plan is to lift the web within the allotted time.

One approach is to use action plans as the initial attempt to solve the problem. We call this the "Nike" or "Just Do It" principle, since we recognize that the problem will be quickly solved if the client system directly takes the action necessary to solve it.

A good number of cases can actually be handled in this fashion. We have found, however, that these cases have successful outcomes within a few sessions because what is involved is a simple web of readily identifiable and straightforward constraints, which do not include strong constraints of meaning and emotion. Nevertheless, when the constraints cannot be lifted within the allotted time, the therapist is still in a strong position to get more sessions approved: he or she can establish that the most efficient approach was tried first and can then argue that more sessions are indicated, given the presence of constraints that could not reasonably be lifted within the original time frame. With the metaframeworks perspective, therapists can document how they have tried to apply the guidelines of managed care, and why there are compelling reasons for additional sessions.

The Future of the Metaframeworks Perspective

We have found the metaframeworks perspective flexible enough to accommodate our personal growth as therapists, as well as the changes in the field of family therapy, and we are encouraged to continue working with and developing it. Now that others are actively struggling with the perspective, we also encourage you to tell us what works and what does not work for you in your own context.

References

Anderson, C. M., Reiss, C. J., and Hogarty, G. E. *Schizophrenia and the Family: A Practitioner's Guide to Psychoeducation and Management.* New York: Guilford Press, 1986.

Anderson, D. A., and Worthen, D. "Exploring a Fourth Dimension: Spirituality as a Resource for the Couple Therapist." *Journal of Marital and Family Therapy,* 1997, *23*(1), 3–11.

Anderson, H., and Goolishian, H. "Human Systems as Linguistic Systems: Preliminary and Evolving Ideas About the Implications for Clinical Theory." *Family Process,* 1988, *27,* 371–394.

Aponte, H. J., and VanDeusen, J. M. "Structural Family Therapy." In A. S. Gurman and D. P. Kniskern (eds.), *Handbook of Family Therapy.* New York: Brunner/Mazel, 1981.

Assagioli, R. *The Act of Will.* New York: Viking Penguin, 1973.

Bateson, G. "A Systems Approach." *International Journal of Psychiatry,* 1970, *9,* 242–244.

Bateson, G. *Steps to an Ecology of Mind.* New York: Ballantine, 1972.

Bateson, G. *Mind and Nature.* New York: Dutton, 1979.

Berry, J. W. "Acculturation as Varieties of Adaptation." In A. M. Padilla (ed.), *Acculturation Theory, Models, and Some New Findings.* Boulder, Colo.: Westview Press, 1980.

Berry, J. W., Kalin, R., and Taylor, D. M. *Multiculturalism and Ethnic Attitudes in Canada.* Ottawa: Government of Canada, 1977.

Bogden, J. L. "Family Organization as an Ecology of Ideas: An Alternative of the Reification of Family Systems." *Family Process*, 1984a, *23*(3), 375–388.

Bogden, J. L. "Rejoinder: Person to Person." *Family Process*, 1984b, *23*(3), 395–400.

Boszormenyi-Nagy, I., and Spark, G. *Invisible Loyalties: Reciprocity in Intergenerational Family Therapy*. New York: HarperCollins, 1973.

Bowen, M. *Family Therapy in Clinical Practice*. Northvale, N.J.: Aronson, 1978.

Boyd-Franklin, N. *Black Families in Therapy: A Multi-Systems Approach*. New York: Guilford Press, 1989.

Braverman, L. (ed.). *Women, Feminism, and Family Therapy*. New York: Haworth Press, 1988.

Breunlin, D. C. "Expanding the Concept of Stages in Family Therapy." In D. C. Breunlin (ed.), *Stages: Patterns of Change over Time*. Rockville, Md.: Aspen, 1985a.

Breunlin, D. C. (ed.). *Stages: Patterns of Change over Time*. Rockville, Md.: Aspect, 1985b.

Breunlin, D. C. "Oscillation Theory and Family Development." In C. Falicov (ed.), *Family Transitions: Continuity an Change over the Life Cycle*. New York: Guilford Press, 1988.

Breunlin, D. C. "Clinical Implications of Oscillation Theory: Family Development and the Process of Change." In C. N. Ramsey (ed.), *Family Systems in Medicine*. New York: Guilford Press, 1989.

Breunlin, D. C., and Cimmarusti, R. A. "Seven Opportunities for Brief Therapy: A Recipe for Rapid Change." In M. Aronson and L. Wolberg (eds.), *Group and Family Therapy*. New York: Brunner/Mazel, 1983.

Breunlin, D. C., Rampage, C., and Eovaldi, M. L. "Family Therapy Supervision: Toward an Integrative Perspective." In R. Mikesell, D. D. Lusterman, and S. McDaniel (eds.), *Handbook of Family Psychology and Systems Theory*. Washington, D.C.: American Psychological Association, 1995.

Breunlin, D. C., and Schwartz, R. C. "Sequences: Toward a Common Denominator of Family Therapy." *Family Process*, 1986, *25*(1), 67–88.

Brown-Standridge, M. D. "A Paradigm for Construction of Family Therapy Tasks." *Family Process*, 1989, *28*(4), 471–489.

Capra, F. *The Turning Point*. New York: Simon & Schuster, 1982.

Carter, E. A., and McGoldrick, M. *The Family Life Cycle: A Framework for Family Therapy.* New York: Gardner Press, 1980.

Cecchin, G. F. "Hypothesizing, Circularity, and Neutrality Revisited: An Invitation to Curiosity." *Family Process,* 1987, *26*(4), 405–414.

Chess, S., Thomas, A., and Birch, H. G. *Your Child Is a Person.* New York: Viking Penguin, 1972.

Combrinck-Graham, L. "A Model for Family Development." *Family Process,* 1985, *24,* 139–150.

Cooklin, A. "Change in 'Here and Now' Systems Versus Systems over Time." In A. Bentovin, G. Garel-Barnes, and A. Conklin (eds.), *Family Therapy: Complementary Frameworks of Theory and Practice.* Philadelphia: Grune & Stratton, 1982.

Davidson, M. *Uncommon Sense.* Los Angeles: Tarcher, 1983.

Dell, P. F. "Beyond Homeostasis: Toward a Concept of Coherence." *Family Process,* 1982, *21*(1), 21–42.

Dell, P. F. "In Defense of 'Linear Causality.'" *Family Process,* 1986, *25*(4), 513–522.

Efran, J. S. Lukens, R. J., and Lukens, M. D. "Constructivism: What's in It for You?" *Family Therapy Networker,* 1988, *12*(5), 26–35.

Ehrenreich, B. *The Hearts of Men.* New York: Anchor Press, 1983.

Ehrlich, P. R., and Ehrlich, A. H. *The Population Explosion.* New York: Simon & Schuster, 1990.

Eichler, M. *Nonsexist Research Methods.* London: Allen & Unwin, 1988.

Eisler, R. *The Chalice and the Blade.* New York: HarperCollins, 1987.

Elizur, J., and Minuchin, S. *Institutionalizing Madness: Families, Therapy, and Society.* New York: Basic Books, 1989.

Engel, G. L. "The Need for a New Medical Model." *Science,* 1977, *196*(4286), 129–136.

Falicov, C. J. (ed.) *Cultural Perspectives in Family Therapy.* Rockville, Md.: Aspen, 1983.

Falicov, C. J. "Commentary: Focus on Stages." *Family Process,* 1984, *23,* 329–333.

Falicov, C. J. "Family Sociology and Family Therapy Contributions to the Family Development Framework: A Comparative Analysis and Thoughts on Future Trends." In C. J. Falicov (ed.), *Family Transitions: Continuity and Change over the Life Cycle.* New York: Guilford Press, 1988a.

Falicov, C. J. (ed.). *Family Transitions: Continuity and Change over the Life Cycle.* New York: Guilford Press, 1988b.

Falicov, C. J. "Learning to Think Culturally." In H. A. Liddle, D. C. Breunlin, and R. C. Schwartz (eds.), *Handbook of Family Therapy Training and Supervision.* New York: Guilford Press, 1988c.

Falicov, C. J., and Brudner-White, L. "The Shifting Family Triangle: The Issue of Cultural and Contextual Relativity." In C. J. Falicov (ed.), *Cultural Perspectives in Family Therapy.* Rockville, Md.: Aspen, 1983.

Farrell, W. *The Liberated Man.* New York: Bantam Books, 1975.

Feynman, R. P., Leighton, R. B., and Sands, M. *The Feynman Lectures on Physics.* Vol. 1. Reading, Mass.: Addison-Wesley, 1963.

Fisch, R., Weakland, J. H., and Segal, R. *The Tactics of Change: Doing Therapy Briefly.* San Francisco: Jossey-Bass, 1982.

Fraser, J. S. "Structural and Strategic Family Therapy: A Basis for Marriage, or Grounds for Divorce?" *Journal of Marital and Family Therapy,* 1982, *8,* 13–22.

Friedan, B. *The Feminine Mystique.* New York: Norton, 1963.

Garbarino, J., and Stott, F. *What Children Can Tell Us: Eliciting, Interpreting, and Evaluating Information from Children.* San Francisco: Jossey-Bass, 1989.

Geertz, C. *The Interpretation of Cultures.* New York: Basic Books, 1973.

Gleick, J. *Chaos: The Making of a New Science.* New York: Viking Penguin, 1988.

Goffman, E. *Relations in Public.* New York: Viking Penguin, 1971.

Goldner, V. "Feminism and Family Therapy." *Family Process,* 1985, *24*(1), 31–48.

Goldner, V. "Generation and Gender: Normative and Covert Hierarchies." *Family Process,* 1988, *27*(1), 17–33.

Goodrich, T. J., Rampage, C., Ellman, B., and Halstead, K. *Feminist Family Therapy: A Casebook.* New York: Norton, 1988.

Gottman, J. *Why Marriages Succeed or Fail.* New York: Simon and Schuster, 1994.

Goulding, R., and Schwartz, R. C. *Mosaic Mind: Empowering the Tormented Selves of Child Abuse Survivors.* New York: Norton, 1995.

Guerin, P. J., and Gordon, E. M. "Trees, Triangles, and Temperament in the Child-Centered Family." In H. C. Fishman and B. Rosman (eds.), *Evolving Models of Family Change.* New York: Guilford Press, 1986.

Hadley, T. R., Jacob, T., Milliones, J., Caplan, J., and Spitz, D. "The

Relationship Between Family Development Crises and the Appearance of Symptoms in a Family Member." *Family Process,* 1974, *13*(2), 207–214.

Haley, J. *Strategies of Psychotherapy.* Philadelphia: Grune & Stratton, 1963.

Haley, J. *Uncommon Therapy: The Psychiatric Techniques of Milton H. Erickson, M.D.* New York: Norton, 1973.

Haley, J. *Problem-Solving Therapy.* San Francisco: Jossey-Bass, 1976.

Haley, J. *Leaving Home.* New York: McGraw-Hill, 1980.

Haley, J. *Reflections on Therapy and Other Essays.* Chevy Chase, Md.: The Family Therapy Institute of Washington, D.C., 1981.

Hall, A., and Fagan, R. "Definition of System" *General Systems Yearbook,* 1956, *1,* 18–28.

Hardy, K. V. "The Theoretical Myth of Sameness: A Critical Issue in Family Therapy Training and Treatment." In G. W. Saba, B. M. Karrer, and K. V. Hardy (eds.), *Minorities and Family Therapy.* New York: Guilford Press, 1989.

Hare-Mustin, R. T. "A Feminist Approach to Family Therapy." *Family Process,* 1978, *17*(2), 181–194.

Held, B., and Pols, E. "The Confusion About Epistemology—And What to Do About It." *Family Process,* 1985, *24*(4), 509–516.

Hillman, J. *Re-visioning Psychology.* New York: HarperCollins, 1975.

Hoffman, L. "Breaking the Homeostatic Cycle." In P. J. Guerin (ed.), *Family Therapy: Theory and Practice.* New York: Gardner Press, 1976.

Hoffman, L. *Foundations of Family Therapy: A Conceptual Framework for Systems Change.* New York: Basic Books, 1981.

Hsu, F. (ed.). *Psychological Anthropology.* Rochester, Vt.: Schenkman, 1972.

Hughes, S., Berger, M., and Wright, L. "The Family Life Cycle and Clinical Intervention." *Journal of Marriage and Family Counseling,* 1978, *4,* 33–40.

Humphrey, F. G. "Changing Roles for Women: Implications for Marriage Counselors." *Journal of Marriage and Family Counseling,* 1975, *1*(3), 219–228.

Imber-Black, E., Roberts, J., and Whiting, R. (eds.). *Rituals in Families and Family Therapy.* New York: Norton, 1988

Jackson, D. "The Question of Family Homeostasis." *Psychiatric Quarterly Supplement,* 1957, *(3)*1, 79–90.

James, K., and McIntyre, D. "The Reproduction of Families: The Social Role of Family Therapy." *Journal of Marital and Family Therapy*, 1983, *9*(2), 119–130.

James, K., and MacKinnon, L. K. "Theory and Practice of Structural Family Therapy: Illustration and Technique." *Australian and New Zealand Journal of Family Therapy*, 1986, *7*(4), 223–233.

Karrer, B. M. "Families of Mexican Descent: A Contextual Approach." In R. B. Birrer (ed.), *Urban Family Medicine*. New York: Springer-Verlag, 1987.

Karrer, B. M. "The Sound of Two Hands Clapping: Cultural Interactions of the Minority Family and the Therapist." In G. W. Saba, B. M. Karrer, and K. V. Hardy (eds.), *Minorities and Family Therapy*. New York: Haworth Press, 1989.

Karrer, B. M., and Burgoyne, N. *Thinking Culturally: A Clinical and Research Perspective and Its Applications,* forthcoming.

Keeney, B. *Aesthetics of Change.* New York: Guilford Press, 1983.

Keeney, B., and Sprenkle, D. "Ecosystemic Epistemology: Critical Implications for the Aesthetics and Pragmatics of Family Therapy." *Family Process*, 1982, *21,* 1–19.

Koestler, A. *The Ghost in the Machine.* London: Hutchinson, 1967.

Koestler, A. *Janus: A Summing Up.* New York: Vintage Books, 1978.

Kozol, J. "The New Untouchables." *Newsweek,* Winter/Spring 1990, pp. 48–53.

Lebow, J. L. "On the Value of Integrating Approaches to Family Therapy." *Journal of Marital and Family Therapy*, 1984, *10*(2), 127–138.

Lederer, W. J., and Jackson, D. D. *The Mirages of Marriage.* New York: Norton, 1968.

Lewis, J. M., Beavers, W. R., Gossett, J. T., and Phillips, V. A. *No Single Thread: Psychological Health in Family Systems.* New York: Brunner/Mazel, 1976.

Luepnitz, D. A. *The Family Interpreted: Feminist Theory in Clinical Practice.* New York: Basic Books, 1988.

Mac Kune-Karrer, B., and Taylor, E. H. "Toward Multiculturality: Implications for the Pediatrician." *Pediatric Clinics of North America,* 1995, *42*(1), 21–30.

McGoldrick, M., Anderson, C., and Walsh, F. *Women in Families: A Framework for Family Therapy.* New York: Norton, 1989.

McGoldrick, M., and Carter, E. A. "Forming a Remarried Family." In E. A. Carter and M. McGoldrick (eds.), *The Family Life Cycle: A Framework for Family Therapy.* New York: Gardner Press, 1980.

McGoldrick, M., Pearce, J. K., and Giordano, J., (eds.). *Ethnicity and Family Therapy.* New York: Guilford Press, 1982.

Madanes, C. *Strategic Family Therapy.* San Francisco: Jossey-Bass, 1981.

Madanes, C. "With a Little Help from My Friends." *Family Therapy Networker,* 1983, *7,* 4.

Madanes, C. *Sex, Love, and Violence.* New York: Norton, 1990.

Manes, C. *Green Rage: Radical Environmentalism and the Unmaking of Civilization.* Boston: Little, Brown, 1990.

Maruyama, M. "The Second Cybernetics: Deviation-Amplifying Mutual Causative Processes." *American Scientist,* 1963, *51,* 164–179.

Maturana, H., and Varela, F. *Autopoiesis and Cognition: The Realization of Living.* Dordrecht, the Netherlands: D. Reidl, 1980.

Mayers, B. "Minority Group: An Ideological Formation." *Social Problems,* 1984, *32,* 1–15.

Minuchin, S. *Families and Family Therapy.* Cambridge, Mass.: Harvard University Press, 1974.

Minuchin, S. "Families and Individual Development: Provocations from the Field of Family Therapy." *Child Development,* 1985, *56,* 289–302.

Minuchin, S., and Fishman, C. *Family Therapy Techniques.* Cambridge, Mass.: Harvard University Press, 1981.

Montalvo, B., and Gutierrez, M. "A Perspective for the Use of the Cultural Dimensions in Family Therapy." In C. J. Falicov (ed.), *Cultural Perspectives in Family Therapy.* Rockville, Md.: Aspen, 1983.

Montalvo, B., and Gutierrez, M. "Nine Assumptions for Work with Ethnic Minority Families." In G. W. Saba, B. M. Karrer, and K. V. Hardy (eds.), *Minorities and Family Therapy.* New York: Haworth Press, 1989.

Neugarten, B. *Middle Age and Aging.* Chicago: University of Chicago Press, 1968.Nichols, M. *The Self in the System.* New York: Brunner/Mazel, 1987.

Nichols, M. *The Self in the System.* New York: Brunner/Mazel, 1987.

Nichols, M., and Schwartz, R. C. *Family Therapy: Concepts and Methods.* New York: Allyn & Bacon, 1997.

Parsons, T., and Bates, R. F. *Family Socialization and Interaction.* New York: Free Press, 1955.

Pearce, W. B., and Cronen, V. E. *Communication, Action, and Meaning.* New York: Praeger, 1980.

Penn, P. "Circular Questioning." *Family Process,* 1982, *21*(3), 267–280.

Penn, P. "Feed-Forward: Future Questions, Future Maps." *Family Process,* 1984, *24*(3), 299–310.

Pinsof, W. M. "Integrative Problem-Centered Therapy: Toward the Synthesis of Family and Individual Psychotherapies." *Journal of Marital and Family Therapy,* 1983, *9*(1), 19–36.

Pinsof, W. M. "The Process of Family Therapy: The Development of the Family Therapist Coding System." In L. S. Greenberg and W. M. Pinsof (eds.), *The Psychotherapeutic Process: A Research Handbook.* New York: Guilford Press, 1986.

Pinsof, W. M. *Integrative Problem-Centered Therapy: A Synthesis of Family, Individual, and Biological Therapies.* New York: Basic Books, 1995.

Rifkin, J. *Entropy: Into the Greenhouse World.* New York: Bantam Books, 1989.

Ritterman, M. K. "Paradigmatic Classification of Family Therapy Theories." *Family Process,* 1977, *16*(1), 29–45.

Rodriguez, A. M. "Institutional Racism in Organizational Settings: An Action Research Approach." In J. W. Shaw (ed.), *Strategies for Improving Race Relations: The Anglo-American Experience.* Manchester, England: Manchester University Press, 1987.

Rohrbaugh, M., Tennen, H., Press, S., and White, L. "Compliance, Defiance, and Therapeutic Paradox: Guidelines for Strategic Use of Paradoxical Interventions." *American Journal of Orthopsychiatry,* 1981, *51,* 454–467.

Rolland, J. "Chronic Illness and the Life Cycle: A Conceptual Framework." *Family Process,* 1987, *26,* 203–221.

Rolland, J. "Family Systems and Chronic Illness: A Typological Model." In F. Walsh and C. Anderson (eds.), *Chronic Disorders and the Family.* New York: Haworth Press, 1988.

Saba, G. W., and Rodgers, D. V. "Discrimination in Urban Family Practice: Lessons from Minority Poor Families." In G. W. Saba, B. M. Karrer, and K. V. Hardy (eds.), *Minorities and Family Therapy.* New York: Haworth Press, 1989.

Scharff, D., and Scharff, J. *Object Relations Family Therapy.* Northvale, N.J.: Aronson, 1987.

Schwartz, R. C. "On Becoming a Familied Therapist." *Family Therapy Networker,* 1982, *6,* 44–46.

Schwartz, R. C. "Has Family Therapy Reached the Stage Where It Can Appreciate the Concept of Stages?" In D. C. Breunlin (ed.), *Stages: Patterns of Change over Time.* Rockville, Md.: Aspen, 1985.

Schwartz, R. C. "Our Multiple Selves." *Family Therapy Networker,* 1987, *11,* 23–31, 80–83.

Schwartz, R.C. *Internal Family Systems Therapy.* New York: Guilford Press, 1995.

Schwartz, R.C. "Internal Family Systems Family Therapy." In F. Dattilio (ed.), *Integrative Cases in Couples and Family Therapy.* New York: Guilford Press, in press.

Schwartzman, J. "Family Ethnography: A Tool for Clinicians." In C. J. Falicov (ed.), *Cultural Perspectives in Family Therapy.* Rockville, Md.: Aspen, 1983.

Selvini-Palazzoli, M., Cecchin, G., Prata, G., and Boscolo, L. *Paradox and Counterparadox.* Northvale, N.J.: Aronson, 1978.

Selvini-Palazzoli, M., Cecchin, G., Prata, G., and Boscolo, L. "Hypothesizing, Circularity, and Neutrality: Three Guidelines for the Conductor of the Session." *Family Process,* 1980, *19,* 3–12.

Simon, R. "Stranger in a Strange Land: An Interview with Salvador Minuchin." *Family Therapy Networker,* 1984, *8*(6), 20–31, 66–68.

Slipp, S. *Technique and Practice of Object Relations Family Therapy.* Northvale, N.J.: Aronson, 1988.

Sluzki, C. E. "Acculturation and Conflict in the Latino Family." *Family Process,* 1979a, *18*(4), 379–390.

Sluzki, C. E. " Migration and Family Conflict." *Family Process,* 1979b, *18*(4), 379–390.

Sluzki, C. E. "The Latin Lover Revisited." In M. McGoldrick, J. K. Pearce, and J. Giordano (eds.), *Ethnicity and Family Therapy.* New York: Guilford Press, 1982.

Sluzki, C. E. "Process, Structure, and World Views: Toward an Integrated View of Systemic Models in Family Therapy." *Family Process,* 1983, *22*(4), 469–476.

Solomon, M. A. "A Developmental, Conceptual Premise for Family Therapy." *Family Process,* 1973, *12*(2), 179–188.

Stanton, M. D. "An Integrated Structural/Strategic Approach to Family Therapy." *Journal of Marital and Family Therapy,* 1981, *7*(4), 427–440.

Stent, M., Hazard, W., and Rivlin, H. *Cultural Pluralism in Education: A Mandate for Change.* East Norwalk, Conn.: Appleton and Lange, 1973.

Stone, H., and Winkelman, S. *Embracing Ourselves.* Marina del Rey, Calif.: Devoras, 1985.

Strauss, W., and Howe, N. *Generations: The History of America's Future 1584–2069.* New York: Morrow, 1991.

Szapocznick, J., and Kurtines, W. "Acculturation, Biculturalism, and Adjustment Among Cuban Americans." In A Padilla (ed.), *Acculturation: Theory, Models, and Some New Findings.* Boulder, Colo.: Westview Press, 1980.

Taggart, M. "The Feminist Critique in Epistemological Perspective: Questions of Context in Family Therapy." *Journal of Marital and Family Therapy,* 1985, *11*(2), 113–126.

Terkelson, K. "Toward a Theory of the Family Life Cycle." In E. A. Carter and M. McGoldrick (eds.), *The Family Life Cycle: A Framework for Family Therapy.* New York: Gardner Press, 1980.

Thomas, L. *The Medusa and the Snail.* New York: Viking Penguin, 1979.

Tomm, K. "Interventive Interviewing. Part I: Strategizing as a Fourth Guideline for the Therapist." *Family Process,* 1987a, *26*(1), 3–14.

Tomm, K. "Interventive Interviewing. Part II: Reflexive Questioning as a Means to Enable Self-Healing." *Family Process,* 1987b, *26*(2), 167–184.

U.S. Bureau of the Census. *Statistical Abstract of the United States.* (109th ed.) Washington, D.C.: U.S. Government Printing Office, 1989.

Varela, F. J. "Reflections on the Circulation of Concepts Between a Biology of Cognition and Systemic Family Therapy." *Family Process,* 1989, *28*(1), 15–24.

von Bertalanffy, L. *General Systems Theory.* New York: Braziller, 1968.

Wachtel, E. and Wachtel, P. *Family Dynamics in Individual Psychotherapy.* New York: Guilford Press, 1986.

Walters, M., Carter, B., Papp, P., and Silverstein, O. *The Invisible Web: Gender Patterns in Family Relationships.* New York: Guilford Press, 1988.

Wantanabe, S. "Cast-of-Characters Work: Systematically Exploring the Naturally Organized Personality." *Contemporary Family Therapy,* 1986, *8*, 75–83.

Watkins, J. G., and Watkins, H. "Ego-State Therapy." In L. Apt and I. Stuart (eds.), *The New Therapies: A Sourcebook*. New York: Van Nostrand Reinhold, 1982.

Watzlawick, P., Beavin, J. H., and Jackson, D. D. *Pragmatics of Human Communication*. New York: Norton, 1967.

Watzlawick, P., Weakland, J. H., and Fisch, R. *Change: Principles of Problem Formation and Problem Resolution*. New York: Norton, 1974.

Weeks, G. R., and Wright, L. "Dialectics of the Family Life Cycle." *American Journal of Family Therapy*, 1977, *7*, 85–91.

Weidner, R. T., and Sells, R. L. *Elementary Classical Physics*. Needham Heights, Mass.: Allyn & Bacon, 1965.

Whitaker, C. "The Hindrance of Theory in Clinical Work." In P. J. Guerin (ed.), *Family Therapy: Theory and Practice*. New York: Gardner Press, 1976.

White, M. "Negative Explanation, Restraint, and Double Description: A Template for Family Therapy." *Family Process*, 1986, *25*(2), 169–184.

White, M. *Selected Papers*. Adelaide, Australia: Dulwich Centre Publications, 1989.

White, M., and Epston, D. *Narrative Means to Therapeutic Ends*. New York: Norton, 1990.

Whitehead, A. N., and Russell, B. *Principia Mathematica*. Cambridge, England: Cambridge University Press, 1910.

Wiener, N. *The Human Use of Human Beings: Cybernetics and Society*. (2nd ed.) New York: Avon, 1967.

Wood, B. "Proximity and Hierarchy: Orthogonal Dimensions of Family Interconnectedness." *Family Process*, 1985, *24*, 487–507.

Wood, B., and Talmon, M. "Family Boundaries in Transition: A Search for Alternatives." *Family Process*, 1983, *22*(3), 347–358.

Wynne, L. C. "The Epigenesis of Relational Systems: A Model for Understanding Family Development." *Family Process*, 1984, *23*(3), 297–318.

Wynne, L. C. "An Epigenetic Model of Family Processes." In C. J. Falicov (ed.), *Family Transitions: Continuity and Change over the Life Cycle*. New York: Guilford Press, 1988.

Index

Acculturation: case example of, 209–211, 217, 222–223; concept of, 206; and cultural transition, 201, 205–212

Action: change of, 357; and emotion and meaning, 354–357; exclusive focus on, 355; in sequences metaframework, 354–357

Action and meaning: in blueprint for therapy, 51–53; and creating events, 299; and emotion, 354–357; in relational development, 186; and sequences, 96–97, 118, 354–357

Adam, 307–308

Africa, dyads in, 216

African Americans, and cultural constraints at biological level, 362

Age, and multicultural domain, 222–223

Aggression, and development, 170–171

Agoraphobia, case of, 166–168, 175

Al, 3–18

Aldama family, 264, 266–271

Anderson, C., 241

Anderson, C. M., 144

Anderson, D. A., 363

Anderson, H., 289–290

Ann, 317–353

Anorexia, case of, 3–10, 12, 14–16, 17

Aponte, H. J., 287, 288

Asia: dyads in, 216; and immigration/acculturation, 206

Assagioli, R., 64

Assessment, and sequences, 114–117

Attention deficit disorders (ADD): and biological development, 179; diagnosis of, 318–319

Attraction, and relational development, 183

Attributes, in systems theory, 29

Autonomy: and routines, 107–108; and society, 161–162

Autopoiesis, and organization, 125

Balance: in case example, 152–154; in domains of action, meaning, and emotion, 357; in gender domain, 248, 361; and leadership, 138–139, 359; in lifting constraints, 354–355; and organization, 135–137; presupposition on, 12–13, 40–42; by sailors in boat, 82, 137

Balanced families, gender balance

in, 251, 254–255, 258–259, 263, 266

Balenciaga family, 209–211, 217, 222–223

Bales, R. F., 130–131, 242

Barbara, 3–18

Bateson, G., 13, 36, 40, 58–60, 61, 136, 244–245, 357

Beavers, W. R., 241

Beavin, J. H., 34, 90, 120, 244, 305

Behaviors, and sequences, 91–92

Beliefs: cultural, 194, embedded, 84, 355; and membership contexts, 359

Berger, M., 166

Bernice, 119, 122, 123

Berry, J. W., 198, 206, 231

Billy, 309–310

Biological system, as constraint, 362; development in, 178–181

Biology: and question of additional metaframeworks, 361–362; as level, 362–363

Birch, H. G., 29, 178

Blueprint for therapy: aspects of, 281–316; background on, 281–285; and case examples, 282, 283, 284, 286–287, 290–291, 297, 299–300, 301, 305, 307–314; case illustrating, 317–353; components of, 287–307; conversing in, 287, 302–306; experience, description, and explanation in, 53; feedback reading in, 287, 307–314; hypothesizing in, 287, 288–292; in metaframeworks, 24, 51–54, 281–316; and models, 285–287; planning in, 287, 292–302; and presuppositions, 281; techniques and interventions in, 53–54; using, 314–316. *See also* Therapy

Boat, sailors balancing, 82, 137

Bogden, J. L., 52

Bornstein, I., 364

Boscolo, L., 126, 236, 244, 259, 263, 288, 299

Boszormenyi-Nagy, I., 111

Boundaries: and balance and harmony, 136–137; case of, 27; and family subsystems, 131–133, 155–157; metaframeworks view of, 10–11; in systems theory, 26–27

Bowen, M., 11, 85, 111, 118, 126, 165, 299

Boyd-Franklin, N., 112, 224

Braverman, L., 241

Breunlin, D. C., 46, 47, 90n, 93, 100n, 102n, 103n, 158n, 164n, 165n, 167n, 169, 172, 173n, 294, 302, 355, 356–371

Brown-Standridge, M. D., 301

Brudner-White, L., 216

Buddhist tradition, and ecological view, 59

Bulimia, family reaction to, 145–146

Burgoyn, N., 206, 207

Calibration, and sequences, 101–104, 111

California: Latin America majority in, 199; proximity in, 227

Cambodian man, transitional rituals for, 227–228

Caplan, J., 164

Capra, F., 24, 203, 238, 239

Carter, B., 241, 243

Carter, E. A., 160, 162, 163–164, 165

Cecchin, G. F., 126, 235, 236, 244, 259, 263, 288, 291, 299, 303

Center for the Study of Transition, 365

Change: consequences of, 263–264; first- and second-orders of, 166; room for, 76, 79; and stability, 31; theory of, and organization, 147–150

Chaos theory: and recursion, 31; and sequences, 97–98

Chess, S., 29, 178

Chicago: poverty in, 212–213; and rural/urban differences, 227–228

Chicago Center for Gender Studies, 360–361

Chronic illness, and biological development, 180–181

Cimmarusti, R. A., 302, 355, 368–371

Circularity, and feminist view, 242–243. *See also* Recursion

Clients. *See* Therapeutic relationship

Collaboration: and internal processes, 73; leadership as, 245, 275–276; in organization metaframework, 141, 147, 149–150; in therapeutic relationship, 284, 286, 288, 292, 293–294, 303, 304

Combrinck-Graham, L., 164

Competence, age-appropriate, 169–171, 174–176

Complementarity, in subsystems, 132–133

Confidentiality, and internal process, 79

Constraints: and achievement of gender balance, 361; of biology, 362; and biopsychosocial concepts of levels, 366; cases of, 38, 39–40; developmental, case of, 190–192; and effects of discrimination, 365; on emotion, 355; and family feedback, 363; in metaframeworks view, 4–6, 11, 14–16, 18, 282–284; more comprehensive concept of, 365–371; in presuppositions, 36–40; and routines, 106–107; and sequences, 99, 355, 357; web of, 366–371

Constructivism: and metaframeworks, 8; and reality, 32–33

Control: and leadership, 138–139; presupposition on, 40–42

Conversing: in blueprint for therapy, 287, 302–306; in case example, 325–327, 330–338, 341, 342, 344, 346–350

Cooklin, A., 101

Coordinating meaning, and relational development, 184

Creating events: in case example, 321, 324, 325, 329, 333, 336, 337, 339–341, 344, 350; and planning, 298–302

Crisis: induction of, 149; as opportunity, 150; and therapeutic approach, 283–284

Cronen, V. E., 51, 52, 184

Culture: in case examples, 48–51, 319–321, 323, 329, 345, 346, 348, 349, 352; concepts of, 195–197; constraints of, 15; domain of, 47, 193–236; feedback on, 313–314; fit of, 230–232; and gender domain, 255, 256; transitions of, 201, 203–212. *See also* Multicultural domain

Curiosity: defined, 291; and feminist view, 244

Davidson, M., 33, 200

Defiance, case of, 312–314

Dell, P. F., 53, 101

Depolarization, in internal process, 68, 71, 82

Depression: case of, 128–130; views of, 19

Description, in blueprint for therapy, 53

Development: aspects of, 158–192; background on, 158–161; biological, 178–181; case examples of, 166–168, 177–178, 180–181, 190–192, 318–322, 330–332, 335–336, 338; clinical implications of, 189–190; clinical relevance of, 169–171; constraints and synchrony in, 188–192; cultural expectations for, 222–223; domain of, 46–47, 158–192; and family life cycle, 163–168; feedback on, 311, 312–313, 314; and gender evolution, 255–256; individual, 168–178; information about, 160–161; levels of,

159–160; microtransitions in, 171–173; oscillation in, 15; relational, 181–188; and society, 161–163
Diane, 312–314
Differentiation, metaframeworks view of, 11
Directives: in case example, 325, 333, 334, 338, 341, 342, 344, 349; and conversing, 304–305; in gender domain, 259–260, 262–263, 268–269
Disabilities, developmental, 178–179
Discrimination, concept of, 224
Distraction, need for, 144, 154–155
Domains: aspects of, 55–277; of culture, 47, 193–236; of development, 46–47, 158–192; of gender, 48, 237–277; of internal process, 45–46, 57–89; in metaframeworks, 23–24, 44–51, 55–277; of organization, 46, 125–157; of sequences, 46, 90–124
Dyad, Self-leadership in, 77–79

Ebb and flow sequences (*S3*): and assessment, 114, 116–117; and biological development, 180–181; and calibration, 104; in case examples, 94–95, 120, 155; class of, 93–94, 109–111; and collaboration, 141; in connecting pattern, 113, 114; and crisis, 283–284; and gender balance, 270; and generation, 101; and meaning, 96–97; and strategic view, 134–135; and tasks, 301–302; and transgenerational sequences, 112; and treatment, 118–119
Ecofeminism, in gender domain, 249
Ecology: and ebb and flow sequences, 110; and internal processes, 59–60, 74, 83

Economics, in multicultural domain, 212–214
Education, in multicultural domain, 214–216
Efran, J. S., 32
Ehrenreich, B., 203
Ehrlich, A. H., 239
Ehrlich, P. R., 239
Eichler, M., 241
Einstein, A., 10
Eisler, R., 238, 239
Elizur, J., 133
Ellman, B., 241
Embedded problems: case of, 20–22; and sequences, 99, 100
Emotion: importance of, in internal family systems metaframework, 355; as legitimate goal of treatment, 355–357
Enactment: and creating events, 300; and interactions, 106, 115–116; technique of, 53–54
Encopresis, case of, 33–34, 177–178
Engel, G. L., 24, 25
Enmeshment, feminist view of, 246
Environment, constraints of, 16
Eovaldi, M. L., 355
Epston, D., 364
Equal Rights Amendment, 204
Ethnicity, and multicultural domain, 216–218
Europe, and immigration, 206
Events. *See* Creating events
Exile part, 358, 359
Experience, in blueprint for therapy, 53
Explanation: in blueprint for therapy, 53; negative or positive, 36–37

Fagan, R., 24
Falicov, C. J., 159, 160, 161, 163, 197, 216, 365
Fallen snowman, and embeddedness, 99, 100
Family: alternative forms of, 162–163; balanced, 251,

Family *(continued)*
254–255, 258–259, 263, 266;
feminist view of, 241–242; gender-aware, 250, 252–253, 258,
260–262, 264–271; and holons,
26; internal family system model
with, 86–88; nuclear and
extended, 217; of parts, internal,
64–67; polarized, 250, 253, 258,
261, 262–263, 265, 271–274; and
reunification case, 307–308; routines of, 106–109; subsystems in,
131–133; traditional, 249–252,
258, 260–262, 264–271; transitional, 250–251, 253–254, 258,
263, 266, 271–274
Family life cycle (FLC): concept of,
158–159; and development,
163–168
Family Systems Program, 367
Family Therapy: and feminist view,
239–241; and internal process,
60–61; pure systems track of,
355. *See also* Internal family system model; Metaframeworks
Farrell, W., 204
Feedback: and hypothesizing,
291–292; in identifying constraints, 366; in internal process,
67, 71; reading, in blueprint for
therapy, 287, 307–314; reading,
in case example, 320, 321, 331,
332, 334, 337, 343, 349, 351, 352;
responses as, 308–309
Feminism: and balance, 12–13;
challenge of, 241–247; and family therapy, 239–241; and gender
metaframework, 237–277; social
impact of, 238–239
Ferber, A., 364
Feynman, R. P., 102
Firefighter part, 358, 359
Fisch, R., 19, 82, 90, 92, 120, 165,
166, 299, 303
Fishman, C., 54, 90, 92, 115, 117,
126, 140, 148–149, 150–151, 165,
233, 298

Fourier theorem, and sequences,
102–104
Fraser, J. S., 32, 286
Freud, S., 29, 60, 61
Friedan, B., 204
Fuentes, C., 363
Function of the symptom: and
organization, 142–144, 156; and
oscillation, 176
Functionalism and family, 130–133,
242
Fybromyalgia, as organizational
constraint, 362

Garbarino, J., 169
Geertz, C., 196, 197
Gender: and acculturation, 207; in
case example, 319, 321, 323,
343–348, 351; constraints of, 15;
domain of, 48, 237–277; feedback on, 313–314; and multicultural domain, 221
Gender-aware families, gender balance in, 250, 252–253, 258,
260–262, 264–271
Gender metaframework: applications of, 247–264; aspects of,
237–277; background on,
237–238; case examples of, 264,
266–274; contexts for evolution
in, 255–257; evolution of,
247–248; and gender balance
evolution, 249–255, 360–361;
implications of, 276–277; and
planning, 257–259, 265–266;
presuppositions of, 248–249;
testing assumptions about,
360–361; and treatment,
259–264, 265–266
Generation, and sequences, 99,
101. *See also* Historical/genera-
tional sequences
Giordano, J., 197
Gleick, J., 31, 97
Goffman, E., 132
Goldner, V., 241, 242, 243
Goodrich, T. J., 241

Goolishian, H., 289–290
Gordon, E. M., 29
Gossett, J. T., 241
Gottman, J., 355
Goulding, R., 358, 364
Grinker, R., 364
Guerin, P. J., 29
Gutierrez, M., 197, 207, 233

Hadley, T. R., 164
Haley, J., 34, 40, 46, 90, 91, 92, 110, 126, 133–135, 158, 163, 164–165, 301, 303, 360, 364, 368
Hall, A., 24
Halstead, K., 241
Hardy, K. V., 225
Hare-Mustin, R. T., 240, 241, 242
Harmony: and leadership, 138–139; and organization, 135–137; presupposition on, 13–14, 40–42
Hazard, W., 198
Hefner, H., 204
Heisenberg, W., 355
Held, B., 32
Hierarchy: and boundaries, 132; feminist view of, 245; incongruous, 176; leadership distinct from, 12; presupposition on, 40–42; strategic view of, 134–135
Hillman, J., 64
Historical/generational sequences (S5): and cultural transition, 201, 203–205, 217, 221; and feminist view, 242; and gender balance, 263, 269
Hoffman, L., 90–91, 92, 101, 240, 289
Hogarty, G. E., 144
Holons: balance and harmony for, 41, 136–137, 154; concept of, 26; and leadership, 137–138; and metaframeworks, 8
Homeostasis: and calibration, 101; and function of the symptom, 142–143; and systems theory, 31; and theory of change, 149
Homework case, 310–312

Hsu, F., 216
Hughes, S., 166
Human nature, in presuppositions, 42–44
Human system: concept of, 24–25; levels for, 25
Humphrey, F. G., 240
Hypothesizing: in blueprint for therapy, 287, 288–292; in case example, 318–324, 328–333, 335–340, 342–349, 351–353

Imber-Black, E., 263
Immigration, and cultural transition, 201, 205–212
Individual: development by, 168–178; internal family system model for, 80–86
Institute for Juvenile Research (IJR), 364, 368, 369, 370
Interaction sequences (S1): and assessment, 114–117; and calibration, 104; in case examples, 94, 120, 121, 152, 321–322, 333, 338, 343; class of, 93, 105–106; and collaboration, 141; in connecting pattern, 113, 114; and ebb and flow, 109, 110, 111; and embeddedness, 99; and enactment, 300; and gender balance, 267, 268; and generation, 99, 101; and isomorphism, 140; and meaning, 96; and routines, 107, 108, 109; and strategic view, 134; and transgenerational sequences, 112; and treatment, 118
Interactions: in internal process, 70–71, 75–77; patterns of, in sequences, 90–124; in systems theory, 27–28
Intercultural beliefs, concept of, 194
Intermittency. See Ebb and flow sequences
Internal family system (IFS) model: applications of, 74–89; aspects of, 57–89; assumptions of,

Internal family system *(continued)*
66–67, 69–72; and balance, 154,
359; and constraints, 302, 359;
evolution of, into healing
process, 359; with families,
86–88; and gender domain, 254,
261–262, 267–268; goal of, 68;
with individuals, 80–86; internal
and external parallels in, 71–72,
75–77, 84–85; and internal family of parts, 64–67, 357–359; and
internal process, 45; and joining,
151; language of, 62, 73, 306;
and levels of focus, 63, 72, 75–77;
linguistic dilemma of, 357–358;
as metaframework, 72–74; and
mind metaframework, 357; promoting Self-leadership in, 77–79;
and relational development,
186–187; and resistance, 73–74;
and spiritual direction, 363; therapeutic relationship in, 88–89
Internal process: aspects of, 57–89;
background on, 57–60; in case
examples, 48–51, 319, 321, 323,
328–331, 333, 336–338, 345, 347,
348; domain of, 45–46, 57–89; and
family therapy, 239–241; feedback
on, 311–312, 313; and gender balance, 250–255; in metaframeworks view, 5–6, 12; and
organization, 142; Self in, 67–69,
70; and systems theory, 61–64
Interventions, in blueprint for therapy, 53–54
Intimacy, and relational development, 182, 185
Intracultural beliefs, concept of, 194
Isomorphism: confirmation of concept of, 366; and levels, 366, 367;
and metaframeworks, 362; and
organization, 139–141; and web
of constraints, 367

Jackson, D., 31
Jackson, D. D., 34, 90 120, 184, 244,
305

Jacob, T., 164
James, K., 242, 244 , 246
Jane, 66, 67, 75, 76–79, 81–86
Joan, 271–274, 367–371
Joe and Sylvia, 356–357
Joe's lying case, 48–51
Joe's sleep disturbances case, 119-
124
John, 75, 77–79, 82–83, 85–86
Johnny's homework case, 310–312
Johnny's internal family system
case, 62, 63, 67, 86–87
Joining, and organization, 150–157
Jung, C. G., 64

Kalin, R., 198, 231
Karen, 48–51
Karrer, B. M., 47, 196, 197, 206,
207. *See also* Mac Kune-Karrer, B.
Keeney, B., 31, 90, 92, 104, 243, 289
Kluckhohn, C., 196
Koestler, A., 8, 26, 126
Kozol, J., 212–213, 215, 225
Kurtines, W., 207

Language: as context, 305–306; of
metaframeworks, 62, 73, 306
Latin Americans: concept of, 193*n;*
and immigration/acculturation,
206. *See also* Mexico
Leadership: as collaboration, 245,
275–276; functions of, 41–42;
hierarchy distinct from, 12; and
internal harmony, 359; and organization, 137–139; presupposition on, 40–42; by therapist, 289
Lebow, J. L., 286
Lederer, W. J., 184
Leighton, R. B., 102
Levels: biology and, 362; biopsychosocial concepts of, 366;
distinction between metaframeworks and, 361–362; in internal
family system model, 63, 72,
75–77; in organizations,
128–130; and planning, 302; in
systems theory, 25–26

Lewis, J. M., 241
Life cycle. *See* Development
Liking, and relational develop-
  ment, 183
Lisa, 132, 134
Los Angeles, proximity in, 227
Luepnitz, D. A., 61, 240, 241, 242
Lukens, M. D., 32
Lukens, R. J., 32
Lying, case of, 48–51

McGoldrick, M., 160, 162, 163–164,
  165, 197, 241
McIntyre, D., 242
MacKinnon, L. K., 244, 246
Mac Kune-Karrer, B., 359, 360. *See
  also* Karrer, B. M.
Madanes, C., 90, 92, 126, 134, 176
Managed care, focus of, in
  metaframeworks, 371–372
Manager part, 358, 359
Manes, C., 239
Maruyama, M., 90
Maturana, M., 125
Mayans, and temporal patterns, 203
Mayers, B., 224
Meaning: coordinating and relational development, 184; and
  historical/generational sequences, 205; and sequences
  metaframework revisited,
  354–357. *See also* Action and
  meaning
Mechanistic and organism views:
  and development, 158; in systems theory, 29–30
Men. *See* Gender; Gender
  metaframework
Mental Research Institute (MRI):
  brief therapy model of, 19; and
  change theory, 166–167; and
  family life cycle, 165; impact of,
  240; and language, 305
Metaframeworks: advantage of, 7;
  aspects of, 19–54; background
  on, 19–22; for biology, 361,
  362–363; blueprint for therapy

in, 24, 51–54, 281–316; building
  blocks for, 22–24; case illustrating, 317–353; combining, in case
  of lying, 48–51; and complexity,
  10, 356; concept of, 23–24; constraints in, 4–6, 11, 14–16, 18,
  282–284; conversation about,
  3–18; domains in, 23–24, 44–51,
  55–277; foundations of, 1–54;
  future of, 372; internal and external views of, 358–362; internal
  family system model as, 72–74,
  355, 357–359; language of, 306;
  and larger system, 368–371; multicultural journey to, 363–367;
  patterns in, 355–358; personaliz-
  ing views of, 354–371; practice
  with, 279–371; presuppositions
  in, 8–14, 23–24, 31–44; refining
  the perspective of, 354–371; systems theory in, 23, 24–31
Metarules, and relational development, 184–185
Mexico: and acculturation,
  209–211, 217; and gender balance, 264, 266–271; multiculturalism in, 363–364
Miami, Latin Americans in, 199
Michael Reese Hospital, 364
Microtransitions: and biological
  development, 179; of development, 171–173
Middle East: dyads in, 216; and immigration, 206; and Islam, 219
Milan model, 118, 240, 244
Milliones, J., 164
Mind: in internal family system,
  57–89; presupposition on, 11,
  34–35; and subpersonalities,
  64–67
Mind metaframework, 355–357
Minority/majority status, and multicultural domain, 224-226, 360
Minuchin, S., 53–54, 62, 90, 92,
  115, 117, 126, 130, 131, 133, 134,
  140, 148–149, 150–151, 160, 165,
  176, 233, 298, 360, 364

Miracles, as therapeutic approach, 283

Montalvo, B., 197, 207, 233

Multicultural domain: and age, 222–223; aspects of, 193–236; background on, 193–196; contexts of, 200–230; and cultural transition, 201, 203–212; and economics, 212–214; and education, 214–216; and ethnicity, 216–218; food as metaphor in, 195; and gender, 221; interrelatedness in, 230–232; and minority/majority status, 224–226; need for, 197–199; opportunities and constraints in, 232–233; pluralism distinct from, 198; presuppositions of, 199–200; and race, 224, 225–226; and regional background, 226–230; and religion, 218–221; and therapeutic guidelines, 233–236

Multicultural metaframework, 193–236, 359–360

Multiplicity: and function of the symptom, 143–144; in internal process, 64–67, 69

Multisystems Applied Research and Training, 370

Muslim family, religious analogy for, 219

Nancy, 3–10, 12, 14–16, 17

Narrative movement: and plan of reauthoring, 364; and reliance on adjunctive supports, 365; and web of constraints, 364–365

Native Americans, and cultural constraints at the biological level, 362

Neugarten, B., 174

Neutrality, feminist view of, 244

New York, proximity in, 227

Newton, I., 29, 97

Nichols, M., 60–61, 354

Nike principle, 372

Nurturing, and relational development, 183–184

Objectivism, and reality, 32

Objects, in systems theory, 28–29

Organisms, and mechanistic views, 29–30, 158

Organization: aspects of, 125–157; background on, 125–126; and balance and harmony, 135–137; in case examples, 128–130, 132, 134, 151–157, 319, 321, 322, 330, 331, 336, 338–340, 353; and change theory, 147–150; domain of, 46, 125–157; and effect of problems, 144–147; feedback on, 311, 312; and function of the symptom, 142–144, 156; and internal process, 142; and isomorphism, 139–141; and joining, 150–157; and leadership, 137–139; level of focus in, 128–130; metaframework of, 135–157; multilevel view of, 126–130, 155; strategic view of, 133–135; and structural family therapy, 130–133, 147, 148, 150; in systems theory, 25; and therapy, 147

Oscillation: case of, 180–181; in development, 15; and family life cycle, 164; and microtransitions, 172–173; and societal development, 162; stable, 174–175; and symptom emergence, 173–178

Papp, P., 241, 243

Parsons, T., 130–131, 242

Parts: and contagion of emotion, 357–358; ecological thinking about, 358; and family members, 356; and family of origin, 65–66, 83–84; internal family of, 64–67; and mind, 35; protective, 74; and variety of emotions, 355. See also Internal process

Patterns of interactions, in sequences, 90–124

Pearce, J. K., 197

Pearce, W. B., 51, 52, 184

Penn, P., 104, 303

Periodicity, and sequences, 93

Perspectivism: and feedback reading, 307; and hypothesizing, 288; and metaframeworks, 8, 11; and multicultural view, 200; and reality, 33–34; and sequences, 95–96

Pessimistic realism, and reality, 33

Philadelphia Child Guidance Clinic, 368

Phillips, V. A., 241

Pinsof, W. M., 286, 304, 371–372

Planning: in blueprint for therapy, 287, 292–302; in case example, 321, 322, 324–330, 333–337, 339–341, 344–346, 348–353; and gender metaframework, 257–259, 265–266

Pluralism, multiculturalism distinct from, 198

Polarization: and acculturation, 207; and balance and harmony, 13–14, 136–137; in case example, 152–157; and effect of problems, 146; and function of the symptom, 143, 144; in internal process, 67, 71, 76, 80; and leadership, 138; and religion, 219; and theory of change, 149

Polarized families, gender balance in, 250, 253, 258, 261, 262–263, 265, 271–274

Pols, E., 32

Power: feminist view of, 244–245; presupposition on, 40–42

Prata, G., 126, 236, 244, 259, 263, 288, 299

Premenstrual syndrome (PMS), and sequences, 99, 101, 109–110

Press, S., 301, 303

Presuppositions: and blueprint for therapy, 281; constraints in, 36–40; of gender metaframework, 248–249; hierarchy, power, and control versus leadership, balance, and harmony in, 40–42;

human nature in, 42–44; in metaframeworks, 8–14, 23–24, 31–44; on mind, 11, 34–35; of multicultural domain, 199–200; reality in, 32–34; summary of, 44

Probability, and sequences, 98–99

Problems: assessment of, 114–117; effect of, 144–147; family reactions to, 145

Protection, and acculturation, 209–211

Proximity, and boundaries, 132, 227

Psychotropic medicine, 362

Questions: in case example, 326–327, 330–332, 335–338, 341, 342, 344, 346–350; and conversing, 304–305; in gender domain, 259, 260, 261, 264

Race, and multicultural domain, 224, 225–226

Radical constructivism, and reality, 32

Rampage, C., 241, 355

Reality: and hypothesizing, 288–289; nature of, 8; in presuppositions, 32–34

Recursion: in blueprint for therapy, 290–291; and microtransitions, 171; in relational development, 185–187; and sequences, 97–98; in systems theory, 30–31

Reframing, feminist view of, 246–247

Refugees, and acculturation, 207

Regional background: case example of, 229–230, 231; and multicultural domain, 226–230

Reiss, C. J., 144

Relating: in case example, 321, 324–326, 344, 345; and planning, 293–294

Relational development: action and meaning in, 186; epigenetic view of, 182–183; and internal family

Relational development *(continued)* system model, 186–187; metaframeworks view of, 183–185; processes of, 181–182; recursion in, 185–187; and therapy, 187–188

Religion, and multicultural domain, 218–221

Resilience, and sequences, 104–105

Resistance: and conversing, 303–304; and internal family system model, 73–74; metaframeworks view of, 17

Rifkin, J., 239

Ritterman, M. K., 29

Rituals, in gender domain, 263

Rivlin, H., 198

Roberts, J., 263

Rod, 20–22

Rodgers, D. V., 197

Rodriguez, A. M., 224

Rohrbaugh, M., 301, 303

Rolland, J., 144

Routines sequences (*S2*): and assessment, 114, 116–117; and calibration, 104; in case examples, 94, 120, 121, 122, 345; class of, 93, 106–109; and collaboration, 141; in connecting pattern, 113; and ebb and flow, 109, 111; and embeddedness, 99; and feedback, 311; and generation, 101; and meaning, 96; and protection, 211; and strategic view, 134; and transgenerational sequences, 112; and treatment, 118

Rule setting, and relational development, 184

Russell, B., 24

Saba, G. W., 197

Sailors, boat balanced by, 83, 137

Sands, M., 102

Satir, V., 240, 364

Scharff, D., 60

Scharff, J., 60

School behavior case, 309–310

Schwartz, R. C., 45, 46, 61, 64, 68–69, 80, 90n, 93, 100n, 102n, 145, 147, 169, 285, 354, 355, 358, 359, 364–365

Schwartzman, J., 197

Segal, R., 90, 92, 303

Self: and common roles of inner parts, 357–358; differentiating, 81; in internal family system, 57–89; in internal process, 67–69, 70; leadership by, 35, 42, 68, 70, 77–79; as path to spirituality, 363–364; subpersonalities of, 357

Sells, R. L., 102

Selvini-Palazzoli, M., 126, 236, 244, 259, 263, 288, 299

Selvino family, 317–353

Sequences: and action and meaning, 96–97, 118; adaptive, 113; applied to therapy, 114–124; aspects of, 90–124; and assessment, 114–117; background on, 90–95; and calibration, 101–104, 111; cases of, 48–51, 94–95, 119–124, 319, 321–323, 333, 336–338, 342–345, 347, 351; characteristics of, 95–105; classes of, 93–95, 105–113; combined, 103; as connecting pattern, 113–114; constraints and, 99; domains of, 46, 90–124; and embeddedness, 99, 100; and generation, 99, 101; in metaframeworks view, 9, 15; and microtransitions, 172; and perspectivism, 95–96; and prioritizing, 116–117, 121; and probability, 98–99; and recursions, 97–98; and resilience, 104–105; and Self-leadership, 78; as sine waves, 103–104; and treatment, 117–124. *See also* Ebb and flow sequences; Historical/generational sequences; Interaction sequences; Routines sequences; Transgenerational sequences

Sid, 38

Silverstein, O., 241, 243

Simon, R., 62

Simons, V., 360

Sleep disturbance, and sequences, 119–124

Slipp, S., 61

Sluzki, C. E., 112, 197, 206

Snowman, fallen, and embeddedness, 99, 100

Society: and development, 161–163; and feminism, 238–239

Solomon, M. A., 158, 163

Spark, G., 111

Speck, R., 364

Spirituality: and meaning, 363–364; and psychotherapy, 363

Spitz, D., 164

Sprenkle, D., 90

Stability and change, in systems theory, 31

Staging: in case example, 324, 326–330, 333–335, 339, 340, 345, 346, 348, 349, 351–353; and planning, 294–298

Stanton, M. D., 286

Starkman, S., 360

Statements: in case example, 325, 330–338, 341, 342, 344, 346–350; and conversing, 304–305; in gender domain, 259, 260

Stathos, K., 360

Stent, M., 198

Stone, H., 64

Stott, F., 169

Strauss, W., 204

Structural family therapy, and organization, 130–133, 147, 148, 150

Structure. *See* Organization

Sylvia, 229–230, 231

Symptom: emergence of, 173–178; function of, 142–144, 156, 176

System, concept of, 24

Systematic approach, in therapy, 284

Systems theory: attributes in, 29; boundaries in, 26–27; core concepts in, 24; and gender domain, 237–277; interactions in, 27–28; internal process in, 61–64; levels in, 25–26; mechanism versus organism in, 29–30; metaframework in, 23, 24–31; objects in, 28–29; organization in, 25; recursion in, 30–31

Szapocznick, J., 207

Taggart, M., 242, 243

Talmon, M., 132

Taoist tradition, and ecological view, 59

Tasks, and creating events, 300–302

Taylor, D. M., 198, 231

Taylor, E. H., 359

Techniques: in blueprint for therapy, 53–54; and metaframeworks, 18

Ted, 229–230, 231

Temperament, and biological development, 178

Tennen, H., 301, 303

Tennis, analogy of, 295–297

Terkelson, K., 171, 173

Therapeutic relationship: collaboration in, 284, 286, 288, 292, 293–294, 303, 304; gender in, 274–276; in internal family system model, 88–89; and joining, 150–157; leadership in, 289; and sociocultural contexts, 234–236

Therapy: approaches of, 283–284; family, 60–61, 239–241; gender in, 274–276; goal of, 68, 147, 283; internal family system model for, 74–89; and multicultural domain, 233–236; and organization, 147; as political, 243–244; and relational development, 187–188; sequences applied to, 114–124; temporal dimension of, 139–141. *See also* Blueprint for therapy

Thomas, A., 29, 178

Thomas, L., 101
Tim, 128–130
Timberlawn study, 241
Time: and development, 165–166; and sequences, 91, 102; and therapy, 139–141
Tom's gender balance case, 271–274
Tom's Tourette's syndrome case, 151–157
Tomm, K., 259, 287, 303, 304
Tough love, as misguided, 42
Tourette's syndrome, and organization, 151–157
Toynbee, A., 203
Traditional families, gender balance in, 249–252, 258, 260, 261, 262, 264–271
Transgenerational sequences (*S4*): and assessment, 114, 116–117; in case examples, 95, 120–121, 122–123, 155; class of, 94, 111–113; and collaboration, 141; in connecting pattern, 113; and gender balance, 263, 269; and protection, 211; and respect, 287; and treatment, 118
Transitional families, gender balance in, 250–251, 253–254, 258, 263, 266, 271–274
Transitions: and development, 159, 163–168; micro-, 171–173, 179
Treatment: and gender metaframework, 259–266; and sequences, 117–124
Trust, case of, 39–40

Unbalancing, feminist view of, 246
Unburdening, 359
U.S. Bureau of the Census, 199
Universal beliefs, concept of, 194

Van Deusen, J. M., 287, 288
Varela, F. J., 106
Veterans Administration, 43
von Bertalanffy, L., 8, 24, 29, 30, 33, 44, 125, 130, 200, 364

Wachtel, E., 60
Wachtel, P., 60
Walsh, F., 241
Walters, M., 241, 243
Watanabe, S., 64
Watkins, H., 64
Watkins, J. G., 64
Watzlawick, P., 19, 34, 82, 90, 92, 120, 165, 166, 244, 299, 303, 305
Weakland, J. H., 19, 82, 90, 92, 120, 165, 166, 299, 303
Web of constraints, 366–367. *See also* Constraints
Weber, M., 197
Weeks, G. R., 166
Weidner, R. T., 102
Weigel-Foy, C., 360
Whitaker, C., 290, 364–365
White, L., 301, 303
White, M., 36, 144, 146, 364
Whitehead, A. N., 24
Whiting, R., 263
Wiener, N., 24
Winkelman, S., 64
Wormen. *See* Gender; Gender metaframework
Women's Project in Family Therapy, 243
Wood, B., 132
Worthen, D., 363
Wright, L., 166
Writing block, sequences in, 94–95
Wynne, L. C., 181–182, 183, 184, 185, 186, 188